NEW POLITICS

New Politics

JOHN PAPWORTH

GARLANDFOLD LTD
in association with
VIKAS PUBLISHING HOUSE PVT LTD

GARLANDFOLD LTD
51 Manchester Street
London W1M 6JD U.K.

Published in U.K. by special arrangement with:
VIKAS PUBLISHING HOUSE PVT LTD
5 Ansari Road, New Delhi 110002

ISBN 0-7069-1273-X

1V2P4301

Printed in India

Preface

This book is not a work of scholarship, much as I would like both the leisure and the facilities to make it so, it is an extended exercise in journalism designed to challenge the thinking of the average person of an ordinary enquiring turn of mind who is seeking to get the hang of the troubled and disastrous confusions of the twentieth century.

It is appropriate that it should first see the light of day in India for it owes much of its genesis to the thinking of Mahatma Gandhi and in a more pointed sense, to that rare embodiment of integrity and vision, the late Jayaprakash Narayan, with whom I was privileged to enjoy a friendship of more than twenty years. To say that I loved J.P. is simply a bald statement of the truth, and one which would be echoed by millions of his countrymen; he was that kind of person and the debt I owe to his thinking and his inspiration, especially his writings in Sarvodaya is one I am happy to record.

I have also to express my grateful thanks to many friends, not least to Professor Leopold Kohr, whose writings ante-date other much more recent discussion on the issues discussed here and whose book *The Breakdown of Nations* was recommended to me by a friend to whom I was propounding not dissimilar but far less systematic views nearly a quarter of a century ago; to my former chief, and one whom I do not hesitate to describe as a spiritual mentor, Dr. Kenneth Kaunda, the President of the Republic of Zambia, for the inspiration of his published works and for numerous exchanges over a long period, especially at times when he was hard pressed with the burdens of office; to the late Dr. E.F. Schumacher and the late Paul Goodman, to professor Carlo Doglio, John Seymour, Frau-Dr. Lavinia Merz-Foerster, Roger Franklin, Lord Macleod of Funiery, Michael North, Hugh Sharman and, not least, my wife Marcelle, all of whom through discussions and exchanges have contributed to the development of my thinking as is in part here expressed.

I am also under a heavy obligation to those who helped with the typing, notably Rita Goma, Grace Haketa, Betty Han'gumba, Grace Mubeya and Gloria Sleep, all of State House, Lusaka, and to Nicholas Albery and Toni Pinschoff for help with the proof-reading.

But whatever ingredients these and other persons may have contributed to the cake, responsibility for their selection and mixing, and the baking of the finished product, is of course mine alone.

JOHN PAPWORTH

Contents

This is a very important book. An original book on political theory is a very rare event, and I think Mr. Papworth has succeeded in mapping out a new and hopeful approach to the problems of modern politics. It is a book which demands the careful consideration of every person with any claim to political literacy.

Patna
9 August 1979

JAYAPRAKASH NARAYAN

CHAPTER I

Why ?

What have we approached or conceived
When we have conquered and built a world? Even
Though civilization became perfect? What then?
We have only put a crown on the skeleton.
It is the individual man
In his individual freedom who can mature
With his warm spirit the unripe world.

Christopher Fry
The Firstborn

Life in the past, we commonly suppose, was barbarous, primitive, and technologically at a generally low level; in Hobbes' words, nasty, brutish and short; the present is refined, civilised and enriched by stupendous forms of progress in many fields, especially that of technology.

This is the kind of picture most people have of their present situation and its relation to the past, yet it is almost wholly false. There has never been a time in which human life has been so precarious, held so cheaply and lived out in terms so demeaning of human stature; there has never been a time when killing, torture and destruction have been so commonplace, where suffering and want have been so widespread, and where creativity of the finer arts has relapsed so greatly from what has been achieved in earlier centuries.

One can see this contradiction between supposition and reality very clearly in the sphere of race relations in South Africa. White people there believe they represent civilisation, culture and progress, and even a great many black people believe them. Yet again, the boot is on the other foot, black civilisation in terms of its family, clan and tribal structures, its social patterns and its cultural manifestations, marks itself out as a very finely balanced concept of organised social life, one which white people once shared in large measures, as witness the glories of English village civilisation until it was destroyed by the advent of mass technology, and as a similar scale of civilisation is now well on the way to being destroyed in Africa by the cash economy, misapplied technology and a general failure to put human beings, as distinct from ideas such as the rate of economic growth, economic efficiency, and so on, in the centre of the picture.

It should be made clear that it is no part of our concern here to send up a wail of despair about technology and to plead for a return to a simpler past where technology was less imposing; our concern is to probe why is it that despite all the advances in technology, life for millions of people is so horrible when it is not simply frustrating and unsatisfying to a degree unknown to our forbears, and why our future prospects look so bleak and ominous.

Such questions inevitably open up many others. Why is the age of abundance which technology is presumed to have made possible not being realised? Why is the gap between rich and poor, and the multitudes of people who are starving, or living in wretched, ramshackle and insanitary conditions, growing instead of diminishing? Why is the failure of mass education to enlarge and make splendid the adventure of living so patent? After all, the arguments advanced for mass education were based on the idea that by bringing more people to an understanding of great literature, music, art, sculpture, philosophy and so on, the general degree of responsiveness to these and other refinements would increase proportionately and that as a consequence our achievements in these fields would outsoar the shadow of the past and lead us towards even brighter vistas of creative adventure and achievement in the future. Why has this not happened?

Why, despite the growth of literacy, is the general quality of our newspapers and journals so demeaning, trivial and unworthy? Why is modern architecture so squalid? Why is modern music so impoverished, and modern taste in almost everything so vulgar? Why are our church leaders so silent and unresponsive when confronted with the horrors of modern life and the armageddon of social collapse towards which civilisation is so clearly moving? Why are our democratically elected parliamentarians so ineffectual and pusillanimous in face of the terrible dangers confronting us and so manifestly unable to map out a path which will give people hope and a justified sense of purpose? Why, for that matter, are they so powerless, despite the power they appear to wield, power which is so often enshrined in written constitutions or constitutional conventions?

Why is the incidence of ill-health, especially the ill-health of the mind, increasing rather than diminishing? Why are we confronted with a population explosion for which we have no answers other than specious ones which merely diminish the human stature as much of those who propose them as of those who are persuaded to apply them? Why are we confronted with such an awesome spectacle of ecological disruption in almost every sphere in which people today are working, whether on the land, at sea, in the air, in factories and workshops and so on? Why such disruption when for thousands of years human beings have satisfied their needs without setting such a disaster in train? Why are we poisoning the land, poisoning the air, poisoning the waterways of the world and, of course, poisoning ourselves so assiduously? Why are we blindly and collectively consuming at an increasing rate the rapidly diminishing stocks of many finite resources in a way which cannot fail, as we must surely now be fully aware, to beggar our grandchildren and affect so adversely our whole posterity? Why, for that matter, are we apparently so uncaring about our posterity (which is really a reflection of the fact that we don't care very much about ourselves) when we ourselves are the heirs of the fruits of peoples' strivings through countless generations of the past? Why are we behaving with such unsmiling insensitivity towards the other animal species of the planet (and is this a reflection of the fact that we have come to have the same attitude to our own species, to each other)?

Why are our economic affairs in such manifest disorder? Why, despite the fact that we probably have today more colleges, students, professors, textbooks, lectures and seminars devoted to the subject than there has ever been in all the past history of mankind, are the workings of economic forces so clearly out of control and so little understood? Why is a growing proportion of workers unable to find work while our leaders inform us that our salvation can only come through greater productivity and an accelerating rate of growth? Why is it that although all governments set themselves the target of economic stability they are so manifestly unable to reach it? Why is the value of money so unstable, and inflation so rampant? Why, despite the Charter of the United Nations, are world trading arrangements so blatantly unjust and favouring rich nations so emphatically that a global political revolution of protest by the less advantaged nations is only too likely to ensue?

What has gone wrong? Why is it that no leading body of academics or politicians or churchmen or other forms of educated opinion is prepared to point the way out of this morass and why, for that matter, do they persist either actively, or in the case of churchmen, with silent acquiescent spinelessness, or in the case of academics from sheer intellectual inadequacy and confusion, in pushing us further along the primrose path to some everlasting bonfire of destruction, and why do millions upon millions of people allow themselves without protest to be herded along this path in defiance of all reason, of all sanity and of all morality?

Why, despite the fact that the overwhelming majority of mankind desires nothing more ardently than to live in peace are the governments of the world arming and preparing for war to such a degree as to make yet another global conflict a natural outcome of their labours? Why in an age of progress and general desire for peace have millions and millions of people died in one war or another, or in one social upheaval or another, around the globe? Why does the whole gamut of scientified endeavour today seem like witchcraft become rampant in the hands of a Sorceror's Apprentice? It is probable that more people have been killed through human action in this century than in all the previous centuries of human experience added together; why has science and war fostered the bitter fruit of so much suffering and sorrow onto multitudes of innocent people? Why are we unable to turn towards the light, towards genuine peace, real plenty and durable forms of progress? Why, above all, is our age of technological triumph one of such manifest spiritual defeat?

Any book on politics today that is not concerned in finding answers to these questions is surely not worth the paper on which it is written. What follows is an attempt to view these problems and many others in a perspective which may give us a clearer picture of their import and which may in consequence be able to project some solutions. But the reader ought perhaps to be warned that he will probably want to agree with very little of it, and indeed he may find the views expressed here run counter to nearly everything he has come to associate with such words as progress, efficiency and civilisation.

On the other hand he ought not perhaps be too surprised at this. If our civilisation is falling apart despite the best wisdom we can produce to stop it, it is surely just possible that there may be something fundamentally amiss with the nature of the wisdom we are applying, and not least in matters relating to politics and economics.

One must suppose the object of the political process is that it should resolve the problems created by the mere fact that human communities exist at all. In the past these problems have centred on such issues as peace and war, scarcity and abundance and on what may be summarised as liberty, equality and fraternity. Today there must be few people with an ordinary interest in the political process who are unaware that these traditional issues of politics are being superseded by new forces which are creating problems of which our forbears had hardly any inkling. The problem of war, for example, has assumed such novel forms that it has become a quite different type of problem altogether. It is no longer a question of controlling ordinary human behaviour, but of finding ways of controlling the technology of war before it destroys us. In the past the main problem might well have centred on how best to start a war, today for the vast majority of mankind, now that its destructive import has become so horrendous, the main preoccupation has become how, at almost any cost, to prevent it.

There are, of course, exceptions to the general desire for peace, the Arabs appears not to want peace *and* the existence of Israel, the rulers of the Russian Empire seem bent on promoting world conquest, and there are doubtless other countries which would prefer war rather than peace for one objective or another. Nevertheless they remain exceptional. In any case, the rulers of the Russian Empire—the only colonial empire to have survived intact into the last quarter of the twentieth century, can in no honest sense be said to be representative of the people over whom they rule. (How indeed can they when Stalin seems some-how to have obtained the power to encapsulate some of the most violent features of several centuries of history, from the Black Death, the Peasants Revolt, the Hundred Years War, the Tudor despotisms, the Reformation and the Dissolution of the Monasteries, the Civil War and the execution of the monarch, the Colonial Expansion, the long-drawn-out defeat of Napoleon to the heroic Luddite revolts, all into a mere couple of decades?)

The tiny minority of governments around the world which seem to want war are in fact utterly unrepresentative of the yearning of the vast majority of mankind for peace. Why then, we need to ask insistently, are we confronted with a prospect of war which our political processes seem able to do little more than to make a statistical inevitability as the extent of destructive armaments increases year by year?

A similar ineffectuality is apparent in relation to other problems which traditionally people have looked to their political processes to solve. Poverty is not being abolished, it is on the increase everywhere except in some especially favoured nooks and crannies of wealth and development; despite all our technological advances, (and it may well be *because* of them), sheer, brute, physical starvation has become the daily lot of increasing millions of mankind, and the verdict of most people who have studied the problem is that it is likely to continue to grow.

And what of the crucial area of liberty? All over the world legislators are busy churning out ever increasing volumes of new laws, and the number of regulatory bodies to give effect to them is growing everywhere like the rash of some noxious disease. Who would claim that this Victoria Falls of legislation spells more freedom for people? and not less?

But even these problems are simply but some of the manifestations of the failure of the political process to do its job, to tackle, that is its basic problem, which we may take to be, how to ensure its everyday processes, never mind its results, reflect the general citizen's interests as they are seen and understood by the general citizen. Why then, despite the widespread acceptance of the ballot box as a basic item of constitutional furniture, are the fruits of the political process so contrary to what people really want, and for that matter what they need?

Politics is, after all, one of the supreme arts of mankind; upon its development and the numerous ways in which it comes to be exercised depends in very large measure all the other forms of social enrichment which man has been able to accomplish. Yet the basic problem of politics has scarcely changed down the centuries; wherever people aggregate themselves into communities, of whatever size, this overriding problem is created which presses insistently for solution: How to dispose of the power inherent in the very existence of the community, by the mere fact of its coming into being, in such ways that the interests of the generality of its members are safeguarded and advanced? This central political problem has defied the best efforts of successive generations of men through history, although not, it is important to note, to the same extent at different times or in different places. Yet however much it has defied them a deeper look at history suggests that despite the despotisms of the past and the abundant ballot boxes of the present, our forbears grappled far more successfully with this problem than we are able to do today. Again it must be asked, why?

Although the record is marred in many ways by the rule of tyrants, dictators, conquering invaders, corrupt princes, cabals of money or military interest, revolutionary despotisms and other forms of usurpation, yet there is a common thread running throughout to which men have always sought to return, and against which the various forms of usurpation have always, ultimately, been judged. That thread is the idea that democracy is the most appropriate method, and the one most likely to yield the most enduring and acceptable results, and for resolving the always dangerous problem of the safe disposal of political power.

Although the idea, possibly because of the word which conveys it, is commonly reputed to be of Greek origin, it is probable that the practice of democracy, if we take Lincoln's classic but somewhat verbose definition for it of 'government of the people, for the people and by the people' must have prevailed from the earliest times. There must be many parts of the world which were once settled by a score or so of families in remote parts and who conducted their affairs on the basis of a general consensus, so that even if they chose to be ruled by a leader, a chief or a monarch, the face-to-face nature of power relationships in such communities meant that no ruler could move far out of step of the wishes of the ruled for very long. We may take it then that the very idea of democracy centres on a general consensus of what constitutes the general well-being; it is an affirmation, if only by implication, that since society exists for people, then people themselves must decide its goals, and the means by which they shall be sought and if possible attained.

This was not the result of any theoretical insight of our forbears; it was a pragmatic consequence of common practice. Human groupings were modest in scale and it was this factor above any other which enabled them to be human-centred and thus closely orientated to the common stock of wisdom and moral precept of their members. These systems of localised, small-scale democracy appear to have prevailed for many more years than we have record among the Indians of the Americas, the sub-Saharan tribes of the continent of Africa, among the Aborigines of Australasia, and the tribal peoples of Burma and the Indian sub-continent.[1]

These instances, and many others there is no need to quote, indicate that the practice of democracy is part of a general disposition of mankind, and one that did not need the enlightenment of the Greek philosophers in order to secure its initial adoption. They also indicate that the idea was a living reality long before the modern era, and that in many respects, if their durability is any guide, it was a more effective method of government than those modern forms which boast the name today. So that if the *idea* of democracy is much older than the Greek origins of the word itself, we may guess it must have

[1] See for example, John Collier, *The Indians of the Americas* ; Jayaprakash Narayan, *History of Gram Swarg* ; Margaret Mead, *Growing up in New Guinea*; Basil Davidson, *Africans in History*.

been not only a common enough practice among numerous isolated tribes and clans long before the Greeks projected it systematically as a theory; as a social instinct it is probably as old as human society. And for a very good reason, it was the obvious and most effective means by which the problem of the disposition of the power inherent in the existence of any society was resolved in a manner which met the general wishes of its members *and also best ensured its survival as a unit.*

Quite clearly there have been long periods when democracy has scarcely prevailed at all, although this must not lead us to assume it has been entirely absent even when the stage has been dominated by some colourful historical despot. Democracy is after all, not just a matter of voting on public issues or of helping to elect representatives to the legislature, it is also, we need to insist, a matter of making decisions, free decisions, on the numerous matters which the citizen will ordinarily encounter in the normal course of his daily life, in his work, as much as in his family, social and cultural life, and there is probably far less scope for an ordinary citizen to do just this in one of our modern 'mass democracies' than there was for a villager in the Egypt of the Pharoahs.

Again many of the city states of Renaissance Europe were often more effectively democratic in this sense, as well as in Lincoln's terms, than the forms of democracy commonly known today. It is true that representation was largely through the trading and craft guilds, so that whilst the skilled workers of every calling had some measure of representation, those who are unskilled or unemployed, or who suffered the misfortune of not being born men, were not formally enfranchised at all. There was indubitably also another side to Renaissance politics, made up of thuggery, assassination, vendetta, corruption and mob violence. The rivalry of the Montagus and the Capulets was not simply, we may be sure, a business of mere personal antipathies, running through it must have been strong elements of political and economic motivation which were too deep to be resolved by intermarriage; and such rivalries, always threatening to erupt into street brawls and murder, were part of the very stuff of renaissance city life, and in acknowledging this double aspect it presents, we surely have cause to marvel the more that the positive element was so full of such splendour.

Yet government was generally small-scale, and if well-to-do families were apt to dominate the scene, their power was liable to wax and wane, whereas that of the guilds tended to remain fairly constant; the power of the wealthy was tempered too by the need always to find allies in the mob, a need which, since it was presumably shared by more than one family, would often have the effect of a mutual cancelling out. So that if government of the people needed to be *for* the people, there was a real, direct sense in which it was government *by* the people. Indeed, there is something to be said for the fact that Lincoln's triad of postulates is superfluous; the concern of democratic government is after all to achieve government *by* the people, for if it is so it cannot fail to be *of* the people and, unless we are to assume the generality of people are not altogether in their right minds, an eventuality occasionally not unfortunately quite so unthinkable as we might like to suppose, it can scarcely fail to be *for* the people.

Both Greek and Renaissance city states depended for the excellence of their achievements on the existence of a relatively large class of wealthy and leisured people, bearing in mind that the tempo of life was such as to make almost anyone with an assured income, even if only of middling proportions, a person of leisure. When journeys by sea or land were matters of weeks rather than hours, when wealth came from the land or from things made by hand, both of which could only be produced by due process of the seasons or of men's labours, there was time not only to make money, but to enjoy it. The spectacle of people giving up the best years of their lives to pursuits such as advertising or stockbroking at a hectic pace in order to enjoy the fruits of such scheming on retirement in a state of marked physical and mental debility, would have struck our Renaissance people as something truly esoteric and possibly slightly mad. In turn, however, they depended greatly on the toil of a labouring class, many of whom in Greece were slaves, and even in Renaissance Europe, were little more than serfs. The twentieth century has enlarged the need for such a class—indeed most people of all classes are slaves in one guise or another today, but in doing so it seems too to have destroyed anyone's capacity to enjoy leisure creatively at all.

An euphoric state of unreflecting, bovine well-being seems to be almost the dearest thing masses of people will now own, and in terms of creativity Europe seems to have slipped back by about three or even four centuries. It is true slaves are no longer bought or sold individually, the power of advertising and other forms of manipulation now enable this to be done more subtly and indirectly *en masse*. It might be thought the development of machines to replace labour would have had the effect of emancipating what used to be called 'the labouring classes' culturally and socially, as well as politically. This clearly has not happened. What has happened is not so much emancipation as disenfranchisement (whereas in pre-technological societies the terms were almost exactly reversed so that people were enfranchised in almost every sphere *except* the ballot box). This process of disenfranchisement from decision-making from nearly all spheres except the ballot box has resulted in a grim process of cultural alienation which seems to have spread to nearly all classes. There will be occasion to discuss the social and cultural effects of this process elsewhere, here we need to focus on the political effects.

Formally, the evidence seems to point the other way, masses of people now have the vote, the scene is dominated by the leaders of mass parties, who take it in turns to occupy office after heady election campaigns in which there is apparently the maximum freedom for anyone to put forward any proposal or any candidate in the hope of securing support and acceptance. And yet, and yet, something is clearly amiss. Behind the facade of mass party organisations and assumed mass aquiescence there is a marked degree of citizen non-involvement in much of the entire governing process.

The modern era has thrown up a variety of forms of political power which were unknown to former ages, forms such as radio, television, mass newspapers, mass advertising, public utilities such as telephone and postal services, air, rail and road transport, electricity, gas and water services, health and welfare services, pension schemes, and also the sheer fact of organisation itself as expressed in mass party structures, trade unions, retail and whole-sale marketing, semi-monopolies and so on. Most of these factors are so huge as to embody as much political power as was formerly embodied in the entire structure of the state and it might be supposed, in a democratic context, that as they emerged in history each in turn would be the subject of varying forms of democratic enfranchisement of the citizen. This of course has not happened, instead these new forms of power have for the most part simply been added to the already imposing power of the state, or they have not been brought within the area of citizen enfranchisement at all; this in turn has created a burden of ministerial functions which is beyond the capacity of any legislature to render accountable either to itself or to those who have elected it. As a consequence, and it is a very unnatural and undemocratic consequence, government has come to mean, for the most part, policy-formulation and decision-making by non-elected persons behind closed doors in one committee or another.

Not surprisingly, such public discussion as ensues, especially during elections, tends to centre on issues which are either trivial, irrelevant, or simply immoral. As these lines are written an election campaign is underway in Britain and almost the entire burden of what the leading party spokesmen have to say centres on how they propose to make people richer in material goods—not how to make life ecologically cleaner and safer, not more just in response to the tidal wave of revolutionary anger which is mounting in the disadvantaged countries of the world, not more satisfying and meaningful in terms of the transcendent problems of existence which confront every individual, not more dignified or even nobler, just richer in material goods.

It might be supposed from this that rich people and rich nations were happier than poor ones, less prone to suicide, drug addiction, divorce, mental and physical breakdown, delinquency and other manifestations of psychic despair. If there is any evidence to support such a supposition it seems to be remarkably well-concealed. It might well be urged that only by promising to make people richer can politicians obtain the votes they seek, and if this is true it is at least worth asking what has gone wrong with a political process which reduces masses of people as a matter of course to a condition of mindless, blinkered moronism and which makes them incapable of seeing any issue of public policy other than in terms of their immediate creature comforts? If this really is the end result of democracy in action it can surely only presage events which spell the end of democracy itself.

The only way Britain or any other rich country can be made richer today in any human sense of the word is by organising itself to consume not more of the remaining stocks of the world's finite resources, but less, to restore creativity and dignity to work, to opt for a simpler and less demanding lifestyle, to disperse the power of decision-making away from one centre and to create a multi-cellular structure which will be able to challenge the powers of mass parties, mass unions, mass manipulators, various economic monopolies and other anti-democratic structures simply by existing and functioning. Such an approach is probably the only one which will resolve the incidental problems of inflation, balance of payments deficits, indebtedness and unemployment.

Even if this was not true we need to take cognisance of the far more imposing fact that it is the political process, especially in the overdeveloped nations, which is *producing* results which are putting into hazard the whole import and direction of civilisation, a hazard which can scarcely fail to engulf our prevailing democratic institutions if steps are not soon taken to steer a different course.

To put it briefly, our political processes have produced or failed to avert a number of problems of which there are no historical precedents and to which men should be achieving clear-cut and decisive solutions if they want to go on living in civilised societies at all. These problems can be summarised in their modern form as war, population excess, pollution, starvation, resource wastage and alienation. Any one of these problems relates to factors which could destroy our civilisation, any one of them, yet here are listed six, and it would be a bold spirit who would aver the list is complete.

The mere existence of these problems bespeaks of a quite shattering degree of failure of our political processes to do the job for which they were presumably established, as much as a healthy man dying in his prime may bespeak a failure of medical practice to prevent or cure his symptoms. What then has gone wrong? How has it gone wrong ? And far more important, how can we put things right?

CHAPTER II

War and State Power

War is a judgement that overtakes societies when they have been living upon ideas that conflict too violently with the laws governing the universe... Never think that wars are irrational catastrophes: they happen when wrong ways of thinking and living bring about intolerable situations.

Dorothy L. Sayers
Creed or Chaos

Let us consider first the problem of war. If Ardrey and others are to be believed, we all of us have an instinct to fight when our homeland is invaded, rather than to accept Gandhi's advice to invite the invader into our homes, to give him refreshment and rest, and then ask him to leave; our natural tendency is to take arms and seek to defend ourselves by putting him out of action. If this is accepted then clearly the instinct to fight is deep-rooted and, it might be supposed, gives a convincing explanation for the prevalence of war, especially in modern times. Yet this is precisely what it does not do, for modern wars are only incidentally about territory, their dominant focus centres generally on the ideology of the government in power.

The fact that a few 'colonial possessions' changed hands at the end of World War I and that there were some frontier changes in Europe should not blind us to the fact that the major contestants were not bent on conquering, subjugating and occupying one another at all. That particular war, one of the most futile, ruinous and horrible in all history, was sparked off by considerations which were purely imaginary and even hallucinatory, and accomplished nothing except the slaughter of the most ardent spirits of an entire generation and the destruction of a fund of moral capital it had taken Europe centuries to accumulate, and more than half a century after the event there has yet to appear a worthwhile explanation of what the conflict really was about anyway.

The Second World War, itself a product of the moral debility stemming from the first, was more obviously ideological. It is true that Hitler's territorial ambitions were those of a demented Roman Emperor, but none of those who resisted him, if one excludes the utterly unrepresentative and barbarous Stalin, were bent on grabbing Germany for themselves.

The overspill of power is not now finding an outlet in actual wars between states, states are now making war on themselves. This is the real meaning of mass motoring, inner city 'redevelopment' —often the cause of more destruction of our architectural and social heritage than all the military conflicts of modern time have been able to accomplish in toto, nuclear energy, 'Concorde', armaments and all the frantic swinishness of mass advertising—engendered consumerism, and they are winning! The awesome degradation of the habitat, the only one we have, is so extensive, and in some cases so irreparable as a consequence as to make its continued functioning in respect of supporting life, and not least human life, a matter of serious doubt.

Any rule in politics must in the nature of things admit of exceptions, and in this matter of war and ideology there is obviously a major exception in the Arab-Israel conflict; but even here there are extraneous forces at work not immediately involved in the problem. In establishing the state of Israel in the former territory of Palestine the Jews compelled many of the former Arab inhabitants to leave. This was a real old-fashioned war of invasion, conquest and settlement at the expense of those inhabitants who formerly occupied the territory. There have since been a number of 'frontier adjustments' as they are called, involving the displacement of yet more Arabs. This has inflamed the feelings of the entire Arab world, partly in terms of Arab nationalism, partly in terms of a failure of Arab Governments to resolve the pressing domestic problems of poverty and social squalour, partly in terms of religious bigotry and partly, one must suppose, in terms of Ardrey's 'territorial imperative'; the strength of these feelings is such that the refugees instead of being sensibly resettled in other parts of the Arab world, have become pawns in the world power struggle, a factor to be juggled with the manoeuvrings of other power groups.

And yet, it remains an exception, and even as an exception it has been modified by the massive sanity of the Arab-Israel peace treaty of March 1979. Within the same historical period there have been far bigger displacements of population in Europe as a result of the Hitler war. Millions of Poles, Germans and other nationalities have been pushed from their homeland, yet why is the European response to this so different? Why has it not provoked, along with an upsurge of European nationalism, a crusading spirit to rectify these wrongs? Why are German and French students, for example, not demonstrating in favour of war to put right the wrong done to their fellow Europeans in Poland by the forces of Russian Empire, even if it does mean another world war, as Arab students are apt to demonstrate in, let us say, Tehran, for the Palestinian Arabs?

The answers to these questions point to a quite different outlook between the peoples of the two regions. Life is harsh in the Arab world, geography gives it a cruel climate and exceedingly tough conditions of life, and has also made it a nucleus of trans-continental trade routes which has meant it has long been a frequent scene of invasion and conquest; its oil resources have made it a favourable target for colonialist exploitation and its poverty is a byword of wretchedness. The Arabs have none of the modern means of production to alleviate their lot, their economies are still largely based on small peasant farming and the frustrations of their lives need to be seen against a background where much of their poverty, despite the wealth yielded by their oil, is destined to remain a chronic feature of life. In these circumstances what is more natural than to visit their frustration against an alien people who, after a long historical interlude, have again come to settle in their midst.

Yet the facts, if facts can be said to speak, point to a different logic. Until the Arab-Israel peace treaty Israel occupied an area of Egyptian territory as far as the Suez Canal which constitutes one-fifteenth of the entire desert area of Egypt. It is almost wholly empty. It contains a modest reserve of oil and some minerals and ores which on the whole are not worth exploiting owing to lack of transport. And that is all. Its value lies not in its wealth either potential or actual, but in its position, for it borders one of the major trade routes of the world, the Suez Canal, which was for some years in abeyance since the Egyptians resolutely refused to allow it to be used; in doing so they lost far more income from its revenues, from loss of trade, from the decline of their tourism, and the high level of military spending to which they chose to commit themselves, than ever was to be gained from the desert territories of Sinai. One may well wonder why the Egyptians did not accept the consequences of their military defeat, as the Germans and the Poles have had to do, make a deal with Israel over the canal (to be made four times wider?), revive their trade and devote their resources to exploiting the remaining fourteen-fifteenths of their desert territory.

The stark fact remains that the Egyptians, and several other Arab states, wanted to make war against Israel, and there is a fair amount of evidence that this still remains, with the exception of the Egyptians, a genuinely popular demand. To what extent this feeling is still being fanned by governments seeking to divert attention from domestic shortcomings it is difficult to say, but even so the fact is there and it is a fact almost unique on the modern political scene. For the counterfact is this, whatever glamour and allurement war may have had in the past, people today do not want war, and they have enough reason in all conscience not to want it when moral as well as physical horizons are dominated by weapons of war so insanely destructive as to constitute an ecological and biological threat to the entire human race.

Yet almost without exception nations all over the world are arming for war and preparing for war and it is surely a matter of statistical inevitability that one day there will again be a major world war in defiance of this overwhelming desire of the majority of the people of the world for peace. 'A nation armed and prepared for war' said Bernard Shaw, 'can no more help going to war than a chicken can help laying an egg'.

The attempts to resolve this problem are already legion. In the modern era we have had that enormous exercise in futility the League of Nations, followed by the no less futile and even more expensive exercise of the United Nations. There has been a succession of disarmament conferences which have succeeded in disarming nobody, endless peace talks, exchanges of views and so on. In the non-governmental sphere there are over a dozen international organisations working for peace and most countries can boast a fair number of national peace organisations.[1] Over the years there have also been an impressive number of peace meetings and conferences, as well as large numbers of public demonstrations of one kind or another. All this activity is very worthy and creditable, and bespeaks a meritorious concern for an urgent public issue, why then at all levels has it been so singularly ineffective? None of these organisations appears to have had the remotest effect on the wars that have erupted over the last two decades, whether in Korea, the Congo, Burma, the Middle East, Biafra, Burundi, Indonesia, Somalia, the Sudan, Rhodesia, Bangladesh, Algeria or, not least, in Vietnam. None of these bodies has been able to exercise any discernible influence on the stopping of nuclear armaments,

[1] The reader who is curious is referred to an annual publication called *World Peace Diary* in which these bodies are listed. Britain tops the board with no less than 104 organisations, the U.S.A. gets by with a mere 62, the democratic, peace-loving peoples of the U.S.S.R. scrape along with a mere four, whereas the heroic toiling masses of the Peoples Republic of China, all 800 million of them, under the inspired leadership of whatever group has grabbed the reins of power at the moment, can manage its quest for peace quite well with only two. (Available from Housemans, 5 Caledonian Road, London, N.1.)

and the drift towards some kind of global disaster continues with a progress which can only be described as somnambulistic.

War today has assumed a form which constitutes a threat to the existence of the entire human species, its force is such that it can easily destroy the entire fabric of civilised life, its moral import is so obscene as to make a mockery of the entire heritage of the various systems of moral precept and practice which has accrued to man through the ages; when it eventuates (we do not say 'if') it will leave the survivors to live at the level of the beasts of the field; the overwhelming majority of mankind, does not, cannot, want this incomprehensible catastrophe to happen; nearly all people live under forms of government which claim to one degree or another to represent the popular will; yet the growth of nuclear armaments, as well as of thermonuclear weapons, to say nothing of other horrors from the laboratories of science, proceeds without respite and the consummation of these trends has already assumed the mantle of a Wagnerian drama moving towards its inevitable Gotterdamerung and the total destruction of Valhalla.

We need to ask with the most urgent insistence 'why'? Why should the hopes and dreams, the labours and the inspired devotion to truth and beauty of men through the ages reach the kind of fulfillment to be witnessed in the dreadful vision of the future that now confronts us? Why should the whole gamut of human labour and human splendour be mocked today by such a squalid apotheosis of destruction and despair? If men in their hearts reject such a doomladen prospect whilst governments everywhere work remorselessly towards it, what has gone wrong?

Any attempt to answer this question in terms of a conventional description of the presumed issues at stake between the communist and capitalist powers will serve only to mislead and obscure the more fundamental problems. However deeply divided nations may appear to be on grounds of ideology, modern communications have created one world where the fundamental assumptions men are making about the world are increasingly identical. This in turn is making countries supposedly divided by an ideological vacuum in fact increasingly alike in terms of the effects their governments are having on the lives of their citizens. It is the growing similarities which exist between Washington and Moscow today which are important, and they are becoming far more important than their differences. Which people, as between these two, is the more brainwashed by the dominant forces at work in their society? Which people is more free? Has better prospects of life for the future? Is seeking more conscientiously to relate its material needs to the limitations of our planet rather than to the undisciplined propensity of each person to push consumption levels to the limit? Which people are able to exercise more suasion over the forces that control their social institutions?

Simply to pose these questions is to reveal the shoddiness of the assumption that the world is marching towards armageddon because of the irreconcilable ideologies that each of these two major world powers claims to uphold, ideologies which compel each power to adopt an insane level of military preparedness in order to meet the threat to its own ideology the existence of the other is presumed to pose. It is an assumption which is shattered by the course of current history, with an American President visiting the capitals of China and Russia on 'friendship' missions and with a prevailing degree of hostility between the two principal communist powers greater than that which they show towards the capitalist 'enemy'.

Nations derive their characteristics from each other today for more than they think, even when they assume they are ideologically completely at odds with each other. The real cause of the world war malaise goes deeper, whilst being at the same time susceptible to a much more precise degree of definition; it is a definition which, because it is an aspect of our problems which men can directly work upon, can give men everywhere a justifiable cause for hope and courage.

The conclusions to be drawn from the spectacle of such gigantic forces hurtling towards a destiny of destruction despite the wishes of the generality of people *and* the wishes of the forces organising the destruction, can be stated simply. Either people everywhere are in the grip of a pathological drive towards self-destruction which permits of no relief of tension until it is accomplished, or mankind as a whole has created forces in its nation states apparatus which are beyond the ability of anyone to control.

The first alternative can indicate a considerable variety of evidence to justify its plausibility. The work of Freud and many others in the field of psychoanalysis is enough to indicate that the human personality is a battle-ground between the forces of light and darkness, and that each individual has propensities for hate and destructiveness, including self-destructiveness, of a degree which is easily able to negative all the constructive drives the ego may manifest. Certainly there is also ample evidence that aggression and destructiveness are on the increase in our societies but, if a generalisation may be ventured, this negativism appears to derive its dynamic from the nature of the social order itself, in other words it is a generalised propensity in human nature which society itself is provoking to uncommon heights because society itself is frustrating to a novel degree the constructive and creative impulses in man.

There is, in any event, far too much evidence that people genuinely do not want war (let the reader ask himself if he wants it), far too much evidence of concern for human well-being even if, with our so-called welfare states, it is rather ineptly expressed, to sustain such a belief. Men do not want war if only because they are too well aware of the horrors it will evoke and because the will to live is, after all, stronger than almost any other impulse or instinct in man; what still remains unexplained is the mystery why this abundant appetite for life is not finding expression in the political mechanisms of modern society and why instead it is being frustrated by forces of destruction and death. Why?

We need to relate this question to the other major problems of our time. The solutions being propounded to resolve the population explosion threaten to be as numerous, it sometimes seems, as the number of new mouths expecting sustenance with every passing year; but nowhere is any attention being focused on the factor of size in community affairs, and its relationship to the quite evident breakdown of any capacity to control those affairs by community members.

We may be well assured that the merest village in any continent of the world, given the power of self-rule, given the power to perceive that the factor of its own numbers was a problem at all, could be relied upon to evolve those forms of community morality, and the endless and subtle variety of pressures which any community produces as a matter of course to sustain it, which would result in a restriction of numbers to seemly levels with no great difficulty. But without control community action does not begin, and neither does control without power, the power to decide and the power to act.

And what about pollution and resource wastage? Factors which hold the threat of mass starvation for millions within a generation or less. Would the elders of the merest African village knowingly allow these factors to get out of control to such an extent without taking effective measures to reassert that community control, based on community morality, without which no answer to the problem is possible at all?

It is true that African village practice often leads, or has led, to both wastage and pollution, as for example in the Chitemene system of agriculture in Zambia with its waste of soil fertility, or in the common but ferociously wasteful practice of starting bush fires which may consume many square miles of vegetation in order to trap small animals for food. But at least here people are acting from ignorance of factors which are, or were, beyond the frontiers of the common stock of wisdom; what are we to say of so-called advanced civilisations which act in far more wasteful and destructive ways in defiance of the wisdom and knowledge of such matters as they have? Where is the control?

As for the last, but possibly the most important of the problems we have raised, that of human alienation from life, what would be the purpose of any small community in full command of its situation in allowing work to be degraded to the joyless level of factory wage-labour slavery? Or of culture becoming a grotesque and passive parody of its own potentialities? Or of community life becoming almost wholly subordinated to the dictates of faceless functionaries in remote offices in almost every sphere of activity—political, economic, cultural, social, welfare and so on? Why should such a community continue in existence at all if, having, the power to control these factors for the enrichment of its members' lives, it refused to use it?

It is surely a fair statement that in these and numerous other matters this control is no longer in members' hands and that this is largely the source of the malaise. Today the formal institutions of democracy have ceased to be a means of citizen control, they have become instead a means of denying it. We shall need to focus more fully on this problem for it has now become a logjam of all citizen efforts to achieve solutions to many other pressing problems.

For generations radical motivation has centred on the need to capture control of the commanding heights of state power, be they military, economic or political, as a means of establishing citizen control which would usher in an era of economic justice. What has never been understood is that it is impossible to gain control of forces conducted on such a scale as is common to mass nation states without becoming a part of the mechanism, becoming identified with the ends for which the mechanism is already used (generally the more pursuit of power as an end in itself), and becoming as much divorced from general citizen control as are the prevailing wielders of power.

It is as though the citizens elect a force to subdue the tyrant in his castle who uses his power to make a decent life for them impossible. The new force, if revolutionary, storms the castle, executes the tyrant and then at once occupies the tyrant's place and proceeds to act in much the same way. If it is Labour Party or Social Democratic reformist, it negotiates an entry into the castle and proceeds to sit down at table with the tyrant. Later on they may pension him off and occupy the castle wholly themselves. In both cases the general citizen body is as remote from any real control over the main questions affecting its own lives as it ever was. The fact that the castle entrance begins to be adorned with nameplates announcing, 'The Ministry of Education', 'The National Police Force', 'The Ministry of Social Welfare', and so on, is not evidence that the citizens have gained more control, but that they have lost more. Tyranny in the guise of bureaucracy is still tyranny. The mailed fist of naked aggression may be replaced by the spider's web of an endless *minutiae* of bureaucratic rules and regulations, it remains a denial of freedom and an affront to liberty.

If man can find no answer to these problems all his other problems will become irrelevant, for he himself will unleash forces which will undo all he has sought to accomplish down the centuries. His immediate danger is of another kind, it is that he will continue to feel so helpless in confronting the powerful forces which are sweeping all human affairs to destruction that he will lose his will to act and allow himself to give way to despair and to an irretrievable surrender to mere defeatism.

Yet it is in his very sense of helplessness that lies the clue to the solution he is seeking, for in face of these giant forces man *is* helpless and he is helpless for the simple reason that these forces have grown so large as to be beyond his control.

With that peculiar facility for seeing the obvious and ignoring its implications which has dogged human progress for centuries, men are very well aware of this, but since its implications point to an order of affairs wholly different in many major respects to that which prevails, and since what prevails is partly a product of a long process of intellectual and emotional conditioning, men find their reasoning powers today pulling in a direction quite contrary to the situation to which they have been conditioned, and since the pull of conditioning is so much more powerful than conclusions reached by a process of abstract reasoning, men tend to blind themselves to the message of their reasoning and thus to conclude there is nothing they can do about the fundamental problems the situation they have been conditioned to accept is promoting.

Yet there is everything they can do if once they resolve in their minds that the nature of the social institutions around them are not as immutable as the stars in their courses, but that they are the products of human needs and human decisions. So that when it is asserted that the main reason why men have lost control of their affairs is because many units, whether political, economic or social, have become too large for anyone to be able to control, instead of dismissing the implications that follow from this as being impracticable, it is important to grasp that they should be made the central focus of our attention.

No doubt the voice of the parliamentary liberal will be heard to urge that this contention about size is not true and that people do in fact exert control over public affairs; what else it will ask, doubtless with some impatience, is the elaborate machinery of parliamentary democracy, with its free press, its free speech, its free elections with a secret ballot and the rest of it, designed to secure but effective public control?

This argument seems soundly based and is widely accepted, but its basis is entirely false; it is moreover not only false, it is quite inevitably so, for it is attempting to apply the principles of democracy in the sense that they were operated within a Greek city state to the monster mass societies that prevail today. In doing this it is ignoring the principle that a change in quantity always leads to a change in quality when pursued far enough. A sand pit in a city public park, for example, may be a happy play-spot for toddlers, but multiply the size of the pit enough and it ceases to have any relation to its original function and becomes a desert where nothing grows and no human communities can exist.

What then needs to be asked is how the principles of democratic government as applied to a city state cease to be operable when applied to a mass society? We should note first a vital distinction between the two extremes. In a city state its proportions were such that its citizens generally knew one another personally, this meant that the personal judgements of the citizens of each other played a dominant part in their selection of rulers and the judgements they made about public affairs. Inevitably these judgements were moral judgements couched in moral terms and based on moral principles and arguments. Indeed, given the degree of personal knowledge citizens had of one another how could it have been otherwise? It is doubtless for this reason that nearly the whole of the voluminous Greek literature of philosophical speculation, especially in the dialogues of Plato, centres around the need for clarity about moral aims and 'right' conduct, about the difference between spiritual health and spiritual disease, the need to ensure that the principles which regulate the morally healthy society are also substantially the principles that regulate private conduct and so on. It is this concern which gives so much of Greek thought and achievement its peerless qualities of luminousness and clarity, of balance and proportion, and which by comparison makes so much modern political and philosophical speculation so arid, bleak, sterile and confused.

Compare the teaching of Plato's Academy with, let us say, that of the London School of Political and Economic Science today. The teachings of the former were a quest for excellence and a continuous attempt to propound what *should* prevail in the political field, the latter is concerned simply to expound the nature and the history of the institutions that exist from a wholly non-existent standpoint of 'objectivity',[2] which yields an impression that its teachers have been morally neutered. The Academy lasted more than nine hundred years and has had a continuous but beneficial and stimulating influence on thought for nearly two and a half millennia; the main assumptions on which the teaching of the London School of Economics appear to be based have helped to bring our civilisation to its knees less than a century after it was founded; a tribute of some sort both to the extent of its influence and the shoddiness of its principles.

[2]The quest for 'objectivity' is one of the most dangerous, as well as fruitless, preoccupations of the modern academic mind. Yet strangely enough it was the founders of the London School of Economics themselves who exploded the rationale of this quest. 'If', they argued, 'you can find a man without bias, it is due to the fact that he has the same prejudices as yourself.'

There is no debate in modern schools of political thought about moral concepts, which in itself contains the essential difference between the classical Greek world and our own; for today citizens no longer live in a moral relationship to each other.

How indeed can they when they do not *know* one another? It is true that we often 'know' our fellow residents, our fellow shoppers, our fellow taxpayers and fellow churchgoers, our fellow workers and so on, but how often are these the same people? Modern relationships tend to be fragmentary and impersonal, limited often to a functional basis—even if only that of fellow drinkers in a pub! We are no longer fellow citizens in the Athenian sense for we simply do not know one another in such a full context. Yet if we are strangers to each other *how* can our moral judgements develop and reflect in their development the fruits of the experience of their interaction, and how can they be made to be effective in the workings *and the control* of our societies? Men do not develop a moral sense in a vacuum, for morals are primarily a matter of the regulation of relationships, and developments in moral sensibility are a primary fruit of well ordered relationships in the light of considered moral precept and experience.

This surely leads to a quite frightening conclusion, since man in a mass society has no complete identity, in the sense that it is one that relates with a fair degree of completeness to his fellows as they to him, there is no basis in the ensuing citizen anonymity from which a citizen can relate his moral beliefs to the workings of society, and neither is there any way in which the workings of society can be related to the individual citizen's moral framework. This, we must clearly see, is the penalty which man pays for living in a mass society at all. The citizen not only lacks the power to control his society, he lacks even the moral basis to which he could relate its objectives to coherent moral purposes, and it is important to see that for this reason alone, and there are many others, the workings of modern mass societies are quite unable to follow any generationally transcendent courses at all. They cannot be controlled at all for any constructive purposes. In modern mass societies the prevailing morality of power has become locked in a life and death struggle with the power of morality. It follows that the other side of the coin of citizen anonymity, the price man pays in a mass society for his anonymity is powerlessness. Just that.

These problems are alluded to because they share with the problem of war a common derivative aspect, they represent results of the workings of the social order which people do not want, they indicate that it is producing consequences contrary to both their desires and their interests and again we need to ask, why? What is happening within the social order to produce this result?

A social organism develops because it serves certain needs of the people who have formed it, and we may postulate the goals of our social organisms as to help people to achieve peace, bread, liberty and survival. Since however they now have a pronounced tendency to produce war, want, tyranny and social collapse we are surely justified in declaring that they are out of control.

And if they are out of control, why?

To answer this question we need to note a common characteristic which those countries most afflicted with these results share. In a scene so shifting and complex as politics we cannot look for inflexible rules and results such as are found in mathematics or thermodynamics, there are bound to be exceptions to any generalisation advanced, all we can do is to denote tendencies and here the most imposing one to strike us is the tendency of loss of control to go hand in hand with a growth in the size of a unit.

One might of course expect this although nobody seems to; yet after all a short ladder is far more manageable than a long one, a five foot fishing rod is more controllable than a twenty foot rod, an elephant is far more cumbersome in movement than an ant and a twenty ton trailer lorry is more difficult to drive than a mini.

The foregoing is a quite crude theoretical explanation of the nature of citizen powerlessness; the record of contemporary history with its genocidal wars, its nuclear weapons and its gruesome dictatorships is a dreadfully tragic expression of the results of that powerlessness; what is needed now is a description of how the mechanics of the mass society operate to render its members powerless, for otherwise we have no answer to the liberal democrat gesticulating so frenziedly in the direction of our 'democratically' elected Parliaments.

In doing this we shall discuss the problem in general terms as its different aspects relate to the general concept of the mass society. At a subsequent stage we shall relate the conclusions which emerge to a division of the nations of the world in terms of three broad categories which distinguish their sizes, namely the nation, the meganation and the continental meganation.

CHAPTER III

The City State

Economic efficiency is a necessary element in the life of any sane and vigorous society, and only the incorrigible sentimentalist will depreciate its significance. But to convert efficiency from an instrument into a primary object is to destroy efficiency itself.

R.H. Tawney
Religion and the Rise of Capitalism

It is a common-place of economic theorising to postulate two forms of market activity, one known as 'perfect' and the other as 'imperfect' competition. In reality these two extremes, the one where many small independent firms, with no organised labour, no government intervention and no consumer protection associations, ensure that market prices are simply expressing an equilibrium of the market forces of supply and demand, and the other where one monopoly concern dominates the market and fixes prices as it will, seldom, if ever, exist in practice; nevertheless it is a useful framework within which it is possible to get a clearer picture of those forces that do exist, and perhaps the same approach, although with a different construct as applied to political life, may be equally useful.

At one end of the scale we can view the problems of a society which numbers only a handful of people, at the other end we can see how the same problems, in addition to many new ones, are grappled with by a society which may number hundreds of millions. Between these two extremes there exist societies of every graduation of size, and our concern here is to focus on how the factor of size itself affects the nature of the problems which are thrown up. In doing so we may hope to do something to rescue political theory from the dead end of undue focus on the formulation of abstract principles which are divorced from the realities of practical experience, of which the factor of size is not only assuredly one, but one which has possibly been more neglected than any other.

Political power in human societies is a product of human numbers. Robinson Crusoe, alone on his island, represented no political power at all until he encountered Man Friday. Their meeting at once posed the problem of political power; who would dominate whom? Or would they work together as equals for their common good? In the event they seem to have developed a rather amicable tutelary relationship.[1] Nevertheless, before the advant of Man

[1] A relationship, given the widespread popularity of this first novel in the English language, which must have done much to give many white people the peculiar notion that in their relationships with black people this was the natural order of affairs as ordained by Providence. They often overlooked however that even this relationship depended on Man Friday's free acquiescence.

Friday there was no society and hence no problem of determining its nature and relationships, that problem arose as soon as Crusoe ceased to be alone. It is a problem present in every family and it is one which grows in scope and difficulty as the growth in numbers continue and as we move by successive stages from the family to the clan, to the tribe, to the city state, to the nation, to the meganation and to the continental meganation.

Before proceeding we must define what is meant here by these three classes of nation. A nation may be defined as a political unit which can be within the general control of its members if the requisite conditions of freedom exist, and which is able to reflect in its day-to-day workings, its citizens' wishes and preferences. The Scandinavian states are a good example of this, so too are Switzerland, Austria, Luxembourg, Liechtenstein and Iceland. It is noteworthy that all these countries are small, most of them with populations less than half the size of London's.

This factor of population may be taken to be a general key although it is not the only one. If a small population is spread over a vast land area it can, if the country has a powerful central government, make democracy a matter of quite difficult practice. The level of communication and economic development, if low, can also hinder the workings of democracy, as may be seen in numerous underdeveloped nations with small populations. It is, of course, the factor of communication which enables a developed nation the practise a degree of democracy which was formerly confined to units little larger, if at all, than a city state.

A meganation is one, again largely because of its bigger population, which is able to reflect the general will in its workings only with the greatest difficulty, and examples of meganations are West Germany, Spain, France, Britain and Italy.

A continental meganation is one which is so huge that no effective functioning of democracy is remotely possible except for brief interludes such as on the issue of a war or a national crisis. A good example of such a crisis was the one which erupted during Mrs Gandhi's Emergency rule in India. Since, in addition to the general state of political oppression which prevailed, Mrs Gandhi's son, Sanjay, set out to implement a compulsory sterilisation programme which struck at the root of the most personal and intimate part of people's lives, and thus caused profound psychological shock (which most foreign observers appear to have failed to perceive), a general election which overturned her rule may well be said to have been an expression of the popular will. But it was an exception to the general rule of the bureaucrats and the politicians, and must be so, for India, like the other continental meganations, is ungovernable simply because it is too big to be governed by anyone. Again the determining factor is size, in this case in terms of both population and territory. There are really only four units in this class which, to give them their official titles, which is not the titles I would give them, are The Peoples Republic of China, the U.S.A., India and the U.S.S.R. In Europe there is a fifth one in the making, although whether the people of Europe will arouse themselves to stop this suicidal development before it is too late remains to be seen. If a United Europe becomes fully established we shall find it will proceed to live on the moral and social capital which centuries of national developments have built up, just as the meganations have been busy for a century or more in consuming the moral and social capital of the nations and the city states. There will come a time however when that capital (mostly in the form of liberal virtues of honour, tolerance and different forms of freedom) will become exhausted, or incompatible with the practice of the brute realities of the new (bigger) forms of power. When that happens, as has already happened in the U.S.A., the rhetoric of these matters will increase considerably as, it would seem by an inverse ratio, its practice dwindles, until it disappears.

Since we are asserting that with growth in population and territory the power of the citizen declines, just as market freedom disappears with the growth in the size of firms, we need to see exactly how the power implicit in the mere aggregation of human numbers is disposed at the various stages. In doing so we should note that this is a rather novel exercise. Democracy has generally been accepted as a working principle that can be applied to any society of any size. Our concern is to show that the factor of size is crucial to the efficacy of democracy in practice.

To begin at the beginning, at the level of the family, the clan and the tribe, the problem of 'who decides' is not very great and is, or generally has been, settled on a basis of consensus or by tradition. There is, however, a third factor of importance to nearly every stage of growth except the final ones, and that is the element of personal leadership in a given individual. A strong leader can ride roughshod over long-established institutions and usages as a weak one can allow them to be undermined by ambitious associates, this is the stuff of monarchial history down the centuries.

What is of more importance to note is the fact that in societies of this modest size it is possible for the generality of their members to control the decision-making process even when the leadership principle appears dominant. The territory covered is generally not large, and membership is on a personal level, where people are known and judged personally in terms of their personal acts and qualities. Indeed, we may say then that the essential quality of life in such communities is that *they are dominated by the personal relationships of their members*.

Several important considerations follow from this. It means that the institutions and practices of such societies will tend to be a reflection of the moral judgements of their members, as distinct from their individual itch for profit or place-seeking. It means that when decisions are made they will be made in the light of the prevailing moral code and in accordance with the judgements it promotes, and not least, such decisions will tend to strengthen or clarify that code—they will not ordinarily confuse or contradict it. This is not to say that the itch for profit or power disappears, or does not arise, of course not; what it does mean is that they, and the institutions they create or through which they work will, on the whole, be responsive and subordinate to the general community ethic of service, brotherhood, justice, equality before the law and so on.

This is probably still the case when we reach the stage of the city state, although already it is a generalisation which will have begun to be subject to important qualifications. By definition a city state is a fairly large urban centre sustained by the resources of its rural environment or hinterland. Generally such entities have been of fairly modest proportions compared with those accepted today. Even the original Greek megapolis, the word now in currency to denote a large city, had a circumference of only about five and a half miles, whilst the length of its territory was a mere twentyfour miles. By the time of the Renaissance the concept of a city state had developed to a point where the city would be more populous and its territory considerably larger; indeed the factor of trade and conquest enabled Venice, for example, at one time to establish a firm suzerainty over the countries of the Adriatic littoral, to dominate the trade routes of the Levant, to become the supreme power in the Mediterranean, to challenge the might of the Turkish Empire and to impose its will on its North Italian neighbours. Yet Venice, in power terms, is a small city albeit the most beautiful city in the world, built on a swamp.

It is interesting to note that both the Greek city states and those of the Renaissance had an awareness of the problem of size in relation to the problem of government, but they tended to resolve it in different ways. The Greeks, when confronted with a growing population, would impose a levy, build and provision a fleet, and ship off a large number of people to found a new city state—perhaps on the North American coast, or elsewhere. The Renaissance city states tended to meet the danger of growth, and it is important to grasp that they saw and understood it as a danger, by increasing the number of divisions *within* the city. Thus Venice, despite the smallness of the city area, comprised a large number of self-contained parishes, and in addition its civic life, as was common to many cities of the period, comprised numerous self-governing guilds, each of which elected representatives to the city council. In addition, as the city's boundaries expanded it did not enlarge the existing parishes, but created new ones each with its own elected council and its own trade and commercial centres, as well as its own church and schools. In effect, when a city grew, it did not simply become swollen in one amorphous lump, it added new cells to its body, frequently by sub-dividing, each of which was responsible in large measure for the regulation of its own affairs.

One can observe a microcosm of this form of organisation in the Universities of Oxford and Cambridge. When a group of scholars gathered to pursue wisdom and to instruct, they built a quadrangle made up of the library, refectory, chapel and rooms of residence. This was doubtless an unconscious expression of a seeking after the organic principle, with its due observance of the limitations of scale necessary to the function of the pursuit, for scholarship cannot be conducted on a mass scale. It is noteworthy that the rooms of residence were not built in a single block with numerous doors opening from a single interminable corridor on each floor, as is the modern way, but to open on to small landings, which might be shared with two or three other residents at most, which in turn led from a staircase which gave access to two or three similar landings on the other floors. As the college grew it might have added a second quadrangle or even a third, but thereafter it stopped. The college was as big as it could be without losing its essential character and identity, without the bonds between pupils and scholars becoming weakened by the increasing burdens of administration which would arise from a larger unit, and without the claims of scholarship being sacrificed to the pressures of catering for the different needs of larger numbers.

If the need for more accommodation was felt, instead of enlarging one college to giant proportions, another was begun on the same principle, and if that proved insufficient then another was begun in the same way and so on. So that these Universities do not comprise one vast megacollege, any more than the contents of an organ are made up of a single undifferentiated mass, but of a number of distinct units, each of which pursues the principles of division and sub-division right down to the individual student in his own rooms. In this way the multifarious and specialist claims of scholarship, teaching, administration and other aspects of college life are reconciled with a peerless degree of balance and functional efficiency upon which no commercial business-methods consultants, not even from the U.S.A., could possibly hope to improve; indeed, one reason for the frequent employment of such consultants in the business world is that firms are generally pursuing a single goal— profit, and creating a mega-organisation precisely for that solitary end. Of course, the works get gummed up and always will, for it is a myopic objective, of only limited human significance, pursued by unnatural means. The only advice which business efficiency consultants could really give to solve the 'problems of the firm' is that which they dare not: Diversify your objectives, pursue excellence and the public good and beauty, as well as profit, for example, and also diversify your structure. If all firms acted on this advice business consultants at least would soon be out of business, but since modern capitalist business has always been pursued on principles of growth and organisation which are fundamentally irreconcilable with the true balance, economy and efficiency of human well-being we must assume that 'consultants' will be with us for a long time yet. We may note the same principle of division at work in African tribal society. A tribe is not a heterogeneous mass but comprises a number of villages, within each of which is a headman and elders. We may note too the village is 'home' to an African child who grows up in it in a sense which has largely been lost in the western world, despite its considerable importance to the psychic well-being of the individual.

Indeed it is worth pondering the position of an African village child in terms of his relationships as compared with that of one in almost any modern urban setting. The village may be little more than a modest number of thatched huts, but to a growing child this, as we have noted, is 'home'. Well before reaching maturity he will know every tree and shrub in its locale, the footpaths, trodden countless times by barefoot walkers, the bird calls, the animals that frequent it, the waterways and streams, the grasses and insects, the flowers and fruits, the alternations of season, the fluctuations of climate, the prevailing winds and, above everything else, he will know all the people who live there; they will be his immediate family, his relations to a degree of consanguinity which no urban child will ordinarily have a hope of being able to match, his friends and his neighbours. It will be his community; he will have a fair knowledge of its history, its traditions, its customs, myths, taboos, strengths and weaknesses; he will know, perhaps often without knowing that he knows, how his people interact with the multifarious forces of nature around him, especially in the important business of securing food and shelter, he will have a keen and realistic sense of practicalities and know what is possible and what is beyond its scope. All this and very much more will be in his bones and blood, it will be as much part of him as his own physique. Is it any wonder that African village people despite (or perhaps because of) their pronounced lack of reliance on advanced forms of technology, frequently possess an emotional poise and grace of physique seldom to be noted in urban areas?

This is not an attempt to idealise village life, which in Africa is a tough and unending struggle against natural forces which are often far more inimical to human survival, much less its well-being, than anything to be found in Europe. One has only to think of the prevalence of debilitating diseases such as malaria, billharzia, dysentery and sleeping sickness, the wild animals which roam freely and continue to take their toll of livestock and even of human life, the harshness of the climate, and the sheer daily grind of onerous human labour involved in supplying the basic necessities of life, to grasp that such a way of life is very far from being some carefree arcadian picnic. Yet it is against such a background that village and tribal political institutions have been forged, and if one may justifiably pause to marvel at the complexity, adaptability and durability of their workings let it also be remembered that they incorporate a principle without which no political stability or progress is possible: they are small-scale and utilise multicellular forms of control.

By the time communities had reached the size of a city state, and we need to remember their populations rarely exceeded a quarter of a million, a number of important features of government had emerged. As we have seen on Crusoe's island, any form of collectivity involves a problem of the disposition of the power inherent in the mere fact of its existence. At the level of clan or tribal organisation, since the conditions of life were relatively simple, government too was simple. The chief or ruler might be hereditary, or chosen by a consensus of the elders, or even by general acclaim. Sometimes the ruler ruled with absolute power, more often he ruled with the elders in a form of council, but whatever the form of his rule if he proved to be despotic or a drunkard, or showed other signs of degeneracy, ways and means were frequently found for his removal, even if they were that of a knife, a bludgeon, or the inclusion of an unprepossessing substance in the evening meal. Such methods may seem an unacceptable affront to modern democratic susceptibilities, even though we allow men like Hitler or Stalin to continue their course to the bitter end in default of them. In a rough and ready manner, and it was not always rough, the views of the generality of people was enabled to prevail, however fitfully.

With the advent of the city state men were faced with new power problems. For one thing the factor of administration began to be one of considerable importance. The supervision of weights and measures, a local constabulary of sorts, a standing army, legal disputes, customs and excise, street cleaning, drainage, the construction and maintenance of public buildings, bridges and city gates, currency management, fire prevention and control, and other matters all meant that the services of a growing class of professional administrators with their subordinates was required and that simply by virtue of its position at the centre of things as a permanent need this administrative class was a new factor in the power equation to be reckoned with.

The size of the city state, small as it was by modern standards, also meant that rivalry to control the power of government had grown to such a pitch that it could no longer be contained within one group. We should be very clear what this means: formally a community elects, by vote or consensus, those who will order its affairs. Partly because the pattern of life is relatively simple, partly because the degree of face-to-face relationships between the government and the governed is considerable, and partly because the community itself is not large, the nature of the public interest is so clear and so obvious, that the only disputes centre on how best it may be served.

With the advent of the city state there is the growth of classes, the growth of sectional interests as between town and country, and of different trade and commercial interests, all of which make it difficult for the ordinary citizens to determine the objective needs of their collective situation. Policy divisions become so deep, the prizes to be won from capturing control of the government machine so considerable, that the jockeying for place can no longer be contained within a single group. The rival factions divide and form themselves into parties.

A political party is, then, a standing monument to the ambiguity that the mere process of growth of a community cloaks around the true nature of the public interest, it is a confession that a community is no longer united about its own goals and that its leaders will no longer automatically serve those goals because there is no longer a common and automatic acceptance of what they are. The public domain is no longer the sphere in which the public interest is defined and conflicting interests reconciled, but where conflicts of interest are institutionalised and hierarchised on the basis of well-nigh perpetual division. This is bound to make general control by a community of its affairs more difficult and to make higher demands on the citizen body of comprehension about the true nature of the public weal and how best it shall be served.

On the whole these difficulties appear to have been overcome. It is impossible to generalise without qualification, for even the Greek city states numbered thousands and were, in the words of one authority, "...remarkable for their diversity. Every variety of political experiment from monarchy to communism was practised and the fundamental principles of political life were formulated by their philosophers." In Renaissance times the diversity was no less remarkable, so too were their fruits, as a visit to any major museum of Europe will testify, and as a visit to a host of ancient European cities and towns will confirm.

The element of genuinely popular control in all these city states varied from place to place and from time to time, but what is indisputable is that for centuries that control, whether popular or not, was predominantly local and from within. Some of them might well not be included in the normal category of city states at all, especially in England and Spain, where centralised nation-state forms of government came to prevail much earlier, but in England at least, the locally elected mayor and corporation represented privileges and powers, incorporated in the City Charter, which were not lightly to be tampered with. Shakespeare represents Richard III as launching a propaganda campaign upon the mayor and corporation, as well as the citizens of London, to convince them of the iniquities of his rivals in his manoeuvrings for the succession to the throne, and the legitimacy of his own claim to it. He clearly felt a *need* to win them over and this element of civic power played a considerable part in the making and unmaking of monarchs down to the Civil War of 1642, when a different kind of power was affirmed and enlarged—that of the supremacy of a central parliament.

Coupled with this pervasive element of popular control was a pronounced degree of civic seemliness in the provision of hospitals, schools, libraries, museums, theatres, public buildings, street paving, poor relief, care of the aged and the orphaned, apprentice training, consumer protection, the embellishment, to say nothing of the building, of magnificent cathedrals, and of numerous other artifacts of civil life.

We have to face the fact however, that in a general sense, even in a city state, most people were concerned with the political process only in a fitful manner, those who were concerned continuously being in a minority. This is true of any aspect of public life and the scene would surely be strange if things were otherwise. Nevertheless at times of crisis or of momentous change the generality of people seek to play a more prominent part and in city state life this was at least possible, and government on the whole, subject to important qualifications regarding property and the disposition of the economic surplus, reflected in broad terms the general interest, as distinct from the particular interest of those factions which were seeking to grasp or maintain power.

This then was the basis of the civic structure which people established for their needs. It was by no means perfect, being fashioned by mortal, fallible men, but neither were its defects such as to overshadow the daily lives of their citizens to the exclusion of more positive aspects, indeed we do scant justice to history if we fail to recognise that what city-state forms of government achieved in many spheres of human life was a degree of resplendence unmatched by any other form before or since. In music, poetry, philosophy, architecture, painting, sculpture; in dress, furnishing and decoration, and in numerous other ways they bequeathed to posterity achievements which continue to dazzle the imagination of mankind, and to arouse awe, wonder, praise and even joy and ecstasy centuries after their citizens have passed from the scene. To walk into the main square of Florence or Vienna is to experience to this day a profoundly moving expression of civic genius with which absolutely nothing of the modern era of meganation states can possibly compare or remotely emulate, and what those people built, and the way in which they accomplished it, for all the negative aspects of the life of the times, holds the profoundest lessons for all who are concerned to ensure that the achievements of the political process are notched up today in terms of quality, as much as of quantitatively measurable satisfactions.

The people of the city states were no less greedy, sensuous, vicious, cruel, spiteful, violent, selfish and depraved than those of any other time before or since. What must compel our wonder is the way in which they ordered their affairs and kept their vices in sufficient check to enable a civic life of the most matchless achievement to flower from generation to generation in a perpetually rising crescendo of splendour and loveliness which holds the mind spellbound with the richness and variety of its accomplishment. How did they do it? What was the secret which enabled them to produce so easily such a staggering abundance of creative manifestation to which to this day millions of people flock for no other purpose but to gaze at in wonder, whilst scarcely a single city of the modern era does other than bore its own inhabitants with its meanness and mock the wider aspirations men once had and have now, irretrievably it almost seems, lost? Why do we return again and again to these splendours of the past and find none of our own civic forms worth a second look? What went wrong? In what way was the spring broken and the magic circle of men's private dreams and public splendours so rudely snapped?

It is not too much to say that the whole future of civilised society depends on men finding a realistic answer to these questions, and on being able to grasp the full significance of the gigantic wrong turning that history has taken, of being able to retrace their steps and of being able to take up the path of genuine progress where the city states left off when they were destroyed by the nascent power of the nation state. For that a wrong turning of frightening dimensions *has* been taken cannot surely now be contested.

What needs singling out in our city state societies, even at the risk of repetition, the factor which, for all their growth from smaller societies, for all their complexity and the novel forms of power they grappled with, was one which they shared with the older and simpler societies, this was the extent to which their corporate life was dominated by the personal relationship of their members. The personal factor was paramount. The most despotic prince, the most bigoted priest, the most inhuman usurper was but mortal; they did their worst, sometimes strangely mixed with their best, and they passed. What prevailed was the corporate sense of the community and the private judgements men applied to public affairs. This *was* society: no institutions, industries or special interests could replace the unique sense men had of their community and its meaning to them as a home, a work-place, a source of recreation, social life, worship, learning and justice.   •

The city states accomplished this against a background of fairly novel problems in relation to the disposition of power in society. It is commonly assumed that this power is simply the aggregate of the power implicit in each member's relationship to the social structure, but this is only part of the truth. There is a function of power inherent in any social structure which derives over and above the act of membership of any single person. The whole is not simply the sum of its parts, *it is much greater than the sum of its parts,* and the whole generally incorporates aspects of power which are beyond the reach of the general citizen. The atomic bomb is a collective, not an individual, enterprise and represents a degree of power far and away beyond a mere summation of the power of individual members of society, even when they number many millions.

This may be so by default by the mere fact that the citizen does not have a sustained interest in the political process, it may be so from the mere fact that the individual, as an individual seeking to initiate some change, finds he is too weak in relation to the general body, it may be that those who control the levers of power are actively seeking to deny the wishes of an individual—even if he is one of many, or it may be that the conditioning effects of living in a particular form of society are so great that any one person who breaks out of his framework of conditioned response is powerless to influence the others who have not.

Hundreds of people, for example, mostly women, all entirely innocent, and often sick in mind or body, were burned at the stake, sometimes after being horribly tortured, in medieval Europe by people who presumably devoutly believed they were doing a major act of public service, as doubtless did the generality of people. The failure of a more liberal-minded minority, who clearly saw that the whole process was a cruel and utterly monstrous outrage to halt it was total. The minority was not partly powerless, it was, to all effects, totally powerless to prevent it.

A society is also served by institutions which come to embody an awe, a mystique or even simply a common acceptance so deeply entrenched which may make efforts to initiate changes all but impossible, and the same is true of long established customs or usages. The institution of monarchy is a good example of this, but it is observable in more mundane matters. Most Englishmen would probably be horrified at the suggestion that, let us say, their Ministry of Education, should be abolished. The proposal would strike them for the most part as so unreasonable as to raise grave doubts about the speaker's sanity and as an attempt to undermine the basis of civilisation. Yet the people of Switzerland, who can claim to have one of the most efficient systems of schooling in the world, have never seen the need for such a centralised body and the proposal to establish one would strike them as being of the utmost absurdity as well as an infringement of their freedom.

There is another aspect of government which poses considerable problems as the scale and complexity of its operations increases, and this is in relation to the time factor. How much of a community's economic surplus, for example, shall be spent on current consumption and how much on investment for future benefit? When one contrasts a city state with a modern mass society a rather surprising contradiction emerges from the manner of dealing with the economic surplus in each. Despite the fact that in the former it was so very much smaller, its citizens did not hesitate to use it, and commit it year by year, to public enterprises which might take more than a century to complete. A spectacular example of this is the Cathedral of Florence, the magnificent Santa Maria del Flore. It was begun in the 13th Century and not completed until the late 19th Century. How many modern governments would embark on a project which would take but one century to complete—far less six? Yet the principle of initiating works which those who began could not hope to live to see completed was widespread. The campanile of the great Cathedral of Pisa (the famous leaning tower) took over three hundred years to complete, and one could do the rounds of Europe to similar effect. What we are observing here is an unshakable belief men held that society reflected them and their propensities for disinterested endeavour and that it would always do so. It is doubtful in fact if it ever occurred to them that it would reflect anything else; the vast institutions for mere profit-making based for the most part on an accountant's calculations of the *annual* results, which now dominate our societies, and which seem to make us incapable of envisaging a society built on any other terms, would doubtless have horrified them. The very manner in which these institutions operate indicates we have become ignorant of history and that we simply despise the future.

We may note in this context too the durability of the very fabric of some structures and the effect they have had on subsequent social, political and economic developments. This is true not only of old churches and schools; consider for example the 2,700 foot aqueduct in Segovia (Spain) which was built under Trajan in the first century of the Christian era and which is still in working order.

This is a time factor in the work of government and calls into question the whole range of popular attitudes and reactions to the social order. Very few people would voluntarily opt to pay higher taxes for example, but frequently they may support a general proposal to do so when moved by the need for some particular social objective; their reactions to the needs of the social order vary all the way from the most bigoted selfishness to the purest altruism, but the demands of the social order are necessarily constant, and become a consolidated constant with the passage of time. How to reconcile the constant needs of the democratic social order with the variable responses of the citizen body is thus a major problem of government. Today in large mass societies the trick, for it is a trick, is done by methods which involve lies and mendacity unlimited by those seeking to do the reconciliation, and there are powerful weapons in the shape of mass means of misinformation to help them. People no longer have any sense of identity with their political structures and are unable to evaluate its long-term interests or concerns.

In the city states there were doubtless times when forms of political deception were frequently practised by the government on the people; Machievelli's wise and perceptive treatise was, after all, the product of life in one such state, but it was deception which had its limits in the extent to which the social structure was still dominated by the personal relationships of their members; we may indeed describe such societies as 'personal societies' as distinct from the 'institutional societies' that followed. For all practical purposes the millions of today's mass societies drift through a perpetual daze of deception in many essential matters to an extent that makes their experience of life an unending chaos of confusion.

This is a product of the sheer dominance of institutions in today's societies, but in the city states Lincoln's words 'You can fool some of the people all the time and you can fool all the people some of the time, but you can't fool all the people all the time', were only too applicable, if only because such total forms of deception can only be maintained persistently where relationships are dominated by impersonal forces such as are represented by huge institutions.[2]

Hitler at a Nuremburg rally, in the glare of massed arc lights, with the throbbing of drums, the blare of trumpets, the parrot-like roars of an audience which has surrendered its humanity to the conformity of a herd, can stand on a platform in a bullet-proof vest behind bullet-proof glass and rant like one possessed and set the armies of the world on the tramp. In the market place of Athens or Verona, or of Nuremburg itself a couple of centuries earlier for that matter, it is all too probable that his demonic frenzies would have been drowned in laughter, or perhaps in a hail of overripe tomatoes and rotten eggs.

Most of these difficulties relating to the disposal of power in society were successfully resolved by the city states. This does not mean that they were always wisely governed, for since government was a general reflection of the wishes of the people, and people being always what they are, it was inevitable that it should reflect the follies and the vices as much as the virtues and wisdom of the governed. Under city state forms of government there were also undoubtedly bleak periods of despotism, cruelty, oppression and war, but somehow, through the centuries, a balance was struck whereby

[2]This is an interesting example of a common practice of using the value judgements deriving from one form of society to another where they have no relevance. Most of the rhetoric about democracy and liberty stems from the city states and the philosophers they produced; they would doubtless have been utterly bewildered if they could have seen their judgements applied to mass societies which are institutionally quite unable to express them in their workings.

the meaner side of human nature was constricted and the creative and constructive side released. Whatever shortcomings these city states expressed, the record of the twentieth century gives no persona today any just cause for the curiously prevalent attitude of condescension to them and their achievements. The city states had problems, but on the whole, given the prevailing state of technology and knowledge, as well as other factors, they grappled with them with conspicuous success. Government in the modern era can scarcely make any such claim, and we need now to establish why and to pinpoint what has gone wrong.

CHAPTER IV

Power and Growth

The Factor of $\overline{\mathrm{X}}$ in the Power Equation

We have seen that a change of direction in the disposition of power was manifested already in city-state structures, and it was manifested in the way power began to be sought and used not to serve the generality of people, but to serve particular interests within society. What in fact was happening is that with the growth of the size of the structure, the power-at-the-centre began to be pursued as an end in itself, or for ends not related to the general interest, and which frequently proved to be in conflict with it, ends such as economic, military or political aggrandizement of individuals, classes or, more rarely, races. It will be noted that such ends can only begin to be pursued with the help of, or by using, the power-at-the-centre by diminishing the extent to which it serves the general interest.

The main characteristic which marks off a nation, in contrast with a unit the size of a city state, is that power is increasingly institutionalised in a number of spheres. This is true in a military and political sense although in many ways the extent to which it is true will depend in part at least on the prevailing level of technology. The effect of many forms of technology is to emphasise the degree of concentration or institutionalisation of power that may already have been achieved. We may see this quite clearly in the case of the Russian Empire; under the later Tzars government had the appearance of a brutal despotism blocking the main high-way to political emancipation and progress. So evil and brutal was this despotism reputed to be that a fairly large minority, mainly of intellectuals, who in the nature of things could scarcely be expected to apply anything so esoteric as a grain of common sense to their situation, came to believe that only a violent revolution which achieved the complete overthrow of the Tzarist system could possibly resolve their problem. A revolution which promised to create a paradise was duly accomplished[1] and paved the way

[1]Not for one moment must it be supposed that it was in any sense a popular revolution, despite the war-weariness of the soldiers and the desperate economic plight of the citizenry. From start to finish the Bolsheviks were always a minority— which is the literal meaning of the word anyway. But they were a minority with a difference, they were imbued with a common sense of purpose, an utter lack of scruple and a degree of ruthlessness with few parallels in history, and on the *scale*

not so much for paradise as for the most obscene forms of abuse
and misuse of political power the human race has ever witnessed,
a degree of deliberately contrived human suffering which dwarfed
any of the horrors that history can show, and a contempt for the
integrity, the dignity and the stature of man which had and has
no discernible limits. Yet it prevailed. It was enabled to do so by
the power of technology. We need to remember that before the
so-called revolution the Tzarist system was fumbling and stumbling
its way towards modern forms of democracy and freedom. Owing
largely to the vastness and geographic isolation of the Russian
Empire (features it shares with the African continent and which
help to explain the remarkable similarity of the political and
economic developments of both), the Tzars just could not halt
this onward movement of liberation and there can be little doubt
that but for the First World War the peoples of the Russian Empire
would have achieved their liberation from the yoke of Moscow
as fully as the peoples of India did from Britain, within a generation.
The Bolshevik dictatorship put a stop to all such hopeful developments. The tragic centralisation and institutionalisation which
technology enabled the Bolsheviks to accomplish was and remains
the halter which is so firmly clamped on the necks of the Russian
peoples and which enables the Bolsheviks to stop them achieving
the power of self-rule. So that whilst making due allowance for
the way in which technology can influence a particular political
grouping of any size, we need to see what is at work in political
terms as such, as the size of a unit increases to that of a nation. As
we have noted, there follows an institutionalisation of the political
process itself; rival political interests become institutionalised into
nation-wide parties each with its own bureaucracy, hierarchy,
organs of propaganda, its own national struggles for position and
power, its own established pecking order and its own system of
reward for faithful service and penalties for disloyalty. Each political
party professes to speak for the nation as a whole but, of course,
it speaks first and foremost for itself and its own consolidated system
of sectional interests.

It will be noted that the developments within each national party
tend to mirror the developments in the city state as a whole in

---

on which they employed it, none whatsoever, acting in a situation of historically
unprecedented chaos. The Communist Party remains what it began as and what
it has always been, a minority of conspiratorially-minded moral pygmies.

terms of the development of the bureaucracy, the institutionalisation of functions and so on.

The same institutionalisation of power is represented in the army where a far greater power to make war is consolidated into the hands of a single, centralised, authoritarian command. The same again is true of commerce; where, before, the market was generally limited to a single city and its hinterland, the forces of commerce are now enabled to flex their muscles and expand to a nation-wide extent, so that in place of localised trading or manufacturing concerns, there emerges national concerns having a nation-wide position and often with sizeable export markets beyond to other countries. In the field of communications, there is again an institutionalisation and centralisation of power at work, national railway systems, national road networks, national newspapers, national distribution chains for books, journals and the printed media generally, and, in the modern era, national telephone, radio and television services.

Similar developments may be noted in the field of what is called social services (although they are frequently social disservices of the most marked order). Education, for example, once a highly localised and individual matter reflecting as much the genius of a particular headmaster and teaching staff as the wishes of parents of the children they taught, becomes a matter of a national policy (the mere conception of which surely represents a frontal assault on democracy), imposed by a single centralised ministry.

It will be noted that what we are witnessing here is not simply an enlargement of the functions of the city state to a national scale, anymore than it can be argued a steamship is simply an enlarged rowing boat. The mere fact of growth brings into the field of possibility numerous other functions and influences of a completely different kind in respect of the nature of the authority exercised. Four men in a rowing boat would very likely settle the question of who will be in command very briefly and on the basis of a common consensus. In any case the decision, which may well be unspoken, will not normally be a significant one; but when the question of authority on a steamship comes to be considered, we are confronted with a completely different situation involving a multitude of factors which are not present in a rowing boat at all. Here the question of authority is one of major importance and so too is the question of the various channels through which it shall be exercised.

But the nation is not a ship and a ship of course in view of the extent to which it is confronting the elements, and the dangers that may arise from doing so, may be thought to require an authoritarian chain of command, but a nation need not think in such terms at all, even though its rulers frequently do so.

Hence, we need to see that a nation embodies far greater and more complex forms of power than that of the average city state, and we need to remember continuously that since most of that power is embodied in its central and centralised institutions, it is not the citizen body which is receiving the bonus of this additional power to dispose of as it sees fit, that bonus accrues nearly always directly to the centre.

The only exception to this trend is that which has been manifested in Switzerland, which strictly speaking is not an exception at all since it is not a nation but a confederation. It is a confederation of cantons and of cantonal power, and the power of the cantons themselves is derived from the jealously guarded powers of the communes which in turn comprise them. But for the Swiss experience, it might be supposed that the centralisation and institutionalisation of various forms of authority and power, as they developed within a nation, was as natural as the stars in their courses. Fortunately, the Swiss have shown clearly and successfully that a development based on the precise opposite to this works and works well.

These developments would also be affected, of course, by the extent to which a local sense of affinity, loyalty and identity exists. If these factors are weak then the centralising process will be stronger. On the other hand where these factors are strong they can often prevail for a long time against the centralising trends. What is important to grasp is that even when they are strong the general tendency is still towards centralisation and a battle to resist it needs continuously to be waged; the modern experience indicates that it is waged with less and less success.

We may see this very clearly in the case of newspapers. A nation will have national newspapers but they will be very often rivals to local newspapers. For example, in Scandavia, there is still a degree of support for local daily newspapers which, in the light of experience elsewhere, is truly astonishing.

In Denmark (population 5 million), there are 52 daily papers, in Finland (population 4.75 million), there are 62, in Norway, (population 4 million), there are 67, *plus* 77 newspapers appearing

1-5 times a week, whilst in Sweden, (population 8 million), there are 146. Britain, by contrast, with a population of 55 million has a total of 104 daily newspapers, including 14 national dailies based on London.

These figures are surely worth pondering; if a country of only 8 million people sustains roughly 40% more different daily newspapers than a country of 55 million one surely catches a most revealing glimpse of what a small country is able to gain in terms of diversity, localisation and, let us not hesitate to say it, freedom, and what a large country is losing in these terms as its citizens become victims of overcentralisation, giantism, remoteness, standardisation and increasing anonymity and enmassification.

In Britain there has been a continuous decline over the last generation of even national newspapers, to say nothing of a tremendous loss in the number of local newspapers. The factors behind this development are very complex but they do point to a conclusion which is common to numerous other artifacts of power in the nation: With the continuance of the growth of the size of political unit new forms of power are brought into being by the very existence of the nation, these forms are increased as well as strengthened by factors pertaining to technology, and that in almost every case, since it is the centre which is winning in one way or another the struggle to control this power, it is the citizen who loses. This remains true whatever exercises in ballot-box mongering may be mounted.

This is why so often the centre is able to act in ways that are diametrically opposed to the interests of the general citizen body as a whole (World War I, the return to the Gold Standard, the Geddes Axe of 1930, the wholesale bombing of German civilians in the Second World War, the return of Russian prisoners to Stalin's murder squads in 1945, by the British Government, the secret Yalta agreements, the development of the nuclear bomb and nuclear energy, the Concorde aeroplane, the destruction of Britain's grammar school system, high rise blocks of flats, motorways, juggernaut lorries, etc. etc. etc.)

It is true, of course, that there are numerous sectional interests at work in a nation and that there is a widespread illusion that when these are all operating freely their bad effects will cancel each other out, as is presumed by free market apologists to operate in economics. Indeed reams of claptrap have been written on economic matters seeking to show that if each pursues his own good the good of all is thereby assured. There is no need to allude to all the arguments which have been used to refute this, here we need only concern ourselves with those arguments that have a bearing on the political scene and to note that if the argument is not working in the sphere of economics then there are no grounds for supposing it will do so in politics.

The proposition is based on the curious notion that the common good is always equatable with the free quest for individual profit. This *laissez-faire* contention has been a source of argument between socialists and capitalists for generations, and one must assume that on the whole the socialists have got the better of it, or that they would have done if the remedy they had proposed was not so obviously so much worse than the disease, or one which betrayed so little understanding of the meaning of human dignity and freedom.

On the whole it would seem that the free forces of the market achieve superior results in terms of the efficient utilisation of economic resources. Yet this is a very broad generalisation indeed and needs to be subjected to several qualifications.

Economic activity is not an end in itself; the business of getting and spending can only be divorced from the moral framework of a society if society itself is regarded as little more than a colony of ants. Once this is conceded a whole field of debate is opened to determine precisely what place economic activity should have within that framework. One of the most pathetic spectacles of the 20th Century is the extent to which leading churchmen and others seem so readily disposed to confine their endeavours to ascertaining the precise opposite, to ascertaining what role morality should have within the prevailing economic framework.

Again, modern technology has armed the forces of the market with products which involve enormous risks to every living creature and to posterity. The manufacture of DDT, to take but one of a multitude of dangers created by modern chemistry, is exceedingly profitable, but many governments have become so alarmed by the consequences of its common use that they have banned it outright, and many more, backed by international conferences of scientists and of government representatives, such as the Stockholm UNO Conference of June 1972, are considering doing so. As well they might.

The instance points to a consequence of wider application. The mere initiation of certain forms of development tends to secure the

acceptance of tendencies which have enormously harmful consequences for society as a whole. The untramelled proliferation of the
private motor car is one instance of this, a proliferation which has
yielded considerable profits to a whole range of manufacturing and
servicing industries, but it is only recently that people have seriously
begun to consider the social cost of this development in terms of
ruined urban centres, environmental squalour, pollution, landscape
despoilation, stress and strain on the human nervous system and the
killing and maiming of a large and growing number of people on
the roads.

Again we may cite the instance of sugar manufacture, of which
the profits are considerable and assured. The body has a natural
craving for sugar, especially the young body, for it contains elements
essential to growth. The craving is doubtless a consequence of the
fact that in its natural forms sugar is scarce and hard to come by.
Once man stumbled on the possibilities of over-refining the juice of
a tropical cane and transporting it around the world, the way was
open to seeing a sweetshop on every corner and a queue of unlimited
proportions waiting for a vacancy at the door of every dental surgery.
Worse, the way was open for physical suffering on a generational
scale as the excessive daily consumption of refined sugar speeded up
the degenerative process of the body, so that forms of sickness once
associated with the terminal stages of life, such as cancer, diabetes,
varicose veins, rheumatism, heart trouble, arthritis and sensory loss
or decay in teeth, eyes, hearing and so on began to appear in younger
and younger age groups, suggesting a conclusion that people today
are not so much living longer as dying more slowly.

What these and many other instances indicate is that a major
disposition of human nature, economic gain, has been allowed to
assume proportions in the working of society where it now dominates
the political field. One would like to assume that the working of economic machinery in a truly adult society which had liberated itself
from greed, would be of no more account, and arouse no more comment or controversy, than the machinery of a tolerably accurate
clock, leaving men free to concentrate on their real problems (morality, beauty, destiny) at their leisure.

What instead is happening is that the malfunctioning of economic
systems through overgrowth, the displacement of man from the
centre of things and the enhancement of the goals of profit, power,
'efficiency' and national aggrandisement, is creating anti-humanist

procedures which are coming to dominate all other spheres of organised life.

In the political sphere these forces are making the political process
itself one of their chief instruments. There has always been a tendency
to assume this was happening—and a considerable amount of
evidence has generally been available to indicate as much. Rich
people have always tended to oppress poor people, if only by the
way in which they became rich and retained their wealth, and it
has tended to be assumed that rich people will bend the political
process to serve their interests rather than those of the generality of
people as a matter of course, especially as they have nearly always
controlled it. It has been supposed that the power of modern democracy would put a check to this, but in fact the terms of reference
have been changed, new forces have emerged within the structure of
the mass society whose major drive has been the parallel development of an oligarchic form of power. These forces, giant corporations,
multinational companies and associated organisations, and oligar-
chical controlled trade unions, have been foremost in promoting a
corresponding political structure to buttress their activities, and
this in turn has taken two forms. First a tremendous increase in the
degree of centralisation of power, and second in the growth of many
new forms of nation-state power.

If an average Englishman had been told three centuries ago that
his central government would one day assume responsibility for
education, health, local government, police, housing and numerous
other matters, he would have regarded his informant as a lunatic.
No doubt a Swiss citizen today would have the same reaction.
Secondly, there has been a move towards larger groupings of nations
on the lines of the United States of America and the Russian Empire,
as well as through organisations such as NATO, the now defunct
SEATO, the Warsaw Pact, UNO and host of subsidiary organisations. Most of these bodies tend to be viewed as conscious attempts
at multinational or international cooperation, but in reality they represent an excrescence of power which has spilled over from national
units of political and economic power because the size, the scale,
the intensity and the speeded-up tempo of their operations has
resulted in a cardinal lack of control as surely as does milk boiling
over in an overheated saucepan.

It is true that many of the forms of centralised power which today
make a large nation state an uncontrollable aggregate of power were

present in the city state. The difference however is this, that the city state, being fairly small scale, could accommodate such forces and still remain a humanist, man-centred society, whereas a large mass nation-state *cannot*. The most significant consequence of this development from one to the other is that the nation-state cannot accommodate the degree of power it contains and remain within full human control.

Why? For answer we must look to the nature of the power being wielded and see whether or not it is controllable by the members of the unit of society who, where democracy prevails, nominally at least, are presumed to run it. In essence that power is the compounded power of a mass aggregation, compounded that is of military, legal, economic, political and propaganda factors plus the factor of X, the factor that is, that accrues additionally to these elements even if it works through them to a large extent, when a mass comprises one body: A factor that emerges, as we have indicated earlier, as an economic factor of X emerges from the division of labour in the tasks of production which is greater than the compounded former production of each worker in isolation.

To be quite explicit, if ten workers, to take Adam Smith's well-worn example, each in isolation produce ten pins a day, the result of them joining together to work on a basis of a specialist division of labour is not 10 x 10, but an increment which, with the aid of machinery, may run to thousands or even millions. The political implications of this are extraordinary and appear to be wholly unremarked, for if we are right in assuming that political power accrues in the same way as it does by the coming together on the basis of the division of labour in economic activity, we can begin to see how the process of growth leads to the dimunition of democracy, for just as in the case of economics the riches derived from the vastly expanded productivity accrue to the owners of the capital employed and not to the workers, so in politics *the increase in the factor of power from growth accrues to the centre and not to the citizens.*

It is, after all, the centre which controls the military forces, the judiciary, much of the information to the media, if not the media itself, the machinery of voting and elections, the prison system, the police, the education system, the administration and that vast silent pervasive power of patronage for all the top jobs which does so much to establish the appropriate response the power system requires for its smooth functioning.

It will doubtless be argued that this power is countered by the power of the ballot box and indeed this is one of the most widespread illusions of the contemporary world, so widespread that even those countries which are manifest dictatorships pay lip service to it by mounting at regular intervals a charade of voting in which the ruling party candidates are unvaryingly returned with majorities apparently not far short of (and occasionally in excess of !) 100%. The cause of this fallacy lies in a failure to appreciate the extent of the conflict of interest which prevails between the government and the governed, and the extent to which this conflict is intensified by the growth of a political unit in terms of its numbers. (We should note that a growth in territory accompanied by no growth in numbers can well lead to a dimunition of this conflict of interest.)

It is true that modern writers on liberty have always, until the present century, viewed the power of government as a potential, if not actual, threat to liberty and sought to extol the extent of its need for protection via the ballot box and other means. Why then has the ballot box failed to preserve liberty? To state the question is really to run ahead of the argument, for it makes the assumption that liberty has in fact ceased to exist in mass societies where the use of the ballot to settle the apparently contending claims of rival political candidates prevails. Is this true?

It is doubtful if an absolute answer to this may be given, the forces working for and against freedom are too numerous and intangible, too lacking in the kind of qualities that are capable of being precisely defined or specifically measured to be susceptible to definitive statement. The most that may be done is to make an estimate of the nature of these forces and the general direction in which they appear to be moving. What needs to be rejected is the idea that freedom is some sort of passive absence of restraint, when in fact its condition is one of perpetual and active opposition to the forces that would accomplish its negation. In positive terms freedom, for its full exercise, requires minimally citizen access to undiluted information, a way of life that enables citizens to determine things that jointly and locally affect them, and a capacity to discuss, to observe and to consider the tide of events in the community in open fullness among fellow citizens so that the experience of doing this enables the lessons it provides to become part of the common consciousness, experience and wisdom of the citizen body.

This means, inevitably, that citizens will be living in a fairly full

social and political relationship with one another so that the basis
of their judgement becomes the ability to estimate the moral quality
of their own lives and that of their fellows in the light of the general
fund of moral belief in the community. Without the ability to make
this moral judgement there is no way in which assaults on freedom
can be effectively appraised or countered until the anti-freedom
forces have become so massive as to be unanswerable, and often so
dangerous as to be uncontrollable.

We may note in passing how the rise of the Nazi and Communist
dictatorships in Europe exemplified this. The growth of a mass
society makes this capacity for the development of moral consciousness one of its first victims. The daily experience of each citizen
becomes fragmented and, as we have seen, instead of knowing his
fellows to the full in all the aspects of their citizenship, as neighbour,
worker, consumer, voter, churchgoer, ratepayer, hospital patient,
prisoner, traveller and so on, he knows them only in a few, and
sometimes only in one, of these roles; and he will be known to them
under the same kinds of limitation. But a moral appraisal of a fellow
(or even of oneself) can only be made on the basis of *all* his social
aspects. The bad worker may be a splendid parent, a conscientious
ratepayer, a devout churchgoer, a greedy consumer, an indifferent
neighbour and so on. Only a full appraisal of all his social aspects
will permit a balanced picture to be drawn and valid judgements to
be made. The mass society effectively destroys the capacity to do this
and since the enlargement of freedom is a dynamic that springs
from the capacity to make such judgements it is a dynamic that is
destroyed when that capacity is broken.

How is this destruction achieved? We need to see very clearly that
the principal characteristics of man in a mass society are his anonymity and powerlessness. The man in the city crowd is anonymous,
often even when he returns to his apartment or lodgings, which is
why it is a part of modern folklore to recognise that a crowded city
may be one of the loneliest places in the world. Of course, some
people profess to enjoy the freedom that a mass city anonymity
appears to give them; perhaps they would enjoy it less if they could
come to see the full price they were paying for it, for undoubtedly a
major part of it is their powerlessness to influence the course of events
within society, and hence to exercise real freedom. What freedom
they appear to have is the freedom to be alone in a crowd which is
being manipulated and directed towards objectives which no indivi-

dual might choose if he were really free to do so.

The manipulation and direction derived from the fact that the real power to make decisions to determine social objectives and to establish principles of social action, is in the hands of an oligarchy at the centre, and this oligarchy is an inevitable product of the powerlessness of the citizen. We should note it is not citizen powerlessness which is the product of the oligarchy, as so much socialist theorising assumes; the citizen powerlessness springs directly from the size of the unit, in this case a mass society, and since this powerlessness springs as a fact of nature from overgrowth, a vacuum would prevail at the centre if the oligarchy did not rush in to fill it. So that the oligarchy *uses* the fact of citizen powerlessness in order to achieve its own purposes. The citizen of a mass society who revels in the sense of freedom which he thinks he experiences from the fact of his anonymity in an urban crowd does not realise that what he is celebrating is the mere freedom to be isolated and alone whilst others use the power implicit in his membership of the citizen body, and which he cannot use because it is too large, to determine the conditions of his life. This freedom is the freedom of powerlessness and, ultimately, of irresponsibility, it is the freedom to be manipulated, it is the freedom of membership of a herd which has no concern about ultimate goals, not even when they prove to be those of the slaughter house.

The oligarchy will, of course, represent some at least of the dominant interests of society, though not by any means all of them. In many mass societies the interests of religion, art, culture, learning and other non-material qualitative aspects of life for example, are conspicuously under-represented. The interests which *are* represented are those of commerce of nearly all kinds, the military machine, the political party leaderships (but not of course the memberships!), and above all, despite appearances to the contrary, the bureaucracy.

What then are the objectives of the oligarchy within the context of a nation? The question is central to any consideration of its role in the struggle for freedom, and if we fail to grasp that freedom does indeed inevitably involve a struggle, to seek to ensure that certain conditions of life prevail, and to prevent certain other conditions from coming to pass, and that freedom is in a condition of poised tension between these two drives, we will be unlikely to reach any conclusion of value with regard to it.

It may be argued that each of the separate interests that comprise the oligarchy is seeking freedom. Of course it is, freedom for itself and to achieve its own particular interests, and it is part of the curious presumption of these interests that they should seek to maintain with a quite limitless effrontery the pretence that their particular interests are identical with the general interest. It is of course a pretence which is wearing thin, which is not to say it is maintained with any recession of ardour.

How then does it seek to realise its freedom? To establish the power relationship in clearer focus it may be useful to retrace our steps and examine the role of a sectional interest at different stages in the growth of a social unit.

When people pursue a sectional interest it will either be absorbed by the general interest, or it will be negated by the general interest, or it will itself negate the general interest.

In personal communities it will almost certainly be absorbed in or negated by the general interest. In mass societies it can often subdue the general interest to its requirements.

It should be noted that the rationality or morality of a given sectional interest has no bearing on its capacity to impose itself on the general interest. In the mass society the strength of an interest is based not on moral or eithical considerations, but on considerations of power as an end in itself. A sectional interest is, of course, a form of power whether expressed as money, militarism, administration or mass persuasion.

Take first the tribal stage. An African writer has this to say about the kind of society he was reared in in the twenties and thirties:

"The tribal community was a mutual society. It was organised to satisfy the basic human needs of all its members and, therefore, individualism was discouraged. Most resources such as land and cattle might be communally owned and administered by chiefs and village headmen for the benefit of everyone. If for example, a villager required a new hut, all the men would turn to and cut trees to erect the frame and bring grass for thatching. The woman might be responsible for making the mud-plaster for the walls and two or three of them would undoubtedly brew some beer so that all the workers would be refreshed after a hot but satisfying day's work. In the same spirit, the able-bodied would accept responsibility for tending and harvesting the gardens of the sick and infirm.

"Human need was the supreme criterion of behaviour. The hungry stranger, could without penalty, enter the garden of a village and take say, a bunch of bananas or a mealie cob to satisfy his hunger. His action only became theft if he took more than was necessary to satisfy his needs for then he was depriving others.

"Obviously, social harmony was a vital necessity in such a community where almost every activity was a matter of team work. Hence, chiefs and tribal elders had an important judicial and reconciliatory function. They adjudicated between conflicting parties, admonished the quarrelsome and anti-social and took whatever action was necessary to strengthen the fabric of social life. I should emphasize that this way of life was not a kind of idealised social experiment such as may be found in Europe where groups of people take themselves off into pleasant rural surroundings in order to avoid the tension of industrial society. Life in the bush is hard and dangerous and a high degree of social cohesion is necessary for survival. The basic unit of life is not the individual or immediate family (as in industrial societies), but the community. This means that there must be fundamental agreement upon goals and all must act together.

"In the second place, the tribal community was an accepting community. It did not take account of failure in an absolute sense. The slow, the inept and incapable were accepted as a valid element in community life provided they were socially amenable. Social qualities weighed much heavier in the balance than individual achievement. The success-failure complex seems to me to be a disease of the age of individualism—the result of a society conditioned by the diploma, the examination and the selection procedure. In the best tribal society people were valued not for what they could achieve but because they were there. Their contribution, however limited, to the material welfare of the village was acceptable, but it was their presence not their achievement which was appreciated.

"Take, for instance, the traditional African attitude to old people. I remember being horrified on the first occasion I made the acquaintance of that Western phenomenon, the Old People's Home. The idea that the State or some voluntary agency should care for the aged was anathema to me, for it almost seems to imply that old people are a nuisance who must be kept out of the way so that children can live their lives unhampered by their presence. In our traditional societies, old people are venerated and it is regarded as a privilege to look after them. Their counsel is sought on many matters and however infirm they might be they have a valued and constructive role to play in teaching and instructing their grandchildren.

Indeed, to deny a grandparent the joy of the company of his grand-children is a heinous sin. The fact that old people can no longer work, or are not as alert as they used to be, or have even developed the handicaps of senility, in no way affects our regard for them. We cannot do enough to repay them for all they have done for us. They are embodied wisdom; living symbols of our continuity with the past.

"No doubt a defender of the Western way of life might retort that institutions for the care of old people are inevitable in large-scale societies and that but for the efforts of the state and voluntary agencies many old people would starve. This is undoubtedly true but it merely serves to underline my point that in a society which regards person-to-person relationships as supremely important no one can be so solated that responsibility for his welfare cannot be determined and assigned.

"The experts have all kinds of standards by which they judge the degree of civilisation of people. My own test is this. How does that society treat its old people, and, indeed, all its members who are not useful and productive in the narrowest sense? Judged by this standard, the so-called advanced societies have a lot to learn which the so-called backward societies could teach them.

"In the third place, the tribal community was an inclusive society. By this I mean that the web of relationships which involved some degree of mutual responsibility was widely spread. I would describe industrial society as an exclusive society because its members' responsibilities are often confined to the immediate family, and I have noted that the family circle may be a self-entire little universe, preventing the acceptance of wider commitments.

"Let me give you an example of the inclusiveness of the traditional society. I do not restrict the title 'father' to my male parent. I also address my father's brothers as 'father'. And I call my mother's sisters 'mother' also. Only my father's sisters would I address as 'aunt' and my mother's brothers as 'uncle'. My 'brothers' would include not only the male children of my father but also certain cousins and even members of the same clan who have no blood relationship to me at all. Now this, which to the Western mind, is a very confusing state of affairs, is not merely a matter of termi-nology. These are not just courtesy titles. With the title 'father' for example goes all the responsibility of parenthood and in return all my 'fathers' receive my filial devotion. Hence, no child in a traditional society is likely to be orphaned. Should his literal parents die then others automatically assume the responsibility for his upbringing. By the same token, no old person is likely to end his days outside a family circle. If his own offspring cannot care for him then other 'children' will accept the duty and privilege."[2]

I have quoted this long extract to indicate something quite specific about tribal society which is fairly common to all its forms, and that is the near impossibility of a particular interest of any strength that might threaten the unity of the community even coexisting for any length of time with the general interest, far less opposing it.[3] It will doubtless be argued, as though the assertion somehow destroyed the validity of the point, that such societies were much simpler, knew nothing of technology or television and could therefore *afford* the luxury of close human identity with the social order. That this is at best a half truth may be shown by the nature and structure of modern Swiss government, which combines to a remarkable degree the sense of small-scale identity in its cantons and communes with all the trappings of a modern state, plus a remarkably high standard of material consumption![4] It is true that even the Swiss communes do not have the homogeneity of a tribal structure, but this in turn is mainly due to the pressures of the super-scale and the super-centralisation of its neighbouring super powers. The fact remains that a high degree of social homogeneity and humanist quality of society is certainly not incompatible with the complexities of modern government and technology, if only the will is there to achieve it by adopting a suitable scale of operations.

Not only, at the tribal level, were these strong forces implicit in the nature of the social order which prevented the emergence of a sectional interest, the attempt to pursue such an interest at the expense

[2]Dr. K.D. Kaunda, *A Humanist in Africa*, Longmans, Green & Company, London, Fourth Impression, 1969, p. 24.

[3]A vivid description of such a struggle for the headmanship of a village is described in Dominic Muleisho's novel *The Tongue of the Dumb* which is set in the context of Zambia (then Northern Rhodesia) in the colonial era. Heinemann, London, 1971.

[4]*The Times* of 25 September 1972 published a chart of the national wealth of the different countries of the world in terms of their annual *per capita* gross domestic product. Switzerland's was shown as £1,477, the fifth highest in the world, yet its only exceptional resources are in its mountains which besides attracting tourists facilitate the production of hydro-electricity. It has no coal or oilfields, no gold or silver mines, no copper or lead or easy means of getting rich.

of the general interest was liable to the most draconian forms of retaliation. One of these attempts may be said to be stealing, and a thief in some forms of tribal society would be fortunate to escape having his hands cut off, to make no mention of preserving his nose, lips and ears. In modern societies the more important forms of stealing are expressed in politer and more impersonal terms such as 'playing the stock market', 'gambling in futures' and so on, activities which involve buying and selling, usually on credit, at a profit, which contributes nothing to the commodity in question except to push up the price of it to the consumer, and absolutely nothing to the community well-being. In Britain those who pursue their own interest in this way at the expense of the general interest, far from being punished are more likely to be given a seat in the House of Lords.

There could be no question at all of the social structure itself being distorted to accommodate the interests of the power holders. One might say this condition continued to obtain even in the city state, but here we are on much more difficult ground. The tribal society was not very much more than the sum of its parts, but who, with Dante, Michaelangelo, Shakespeare, Titian, Purcell, Montiverdi, to name but a few of a glorious host in mind, could claim as much of the city state?[5] Clearly in some important respects the life of the city state was a reflection of the work of some notable men of genius as much as of the generality of its citizens. The same is true of the economic and political sphere. The pursuit of excellence in a society where the generality of people can employ their creative capacities in their working lives is a general one, but in any *particular* form it is a minority one and is bound to be so. Only a minority will ever be closely concerned with the craftsmanship of good shoes, of good buildings or of painting or sculpture. The same is true of political and economic affairs, and what is striking about city-state

[5] It may be argued Shakespeare was not the product of a city state and in the sense of those that prevailed in other parts of Europe at the time it is doubtless true. But the England of Shakespeare was an early example of a nation state and as such was still dominated by its towns and cities rather than by the central power at Westminster. As we have seen Richard III needed the sanction and approval of the Mayor and citizens of the city of London before he could be sure the crown was his to wear. It was the same citizens who secured the defeat of the Earl of Essex during his abortive revolt against Queen Elizabeth I and it was the power of the towns and cities of England which brought about the defeat and execution of Charles I well after Shakespeare's time.

life is the extent to which it produced individuals who made out-standing contributions to its quality, contributions so outstanding as to alter the social, political and economic horizons of their fellows in decisive ways.

The kind of leadership that gave city-state life its particular quality of excellence was justified ultimately in the only way such leader-ship can be justified—by the results it produced. Yet in many of these forms of leadership there was an implicit or explicit minority interest, not least in the economic sphere; there was, already, a significant gap between the government and the governed, but since the structure of society itself was still microcellular, that gap could not grow and be sustained for long beyond certain limits. Technology and production was small-scale, which meant that there was a pronounced degree of decision-making in numerous ways at the base, which in turn meant there were considerable areas of life not susceptible to totalitarian or oligarchic control. The gap really arose from the increase in the economic surplus, the surplus that is, that accrues from production after the needs of subsistence have been met. This increase was in part a natural result of improved techniques of production and, in many cases, the consequence of an increasing volume and extent of trading operations.

Inevitably a minority was being enabled to enrich itself, sometimes spectacularly, but it is worth pondering the kind of problem which wealthy class would be confronted with in seeking, as clearly it is needed to, to secure and advance its interests as distinct from those of the generality of citizens.

As we have seen, in economic affairs, the mere fact of a microcellular structure meant its capacity to extort, to rackrent, to exploit and generally to squeeze, had certain limits in respect of the degree to which decisions about when and how to produce were made on an individual basis by the producers themselves.

There was also another factor. The man who made money would generally want to spend it, and in the localised communities of the period, whether he spent on food, clothing, jewellery, shelter, furnishings, travel-equippage, gardening or other forms of conspi-cuous consumption, it was generally money spent within the local community and which therefore went to its enrichment. By and large it seems fair to say that whereas a tribal community had a settled way of life within which the elders who governed would do so

largely in accordance with the wishes, or at least needs, of the governed, city state government was of a developing society, a society
developing intellectually, socially and artistically in ways which had
a pronounced impact on all its aspects. As a consequence leadership
was in the hands of small groups or individuals in different spheres.
In many ways this leadership was not so much pursuing a policy of
faithfully sticking to old paths as creating new ones, and although
the gap between the rulers and the ruled often seemed enormous,
especially when despotism and war-lordism held sway, the conflict of
interest was generally limited and on the whole contained by the
limitations of the size of the territory of the community and the
nature of the divisions within it.

These divisions took two main forms, religious and secular. However
the matter may be viewed, it is indisputable that the Church of
Renaissance societies was a formidable power, often in more senses
than one, for in addition to the power inherent in its priestly
functions, it was frequently an extensive landlord, responsible for a
great deal of the welfare and educational provision of the time; when
it spoke it could expect the obedience not only of a large number of
faithful followers who believed it was able to condemn them to, or
absolve them from, the torments of hell, but of many who were
economically dependent on it as an institution. It was not a power to
be trifled with by the secular arm of the state, and indeed some of the
most terrible forms of despotism ensued when the forces of secular
and religious authority were combined as under Savanarola in 15th
Century Florence.

There was also a third power, that of public opinion. Frequently
this power could be suborned, misled, bribed, suppressed or ignored,
but the utterance that "you can fool some of the people some of the
time, you can fool all the people some of the time, but you cannot
fool all the people all the time," although often applied to modern
mass societies, to which it is conspicuously inapplicable, had a solid
basis in Renaissance society. This stemmed from the fact that small
as a city state might be, and Venice at the height of its power and
grandeur did not exceed above a quarter of a million inhabitants, a
number which today would provoke earnest dimwitted enquiries
about its economic viability, was further subdivided in a variety of
ways. To the numerous small parishes which constituted the compo-
nent parts of the city, as did the villages in its environs, we must add
as we have already noted, the key factor of the guilds.

Attempts have been made to belittle the significance of the guilds and the extent, for example, of their precise economic significance, and whether, in their various forms, they played quite the imposing part in the life of the times that their frequently ample records would suggest. Much of this discussion, as well as the one on whether the medieval guilds were or were not a continuation of the older ones of the closing stages of the Roman Empire, is beside the point for our purposes. The fact is that politically they represent the reactions of men, widely spaced in time and space, to a common problem, and it was a reaction which however much it differed in detail, was in principle the same. The problem was the political one of size, how to cope with the factor of growth in their community. In almost every respect they responded to the problem with the principle of division. When things became too big divide, divide so that the unit can continue to be humanist, continue to keep man at the centre of the stage and not succumb to the total control of particular interests working for particular ends.

It is not suggested men saw it quite in these terms at the time. This, if you like, is our gloss on their actions and their situation. But it is frequently the case that men respond to a problem in a particular way, the wisdom of which is often only apparent with hindsight; how else can one account for the emergence of the family, the clan, or early village settlements and so on?

The reason for their appearance at successive stages is quite mysterious and stems from the fact that all human motivation at the primary level is unconscious; men do not know why they kiss girls and marry them, they don't know why they find their babies such an enchantment, at least, during the daytime, they don't know why they want to shorten the distance between A and B, to invent bicycles to help them accomplish this and to master the complexities of riding them and so on, just as, at a much earlier stage of revolution, they do not know why they developed bodies with such attributes as eyelids which possess the quality of rapid blinking. It all seems reasonable enough in retrospect, and the Reasonableness of the guilds lies in the fact that they enabled men to grapple with a large measure of success for more than a thousand years with the new problem of size that the growth of human communities had promoted.

This holds true whatever the guilds existed to promote, a matter on which they varied considerably, for some of them looked no further than the mutual protection from violence of their members, some were religious, some were guilds of merchants, while others again, much the most numerous and widespread, were for particular crafts and occupations. Since they did not exist in a power vacuum, and since the disposal of power was going through considerable fluctuations over the centuries, especially at the hands of monarchs, emperors and other rulers, guild history itself is a chequered and fluctuating affair. We are not concerned here with the extent of their usually comprehensive regulations and how far and how consistently they were applied, what we need to see is that they were a form of power, an attempt for the most part by humble men, to create a nexus within the swelling power of the larger unit, the city, nation or empire, in which they could register their significance and their humanity. As such they represented always a threat, potential or actual, to the larger power. It is not without significance that one of the earliest recorded references to the guilds as entities of power in their own right is at the time of Charlemagne (779) and is in the form of prohibition. This is unlikely to have been the first and it certainly wasn't the last, and that in nearly every case their final eclipse was accomplished by decrees of state power.[6]

To these factors must be added one other at least. A small scale society is one where personal relationships matter in a sense that cuts both ways. They enable citizens to know one another more easily and in consequence they enable them to identify their common problems a great deal more easily. This in turn enables them more easily to project solutions to those problems. Those solutions might at times be drastic; Dostoievesky's father was a landlord whose oppressiveness towards his peasants made him exceedingly unpopular; he was found one morning in a ditch with his throat cut.

The fact is that in such societies, when people were driven to extremes they were driven not by impersonal forces beyond their control, but frequently by individuals whom they could identify and against whom they could often act.

We have perhaps introduced the concept of class rather casually, for clearly the very existence of a class which differs in its economic interest from the rest of society is a division within society of tremendous importance. So important that Marx may be forgiven

---

[6]We find Plutarch speaking favourably of Numa Pompilius and the way he organised the people by their trades into companies or guilds. Plutarch, *Lives*, Vol. 14, Britannica Great Books Edition, 1952, p. 588.

for developing a whole theory of class warfare to account for the evils of the mid-nineteenth century industrialised Europe he lived in. But he was quite wrong all the same. It is probable that a differentiated class structure, far from being an anti-social evil, is a basic necessity to the survival of any civilised society. If even the occupants of a chicken run, with brains the size of a pea, will instinctively establish a pecking order, the infinitely more complex social order of a human society will surely need its divisions for much the same reasons, to ensure the stability and the survival of the unit and the protection of the young; it will need them also to affirm to the individual the significance of his place and contribution to the well-being of the unit, to say nothing of giving a bit more colour and sparkle to life in general. Even the most penurious shoemaker in Venice at the height of its glory must have lived, one can only suppose of course, a trifle more vitally than a 'worker' in a vast suburb of one of the grey, dreary urban conglomerations which afflict our modern classless societies. It seems that as soon as we act on the idea that Jack is as good as his master we make him a pawn of the party boss or the manipulating bureaucrat.

Marx failed to see that the crucial aspect of the problem was not the class division of society but the way the very scale of capitalist operations was ensuring their eventual abolition, so that in consequence the 'worker' became defenceless and tragically exposed either to the giant impersonal economic forces which technology was enabling capitalists to operate, or to the authoritarianism of the party boss. He never seems to have grasped that the real enemy was not capitalism but the scale on which it was operating, a scale which could also be applied to politics with even more horrible consequences, as a whole class of so-called revolutionaries learned to their cost when Stalin engineered himself into the driving seat of the governing apparatus of an entire empire. At this stage we need only summarise that whether an individual, a group or class had a consolidated economic interest which of its nature was opposed to the general interest of the community, such as seeking to profit from high prices at the expense of the generality, the forces which might seek to maintain or affirm the general interest were not negligible and comprised by way of summary, the large area of individual decision-making inherent in a small-scale, microcellular structure of production and distribution, the extent to which riches amassed were spent locally on locally produced goods and craftsmanship, the power of the Church, both in terms of its moral authority and in role as landowner and a general repository of wealth, the power implicit in the structure of the guilds, and lastly, informing all this, the factor of fairly close personal relationship between the government and the governed, which was frequently close enough to put real limits to both oppression and subservience.

There were times when the lives of many people were overshadowed by war, famine, tyranny and oppression, and frequently a compound of several of these factors, but what often seems to be ignored by historians is the extent to which the structural nature of such societies made it possible to resist the impact of many of these misfortunes in ways quite unknown to the members of modern mass urban societies. It would be absurd to suggest that they could resist them entirely, indeed much of history is an account of their failure in their struggles to do so. But the fact of such failure was exceptional; had it been general it would scarcely have been worth recording. History tends to be a record of exceptions.

We can see then that city-state society was one of interlocking and interdependent relationships of many kinds, the character of such societies stemmed from all its parts and it was virtually impossible for any single element to impose itself for long on the rest and to determine its general character.

CHAPTER V

Democracy and the Advertisers

Why do the people imagine a vain thing ?

In turning now to examine this factor of the strength of a minority interest, and its power to pursue its interests even in despite of the general interest in a modern mass society, the first conclusion to be drawn is the rather frightening one that the general interest has almost ceased to be represented. What prevails is a battle-ground on which a host of polyarchic groupings of minority interests of varying strengths are in conflict to influence or wield the vast powers of the centralised controlling mechanism, over which the ordinary citizen is able to exercise only, if any at all, the most vestigial forms of control.

Received opinion has a quite different view of this, it assumes, for example, that the affairs of the community are under the surveillance of freely elected members of local and national legislatures, a free press, a free radio and television service, together with the generalised forms of freedom to speak, write, associate, worship and organise for political, industrial, religious, cultural and social purposes and so on, and that the major forms of mass political and industrial organisation are effective expressions of these freedoms in action.

This picture is widely believed by millions of people to be true in every particular, yet we must reiterate, it is almost wholly false.

A survey of the elements of modern life that actually wield power is enough to indicate that in no wise is that power wielded by the general citizen body. The apparently key focus of power, the national parliament, is not controlled by the people, but by the leading elements of the mass parties whose entire concern is to maintain a tight grip on the party machinery *for their own power-oriented interests*. Similarly the 'workers' in no real sense control their union organisations, most of the leaders of which have long settled in the comfortable rut of self-perpetuating oligarchies. Again, the people do not control industry in any sense whatever, although its operations dominate their lives, they do not control the entertainment industry, banking, insurance, the mortgage market, the mass circulation newspapers, the transport system, the post office or any of the numerous artifacts of community concern in which they are almost continuously involved; even the organs of their local government, which give the appearance of managing local affairs, are in fact answerable to centralised, all-powerful ministerial bureaucracies which effectively ordain teaching policies, school organisation and administration, hospital and health service matters and numerous other aspects of local life.

It may be argued that the people in fact do control all these things because it is they who elect the leaders of mass parties, the members of parliament and the leaders of their unions, and in this way their views are adequately expressed and their powers of control affirmed. This argument needs to be answered in some detail, but before doing so it is necessary to examine the role of one form of power which has as yet scarcely been mentioned, one which has a pervasive and powerful influence on the whole nature of modern mass societies, and which in the former city-state societies did not exist in an organised form at all. That power is the power of advertising.

It has always been held to be a distinct feature of primitive mind that it can maintain quite contradictary concepts on the same subject at the same time without feeling any need to reconcile them; our forbears would pray for relief from the visitation of the plague whilst others would urge that the supply of drinking water be separated from the open sewerage runnels of the time. One might do one or the other, but without decrying the reality of the power of prayer, nobody with the least knowledge of bacteriology would do the former and neglect the latter.

Similarly one might suppose that nobody today with the merest knowledge of motivational psychology would be able to assert that a high-powered advertising industry was remotely compatible with the ordinary decencies of democracy, yet millions suppose it is in blithe ignorance of reality.

All advertising is an attack on people's minds, an attempt to persuade them to believe something to which they would otherwise give neither credence nor even possibly attention. "Advertising" said H.G. Wells, "is the art of teaching people to want things." The justification for even trying to do anything so grotesquely immoral in a world where millions are unable to satisfy their basic needs is justified by one authority, with a bland and total indifference to moral commitment which permeates much of the text-book world of our decaying civilisation, by urging, "But without the widespread dissemination of information that only advertising can provide, and the resultant mass-demand, the availability of such amenities at reasonable prices for the mass market would be technically impossible." The amenities referred to are "ch... eap transport, the advantage of clean, hygenically-packed food and drink, the luxury of modern furnishings, the benefit of labour-saving domestic appliances and the exquisite pleasure of fashionable attire."[1]

One can only marvel, for a variety of reasons, at this list and the major fallacy behind it. Does the author suppose people would cease to travel if advertising ceased? Would people cease to eat and drink? And as for the rest does the author really suppose that if furniture and clothes which really represented good value for money were available that the good news would not travel with far greater rapidity than any advertising could contrive. How does he suppose the mass market is satisfied in the Soviet Empire where commercial advertising is prohibited?

However this may be, it obscures the really crucial impact of advertising on the life of community, which is that given the sums spent on it, it usurps the power of judgement of individuals and substitutes the judgement of those who control the media. If this were not so the vast sums spent on this special pleading, lying pretence and mordant attempts to link a commodity or service to the unconscious and instinctual motivations of people, would be wasted. As it is the attempts to supplant the citizens' private judgement for that of the commercial hucksters' are almost invariably successful, that is why the money is spent and that is why the sums involved have shown an uninterrupted expansion over the last twenty five years.[2]

At one level all this activity may appear quite harmless. A greengrocer bawling his wares in the market place may be said to be employing the art of advertisement, and a series of labels bearing

[1]Leslie M. Gill, *Advertising and Psychology*, Mitchinson's University Library, London, 1954, p. 13.

[2]The following indicates the sums spent on advertising (a) and on education (b) in million pounds in the United Kingdom.

	1960	1965	1968	1969	1970	1972
(a) Advertising	323	435	503	544	554	591
(b) Education	1,058			2,399	2,747	

Source : The Economist Diary, 1974.

The figures for advertising are only for the main forms in the media, it excludes expenditure on outdoor signs and also the enormous sums spent on advertising via packaging, the eye catching devices in shops and stores, the hand-outs and giveaways and all the various forms of promotional art which seek to drown the independent citizen judgement.

legends such as 'choice' 'top quality' and so on indiscriminately stuck into each pyramid of produce may be doing the same thing, but the e are limitations here which are important. Where the advertiser is the same person as he who is personally selling his wares, there is a personal confrontation between the buyer and the advertiser/ seller and a fair chance for the buyer to make his own assessment of what is being offered and of he who is doing the offering. Citizen judgement, whilst being appealed to, remains paramount and operative.

In the world of loaded shelves of branded packages in a modern 'supermarket' none of this remains true at all. The truth is whispered at such a low pitch as to be virtually inaudible, the lies and half truths are blazoned out to catch the attention of the unwary, to misinform and to deceive, and this is the entire drift of the power of advertising.

We need to see that we are in the presence of something wholly new in the record of civilisation, a deliberate, sustained and continuously expanding attempt to misinform and to deceive the citizen body on a mass scale. We are not concerned at this stage to evaluate the sociological effects of this phenomenon, here we need to note the effects on the citizen body in terms of political power, the power, that is, of the citizen to exercise the basic criteria of democracy, to have an informed and discernible influence on the conduct of public affairs and to participate meaningfully in the formulation of policy. Basic to the whole exercise of democracy is the assumption that the citizen has free access to the truth relating to public affairs and that its well-springs are not contaminated with lies and deception before it reaches him. "Democracy," said Laski, "means participation," but in one fell swoop the power of advertising cripples the citizen's capacity to make an informed judgement on many of the key areas of community life, often before he is aware the issues have been formulated.

The idea of a certain detachment from material things, of exercising a sense of economy with material resources, and restraint in one's general pattern of consumption is one that has been expressed in traditional wisdom for many centuries. This is why a practice of bodily asceticism, which sometimes took extreme forms of fasting and indifference to severe physical discomforts, has long been associated with spiritual grace and even saintliness. An outstanding exponent of this view was Mahatma Gandhi. On a sea voyage at the turn of the century he persuaded a friend to throw a pair of binoculars through the porthole; for the same reason, the desire to practice non-attachment to material things, he persuaded his wife to give up her jewellery, took to wearing simple homespun clothing, travelling in third class railway carriages and so on. When he died his total property was reported to consist of a pair of spectacles, a loin cloth, a pair of sandals, a cheap metal pocket watch, and wooden eating bowl.[3]

Gandhi, in common with others, of which Jesus, Tolstoy, St. Francis, the Buddha and Albert Schweitzer, can be reckoned notable in a notable company, saw clearly that the way forward for civilisation lay in the field of simplicity, of detachment and of personal restraint in matters of consumption and sensual gratification. One need not stay to explain here *why* this is so, it must suffice to indicate that some of the noblest minds in the human record have agreed it is so,[4] and to note that the whole burden of modern advertising with its consummately diabolical skills is designed to persuade people of the precise opposite.

In a world where human potential is being destroyed or stunted in its development to an appalling extent by the grossest conceivable forms of poverty, where life-support systems are under cumulative forms of pressure from the technological malpractices of advanced nations, where indeed these nations have made such malpractice a dominant pattern of life, and where the gap between the 'have' and 'have not' nations is rapidly widening, there is something utterly schizophrenic in advanced nations spending sums which can be as much as fifth or more of the Government educational budgets on persuading their citizens to consume yet more of the products of their mechanical industries and services than they might otherwise be disposed to.

---

[3]One must allow here for the power of legend and the use of precisely the kind of techniques we are discussing. When he was alive Gandhi had a small army of helpers in his public work, he used the services of secretaries, of office furniture such as typewriters and filing systems, and his voluminous personal papers were already of very great value. A secretary preparing his financial accounts amused him one day with the comment, "You know Mahatma, it costs a great deal of money to keep you in poverty."

[4]Note especially those great words from the Bhagavad Gita, perhaps the most sublime on the human condition ever uttered, "The whole world is the garment of God; renounce it, and receive it back as the gift of God."

We may note merely in passing that the main reason why such evils proliferate is because our societies have ceased to be bound by any explicit moral code. Such codes existed, even if they were not always followed, before the age of giantism and industrialism, and the church of Christendom for example, denominational distinctions notwithstanding, sought to promote it. For many years now the Church has been silent on these cardinal issues, except in terms so bromidally generalised, or so sociologically insensitive, as to cut no ice at all; in Tawney's crisp words applied to other problems in another era "The Church ceased to speak its mind and as a natural consequence it ceased to have a mind to speak."[5]

What we need to note however is the extent to which the power of advertising is being used to preempt all the major decisions about the pattern of society, its institutional shape and even more the values that inform it. We have noted this already in the way it is seeking to promote the prodigality of the rake in place of the careful sense of restraint of the alert conscience as the dominant ethos of society, but we need to see how it institutionalises this trend in countless ways. A young person entering society today finds, to take a particularly heinous example, that the private ownership of a car is considered a perfectly natural and normal means of transport. This, after all, is what prevails, a mass car-owning public, a multitude of many forms of car advertisements, plus numerous advertisements of car accessories and services, a vast programme of public expenditure on special roads for cars, a proportionate expenditure on the construction of refuelling and service stations, and an inhuman acceptance of a rate of killing and maiming of human life which now pertains to all modern societies and cheapens immeasurably the instinctual regard for the value of life; these forces hang over our society today like a flock of corpse-hungry vultures. There is also the frequent and much boosted incidence of 'motor shows' local, national and international, provoking their due accompaniment of lucrative newspaper and magazine supplements. The shows are usually of course, opened by prominent members of society of quite the most eminent respectability.

Any young person who sought to question this strangely selfish, destructive and life-demeaning form of transport would at once find himself at cross purposes with the dominant values of his society.

[5]R.H. Tawney, *The Acquisitive Society*, London, Fontana Books Edition, Collins, 1962.

If he were to argue about the waste of resources, the disregard of life and the destruction of urban and rural environmental amenity, he would be countered with the apparently inexorable need to increase the gross national product, to boost the current export drive, the need to win a dominant position in the world, to defeat our competitors and, perhaps above all, the need not to stand in the way of progress; and progress, he will find, is a word defined in people's minds (rather than in the dictionary), by the world of the advertisers, and means earning, spending, and consuming goods and services at an ever accelerating rate for the purely personal and sensual gratifications that may accrue as a consequence, however transitory, however destructive and however harmful to private morality or public well-being.[6]

He will find too, and this may well prove the decisive force which leads him to modify his views, that he is at odds with the views of nearly everybody around him, for the advertisers have been spending big money for years, and that their expensive and skilful brainwashing techniques have been successful will be in no wise more apparent than in the way his fellows will seek to repudiate even the need to answer his questions. It is of the essence of such techniques that they are able to plant assumptions in the victim's mind without making him aware of the process, so that he can come to believe that they represent the results of his own profoundly original and entirely unaided mental activities.

The same forces have succeeded in winning unquestioning acceptance of factory farming and all its dangerous and anti-human consequences, the idea of economic growth of almost any kind as a worthy end in itself, the destruction of localised shopping complexes in the hands of local retailers as the price for chains of so-called supermarkets, and modes of packing and presentation which seem to benefit everybody but the consumer, and which with numerous other changes which be speak of transformation of the way of life of millions of people, changes they have neither sought nor initiated, which they have neither freely and soberly assessed, nor been given the chance to freely accept or reject. Over almost the entire complex of corporate life in society its members have been cajoled and tricked into an acceptance of a lifestyle which affronts

[6]In 1971 no less than 8,185 people were killed in road traffic accidents in the U.K. alone.
Source: *The Economist Diary*, 1974.

and rejects their humanity, displaces them from the central focus of consideration in favour of economic and political factors which were previously subordinate, and casts the entire direction of society into a mold which denies the essentially humanistic basis of any sane social order, denies humanity itself except as an element to be exploited or managed for non-humanist ends which are generally as demeaning as they are destructive.

We know full well, in considering the subject of transport, that in Britain the resources devoted to roads and motor vehicles could have provided a fast, comfortable and frequent service of trains to almost every part of the country; for long-distance journeys, there could be special cinema shows, stenographic services, and dining cars equipped to serve meals of a Lucullan splendour; municipal taxi and bus services could be used to service the railway stations, and much of the entire service could operate with no direct charge to the users at all and with a burden on general revenues and private spending which could be trifling compared with the sums devoted to cars and roads. People of all ages could travel easily, comfortably, safely and with some approach to dignity and ecological sanity. Instead we are saddled with a socially savage system of private transport which is wasteful of resources, of beauty, of human life and happiness and indifferent to the needs of the poor and the aged who are often unable to use it at all.

A railway engine with its complement of rolling stock will, in its lifespan of let us say, twenty-five years or more, convey millions of passengers, and carry tons of postal packets and other freight with a minimal hazard to life and limb and a minimal demand on resources. Many railway stations in different parts of the world are palatial works of art in their own right, and the man who has seen a steam train making its own pattern of movement and smoke-puff on the horizon and not known some extra happiness at least, has surely no poetry in his soul. A car in its short span of seven years, and frequently less, seldom carries more than one passenger, seldom indeed that, and, not least of its wasteful peculiarities, is generally stationary for most of the twenty-four hours of the day. In motion it is a perpetual menace to pedestrians, other vehicles, and not least to the driver himself.

Yet what has happened to us that we accept the one and reject the other of these alternatives when so obviously we should do the reverse? The answer of course lies in advertising, which ensures as a consequence

> Each new morn, new widows howl, new orphans cry, new
> sorrows strike heaven on the face. . . .

Yet what politician, once the commercial brainwashers have done
their job, could begin a national campaign against privately owned
transport in favour of publicly owned transport and expect to gain
victory or even votes in an electoral contest?

Here, as in so many other instances, we can see how the power
of advertising is used to undermine the very foundation of democracy. Following its operations through we can see how it projects,
how all such advertising projects, the value assumption that it is
a good thing, an indubitable sign of progress, to expand one's
personal consumption of goods and services to the maximum.

If this is a good thing then clearly any move to increase or enlarge
the means of doing so, by building more and bigger factories, more
atomic power stations, by sinking more oil shafts and so on is also
a good thing. So that institutions, deeply implanted habits of consumption, an irrationally inflated level of consumer expectations, and
an entire psychology of the individual's place in the social order
and his relationship to it is created long before the formal processes
of democratic political evaluation and decision-making have begun.
As a consequence we find that the basis of a great many political
questions is pre-empted by this factor.

There is, for example, not a single instance on record of any democratically convened or elected body ever having discussed whether
the private ownership of a motor vehicle on a mass scale was a good
or bad thing, far less recording a verdict in its favour. The *principle,*
as applied to an individual, and its social effects when multiplied
to a mass scale, was never in the first place considered at all. That
discussion was pre-empted at different stages in the development
of motoring by the power of advertising. As a consequence, since
the principle of the thing was made acceptable, and thus accepted,
all the debates in the political arena relate merely to its consequences. Indeed the very fact that debates in the legislature centre
on road safety, parking problems, motorway construction, car
exports, urban traffic congestion and lead pollution from car fumes,
and that offences against road traffic acts now constitute one of
the biggest single forms of law infringement, all merely buttresses

the success of the advertisers in their campaign to win over the
public mind to an uncritical and unquestioning acceptance of the
place of their product in the scheme of things.

We need to realise that in terms of its impact, however transient
it is likely to prove, and it seems likely that the age of mass motoring
will end as suddenly as it began, and from beginning to end is hardly
likely to last a single century, it has transformed the conditions of
organised human life far more profoundly than any other single
development. Yet despite the fact that this transformation has
been almost wholly disastrous, to this day we insist on discussing its
effects rather than the principle of its acceptance or not.

We can see the evil of this process at work in some of the undeveloped countries, especially those which have only recently achieved
their liberation and political independence from colonial rule.
Zambia, for example, has been under colonial rule for more than
half a century and when in 1964, it achieved the power of self-
rule, it inherited from the colonial era, as did Britain in its time
from the Romans, a defined legal system, a number of towns and
cities, some decent roads, a standard system of weights and measures, a currency, a national language, a system of military training,
a system of government, some elements of a dominant architectural
ethos, and some new concepts of religion, social behaviour, dress,
culinary craft and so on. Yet the British colonialists left behind
in Africa one feature which was entirely absent from the Roman
legacy in Britain, and this was the unspoken message of the whole
world of advertising, that the need to engage in a competitive
scramble for ever higher levels of production and ever accelerating
rates of personal consumption of goods and services is one that
takes precedence over all other aspects of life.

In Britain this concept has developed slowly over nearly two
centuries as production technology developed and required a
corresponding adaptation of consumption habits to absorb its
diverse fruits. In Africa it has suddenly been dumped there, with
effects on social habits and prevailing values which are quite calamitous.

Zambia has about four million people, three-quarters of whom
are living in rural areas in conditions of poverty and backwardness
which has rightly led the government to make the cause of rural
development one of its primary concerns. On the face of it this would
not seem to be a difficult problem; already Zambia has established

the main elements of a locally trained infrastructure of administrators and technical people of many kinds, it earns large revenues
from its copper mines, it enjoys a fair measure of international
goodwill and this expresses itself in different kinds of aid programmes
which embrace hospitals, teaching services, agricultural research,
intensive rural development zones, town planning, self-help schemes,
co-operative experiments and in numerous other ways. All systems
are set, it would seem, to go. But what is the reality?

The development programme is running into the quicksands of
advertising values in a number of ways which are making rural
development look like a lost cause before it is launched, for such
development depends for its success on a certain change of consciousness on the part of rural people, they need to acquire habits
of study, comparison, classification, innovation and contingency
provision, to harness the admirable sense of community and co-operative effort they already possess to certain improved methods of
farming, stock raising, grain storage, marketing and so on. Again
none of this is difficult and in places where it has been tried the
results have been dramatic in terms of higher levels of production
and so on. Yet again none of *this* is so very difficult; what then is
hindering its application? We have to face the fact that in large
measure the 'change of consciousness' has already taken place,
but that change has been away from concepts of rural development
and towards urban consumption standards and values.

The merest village of Zambia may be full of people who are illi-
terate, malnourished and badly housed and clothed, but they will
all know about a certain widely advertised drink of artificially
sweetened chemicals in sealed bottles which first originated in the
U.S.A. and which is delivered regularly to the village store; they
will also know about tinned milk and tinned meat, the blessings
of which are available from the leverage of a bottle or can-opener
after hard-earned money has changed hands. The village may
possess, potentially or actually, numerous fruit trees from which
to make delightful natural fruit drinks, and cattle to provide any
amount of meat and milk, but the advertised goods hold sway in
people's minds and take precedence.

Where do they come from? Where, for that matter do the two
government men come from who visited the village only yesterday?
They came in a gleaming Mercedes, they wore brilliantly polished
shoes, beautifully pressed suits which, even if they did bulge a bit

at buttock and stomach, were carefully cut and trimmed, they wore such white shirts, such dazzling and colourful silk ties, one had a gold wrist watch and gold cuff links, and the other had two jewelled rings on his fingers and carried a camera on his shoulder, both had shining, exotic fountain pens, as well as an air of authority, command, ease, well-being, assurance, affluence ... Whilst they drank their bottle of sweetened chemicals during their five minute stay in the village one of them turned on a big portable radio and there was a news bulletin, just think of it, from Lusaka! And the man said they could even get a voice speaking from London! Where did these incredible men and their possessions come from? Where do the bottles and tins come from? Where did the money come from? It came and it comes, it is manifest, from the city; what alternative then is there for any young man of spirit but to gather his scanty possessions, make a sorrowful farewell to his parents and friends, and go his way too to the beckoning wonders of city life which have begun to invest his imagination with the kind of power that the golden fleece exercised over Jason.

And this pattern of response is registering not only all over Zambia, or indeed all over Africa, but the entire world, and the senseless silent rush of rural Dick Whittingtons to what they imagine to be the gold-paved splendours of city life has become one of the most dangerous and tragic revolutions that mankind, in all its turbulent history, has ever accomplished. Behind it stands the beckoning finger of advertising, like some evil symbol of the giddy pleasures of the eye which will betray all who follow as much as those that remain. For who does remain to invigorate village life with new ideas and new ideals, to experiment, to volunteer, to serve, to inspire and to lead? No government can hope to initiate a rural revolution from a city centre, it can only hope to educate and inspire those in the rural areas who are willing and able to comprehend and respond. The fact that they have largely left the land and are herding into lawless and insanitary shanty towns of the world's new cities, or transforming the centre of old ones into decaying slums, is the bitter medicine of failure which governments take in double doses as they watch the bright prospects of rural renewal being able to revivify urban life with a continuous feedback of vitality and innovation, given way to continued stagnation in one and manifest decay in the other.

Yet what can governments do? Despite the fact that they hold power either because of people's votes or despite them, they must be conscious that the real power is elsewhere, as indeed it is, and that power is in the values by which people live, values which today centre on the mere fact of consumption in increasingly esoteric and unsatisfying forms which the world of advertising has created. And since these are the values by which people tragically have come to live and measure their lives, values now buttressed by vast systems of production and distribution, imposing patterns of foreign trade, and even more imposing problems of foreign payments, what can the politicians do but go along with the general drift—especially since they are, for the most part, as disposed to accept the values prompting that drift, having themselves been subjected to the same conditioning process, and which has indeed made them part of it?

Yet the greatest offence which advertising gives, in the professionalised and highly skilful manner in which it has now become practised is probably the least remarked. A community needs to be aware of itself and of its needs; it needs to have a general mind about its problems and of the ways they should be resolved. Yet what chance does any member of a modern mass society, each of whom is subjected to these skills of mind manipulation, have of becoming aware of these problems at all unless, as is likely as not, he is himself a community problem?

In a crowded modern megalopolis it is all too probable that within any given square mile there will be scores of people who are in trouble of one kind or another, who may be in the grip of alcoholism or some other form of drug addiction, who may be the families of a breadwinner now in prison, ("you have been found guilty of a particularly heinous crime. I sentence you yourself to ten years imprisonment, and your wife to ten years of constant want, penury and uncertainty, and your children to ten years of deprivation of their birthright of male parental care in the not very confident hope that as a consequence they will avoid becoming sexual misfits and delinquent themselves when they are grown up"), who may be on the brink of suicide, infanticide, or of committing some other crime, who may be homeless, hungry, friendless, sick or dying without the mead of fellowship and concern it is the duty of any civilised society to provide as a matter of course. These victims, which for the most part is what they are, if only of circumstance, are known to those nearest to them (and not always then), perhaps to the police, clergyman or a social worker, but for the most part they form a vast secret society of suffering and neglect. Who else knows about their problems? Of the half-starved aged lady in the grip of poverty—loneliness and despair, of the hordes of old people sitting in 'homes' '…staring at radiators and waiting to die.' Of the wide-eyed children, again in 'homes' looking blankly on the world and whose souls are gasping vainly for the love which is utterly indispensable to their growth and fulfilment … who knows, and who in consequence cares?

How can the commuting millions of suburban workers of today's mass societies possibly be aware? It is possible indeed that they are living partly in a cloud of self-induced unknowing simply because their common sense tells them they are powerless to act in any real ameliorative sense even if they really exerted themselves to know; the social mechanisms by which they might so act in any genuine community do not exist in mass societies; what does exist instead is a near-total degree of exposure to the wiles of the manipulators and the message *they* wish to convey. The ignorance of the fate of Miss X, who dies from hypothermia in an isolated bedsitter, or of the small child who is maltreated by cruel parents (themselves the products of what in their behaviour they project?) is part of the colossal price we pay for being all too fully informed about the probably bogus qualities of a certain brand of toothpaste, floor polish or shoes and so on, or of some nutritionally perfectly useless breakfast cereal or chemical drink. We do not even *need* such information, but our exposure to it and our absorption of it blots out every kind of social message we do need to hear.

Not least of the evils which stem, at least in part, from living in a cloud of unknowing about the problems of those who ought to be our neighbours as distinct from being simply isolated units in a mass aggregate, is that even the possibility of remedial measures that would make society more civilised and humane simply go by default.

Quite a number of people go to prison, for example, but this is an experience reserved for a small (but growing) minority, most of whom are unable to cope with the problems of life or of the buildup of pressures within their own personalities. By and large they certainly are not drawn from the ranks of well-to-do middle class people with assured jobs, status and incomes; they are all too frequently the products of single-parent situations, broken marriages, parental alcoholism or other types of drug addiction, poverty, educational inadequacy or the stunting of their possibilities for development and maturation by many kinds of social pressure, of which advertising itself is assuredly one, to say nothing of the absence of many positive forms of social pressure which might have helped them on to a brighter path.

These social 'can't copes' and misfits, what is our answer to their problem? It is an answer which is barbaric to a degree. We lock them up, more important, we lock them *away* indicating all too clearly we don't want to know about them or care about them, being perhaps too busy contemplating the allurements of the bargain offer of the very latest in sound reproduction equipment advertised in the Sunday Supplement of one of our ever so progressive liberal newspapers which costs a couple of acres of ecological devastation each week just to produce.

We lock them away in conditions of the maximum psychological (and often physical) degradation and torment, conditions which constitute a frontal assault on the integrity of their personalities and a determination to stamp out every manifestation of sensibility and refinement they might manifest through the thickets of inner misery, disruption and deformation amid which most of them live.

Even if we had never heard of Freud, Jung and a host of others, and the revelations of the unconscious processes of the personality they have helped to clarify, we must surely be aware that the human personality is something utterly unique on this planet. We continue to regard ourselves as being a mere cut above the beasts and not much more, and God knows the way we behave at times, especially to the less fortunate, can provide a fair share of justification for such a view.

But only consider; at the age of three a human child can speak a language, before it is fully adult it can contemplate mathematics, history, geography, thermodynamics, town planning, television, the workings of a car engine, astronomy, music, theatre, sculpture, painting, poetry, philosophy, the presence of God and hundreds, if not thousands, of other facets of human life and understanding. Compared with the level of understanding of the most intelligent of the beasts, humanity is godlike in its superiority; it is an altogether richer, more complex, innovative and profound form of life, as different as a tree from a rock or a moon-rocket from a seashell.

Yet there is a corollary here which is universally played down or ignored. The personality of a small child which embodies as a matter of course the potentiality of such riches is, it must follow, more delicate, complex, sensitive and finely balanced than any other expression of life. A million computers could not begin to simulate it. This is reflected in the astonishingly long period of protection and tutelage the human young are given; if we take the limit of such parental protection as being with the onset of puberty, and it frequently extends well beyond, it constitutes about a fifth of a normal life span. It follows the fulfilment of the *need* for this protection is utterly paramount to the well-being of the personality. We may put it even more strongly, especially since the idea of 'protection' may suggest nothing more than a city wall; it is part of every child's birthright to be loved and to have a sense of security. Yet how many of our prison inmates, on whatever side of a cell door they may be, for like always attracts like, have ever known either?

Why then do we continue to behave to these unfortunates with such barbaric abandon? With buildings, regimes and regulations that assume the needs of the human personality are on a level with the bovine inmates of a cowshed? Part of the answer lies in the sense of insecurity we all feel and which stems from the pressures and the patterns of modern life; any factor, even a human one, which may add to that sense of insecurity arouses deep levels of hostility, which is partly why proposals for 'prison reform' (can any prison be reformed without being abolished?) are endlessly sidetracked with assertions that life must not be made comfortable for 'criminals', and anyway, 'what about the victims?' Most people have never been to prison, not even as visitors, and have very little idea of the extent of the emotional suffering they generate, the wilderness of misery in which most of the inmates wander as they sit in their cells, nor of the depth of psychological degradation they perpetuate. Few people pause to think that prison inmates have all too often been denied in their formative years the kind of love and protection a farmyard hen, with a brain the size of a pea, will give its young as a matter of course, or of their responsibility for what goes on behind prison walls. This responsibility stems not simply from the fact that we are all members of a society which perpetuates such needless misery but because in our concern to join the rat race of higher earnings and increased consumption we simply shore up the institutions which are creating the tensions, especially in family life, which are tearing our society apart. It is of course the victims of these tensions who are most likely to find themselves behind prison walls. We want to forget and to ignore all this suffering, and the consequent blunting of sensibility, we want to regulate prisons to the dark, remoter reaches of our minds along with torture cells, gas-chambers, hangman's ropes and the like, and the seductive power of advertising is there on every hand to help us.

The outraged middle-class conscience, so active to secure the abolition of the slave trade, let us say, and which awoke with a fitful start for a brief spell in the fifties to protest about atomic bombs, has been lulled to sleep by the endless lullabies of consumerism orchestrated by the conductors of high-powered advertising. The moronic inhumanity of modern prison life continues not because we lack the money for new buildings (which would doubtless house as much psychological torture as the old), not because public opinion won't stand for a change (when has public opinion ever been in the modern era but a factor to be juggled with and manipulated?), but because we are not getting the message; we have been cajoled into a corrupt overconcern with our creature comforts and above all we lack the will to act. At the very least, if the concern for prison inmates was real, that concern would by now have raised its own funds to ensure there was at least a comfortable hotel outside every prison for the prisoners' wives and families, a place where they could get advice and help, and which were active campaigning centres for prisoners' rights, for the checking of abuses and the assistance of the prisoners.

But we ignore all this suffering and torment, or we leave it to bodies such as the Howard League for Penal Reform, itself waging the battle against medievalism with nineteenth century ideas, just as we largely ignore the inhumanity of our mental hospitals and old people's homes, where staff shortages sometimes mean old people cannot be helped to dress, so they simply lie in bed and vegetate week after week, and sometimes for hours at a time in their own excrement. What community, what genuine community, a social unit whose predominant and most powerful aspect was the personal relationships between its members (as distinct, let us say, from increasing the gross national product), would be *unaware* of such suffering if it prevailed, and would not act swiftly, as swiftly as a hen would rush to protect its chicks if need arose, to remedy matters?

Saturation advertising is an entirely new development in the history of civilisation, by displacing the social message from the central focus of concern and intruding the voices of the huckster and special market-place pleading, it is making our entire society a stranger to itself and to its own purposes, and by usurping the power of morality for the power of salesmanship it is cheapening and demeaning the entire adventure of life.

The real price of high-powered advertising is unending social degradation.

CHAPTER VI

Bureaucracy and the Ballot Growth, Power and Control

I swear to the Lord
I still can't see
Why democracy means
Everyone but me.

Langston Hughes
The Black Man Speaks

Having established the limitations of democratic power implicit in the power used to condition people's minds which the manipulators of mass-advertising possess, we must next look at the nature of the power wielded in mass societies through the established political process. Crucial to most prevailing thinking on this subject is the idea that liberty is enshrined in people having free and secret access to the ballot box and that so long as this obtains, together with the right to associate in political groups and to select freely candidates for elections, then it is virtually inviolate. That this is true of a genuine community is not to be gainsaid, but a mass society is not a genuine community, it is not indeed a community in any sense, for reasons to be explained, and it has to be asserted quite explicitly that in relation to a mass society this just is not true at all.

A community, for the purpose of this discussion, may be defined as a social unit where the relationships of the members are more important and more powerful than the mechanisms of control that are used in determining its general nature and direction; contrariwise a mass society may be defined as a unit where the mechanisms of its control are more important and more powerful than the relationships of its members in determining such matters.

Why is it necessary to counterpoise these two aspects? Primarily because any social grouping is an expression of human relationships and it is the nature of those relationships which defines and determines the nature of the group. When, however, forces emerge within the grouping which displace the determinant nature of the personal relationships of its members it is necessary to isolate and define those forces, and in modern mass societies they are in every case, with no exceptions, derived from the central and centralised controlling mechanisms to which reference has already been made.

What is being asserted is that it is in fact the central controlling forces in mass societies which determine the nature of people's social relationships and not vice versa, and we need now to make clear in detail how this portentous conclusion is established.

We have already stated that a city state, because of the factors outlined earlier (Chapter III) is able to be democratic if the democratic spirit of its members is strong and persistent enough to ensure it prevails. In a mass society these factors are displaced or destroyed by others, and as a consequence a mass society *cannot* by its nature be democratic; a mass democracy is simply a contradiction in terms.

A community of, let us say, one hundred thousand people can, as we have already suggested, be democratic because the conduct of public affairs will be based very largely on the knowledge people have of one another as fellow citizens and because this fact alone will tend to determine the nature and the quality of the social order. As a growth in numbers proceeds a number of potential or actual anti-democratic factors begin to emerge:

1. The size of the central controlling mechanism begins to grow and its functions and powers to expand.
2. The need for representative rather than direct decision-making increases to a point where representatives elect representatives to represent *them*.
3. Differences of economic status begin to develop which tend to create differences of class interest between the members of the formerly relatively economically homogeneous group.
4. The central controlling mechanism becomes more remote from the individual citizen.
5. The mere increase in numbers means that the power to decide becomes more thinly spread, that each individual citizen is able to wield less of it, despite the fact that the total degree of the power inherent in the community is increasing at least proportionately to the increase in its numbers.

Taking each of these factors in turn we need to see clearly not only how the central controlling mechanism grows, but that each stage of growth is a progression of increasing inroads into democratic power. Proceeding by analogy we can see that if a number of vehicles in an urban community is not more than a score or so the drivers are perfectly able to establish amongst themselves certain rules of the road and certain rules of precedence at road junctions to ensure that traffic flows freely and without danger. But once the number increases to hundreds or thousands this will not do, controls will be needed, at first human, later frequently operated by robots which (not whom!) the citizen will be bound, under penalty, to obey.

It may be argued in this instance that the driver surrenders some freedom in order to acquire the wider freedom of being able to travel longer distances and in greater safety. This is a half-way argument, the end of this particular road is a growing multiplicity of vehicles which comes in time to dominate and largely destroy the urban scene as fashioned for man and to create a special motoring environment which is well-nigh identical wherever one chooses to travel, and which largely cancels out the point of travel altogether. If A becomes the same as B or C or D *ad infinitum*, what is the point of leaving A at all? The point is sharply applicable to politics, for to surrender real freedom to choose in order to acquire more apparent freedom—let us say, to consume, is to find one has surrendered reality for a chimera in which one has no freedom worth the name and where one's destiny becomes the creature of forces one cannot control and ultimately not even question.

There is no equivalent in a city-state to, for example, the Pentagon military machine or the Central Intelligence Agency of the U.S.A., which have both grown to such dimensions of power as to be not simply empires of power in their own right, but capable of wielding enormous, and at certain crucial stages, decisive influence on the supposedly democratic political process.

Part of this loss emerges from the mechanism of selecting and electing representatives instead of making one's own decisions. In mass societies we may see how the validity of the principle of election is altogether subverted by the mechanism of mass political parties and their disciplining procedures, and the play on political forces of the influences of the media, political charlatanism and so on. We shall need to develop this point in detail.

The question of class structures and class interests, and the conflicts they engender, has been the subject of much discussion and contention for more than a century, much of which has been sterile simply because real though the conflicts of interest are, and indisputable though the loss of power vis-a-vis the stronger at the expense of the weaker is, the fact that this discussion has ignored altogether the question of size and how a growth in the size of a unit decisively determines its character, is what has led to the horrors of Soviet Communism and the conservative ineffectuality of social-democratic and labour type socialism.

Differences in income and economic status can never be abolished, and there are a host of good reasons why they should not be, for merely to seek to do so would require an army of police and private investigators, and volumes of detailed government legislation which would end in making a farce of freedom and the remedy worse than the disease. This is not to condone excess at either end of the scale, whether of consumption or of economic deprivation, it is to recognise men are different and that they have different propensities and needs over which any social order should refrain from riding roughshod, especially at the expense of its own stability and well-being. All that is being asserted here is that if economic polarisation into contending classes goes beyond certain tolerable limits the more powerful will come to deny the weak the reality of democratic experience itself.

Our fourth and fifth points are really obverse to each other. In geometry we say that a point is represented by the intersection of two straight lines and that the sum of the angles meeting at any given point is 360°. If we think of 360 lines meeting at the centre, rather like spokes of a wheel, we may project the lines away from the centre to any distance we please so that whilst the lines meet at a point so small as not to be susceptible to measurement, they can stretch out to infinity.

If we seek to particularise this concept with numbers and assume the centre is the shape of a wheel one yard, let us say, in diameter, we may then calculate the circumference and the radius. Let us assume that this is a diagrammatic representation of a village community of 360 families; the 360 lines will then be little more than lines of communication which will not so much meet at the centre as cross it as they will in a village street or square, and what exists is a definable and measurable community.

The city-state will enlarge this diagram to a stage where each line, now on the same assumed scale several yards in length, giving the wheel a correspondingly larger circumference, will represent a small village or parish, but at the centre there is now a power nexus where they terminate in city hall, law court, university, cathedral or wherever. Transposing this to the mass society the lines making the 360 degrees, now measured in miles rather than yards, become endlessly sub-divided to take account not of cities, nor of villages and parishes, nor even of families, but simply of individuals! In a key respect the mass society represents not progress but a distinct form of regression to the lone nomadic hunter of prehistory, a conclusion confirmed when we reflect that the mass society is the child of capitalist aggrandisement which, as intellectually systematised by Adam Smith, assumed the pre-eminence, in Keynes' words, of 'a mere congerie of pursuers'.

Man is not in these circumstances enjoying the security (which may be as much emotional as physical) of a genuine parish or village community, in psychic terms he is naked, isolated, totally dependent and terribly alone within the maw of the mass society which can only in fact come into being by destroying community.

A diagrammatic representation can only convey the static realities of the remoteness of the central controlling mechanisms from the citizen, and the extent to which the power of the individual citizen is undermined by the sheer multiplicity of his numbers on a grossly inflated scale of living accompanied by a breakdown of the small divisions which represent to him community, home and roots; what it cannot show is the dynamics of power and how they are affected by the growth in scale, a point to which we now need to turn.

The first thing we need to note is that with growth there comes a change in the functions of the 'lines' which attach the individual to the centre. At village level they are lines of mere communication, at city-state level they carry decision-making power and also an element of acknowledgement of authority through payment of taxes, acceptance of conscription, answering summonses to a court and so on. In the mass society the function of these lines is transformed. Communication *to* the centre becomes residual, it is communication *from* the centre which is now paramount. These lines do not run direct from the centre to the citizen, they run through localised centres which were once the expression of the citizen's needs and powers and *which are now that of the controlling mechanism itself*. Communication, decision-making, planning projection, control of the media and control of elected representative, this all emanates from the all-powerful centre. For the citizen, an apparent growth of democratic apparatus notwithstanding, acknowledgement of authority is all.

It need not be supposed that this development has been plotted by some evil genius, rather is it the consequence of a failure of men to revise some basic concepts of government in the light of some utterly unprecedented developments in human history, so that more than two and half millennia after their first appearance, we are vainly seeking to fit the phenomena of the mass society in terms of democratic practice to the theoretical construction of the Greek city states. We have to see that quantitative change if pursued far enough leads to qualitative change in politics as in anything else and we need to adapt our theoretical framework to such change if we are to avoid needless trouble and confusion.

Let us, for the purposes of simplicity, imagine a progression in size, in terms of numbers of inhabitants, and seek to indicate the power attributes that pertain to each unit as its numbers are multiplied by ten. If we start with a community of 100,000 we can see at once that with such a number certain mechanisms of control are already a social necessity. There will be a need to organise water supplies, sewage services, traffic controls, a currency, weights and measures, a legal system, a system of law enforcement, and so on. Yet with all these requirements the general body of the citizenry is able to share as fully as it may wish in the decision-making that governs such matters even though the simple process of direct democracy may have given way to that of elementary representative forms.

We should note here that in any free society decision-making is not confined to one sphere called 'politics', but is operative in numerous forms and at numerous levels. For some reason there is a disposition to assume that if people are not interested in 'politics' they are not interested in decision-making. The present writer happens to have a disposition which makes him fascinated by the political process and the problems it promotes, but he would be unable, say, to run a school, to conduct an orchestra, at least in a way that anyone would want to listen to it, to make a pair of shoes, to operate a capstan, to build a house, administer a factory and so on. Yet all these and many other spheres are important areas of decision-making. If he could do some of these or other tasks he would probably be less interested in the political process. The point is that nature seems to provide an abundance of capable 'leadership', by which is meant simply the capacity to consider a problem and give a lead to its solution to others, in every sphere of life. Yet this diversity is somehow taken to be an indication that authoritarianism in politics is thereby justified.

Mr. Colin Wilson, for example, was wont to dwell on the apparently anti-democratic political implications of the fact that in the American prisoner of war camps in Vietnam only a very tiny percentage of the prisoners ever busied themselves with the problem of escaping, the rest being content to accept their lot like sheep, with no more than an occasional bleat of protest. It never seems to have struck Mr. Wilson that if the same inmates were asked to build a cathedral, cook a banquet, stage an opera or organise a supply of clean drinking water, that again, doubtless only a very tiny percentage would respond, but that in each case the percentage might well comprise a quite different set of people.

If we increase the number of inhabitants tenfold to one million we find that somewhere along the road a number of important changes begin to appear if, that is, they have not already done so. Chief of these is that among the elected representatives, the differences of opinion about the conduct of public affairs, and the struggle for power among them become so intensified that the former factions are no longer willing—largely no doubt, because the fruits of success are so much greater, and the struggle for power therefore so much more intense—to wage the struggle within the confines of one party. The ruling group divides.

This, as we have noted already, is an event of the utmost significance. Hitherto the ruling group was elected, if it was elected, to conduct public affairs in the general interest. Since the scale of public life was relatively small a speedy and more immediate grasp of the true nature of the public interest was not difficult to establish on the basis of a general consensus. Now, it appears, this is no longer the case. The mere growth in the size of the community makes a consensus of view on any given subject more difficult to ascertain, so difficult in fact that in accordance with a long established precedent, one going back to the Greek city states, a clear need arises to divide the unit so as to ensure that the former healthy situation prevails. This is not done; instead a division is made not of the unit itself, as in nature, but of the ruling political group, and with this fateful step the unit is launched on the path towards the most evil, destructive and disastrous political structure to which mankind has ever been subject, the mass society.

By means of this step a large section, those who will have voted against the ruling group, sometimes by a quirk of voting machinery— even the majority, is disenfranchised from any effective controlling voice in the political process! Yet even this is part of a trend towards an even more imposing result.

All subsequent history has shown that once this step is taken it is but a prelude to the effective disenfranchisement of the general citizen body regardless of the formal voting and elective process that may prevail or the political ideology that is pursued.

This tenfold increase also results in both an enlargement in number and a further professionalisation of the officials responsible for the administrative machinery at the centre. The bureaucracy at this stage of the growth of the political unit is already a considerable power in its own right, and in this regard it is worth listing some of its main characteristics, bearing in mind they appear to be constant from century to century and as common to London as they are to Liechtenstein, to Los Angeles, Lucknow, Lagos, or Leningrad.

1. A bureaucracy will serve *any* master of any political complex so long as its own prerogatives are observed.
2. It is the most profoundly conservative force in any community.
3. It will be the main agent in defusing the will-to-change of any revolution.
4. Its working rule as a body is always 'self first' on the basis of the conservation of its own energies regardless of the extent to which it involves the expenditure of the energies of others.
5. The ties of loyalty between its own members are always stronger than the service of the public interest or that of its ostensible political masters.
6. The politician who seeks change is the bureaucrat's enemy.
7. The politician who is concerned to maintain the *status quo* is the bureaucrat's friend.
8. All bureaucracies are 'non-political' so long as this is interpreted as being the upholding of the 'status quo'.
9. To the politician in office the bureaucracy is there to serve him by applying his policies. To the bureaucracy the politician in office is a transient inconvenience who must be kept out of mischief by piling up his desk with papers he dare not ignore whilst the bureaucrats pursue their policies-as-usual.
10. In any conflict of interest and opinion the bureaucracy is always the ultimate victor.
11. The power of the bureaucracy may be measured by the degree of dependence a government minister has on it. A minister rightly fears the power of the bureaucracy more than that of the ballot box.
12. Governments come and go, the bureaucracy goes on for ever.

There is no need to add to this list, easy though it would be to do so, what needs to be observed is that the bureaucracy is a special-interest group, perhaps the most powerful there is, which has a permanent, consolidated, entrenched and virtually indestructible position at the apex of the power structure and which in no way is dependent on the turn of the wheel of either political or economic fortune for its survival. Indeed one may well say that far from being an appendage of state it is the one factor of any state which is its embodiment more than any other.

It should not be assumed that these strictures are a personal charge against every single member of a bureaucracy. Far from it. The high level of administration achieved by many governments could not be attained without a considerable degree of able, disinterested and devoted service to the public weal by many public servants of exceptional capacity and integrity—especially in the higher echelons of the civil service. What we are concerned to do here is to locate the nature of the forces that mould such institutions and the forms of power wielded within them and by them in relation to the unending struggle of the citizen for his democratic rights and liberties.

Yet even a state of one million inhabitants need not be debarred from achieving a condition of affairs where the process of government reflects the general wishes of the people. Representative government *in itself* is no barrier to democracy, indeed the very fact that in smaller societies it can be a successful means of achieving democracy is one of the reasons why in the mass society it has become a means of aborting it. A minor road in a small community can be a very effective means of communication, but if the size of the community multiplies with no corresponding increase in the size of the road, then the road itself can become so crowded as to defeat one of its principal objects and far from being a useful means of communication becomes a barrier to it.

In the same way the power of the bureaucracy need not be a barrier to democracy in a society of around, let us say, one million inhabitants; (the reader will understand that politics, the absurd title of a certain scholastic institution in London notwithstanding, is not a science and no attempt is being made to make exact statements about precise numbers); provided that power is recognised and its capacity to thwart democratic forces is understood, it can be confined to its proper function of being an instrument of democratic intention. This can be so even if the society in question is, so to speak, in a lump rather than sub-divided into small communities, but if the principle of division is ignored it will of course tend to be that much more difficult.

Nevertheless, in a society of one million, as contrasted with 100,000 the changes at the centre will be of considerable significance. The central bureaucracy will naturally be stronger, the power of political party machines, as distinct from the power of the individual members, will begin to be much more pronounced, political leadership will begin to be a matter of the *projection* of a personality rather than the personal knowledge people will have of the leader, and this in turn will give emphasis to the power of media to distort rather than to report.

These factors are, as it were, the institutional expression of the arithmetical projections of the growing weakness of the individual vis-a-vis the centre made earlier, but to it we need to add another quite salient consideration; for if it is possible to say that the share in the power wielded by each individual in a community that grows from one thousand to one million declines from one-thousandth to one-millionth, it may be argued it will be one-millionth of a much larger integument of power, an equally large slice of a much larger cake. The logic of this may appear unexceptionable, but it does not hold for reasons already explained. First the individual is further from the centre and therefore less able to influence it; second there are influences playing on the centre which are much more powerful than any individual can hope to challenge—the dominant ruling group, the bureaucracy, the economic interests, the military machine, the media and even by now otherwise politically innocuous religious, cultural and social forces. A citizen who is not a member of one of these top interest groups, and in a mass society this is inevitably the overwhelming majority, is only able to influence them in one way, and that is through the political process. Most of the cake is in fact not susceptible to division at all, it is congealed to a central mass, the power of which grows larger *more* than proportionately to the growth in the size of each citizen's share of the cake itself.

If this general operative principle is acknowledged, that individual citizen power declines with the growth of the political unit, then it would seem there must come a stage when with continued growth the citizen may end up with no power at all. Clearly this cannot be. One has only to reflect on the extent to which a gifted man can, through his writings and other modes of expression, influence dominant currents of thought on a world scale to see this is so.

Since every man can speak, if only to those nearest to him, and exert himself to voice his opinions in other ways, we may say that some residue of power always remains to the individual in any political complex however giant or repressive. Perhaps we may view it as one of those mathematical phenomena which in a given reductive progression never quite reaches zero but stretches out to infinity. Nevertheless we must recognise that to increase the size of a community from one million to a hundred million, for example, is to reduce the power of the ordinary citizen to influence the direction of the affairs of his political unit to a level where for all practical considerations it is zero. What in practice confronts the citizen, frequently in units far removed from his stage of giantism, if he wishes actively to dissent from some prevailing political trend, is a series of inhibitory questions. 'Why should you be different from everybody else?' 'Why should you want to obstruct the wishes of the majority (or the 'masses' or the 'party')?' 'Why should you make a lot of needless trouble?' 'Why don't you trust the leaders, or the experts, or those who know best?' 'Do you realise that if you persevere you will create doubts about your loyalty (to the state, the teachings of our inspired leader, to the party) and that it will create difficulties about your employment, your union membership, your promotion and pension prospects?' And so on and so on. It will be noticed that all these questions are loaded with a bias in favour of the centre and against change which the citizen may desire, and which represents a threat to human liberty now prevalent in nearly every existent political structure.

The basic drive of man in politics is to create a form of social machinery which will serve his needs. Man's basic need in society, indeed, his basic purpose in sanctioning any form of political organisation, is to pursue his quest for his individual self-realisation. This means there is a need for a form of unity to be achieved which recognises and promotes the diversities of those individuals who comprise it. Once the mechanism of that unity is used to suppress or abort the diversity of its members it is destroying the fundamental assumption on which it is based, and indeed its own validity, for to suppress individuality is to suppress the quintessence of any human being and block the path of self-realisation. This in turn is to block, or at least to attempt to block, the only road by which man may achieve genuine self-improvement and progress.

We need to reflect on this in the light of common governmental practice towards the citizen today. Sometimes such practice suggests an inversion of reality, that government, far from being made by man for man, is in fact some kind of natural element like fire or water which in this case has created man for its own purposes.

Well within living memory a man could travel freely about the globe without let or hindrance of any kind from his own government. With the expansion of travel he began to find it a matter of personal convenience to furnish himself with some kind of identity document which would enable him to pass through foreign parts with greater facility. A passport thus became a matter of personal convenience to the traveller, something backed with the authority of his own government to help him in his dealing with the officials of other governments *and nothing more.* An everyday service which any citizen could reasonably expect his government to provide as a matter of course to help him on such journeying about the globe as it would occur to him to make.

Somewhere along the road some quite new considerations appear to have insinuated themselves into the matter; what was once a citizen right has now become a privilege to be granted or withheld by the government in question. To a greater or lesser degree this infection of bureaucratic presumption afflicts nearly every government in the world. In many countries, notably those with democratic, peace-loving, people's governments, the mere granting of a passport is regarded as the bestowing of some rare act of political grace and favour, a reward for good political behaviour perhaps, to be withdrawn at once if the merest sign of recalcitrance is expressed. Many governments positively forbid their nationals to travel to certain places and punish them if they do not obey the prescription. The American Government, for example, at one time sought to forbid its citizens to travel to China, a ruling only overturned after an arduous battle in the courts and the delivery of a Supreme Court judgement. But perhaps the most sinister development is that which seeks to relate the possession of passport to the right of a citizen to his citizen identity at all.

In December 1972 a Soviet Embassy official called on Mr. Valery Chalidze, a Soviet lecturer in physics in the U.S.A., in his Manhattan hotel, and requested him to identify himself. He produced his passport, whereupon the official passed it to an aide who promptly pocketed it. He then informed Mr. Chalidze that he had been stripped of his citizenship by order of the Presidium of the Supreme Soviet.

This surely is the ultimate inversion of all the assumptions about the existence of government; a growth in the power of the state to a point where citizens, far from being protected by what they created, are repudiated and declared not even *persona non grata,* but *non persona*.

The citizen must of course accept the need to make a uniform response to certain situations and demands in order to achieve the wider possibilities that the existence of society makes possible. This remains true even though it is a truth which has been used to justify an endless succession of quite unjustifiable forms of presumption by those who wield the various forms of state power, presumption which has led to a situation where the citizen makes an ever-increasing surrender of his individuality to the forces of the state and in return finds that because the whole pattern of his life in society is predicated by forces beyond his control, and frequently beyond his ken, the spectrum of possibilities for the development of his individuality far from increasing, as a compensatory justification, is constantly shrinking. The name of this road is 1984, and we need to see how, despite the apparent differences of the various state systems of the world, they are all moving along it at varying speeds, the larger ones being the ones moving most rapidly.

In a genuinely humanistic society we must surely expect a balance to prevail between the forces that promote the interest of the collectivity and those that enable the individual members to express their humanity and individuality. It is noticeable that not only did this balance prevail to an exquisite degree in many of the former city states, but that the forces of the collectivity themselves were part of the expression of human individuality and creativity. This is why the 14th Century city hall of Sienna is a consummate work of art which has given visual joy to generations of people for over half a millennium, whereas the new city hall of the Westminster City Council is a machine-produced building produced for machine-like administration and is merely a source of despair for those who care for the things of the spirit and is incapable of giving a vestige of joy to anyone.

It may be though that the cities of the renaissance figure too prominently in these pages and that there is nothing to be gained by harking back to the past. This feeling alone indicates how we moderns tend to be afflicted by a terrible blindness about our true situation and with a lack of any scale of values about the achievements of the past which would enable us to see them in true perspective and in a way which would help us to resolve our present predicament.

It is probable that a human society that lacked any defects would not be worth living in. The well-spring of life is expressed in the

tensions that are created in the constant battle between good and
evil in every human being as much as in the forms of corporate life
that humanity creates and which, however insensibly or inadver-
tently, reflect it. So that it is no answer to the problem of explaining
the manifest excellence of these city states, and their unquestionable
superiority of political, economic and social form, to point to certain
indubitable defects with which they were afflicted. For if slavery was
a feature of Greek city life, for example, how is it that that Greeks
made such astounding advances in the adventure of civilisation
despite it? And it is held, as some perversely do, the Greek excellence
was a product of slave labour, if, for example, the stunning serenity
of the Parthenon, or the crisp and lofty clarity of the Platonic dialogues are really attributable to the existence of slavery, why cannot
we moderns, with hundreds of millions of our fellows tied to the
more subtle forms of degradation of wage slavery, do better? And
if we feel we can dismiss the spectacular achievements of the renaissance with references to poor hygiene, visitations of the plague and
other matters in which we moderns profess to be superior, why are
we powerless to achieve with our forms of superiority what the people
of the renaissance were able to achieve despite their drawbacks?

Yet a peculiar form of condescension afflicts us, as though our central heating systems and flush lavatories were somehow a justification
for permitting such a marked decline in our standards of civic life in
nearly all its forms as compared with what our forbears achieved.
Our buildings mock us with their moronic indifference to questions of
scale, proportion, seemliness, embellishment, expression, inspiration
or any attribute of the deeper, more sensitive and more refined
aspects of human sensibility, whilst to walk through no more than
two or three hundred yards of a renaissance city is to be made compul-
sively aware that what was at work here once and has since died,
was a manifestation of human excellence, in design, in creativity,
in colour and assembly of materials and buildings alone which is
quite literally matchless if only because it is utterly beyond our
present powers to even emulate, far less surpass.

We really must learn humility here. These people of former times
worked on a basis which we have lost or abandoned and we must
make it our business to explore the nature of that basis if only because
it holds the key to the solution of so many of the problems that now
press so insistently upon us. So instead of treating these achievements
with a condescension which acts only as a measure of our ignorance

and constitutes a barrier to our understanding, let us open our minds to the true nature of the astounding reality that they embody and ask ourselves where it is that *we* have gone wrong. Again and again we are back to a consideration of scale and size, for this, the most neglected factor of all political studies, is the key to all that the city states achieved as much as it is the key to what modern mass societies have failed to achieve, failed despite the enormity of the increment of mechanical power they have produced and the wonders of technology, especially in the field of communication, they have accomplished. For implicit in the factor of size is that of control. Even city states had their impersonal forms of power to contend with, the forces of the market, of tradition, economic expansions, legal systems and so on, but *because they were of a size that enabled the relationships of the members to predominate as a force over the central controlling mechanisms,* it meant they were also able to control the other impersonal factors that were present.

This is the major distinction that needs to be observed in contrasting the city states with modern mass societies, for in the latter, since the members are no longer able to control the central mechanisms, they become inevitable victims of a process of overgrowth from all the other impersonal forms of power which only the centre can control. At the risk of repetition we need to see with stark clarity the reason why it is impossible for ordinary citizens to control the power nexus of a mass society—the only means by which they can control the other impersonal forces which come to dominate their lives.

We need to bear constantly in mind the two forces that are set in motion as the growth of a political unit proceeds; first the national share of power of each individual to determine its nature and its direction declines by a mere process of mathematical division, bearing in mind that each person as a citizen can only presume to embody a certain limit of power for himself; secondly there is a gravitational pull of power to the centre which itself increases with growth much as the force of attraction of water to the centre of a whirlpool increases as the size of the whirlpool itself expands.

With this development there emerges another factor pertaining to the uses to which power is put. In the city state power can be used for a variety of ends, for self-aggrandisement, war, tyranny, community, enrichment or even simply to enable everyone to have a good time all round. In the mass society power serves only one basic purpose, and that is power itself. It may be argued that this is to

overlook the drive to seek profits, which may be said to be a much
stronger drive, yet even profit, in the form of capital especially, is a
form of power, whereas people quite often seek offices of power which
yield only the most trifling pecuniary gains, especially when compared with what can be obtained in industry and commerce and
other fields where the path to power is similarly indirect. Both Stalin
and Hitler enjoyed wielding enormous aggregates of power, but
neither was interested in amassing personal wealth.

Perhaps this is why such political units are often referred to as 'the
great powers'. Even war is similarly an expression and a servant of
this drive. Who then, it will be asked, controls this power? The
question is susceptible to two answers, neither of which includes any
reference to the ordinary citizen. If the mass society is relatively
modest in size, say, of the order of ten million, the power will be in
the hands of the top groups, the political, bureaucratic, military and
economic oligarchs and the media controllers.

If the mass society is a mammoth one of a hundred million, or even
several hundred million, then, even if the power of these top groups
increases, the real controlling power becomes non-existent, for the
process of growth has reached a stage where no group can use the
power for socially comprehensible or even at times morally defensible
means. Quite literally such societies are out of control.

Even so, in mass societies life must go on, and it is not suggested
that this lack of control means that life becomes impossible for all its
citizens all the time. Yet we must face the ugly fact that Stalin and
his purges, involving the deaths of millions of innocent people, has
happened in this century of progress and human enlightenment
despite the fact that the generality of the people of the Russian Empire had no interest in promoting such barbarism and were horrified
when its full dimensions were revealed to them, if indeed they were
fully revealed, in Khrushchev's speech to the 20th Congress of the
Russian Communist Party.

And who dare say that the peoples of Europe, any of them, *wanted*
to see the monstrous and demonic cruelties of Hitler, Mussolini and
Franco, the shameful evasions and pusillanimities that allowed these
unprincipled adventurers to pursue their courses, the inevitable war
which followed with the mass bombing of helpless citizens in overcrowded cities, the utterly unprecedented horrors of the extermination camps and the general blight of organised depravity that
settled on human life for a spell? Wars there have been in plenty in

the past, but they were wars which had obvious limits of destructive capacity, wars which many may well have wanted if only to relieve the boredom perhaps of what men might have felt to be an otherwise tedious existence. Besides, with victory there were spoils, jewellery, wine, women and perhaps an orgy of debauchery. What possible comparison is there here with the modern equivalent when the fruits of peace are so much more resplendent and abundant and when destruction is so all-encompassing? Why was the overwhelming desire of the peoples of Europe for peace not translatable into action which would have stopped the dangerous fanaticism of obvious psycopaths such as Hitler from pursuing their destructive courses?

The same question may well be asked about the United States and its orgy of senseless destruction in Vietnam. Which American people wanted this meaningless and monstrously inhuman bout of killing and wasting? And who in their hearts, of the millions of people around the world, wants a world of atomic and thermonuclear weapons? Yet who can stop France (liberty, equality and fraternity) from conducting atomic bomb tests in the Pacific or elsewhere? Assuredly not the 50 million French people, who, conditioned to an unquestioning acceptance of the destructive values of the mass society, probably think they serve a useful purpose anyway; and certainly nobody outside France. The same is true of the Chinese and Russian Empires, (Workers of the world unite! You have nothing to lose but your chains) 730 million and 238 million respectively, cannot stop them and neither can anyone else.

All the super powers are out of control in other important respects as well; if one looks for example at the figures of production increases and other indices of national wealth it may appear that all is well and that they are in a perpetual euphoria of expanding standards of consumption. Yet a closer view of the facts reveals at least two trends which indicate that the capacity of the government machine to get the results it presumably wants is non-existent. In all these countries (to which may be added India) the gap between rich and poor is not closing but is getting steadily wider. Secondly, all such countries are showing one of the most ancient and elementary symptoms of decadence and disintegration in the record, a failure to control inflation and an erratically accelerating depreciation of their currencies.

The need to reduce the gap between rich and poor is regarded as one of the most pressing problems of the modern world, yet why is it that a solution, which is required if only to avert serious eruptions of social unrest, is beyond the reach of its capacity? One cannot say the desire is not there, or that there is not available a sufficient degree of economic expertise. What is missing is the political capacity to translate a desirable economic objective into political fact, and this in turn is part of a general incapacity to control the forces of the economic machine. The same is true of inflation. Britain, at the time of writing, is in the grip of an inflationary pressure which in recent years has reached the startling figure of 25 per cent per annum. The rate of depreciation expressed is not in itself very meaningful because behind any inflationary tendency are forces which operate rather on the scale of a geometric progression. A small inflationary tendency, like a small fire, can easily be damped down, but once allowed to develop it creates a conflagration which, because it is more difficult to control, may result in disaster. Yet again, despite the enormity of the consequences of failure, no large country is able to avoid such disasters. Yet small ones can and do.

At the end of World War I the tiny Principality of Liechtenstein, population 22,000, was virtually bankrupt as a result of the invasion of its territory and the general economic collapse of Europe. Yet today it has no poverty problem, no unemployment, no homeless, no illiteracy, no hunger or malnutrition, no crime to speak of and no problems of political disruption. The Government has a comfortable surplus of income over expenditure and the Principality is probably one of the most stable, prosperous, well-educated and well-governed corners of the world. Why? It has no exceptional natural endowment of riches, and in winter the agriculture of its 65 square miles comes to a virtual stand-still owing to its elevation (it is situated on the banks of the Upper Rhine between Switzerland and the Austrian Province of Vorarlberg). Diminutiveness is no guarantee of stability and general prosperity, *but it does nothing in itself to hinder such objectives;* what needs to be noted is that overgrowth, however portentous production and other figures may sound when reeled off in grand totals, (and we need to remember that the U.S.A., if measured only in terms of its gross domestic product, is the wealthiest country in the world), is itself an effective barrier to the realisation of political and social objectives. The pragmatic evidence is too abundant to be denied and the reasons which are being related here to the question of size itself are too conclusive to be ignored. The U.S.A. is powerless to accomplish the objectives its spokesmen are so prone to trumpet with leaden, saturation oratory—miniscule objectives that

Liechtenstein accomplishes without comment.

Behind the whole range of economic activity is another problem which indicates even more eloquently the extent to which 'the great powers' are out of control. Quite suddenly there has appeared on the human scene an issue so unexpected, so unprecedented, so utterly pervasive in its denial of the validity of the assumptions on which current economic practice is based, that not a single government has even begun to formulate any fresh assumptions. So swiftly has this issue appeared that governments are in the curious position of decapitated hens who are reputed to continue to run around the farmyard for several minutes after they have all too literally lost their heads.

The ecological bombshell exploded on the intelligence of educated mankind somewhere towards the end of the sixties. It comprised a message compounded as follows:

(a) The most unequivocal warning that present forms of planetary pollution will, if not halted, render mankind's only home uninhabitable within a space of time so short as to put the survival prospects of the generation now being born in doubt,

(b) Similar warnings about the exhaustion of numerous resources on which our machine-civilisation is based well within the lifetimes of most people now living,

(c) A population 'explosion' which will far outstrip the earth's food production capacity within a generation or so,

(d) Warnings that the mechanisation and subversion of agriculture by the use of inorganic chemicals, with its accompanying destruction of soil fertility and its effects of driving men off the land to dangerously unviable and uncontrollable megacities, is leading to a predictable and inevitable collapse of both rural and urban-based forms of economy.

Why then has there been no rapid agreement to shut down every advertising agency on the planet; or to the abandonment of the very idea of economic expansion as a rational goal,[1] at least in terms of the consumption of the remaining reserves of the planet's finite resources. One might suppose that any continued attempt to *increase* consumption, at least in the developed countries, would be greeted with the same opprobrium a beleaguered and starving city would display to someone who was selfishly acquiring as much food

[1] In his famous letter to the Soviet leader Alexander Solzhenitsyn urges precisely the same point.

as he could eat from some illegal private store. Yet nothing of the sort has happened, and life is pursuing the far from even tenor of its way as though the new awareness had never dawned. There is no doubt a highly technical term buried in the lore of psychoanalytic literature which serves to define this phenomena; there is also a much older one, for it has long been recognised that those whose dominant behaviour patterns no longer correspond with objective reality are, quite simply, mad.

The smaller nations can declare, with some justice, that if they ceased to behave unecologically, that their economies would suffer tremendous disruption from the continued expansionist insanity of the bigger powers; there can also be little doubt that even if a number of big countries began to set limits to their consumption of finite resources they might well provoke a downward spiralling of economic activity, especially among the bigger powers themselves, which would be as uncontrollable as the present boom situation.

The mechanics of this are all too familiar. If, let us say, several small countries decided they would cut down by 50 per cent their imports of cars, this would almost certainly lead to production cutbacks among a number of manufacturers; this in turn would promote a contraction of demand in other sectors of the economy, leading to more unemployment, further contraction of demand and so on. The car industry is of course abnormally sensitive to these fluctuations, for despite the complexity of a car and the number of subsidiary industries dependent on its manufacture and use, it still represents a marginal form of expenditure. Even so, it accounts, for example, for one-tenth of the total value of Britain's exports and is indeed its largest single export item.

Clearly then there is need for concerted action by these big powers to stop the present colossal waste of resources, but, to assert yet again, it is impossible to take this step. The major powers are like passengers on a fairground switchback-railway who are beginning to feel sick from the continued upswing and downrush of the car's motion. To stop is impossible, motion is all, and if they try to jump off they risk being broken to pieces.

Or one may cite the instance of mass air travel. This phenomenon is unlikely to endure for more than two or three decades more at most (since this was written boom has given way to an equally uncontrollable slump); by then no doubt bewildered farmers will be mourning the way we squandered oil on such mirthless frivolities as they sit beside idle tractors which for lack of fuel cannot grow the food which surely the world will then need more desperately than ever. The logic of our situation cries out for a world air authority which will replace the present wasteful national airlines which duplicate routes all over the world and frequently fly planes less than half full for long distances, but such an approach is the antithesis of the uncontrolled drive for economic expansion that now dominates the world despite all moral considerations of material restraint and economy.

It is pointless to ask 'who controls these forces'. Those young people who opt so stridently for anarchism have missed out, as most other people have missed out; the world is already in the grip of a general convulsion of anarchy of historic dimensions and only an attempt to restore social control will save us from the evil consequences which are likely to ensue.

Moral considerations are not factors which are somehow suspended in mid-air, they are part of the framework of private judgement of every individual, and if in the mass society the citizens' private judgements cannot be projected into its general workings because it is too big, too centralised and operating at too rapid a tempo, and reduces his individual significance to a virtual nullity, then the question becomes one of how to make the unit concerned, generally the state, smaller, more non-centralised and operating at a seemlier tempo so that citizen control can be operative.

It really will not do to dismiss this conclusion as unrealistic or impracticable. The adventure of civilisation does not acquire its momentum from what may or may not appear immediately practicable, but from the vision men and women cherish of what they believe to be right.

So that if we can envisage a world comprised of genuine human communities the workings of which are controlled by their members, then it is surely obvious that the question of the moral criteria by which each will be governed does not lend itself to any single answer. How indeed can it? It will indeed be a matter for the members of each to decide for themselves, a prospect at present utterly beyond the reach of any member of a mass society.

It is surely indubitable that when such power is operative men will make mistakes and sometimes very big ones and even bad ones, but at least such mistakes will be their own, and as such part of their common stock of experience from which they can learn the kind of wisdom necessary for the successful conduct of public affairs, often in the only way in which it can be garnered.

We are driven back in any case to a more basic consideration; any massive changes in production patterns in response to, let us say, ecological and resource considerations presupposes the acceptance of a quite different body of social values. At present nearly all economic activity stems from a drive for profit and power and the much-vaunted goal of 'efficiency' is measured in these terms. The giant machine of economic activity blunders on in response to no other criteria.

Yet if there is to be change, change to take account of ecological perils, among many other factors, this cannot be done piecemeal or without revolutionising the whole basis of economic activity as currently accepted.

Yet we need to be very clear what we are talking about here; at present the system is still largely governed by the traditional market forces of supply and demand, which in turn are based on the assumed division of the so-called 'factors of production' into land, labour and capital: It is true that the automatic operation of these forces has been greatly modified over recent years by a number of factors such as government fiscal and tax policies, the growth of semi-monopolistic forces in the labour market as a result of trades union power, in the capital market by the consolidation of banking operations, in the investment world by the expansion of institutional investment through bodies such as 'unit trusts' and giant insurance corporations, in the marketing field by the emergence of 'chain' stores and 'supermarkets', and not least in the productive field itself by processes variously described as takeovers, mergers, horizontal and vertical integration, consolidation, diversification and so forth.

Despite these modifications, and many more factors could be listed, the basis of the system is still presumed to be that of a mechanism which is largely self-regulating, and on the whole this assumption is justified. Government or semi-monopolistic[2] action may distort its workings and bend it in a given direction, but they do not break it.

The moment we seek to inject a value consideration into the working of the system we open up a Pandora's Box of debate as to what

[2]The term 'semi-monopolistic' is not strictly accurate. Science seems to be a breeding ground for ugly words and the pseudo science of economics is not immune to the practice. To describe the phenomena of a number of large firms having a monopolistic effect on market forces economists have coined the word 'oligopoly.'

that value consideration shall be. Once we assume that economic activity shall serve a given social end, instead of serving social ends incidental to its main business of maintaining an equilibrium of market forces, we must be clear that we are abandoning a theoretical basis which has been the yardstick of economic forces for several centuries and in fact reverting to a medieval concept (the term is used in its historical rather than pejorative sense) where economic activity was regarded as being subservient to moral precept.

What then shall be the body of moral precept which guides economic activity? Socialists and communists have been alone in seeking to pose this question and in finding an answer to it, and it must be said that both have failed. The socialist, or social-democratic, position is so riddled with contradictions that it has no theoretical position worth the name. When socialist governments achieve power they find their power to act and govern is based directly on the momentum of the relatively free play of market forces and they tamper with those forces at their peril—a peril spelt out in terms of inflation, depression, a balance of payments crisis, pressures on the currency from foreign bankers (and sometimes foreign governments) and so on. Hence they are driven to talk in terms of such windy generalisations as 'nationalisation' and at the same time concocting a variety of measures designed to make private industry 'more efficient'. More efficient than what is seldom specified and the confused grammar is but a token of the confusion of thought behind it.

The fact is that any government of any persuasion which sought to operate economic activity on the basis of the contemporary imperatives for ecologic sanity, a careful husbanding of the remaining stocks of the world's finite resources, some regard for the population explosion and not least a concern for elementary global justice between rich and poor, would be destroyed by both extraneous and domestic political forces in a matter of months if not weeks.

And it would probably deserve to be so out of regard to a much more profound consideration, that of freedom.

The communist experience indicates clearly something that even socialists even today fail to heed, that state management of an economy in a mass society is quite incompatible with freedom and can only lead to tyranny.

In the communist empire of Russia the economy is presumed to be planned on the basis of the simplistic slogan, from each according to his ability, to each according to his need. With this there is usually added the curiously capitalist rider that when full communism is finally achieved the slogan will become 'from each according to his ability, to each according his *wants*', which must be about the most succinct expression of pie-in-the-sky ever mouthed.

In reality Russian planning is merely based on a blind belief in the virtue of producing more and more and more for the goals of military aggrandizement and the gratification of an open-ended consumer propensity among its subjects. The denial of the reality of market forces simply leads to these forces expressing themselves in unusual and frequently illegal ways, so that partly in consequence, the system is shot through with a ponderous degree of sheer waste, corruption, nepotism, elitism and self-serving. Not unnaturally the capitalist beast is reasserting its prowess and it can only be a matter of time, well, I believe, within a generation, before capitalism is re-established, accompanied no doubt by reams of inspired comment from the ruling gang as to the marxian correctness and historic inevitability of permitting it to do so.

None of this means that the answer is to be found in the untrammelled working of economic individualism, if only because it is precisely these forces which have played such a large part in creating the problem.

What in fact we are confronted with in any attempt to inject given moral considerations into the workings of the economic process, as we seek to argue throughout this essay, is an imperative need to focus on the factors of size, scale and tempo. For if under free enterprise in a mass society we find a number of oligarchic groupings struggling for power and profit whilst the political and economic process ceases to be susceptible to control by anyone, whilst socialism and communism both promote unacceptable threats to citizen freedom with batallions of bureaucrats or commissars, it is evident that what is being called into question is not the given form the mass society should take, but the mass society itself.

CHAPTER VII

The Morality of Power

I believe that the essential foundation of liberty is freedom to *choose*, and that any 'good' society must be of such a nature as to allow and encourage this freedom and to include within it a wide diversity of autonomous institutions, each at liberty to shape its own policy within the general framework of a flexible structure of institutions between which real disagreements can find expression and be resolved by open discussion.

G.D.H. Cole
History of Socialist Thought
(Part I, Vol. IV, p. 7.)

We can now look a little more closely at the power equation and how it works. We have seen that the growth of a political unit creates centripetal forces which increasingly rob the citizen of his decision-making power. It is not only that the power of the citizen declines as such, even though in some ways the power of an individual in a mass society, especially for example, his purchasing power, may actually increase, (even if an Indian peasant may be forgiven for failing to grasp the point); but that in general terms his *relative* power, his power relative to that of the central organs of power, declines.

This relative decline is expressed in a variety of ways. In pre-technological societies it would be expressed in crude terms of physical submission to a conquering invader and to onerous forms of taxation and tribute to the imperial power or its local proconsuls or Pilates. With the advance of technology the increase in powerlessness begins to be expressed in more subtle ways; the citizen begins to find he loses the unity of his own identity in society, he becomes, for example, a worker, a consumer, a commuter, a trade unionist, a voter, a resident, a worshipper, a listener, a viewer, an applicant, a taxpayer and so on and so on. The citizen becomes increasingly divorced from his former integrated role in society and his life begins to be compartmentalised so that he is confronted at *each* division with forces over which in turn he is unable to exercise any real control.

Think, for example, of his role as a worker. As a master craftsman in a city state, let us say, he really was master of his work situation; if he were a journeyman, or an apprentice of a master, he would stand in a personal relationship to his employer, would like as not lodge with his master's family. There were of course masters who were cruel, mean or otherwise oppressive, but it is in the nature of a personal relationship—especially when established for utilitarian purposes, that it tends to put a limit on extremes of behaviour of either party, whether the relationship is that of a master and servant, or of equals. The dependence on the relationship is generally mutual, for a bad master will tend to get bad results from his workmen just as a good one will tend to get good results. In any case an apprenticeship was generally regarded as a preparation for being a journeyman just as the latter was seen as stepping stone to becoming a master.

The contrast with, let us say, the modern factory 'hand'[1] could scarcely be more complete. Who runs the factory? Who owns it? Who controls it? Who decides the conditions and tempo of work? Who decides about the economic surplus it produces and its disposal? Assuredly not the 'hand'. Nor is the 'hand' moving upward to a self-fulfilment of himself as a citizen through his work to a fully-fledged mastership or anything like it. He is a 'hand', a fate decreed by the excessive specialisation of labour which robs work of its real meaning and joy for him, and it is very likely that he will spend his entire working life in no other capacity.

This kind of powerlessness is not confined to 'hands' on the factory floor, it is the life-sentence of wage-slavery to which almost every employed person in a mass society is condemned as a matter of course. The essence of the change is that in a city state a man influenced the nature of his society through his work, in the mass society it is society itself which through the work process influences man. The *results* in both cases provide a most eloquent verdict on which approach can best be described as progress.

Or take the citizen relationship to the extremely important matter of shopping in the market. Formerly, when the scale of operations was smaller, shops themselves were not only smaller, but highly specialised and much more numerous. England, said Napoleon, in a notorious instance of the pot calling the kettle black, is a nation of shopkeepers. These factors, the number and specialised nature of the shops, and the fact that shops were usually crowded into one quarter, as well as the fact that particular kinds of shops, for meat say or for vegetables, would occupy a whole street, meant that the concept of 'the sovereignty of the consumer' was based on an observable reality.

The consumer really did have a choice and his choice reflected the order of the market and the nature of the goods offered, as well as a measure of control over their prices. We can see here how the concept of consumer sovereignty is an essential ingredient of political freedom, not so much perhaps with regard to the absolute virtues the concept contains as to what happens to the power of the market when the citizen ceases to be able to influence its workings.

Again, the contrast with a modern 'super-market' could scarcely be more complete. In former times a milkman who watered the milk

[1]The question of the power influence of the 'hand' through his membership of a trade union is discussed in a previous chapter.

would be lucky if he escaped being up-ended in one of his own churns, today a variety of deleterious and skilfully concocted chemical substances are projected as substitutes for milk and presented to the consumer with a barrage of fanfares which would have served in former times for a monarch's coronation. By the time he reaches a 'supermarket' the consumer is as familiar with the names of the different brands of these minor horrors as he is with his own. Inside the 'supermarket' he is confronted with a massive range of similarly trumpeted and equally worthless wares, a din of something moronically described as 'music' to further confuse and distract him and generally lower his perceptive and critical faculties, and a maddeningly slow queue at the cash desk. The queue is nearly always there, the number of cash desks operating being carefully and artfully calculated to ensure that each 'consumer' spends several minutes surveying nearby stands which have been judiciously stocked with the kind of wares which prompt what is known to the trade as 'impulse' buying. Bars of chocolate to pacify perhaps a fretful child whose demand for one has become more insistent than parental patience can stand, a stock of highly coloured picture books, a plastic toy .... By the time the consumer is out of this revised version of hell-on-earth he (it is of course more often 'she') is generally enervated, irritable (somebody should count the occasions of parental bullying, slapping and other forms of oppression, that occur outside the portals of these palaces), and heavily laden. The immediate objective is to reach home, besides, the car is probably parked by a meter ... with a dutiful traffic warden hovering around ....

Clearly, consumer sovereignty here has virtually disappeared and again, it is not the consumer and his preferences which are determining the nature and conditions of the market, rather it is the forces of the market which are determining the tastes and preferences of the 'consumer'. A shopkeeper in former times would never have dreamt of calling his customers 'consumers'. As likely as not they were his neighbours; only modern corporations are capable of this kind of insolence.

What we have to note here is the new forces that are playing on the political process, for if the power inherent in the sovereignty of the consumer has slipped from the grasp of the ordinary citizen it has not disappeared altogether. Quite the reverse, it has become institutionalised in the controlling forces of those giant firms which today dominate the wholesale and retail markets. It represents as a

consequence a new consolidated form of *political* power, a power used
to influence the political process away from that of the general
citizen interest towards whatever conduces to its own. In this we are
simply seeing yet another instance of the truism that as the size of the
political unit increases that of the individual declines. Where power
in the small unit is generally dispersed, in the large it becomes
concentrated at the centre.

These principles are equally at work in almost every other field of
human activity; in the field of entertainment, for example, we may
reflect on the extent to which, when societies were more susceptible
to control by the general citizen body, it was precisely that body
which provided its own entertainment in a variety of ways. Even so
recently as the nineteenth century Thomas Hardy could relate in
one of his novels how a village church choir was led not by a college-
trained organist, but by a small ensemble of various instrumentalists
who were ordinary village labouring people for whom sign-reading of
music was a commonplace minor accomplishment. In a variety of
ways it was an active, creative process stemming from the roots of
society and as such in terrible contrast to the passive acceptance of
an unending diet of the dubious and the second rate which the
powerless citizen today accepts from the moguls of what has become
a centralised and highly profitable 'entertainment' industry.

Or we may note how holidays, once a plentiful scattering of feasts
and saints' days throughout the year, in which local people celebrated after local custom and fashion, as locally determined, have now
been lumped into a two or three weeks' annual 'holiday' which
becomes part of a mass migration to other parts of the world on
'package' tours and the like. So that instead of the holiday being
an opportunity to express another many-faceted aspect of citizenship
life and citizen values, it becomes simply an occasion where the
individual is involuntarily led to emphasise yet again his anonymity
in the herd.

Even newspapers, something begot by the age of technology, have
become part of the same trend. The time was when every region
could boast its own daily news-sheet, and often more than one.
Today their number shrinks steadily before a tide of advancing mass
conditioning which begets its own force of acceptance from the
minds of those it plays on. Daily national papers shrink in number
and even more in variety of opinion and expression.

The astute reader will doubtless be quick to point out that all these factors are operating in many small countries as well, so that as evidence of the way the powerlessness of people in big countries is accomplished they are neither here nor there. There is some truth in this, but we need to note that all tendencies have a point of origin, and further, that once those tendencies are established what ensues in other places where other norms prevail is, in a world of multifarious dynamic relationships, that either the new forces come to prevail over the old or *vice versa*.

In this regard we need to ask whence this tendency to oversize and citizen powerlessness originated? It is probable that the small nations of Scandinavia are the best-governed, democratic, prosperous, peaceful and stable communities in the world, yet even if this is not saying very much (and it is surely saying a great deal), it is perfectly obvious that the dynamics of overgrowth and anti-democracy are not originating here, as our thesis might in fact suggest, or indeed in any small nation at all, but in the bigger, in fact in terms of national wealth, the biggest continental meganation.

In nearly all cardinal respects the world is being rapidly Americanised in terms of organisation, centralisation, standardisation, techniques of production and patterns of consumption. But above all, when we say Americanised we refer to the *scale* on which Americans tend to operate. Whatever the real origin of the multi-national corporation, for example, it is the extent of American practice which has made it today a world-wide phenomenon and one of the most ominous anti-democratic forces now existing; it is one with which ordinary citizens must one day learn to battle if they are ever to regain their liberty to fashion their own destiny. The mere existence of the multi-nationals is evidence that we no longer live in tidy compartments of economically sovereign nationhood, and that such frontiers as still remain are becoming increasingly powerless to protect their citizens from the effects of the follies of giantism practised elsewhere.

One day, when men learn wisdom in these matters, they will return to the smaller scale and discover that despite its apparent drawbacks it offers them means of economic and political control of their affairs they can obtain in no other way; they will find too that the fruits of that control will be every bit as varied, abundant and delightful as earlier human experience suggests it can be. But until the generality of citizens is conscious of the real issues of the freedom struggle as presented in these terms we are unlikely to make such headway, and even those smaller political units that still prevail will find themselves in increasing danger of being swamped by the sick and unhealthy dynamics of the meganations and their larger brethren.

This is especially true of the play of large-scale economic forces on the political life of small-democracies. Switzerland, for example, possesses probably the most revolutionary democratic political constitution and political institutional structure of any country in the world, yet no visitor to that charming corner of the world can fail to be struck by the extent to which its political framework is being undermined by the values being promoted by large-scale economic units which it allows to encumber its horizons.

If the economic forces of Switzerland were subject to the same forms of control as are its political forms, that is, controlled from the base by its village communes and its district cantons, there is no doubt Switzerland would be showing mankind the way forward to an altogether new and more hopeful phase in its affairs.

As it is, massive industrial, commercial and banking corporations, centralised chain-stores, and even multinational corporations are prompting the same kinds of civic decline, the same standardisation and uniformity visible in monster countries such as the U.S.A., and in its bigger neighbours France and Germany. The lesson here is that life is all of a piece and that economic giantism will make nonsense of political democracy if allowed to, even in countries of modest dimensions or where genuine political democracy exists.

It may well be said that a fairly obvious point has been ignored which puts the skids under the whole case as thus advanced, for in all the foregoing no mention has been made of the quite obvious means of redress which it is assumed the citizen can claim to have, at least in those countries where the freedom to wage elections and to vote secretly is taken seriously, and that is, in the ballot box itself. Here surely, it will be argued, the citizen has a historic means of redress and of exercising his sovereignty which he is still free to use.

This is possibly one of the most widespread fallacies of modern life, the idea that in banding together into a mass party citizens can elect members of parliament of their political choice and so secure a rational control of the legislative process for considered social ends of their own preference. The theory of all this appears impeccable and had deluded generations of social reformers and revolutionaries of all complexions, with the possible exception of the anarchists, who have never had any ideas on the subject worth talking about anyway.

Yet what is the reality? In a mass society political parties dominate the political process and, of course, these are *mass* political parties. This factor alone means that the individual member is confronted with all the problems of power, and of powerlessness, and of doing battle with entrenched interests such as the bureaucracy, in his dealings with the government of his party as he is with the government of his country.

We have already noted how when a social unit reaches a given size there is a tendency for the leadership group to split rather than for the unit itself to divide. In a sense this is a division of the social unit itself since henceforth both sets of leaders, in professing to speak for the unit as a whole, can in reality speak for only part of it, although of course, once in power they *act* for the whole of it.

Broadly speaking the average citizen does not like change, although he will be disposed to it occasionally when a combination of circumstances prompts him sufficiently. Hence the line of division will generally be between a group that does not favour change and one which does. In point of fact so great is the pace of change in the modern world that it is sometimes necessary for the two groups to change roles, although not labels, if only to enable them to maintain some meaningful relationship to the passage of events and their prospects of power. But it will occasion no surprise to learn that since people who have comfortable incomes dislike change more than those who haven't, they tend to call themselves conservatives, and since the options of change are somewhat more varied it follows that their opponents tend to reflect this in the variety of labels they adopt, be they socialist, liberal, radical, democrat or whatever.

The dynamics of role-changing in political groupings are too complex to be entered into here in detail, and but one example must suffice. The writer is still young enough to recall that the cardinal point in the credo of the no-change party in Britain was wont to be summed up in the phrase, "For King and Empire". Its public meetings were solemn rituals at which serried ranks of supporters would sit facing what, at first sight, seemed to be a bier but which was in fact a table draped with the national flag. The meeting would portentously stand and sing the national song, as well as others denoting, for example, the ineffabilities of a certain land of hope and glory . . . . During the speeches it was not uncommon to hear orotund declarations about 'our Empire' which, in due course, as a consequence of external rather than internal pressures, became, 'The British Commonwealth of Nations'. If this kind of detail seems tedious it is necessary to dwell on it if only to catch the full savour of the contrast, for within the space of a decade or so a new credo has emerged with an orthodoxy which centres on the concept of a united Europe and which, much rhetoric to the contrary notwithstanding, decisively repudiates the whole ethos of the Commonwealth.

This involves a change of all the symbols; the national flag is now a positive embarrassment, themes of hope and glory have somehow suddenly lost any savour of either, the monarch has become a useful reminder perhaps of a narrower, more lack-lustre past, a retired retainer who can sit in the corner but who must not get in the way, and the Commonwealth has begun to acquire an aura of faded respectability, all right in its time, but like the issue of suffragetism or conscription, or even perhaps the corn laws, something over and done with as a new age dawns .... The party of non-change became suddenly the party of change, and whilst the transition period prevailed thrust its traditional role upon its opponents.

It happens that this shift was the expression of deeper changes of considerable historical significance. In a number of respects the no-changers had been on the defensive for more than a generation as popular distrust of their governing capacities during the interwar period of the depression years, their ineptitude in their dealings with the nascent dictatorships of Europe, and the clear capacity of the Soviets to organise and fight with no more inanities and blunders than a traditional ruling class, brought a party wedded to change of sorts to power when the fighting in Europe was over. It was shortly afterwards that roles changed, and the Labourite changers became increasingly on the defensive; whereas the former conservative no-changers were sensing with a growing intoxication of greed the possibilities of self-enrichment from the application of technology to hitherto virtually untouched aspects of consumer life, in expanding mass markets for an increasing availability of wares from mass production, and other forms of institutionalised robbery of consumers.

With political independence in the former colonies and other difficulties arising largely from this move to independence, the 'Commonwealth' (whose members never ever had even dreamt of holding its wealth in common) suddenly lost much of its enchantment, and the rich pickings, made possible by enlarging the still only half realised possibilities of the European market behind a high tariff wall and the need to protect these bright prospects from any military adventures that might be mounted from the Soviet Empire and its enforced East European dependencies, suddenly made the cause of the unification of Europe one of overriding urgency and attraction.

What made it successful in the immediate sense as far as institutional organisation is concerned was none of its merits, for in terms of liberty and democracy none it has, but a total failure of the socialising forces to grasp the realities of power—either theoretically or in practice. Its chief theorists, Marx, Cole, Laski, the Webbs, Tawney and Strachey had all, whether they accepted or rejected the class struggle as the bedrock of their theorising, been concerned simply to inject a fairly old concept of brotherhood, justice and peace into a situation where these things were manifestly lacking. Not one of them had grasped that the problem of size and scale in political units was also *the* problem when applied to the organisation of a mass political party, and that because they saw nothing wrong in planning and organising in mass terms they were unwittingly handing over the moral considerations with which they were concerned to the mechanics of mass party organisation, which in turn were concerned with power first and moral principle a long way second.

As in the political unit itself, what began to loom most large was not the moral objectives for which power would be used but who in fact wielded the power? Was it A or B? To such questions were all considerations of principle inevitably subordinated and finally buried.

The intellectual and moral confusion thus generated still predominates and has made the Labour Party, for example, quite incapable of plotting any coherent course through the quicksands of contemporary life. Is it for, or against staying in Europe? It does not know, and would not know what it meant by an affirmation either way if it made one. If it is *for* such a step how does it reconcile it with the ecological catastrophe emerging from the wings to engulf us, or with the socialist ideal of justice for the underdog in the third world? It doesn't know and is too busy weighing the pros and cons of how to get power and keep it regardless of fidelity to any other principle to care. If it is against such a step then on what basis of principle does it propose to contain the new bandits of change who have held the fort? It does not know and if pressed would fall back on the not ignoble slogans which have been of such inadequate service to it in the past.

To avoid any possibility of misunderstanding, even at the risk of repetition, let us recapitulate the essence of the predicament; as the unit grows larger the power of the individual to influence or control it dwindles. The power itself does not vanish, for in fact it grows to enormous proportions, *but it grows in the hands of those who control the central levers of power.* Since the members of a mass party are divorced from power they cannot do more than marginally influence how it shall be used. It is a condition of any mass organisation that its members are powerless, and mass democracy is thus a contradiction in terms and a cant phrase in the mouth of whoever uses it. Hence the position at the centre is not one of leaders zealously seeking to apply these principles of their party, out of fidelity to which the members have joined the organisation, but of power-seekers using every trick in the circus to obtain power and keep it, and to manipulate the membership into following them and supporting them in their quest for the holy grail not of moral principle but of political power.

Men are not automatons and societies are not machines, so it must not be assumed that these general propositions have the inflexibility of the rules of German grammar or the laws of thermodynamics. Exceptional men will arise at times to act very much contrary to the grain, and times of exceptional stress will ensue, such as war, revolution or some national disaster, when the views and feelings of the generality of people will, for a brief phase, determine, or help to determine, the course of events. The point to note is that these *are* exceptions and that we are seeking to establish here the prevailing general drift of the forces within society, and these are such that in any eventuality it will be only a matter of time before the centre resumes its control.

Theories of democracy, or indeed of any school of political thought, are not concerned with magnitudes, only with principles of political action, yet we have to see that the great unlearned lesson of the modern era, one which has destroyed the effectuality of all the modern attempts at revolution or even reform, so that today their protagonists are helpless to grapple with the problems of the modern age, is that the mere process of growth of a political unit leads to the invalidation of all attempts to apply democratic principle owing to the shift of power away from the citizen at the periphery to bureaucrats and others at the centre.

It does not follow at all that no superior moral principle will be considered or applied in a political process conducted on a mass scale, this is too crude a reading of events. A body of citizens which is perturbed by some issue of public policy enough to make representation to, let us say, a cabinet minister, will confront him with at least two problems. Will his concurrence with their proposals harm his prospects of power? And if it does how can he appear to concur without intending to take any action? It is quite possible that the minister will be helped in his power quest by acceding to the proposals, which will simplify his problem and leave his petitioners with the comfortable feeling that he is using his power to support their moral principles. The case is really otherwise, he will simply be using their concern for moral principle to buttress his power situation. If it were not so, if his power prospects were to be weakened by accepting them, he would not support them.

Isolated occasions will readily spring to mind to suggest the contrary. In Britain in recent years a number of measures have been enacted to which a considerable majority of people are or were opposed; the abolition of capital punishment, homosexual law reform, divorce reform, even perhaps the raising of the school-leaving age. What is noticeable about all these issues and many more is that they did not involve serious danger to continuance in office of the Government. Had they done so, had any single issue involved the defeat of the Government, it would not have been proceeded with.

This points to a cardinal rule about the play of power. Since the aim of power in a mass society is simply power itself 'leaders' will not wittingly pursue courses which result in the loss of power or the failure of any attempt to obtain it. However important any issue of moral principle may appear to the members of a party, the leaders can do nothing about it if they do not have power. Power comes first, it is the overriding principle which is applied first to the consideration of any issue.

It may be said, "well, of course, how else can a leader, or indeed any politician function if he has no power, and since this is so obviously the case what is the point of going on about it?" The point is this. That in a small-scale society the wielding of power can be, and frequently is, intimately related to the broad principles of public good, whereas in a mass society they are separated by a welter of conflicting special interests exerting pressures which converge on the central controlling mechanisms to the exclusion or attempted exclusion of the public good. So that in the former case power is a means to an end, whereas in the latter it becomes pursued simply as an end in itself. This conclusion should occasion no surprise even if it is drawn simply from a casual observation of the behaviour of those who occupy political office, but it can be made more explicit perhaps if we consider the pressures to which politicians are subjected inside the political structures.

What needs to be emphasised here is that on such a basis the citizen is responding to a media which is manipulating his mind and conditioning his responses at every turn, to a party machine of one persuasion or another which is staking out its own priorities in terms of power whilst he blissfully supposes that they are being ordered according to moral precept, to political programmes based on the usurpation by political placemen of his capacity to make his own judgement, to a pattern of life which in almost every particular has been predicated for him, and to options which bear little or no relationship to his real well-being. In these circumstances he can scarcely fail to find the ballot box not an expression of his power so much as a confirmation of his powerlessness. What choice can the ballot box offer him when those seeking election are invariably concerned not only to buttress the thraldom of the mass society in which he is trapped, but are themselves, and in their aspirations, an expression of that thraldom?

CHAPTER VIII

Democracy and Party Power

Do you not know my son, with how little wisdom the world is governed?

Axel Count Oxenstierna.
Letter to his son, 1648.

We have already discussed the largely personal nature of the relationships that dominate a city state; one effect of them is that the citizens at least know where they are. If they have the vote and elections are free they can begin at least to claim they are living, according to the principles of democratic practice; on the other hand if they do not have the vote, or if elections are influenced by violence or the threat of violence to secure the return of particular candidates, they will *know*, they will know as a matter of course from their personal experience, that this is so and will be able to conclude they are not living in accord with such principles. The political struggle then becomes not a matter of the citizen deciding for what purposes the political machinery shall be put, but about the citizen's right to decide at all; the issue centres not on the fruits of democracy but on democracy itself.

For the politician in office in a city state, or who aspires to it, he is a man serving the interests of his fellows on the basis of their free choice, or he may be the representative of a corrupt prince or of some moneyed interest, who is obeying the kind of pressures they can mount from fear of loss of office or even perhaps of life or limb from some act of violence they may not hesitate to instigate. In which case we are not talking about democracy at all and there is an end on it. But if the voting and elective mechanisms are free, and unfettered by other than concern for the general citizen well-being, then the representative is in a continuous confrontation situation as it were, with those who elect him and will be in some position to claim his situation depends on a democratic choice. He is, he may claim, a servant of the people.

He might have enjoyed a number of privileges from his elective office and certain forms of social precedence, but he was generally an unpaid public servant and almost certainly not dependent on his emoluments for his everyday means of subsistence. Inside the legislative chamber, if he sought preference to a higher rank, to membership of the inner Council, or to the apex of power itself, he was dependent on nothing more than the votes of his fellows; and it was their personal estimate of him which played a large part in his advancement or otherwise. It might well be of course that he was

bent on corrupt courses, but then he would need to strike a balance
between his personal interest and that of his office. It is conceivable
that these might be the same, and even if it is more easily conceivable
that they were not he would doubtless find no difficulty in persuading
himself otherwise; but still he would need to strike a balance, to take
adequate account of public opinion, bearing in mind the emphatic
personal relationship he has with it and the extent to which he is dependent on it. And we need to bear in mind too that however much
other pressures might bear on him, such as the wishes perhaps of a
titular ruler or of some wealthy interest, or his own veniality, ultimately he would need to return to the bar of popular appraisal of
his office and be judged.

Even this is to put the worst possible gloss on things and to ignore
the fact that selfless service to the public weal has always played
a tremendous, perhaps a preponderant, part in the political process.
Mankind as a whole has benefited from the fact that generation
after generation has always found a goodly number of dedicated,
selfless people who have striven and sacrificed for no other goal
than, in that banal phrase, to leave the world a better place than
they found it. Such progress as we have known is due almost
entirely to their efforts and one of the major problems of society
today is to find a way in which this abundant generosity of spirit
can find a means of being heard and of making a due contribution
to the problems of our time. The important point here, however,
is clear—whatever the personal disposition of a man in office might
be, he had real power to make decisions or to influence debates,
either with his vote or his powers of persuasion within or without
the elected assembly.

Where is that power, stemming from the ballot box, today?
How much power does an elected representative have in a mass
society? These questions may be answered at two levels, by considering the dominant problems of our time and the capacity of
the elected person to influence their solution, and also in examining
his path to power and office. For fairly obvious methodological
reasons we shall need to clarify the latter aspect first and here we
shall need to descend from theory to everyday practice.

Let us assume that an aspirant for public office desires to serve
through the structure of the Labour Party in Britain.[1] If he desires

[1] The present writer was a member of the Labour Party for nearly twenty years
and served as a ward secretary, constituency secretary and as a parliamentary candi-

to be elected to Parliament as a Labour member he must, of course, first join the party. In this he must join a particular section of it. The party is made up of constituency organisations corresponding to the constituency boundaries of the parliamentary elections, and the constituency organisation itself is based on a division into wards which in turn correspond to the ward boundaries of local government election. Hence in 'joining the party' he will in fact generally join the ward organisation functioning in the area in which he lives. The ward generally meets monthly and, among other matters, will elect delegates to a constituency management committee which is generally the real focus of party organisation in the constituency.[2]

The management committee is made up of elected delegates from the wards and from various affiliated bodies such as local trade union branches, local co-operative societies and so on, and its tasks are usually quite considerable. Its main objective will be to seek to secure the return of a Labour representative to parliament for the constituency, and to do the same for the local council. To this end it will collect funds, organise social, propagandist and educational functions, conduct membership campaigns and so on. It will also, from time to time, consider nominations from the wards and affiliated bodies for inclusion on the list of prospective parliamentary candidates which it will transmit to the party's national headquarters.

So this is one route by which the aspiring Member of Parliament may reach his destination. In point of fact this route is something

date at a general election. The details given here do, of course, differ from those of mass parties in other countries, but the general principles to which they relate are markedly similar. Even though it was written over half a century ago, the work by Robert Michaels, *Political Parties—A Sociological Study of the Oligarchial Tendencies of Modern Democracy*, derived largely from his experience of the German Social Democrats, was a pioneer work on the theme of political organisation in a mass society. But it was pioneering which has been largely ignored by most political theorists and even now its lessons have scarcely begun to be considered, far less applied. This is not to say the writer shares Michaels' conclusions, which were even more right-wing and authoritarian than those of social-democrat and labourite leaders today. He did in fact become an ardent fascist and a supporter of Mussolini. The work was republished by the Free Press, Collier Macmillan. London, 1966, with a lengthy introduction by Martin Seymour Lipset.

[2] There are differences of detail here as between rural and urban areas, and as between large and small urban areas. Although these details are ignored, if only for the sake of clarity of exposition, they do not affect the analysis or the inferences to be drawn from it.

in the nature of a cul-de-sac, for the party maintains two separate lists of prospective candidates, one of which is for 'nominated' candidates and the other for 'sponsored' candidates. The distinction is crucial, for the former, list B, is made up of those nominated by constituency management committees but having no financial backing, whereas the latter, list A, is comprised of those whose election expenses will be paid in large part by the sponsoring organisation, generally a trade union.

In practice what happens is that voting behaviour over a series of elections has established that some constituencies repeatedly return a Labour member, that others never do, and that some fluctuate as the prize of different parties from one election to another. Hence, there are 'safe', 'hopeless' and 'marginal' labour seats. The 'nominated' candidate is unlikely to be selected for more than a 'hopeless' seat, one, that is, on past voting form, he is unlikely to win. The 'safe' seats will generally go to sponsored conference of the constituency management committee is called and all duly elected delegates from ward and affiliated organisations are free to attend and all member bodies are free to make nominations. The nominations will usually be reduced to a short list by the executive committee of the management committee and they, like the members at the selection conference, will be guided mainly by one consideration; who will pay the election expenses of several hundred pounds which a local party is unlikely to have? This will weigh the list in favour of those candidates on list A whose expenses will be largely paid by the trade union, or any other body, sponsoring them. If an unsponsored candidate is chosen then the constituency party itself will have to find most of the election expenditure, which may be a matter of some difficulty.

At the selection conference itself the final choice will be likely to be weighed by another factor. The general management committee is normally a very hard-working body. Its *active* members are likely to be the ward delegates, who generally do all the donkey work of party organisation and of taking the party to the people, as it were. Without their labours there just would be no party worth the name. It is these members, often imbued with idealism and a keen sense of public duty, who spend long hours in dull organisational meetings and who are prone to labour assiduously at preparing resolutions on world affairs and other matters to be discussed at ward and management committee level before, if adopted, being sent to party headquarters or to the party leaders. There is hardly a shred of evidence to suggest that any of these resolutions has ever had the slightest influence on any government in office whether of the party or not, but this does nothing to deter this form of expression. It is not for nothing that the Labour Party has come to be called the 'resolutionary party'.

At any rate it is these hard working members who are the mainstay of the central management committee and who will have a disposition to look at a prospective candidate not simply in terms of the financial backing of the sponsoring organisation, but of what he actually stands for in terms of political policies. Is he for or against Britain being a member of the Common Market? What are his views on comprehensive schools? Unilateral nuclear disarmament? More nationalisation? And so on.

At the selection conference the ward delegates are likely to be surprised to find the meeting has grown well beyond its routine proportions by the attendance of 'delegates' of the local trade union branch whose national body is sponsoring one of the candidates. It is the practice of local branches of a union to affiliate to the local constituency Labour Party, but it is seldom indeed that these union members will take any active part in the routine organisational activities of the Party, but since the branch is affiliated it is entitled to send a substantial quota of delegates to the (generally) monthly meetings of the management committee, a privilege of which it seldom avails itself. It should be noted that the distinction between the party militant and the trade union delegate is not all that clear-cut since all wage-earning party members are expected to be members of a union as a matter of course. It is the votes of these perfectly legitimate, but otherwise usually totally inactive, union affiliate members which are likely to decide the issue. Having cast their votes and secured the adoption of their men they are all too prone to disappear until with the passage of the years the sitting member is removed by death or resignation and another selection conference is called. This helps to explain why such a large proportion of the members of the Parliamentary Labour Party (i.e. the Labour members of Parliament), consists of elderly trade union officials whose active days at the negotiation table are over and for whom a safe parliamentary seat is regarded as the due reward for services long rendered.

It is possible that our aspiring 'Member' will be selected even for a safe seat, or that he may be chosen to contest a marginal or hopeless seat and then succeed in being elected to parliament. Such freak results are not unknown, but however he makes it one thing will be impressed upon him from the start, that his selection and election will be entirely a matter for the party machine. Without the active and organised backing of the machine, which extends to the provision of funds, literature, organisation help and prominent speakers from central sources, his campaigning could scarcely have begun. At some early stage, probably shortly after his selection, he will have to sign a paper solemnly declaring he accepts party policy, and to this boy-scout ritual is added the necessity of the central party machine to approve his selection before he is formally acknowledged as the party's prospective candidate.

Even at this early stage his situation is thus dominated in every important respect by the party machine, so it may be in order to ask 'What is the party machine?' To do the top echelons of the party justice its constitution was framed from the very beginning to emasculate the power of the constituencies to have any serious effect either on its structure or its policies. The method used was crude but extremely effective. The zeal and devotion of the party come, have always come, from the constituencies. But not the money. Elections are expensive affairs, and so are centralised party bureaucracies with their salaried, full-time officers, and it is doubtful if constituency fund-raising could have produced more than a modest fraction of the money usually spent. This is the source of trade union power in the Labour Party, for with their memberships frequently running into hundreds of thousands, and sometimes millions, a modest *per capita* political levy on such membership is able to produce the kind of sums that make modern electioneering on a mass scale possible.

The influence of the Unions is ensured by the manner in which power in the annual Conference of the Party, supposedly the supreme policy-making body of the party, is disposed.

The membership of the Labour Party in 1971 was as follows:[3]

Trade Unions	5,559,371
Individual (constituency) members	699,522
Socialist & Co-operative Societies	23,360

[3] *Report of the 71st Annual Conference of the Labour Party 1972* and *The Labour Party Constitution and Standing Orders.*

The preponderant weight of the Trade Union membership is apparent and this is reflected in its financial contribution. Under the present rules each Constituency Labour Party must pay £5 per member per year party funds. Trade Union affiliated members pay 40 p per year.

In 1979 affiliation fees were paid as follows:

	£
Trade Unions	1,842,383
Labour Parties	208,182
Socialist & Co-op. Societies	12,973
	2,063,538

In addition the Unions make hefty donations to Party funds at elections and on their special occasions, as well as to local parties when their own sponsored candidates are election candidates.

Voting at annual conference is by cards on the basis of one 'card for each 10,000 members or part thereof'. It is a sharply political occasion, in many ways it is the consummation of much earnest thought and discussion: like as not the local party will have debated at length a resolution at ward and general management committee level which may appear on the agenda and to which the constituency delegate will be expected to speak. It will be a matter on which he and his local comrades will feel strongly, a concern likely to be shared by many other constituency members.

The contrast with the trade union element could scarcely be more marked. Numerically the union delegates will far outnumber the constituency delegates, but the union delegates will be divided in terms of their approach between the leaders who represent in their own person a virtually irremovable and self-perpetuating oligarchy, and a large number of acquiescent followers for whom the occasion is little more than a free week in a seaside hotel with all expenses paid by the union. Generally their interest in political matters is peripheral and tends to be aroused only when pocket and stomach issues are touched on, for the rest they tend to be acquiescent, elderly, easy going, fairminded and decent; voting-fodder for issues on which they are seldom, if ever, aroused to take more interest than is involved in scanning a newspaper headline. Yet their votes, lumped together to form the 'block' cast by their leader, a block that may run to millions, is what determines the outcome of most of the conference proceedings.

We shall have to discuss the nature of the pressures which operate within the trade union world, here we need to note whatever the form of those pressures, even if it is no more than the threat of being dropped from future delegations if the leader's wishes are not followed, they suffice on the whole to enable the trade union world to present a fairly solid front to the 'wild' men of the constituencies on nearly all key conference issues.

It is true that of recent years this front has shown some signs of cracking, but this is something which is happening to authoritarian structures all over the world, largely as a result of what is called the youth revolt. But youth clearly does not yet know what its own revolt is for, and since the other side of this equation, the constituencies, have ceased to have anything significant or coherent to say, the matter is of much less importance than it might be. Once the member is elected to parliament he finds that his quest for the locus of power, if he is seeking it, and many trade union M.P.s tend to be elderly T.U. officials whose active days are done, and who would be no more dream of conducting such a quest than in taking up cross-country running, is as far from attainment as ever. One former British cabinet minister comments on this question as follows:

"Everybody knows the story Nye Bevan used to tell. Political power was his grail. He got himself elected to the Parish Council in order to find it but when he got into the Council Chamber it wasn't there. So he got himself elected first to the Urban District then to the County and last to Parliament and he couldn't find it anywhere in the Palace of Westminster. He fought his way into the Cabinet and then into the sanctum of the inner Cabinet—and always it had eluded him. Partly, perhaps, because I spent seven years as an Oxford don, my quest has been not so much for the secret place where power is concealed as for the Committee whose decisions are taken in the light of the available evidence. And all my life the vision has eluded me. Wherever I got myself elected, to the Fellows Meeting at New College, to my Faculty Meeting, to the Oxford City Council, to Parliament, and finally to the Cabinet, the higher I climbed the more certain I was that on the next storey of the pyramid of power I would find a body of people making their decisions not on hunch and guesswork but on the basis of reliable information. Now I know that in Whitehall at least I was searching not for a will-of-the-wisp but for a pot of gold which is extremely difficult to find—except of course in wartime."[4]

Parliament, the new Member soon finds, is a highly disciplined machine; it has to be if only to carry, or pretend to carry, its utterly fantastic work-load and to reduce to some sort of order the competing appetites for power of many of its more than six hundred members. The member soon finds too that his power to exercise any influence over events could scarcely be more residual. This is due to two principal factors; the insistence, first, of the central government in presuming to extend its authority into numerous fields of social affairs which are none of its business at all. For historical rather than practical reasons it concerns itself with education, details of health service administration, local police organisation, what is blissfully called 'social security', housing, town and country planning and a host of other matters which, in the name of liberty as well as efficiency, are the obvious prerogative of locally elected councils. In fact of course its capacity to give more than a cursory survey of these matters is manifest and the occasions grandiloquently described as 'debates', when these matters are discussed in the legislative chamber, are remarkable only for the extent of their general failure to effect any real remedies for the problems under review.

How indeed could it be otherwise? Education, for example, is a matter of a parent's decision about the intellectual nurture of his child. He may, indeed common sense suggests he will, combine with other parents to solve problems which are fundamental in any case to the course of civilisation, and with them work out a common programme of schooling for the children of the neighbourhood. The 'educational policy' will then be what this particular group of parents decides is best for their children, and that policy may give emphasis to music making, mormonism, money making or mineralogy. Whatever it is, that is their business; it is not, it cannot be, a matter of decision-making concern for any other person or body, without infringing their democratic rights and liberties as free citizens.

The different policies of thousands of neighbourhoods will be as varied as the fish in the sea and it is these often profound and exciting differences which should be giving the whole process of civilisation a particular sense of multiple individuation and riches of character and gifts. But simply to suppose that a few score salaried

[4] R.H.S. Crossman, *Socialism & Planning*, the Fabian Society. 1966, p. 5.

placemen in a centralised parliament can pretend to usurp this parental power is not only to open the door to the comedy of debate about
'educational policy', as though every vestige of genuine freedom to
decide is not being snuffed out, but to assume further that the whole
process is likely to reflect parental wishes after the bureaucratic
machine has done its work. How can a situation involving the centralised expenditure in Britain of £845 million per *annum*[5] and
the employment of an army of teachers and inspectors be equated
with the merest notion of individual freedom or of democracy through
parliamentary control, when parliament is also loaded with responsibility for the general state of the economy, foreign policy,
disarmament, currency management, taxation, Scottish affairs,
the white fishing industry, sewage in Manchester, civil aviation,
and the telephone service? It would be possible to extend this
list through several pages and all it would serve to show is that far
from exercising any real control Parliament is simply handing over
such control to the fantastic degree of bureaucracy that such a
presumed involvement in a multiplicity of affairs at this level involves.

Indeed, and again, how can it be otherwise? Parents in one
village may be up in arms about the defects of a school in their
area. But they decide nothing. And to admit the member of Parliament can bring his 'power' to bear—he is, after all, the elected representative, which no one else in the locality is—is to admit the
principle that all M.P.s can talk about all schools. In theory they
can, but what we are concerned with here is not theory but actuality,
and when it comes to the nitty gritty it is not the Member, nor the
parents, nor even the Minister who really decides, but the people
with the real power, the bureaucrats.

If one could suppose that Parliament were simply concerned to
handle those matters which could not be handled locally, such
as defence, foreign affairs, certain forms of taxation, customs and
excise, legal affairs and economic and fiscal policy, there is at least
a chance that the hapless Members might be able to focus attention
on something of substance. But in Britain there are over twenty
major offices of State and each of these involves numerous portfolios.
Parliament meets approximately 165 days in a year, rarely before
2.00 p.m. in the day and its timetable is so loaded with procedural

---

[5]It will be appreciated that local authorities are also involved in considerable
expenditure on education within a detailed framework fashioned by the central
machine.

formalities that the actual amount of time spent in debate will be about half of that. What in fact has happened is that owing to its grossly over-extended field of surveillance the locus of discussion and resolution of policy has largely been taken out of parliament. It just could not be otherwise if parliament's own machinery were to function with any sort of order under this absurd degree of centralisation.

It must not, however, be supposed, that a member of parliament is therefore entirely powerless; there is always some scope for the member with exceptional gifts of expression, or of intellectual penetration or of sheer assiduity, but that is what he will need to be, exceptional. By and large the working of parliament is a formalised ritual which puts the seal of approval on matters which have been discussed and decided elsewhere. Some, as we have seen, have been decided in the boardrooms of advertising executives, especially matters which underlie the policy assumptions of those who believe policy-making is their business, but for the rest these decisions have been made for the most part in the cabinet, by the Prime Minister, and, undoubtedly in the most dynamic centre of all, within the upper reaches of the civil service. Yet not even this dispersal of the decision-making function to areas outside parliament will enable parliament to function without another factor which severely limits the power of the individual member to influence affairs, and this is the highly disciplined machinery of the party system.

We have seen that the member, once having been selected as a prospective candidate by a relatively small group of people in his constituency, owes his election almost wholly to the functioning of the party machine.

At this stage we do well to grasp a basic truth about the workings of any mass party which makes much of their operating methods, which are otherwise incomprehensible, explicable. It is simply this, that the organisation of a mass party, vis-a-vis the power relationship between its central controlling organs and that of the individual member, follows the same laws as those which apply to the working of the society as a whole of which it is part. So that we must expect to see the same effects.

As the *party* grows in size the power of the individual member declines in relation to the power of the centre. He is less able to control it than it is to control him. Since the centre is removed from all but residual and spasmodic efforts by the members to control it, it follows that moral principle will be of less moment at the centre than the main business in hand, which is inevitably the quest for **power** *as an end in itself.* What power is used *for* is of infinitely less importance than the mere business of getting it and retaining it. This is the main reason why it is virtually impossible to predict how a party will behave in terms of its manifestoes, its label, its election promises, its credo, or the rhetoric that may be embalmed in its constitution.

In 1907 an historic conference took place in Stuttgart of the socialist and social democratic parties of Europe; mindful of the war preparations of the great powers they passed a carefully worded resolution, the final paragraphs of which are worth quoting in full:

> If a war threaten to break out, it is a duty of the working class in the countries affected, and a duty for their parliamentary representatives, with the aid of the International Bureau as an active and co-ordinating power, to make every effort to prevent the war by all means which seem to them the most appropriate— means which naturally vary according to the intensity of the class-struggle and to the political situation in general.
>
> Should war none-the-less break out, it is their duty to intervene in order to bring it promptly to an end, and with all their strength to make use of the economic and political crisis created by the war to stir up the deepest strata of the people and precipitate the fall of capitalist domination.[6]

These paragraphs were mainly the work of the Russian Social Democrats (under Lenin!), and the Polish socialists, under Rosa Luxembourg, and deliberately avoided any reference to such matters as insurrection or a general strike out of deference to the German delegates who were, of course, the hosts, who feared trouble with their own government. The resolution was regarded (and still is) as a landmark in socialist cooperation and yielded everybody present a profound sense of accomplishment, one delegate, after it had been unanimously agreed, jumping on the table to signify his enthusiasm.

Yet within seven years a general European war had indeed broken out, and with scarcely any hesitation the workers' parties, with the

[6]Quoted by G.D.H. Cole in *The History of Socialist Thought,* Vol. III, Part One, 'The Second International', Macmillan and Co. Ltd., London, p. 69.

solitary and temporary exception of the Italians, were fully aligned with their capitalist masters' fighting a capitalist war and shooting and killing one another to an extent to which men in all history had never before engaged. Within a few days the Second International which had so solemnly passed this resolution was virtually extinct.

What caused this sudden about-turn of the major socialist parties? What prompted them, after all the high-sounding declarations of principle of less than a decade earlier, to suddenly give their blessing to the fighting and all that followed? This is a crucial question; we are so used to seeing the abandonment of principle today by politicians either in office or seeking to attain it we are tempted to forget what high hopes were placed on the shoulders of these leaders, and how much genuine idealism and readiness to sacrifice for noble ends prevailed in the parties they led. If a mere handful of them had shown themselves ready to sacrifice imprisonment or worse rather than consent to the fighting it is first possible that millions of lives might have been saved and mountains of human agony might have been prevented, and Europe might have retained the centuries of accumulated moral capital which was squandered in the ensuing four years of cumulative horror. What went wrong?

The answer is simply that with the outbreak of war something like a contagion of war-fever gripped the capitals of Europe. For years, indeed for more than a generation, European rivalries had been fostered by the new 'popular' press, in turn inflamed by successive stages of rearmament of the major powers, each new stage in one provoking an armament increase in the others. It would be impossible to lay the blame for the war on any one country, all the major contestants were up to their necks in the power game and either seeking fresh advantages in terms of colonies, markets, alliances and new degrees of armaments, or preparing to defend advantages they already possessed. The underlying tensions generated in masses of people by decades of persistent propaganda designed to persuade them that the 'others' were war-making barbarians whilst 'we' were the soul, as well as the saviours, of civilisation, reached a climacteric apogee in 1914 which caused millions of people to pour into the streets of their cities and cheer to the echo the fact that now, at last, 'we' were going to give 'them' their just deserts.

Confronted with this degree of sustained popular hysteria the socialist leaders had two clear courses, either to repudiate it, or to join it. Either to affirm the basic decencies of life which until then had largely prevailed over much of Europe, at whatever cost in personal terms, confident that in due course the tide of popular feeling would change, or to betray the so recently affirmed and still nascent 'brotherhood of man' at the behest of more immediate factors. Almost to a man they chose betrayal. They did so because they felt that to stand out against this tide of feeling would be to rob them of any prospect of obtaining office. In point of fact their strategy was false even in terms of their own power-quest, for none of these parties achieved majority office for nearly a generation. In playing the power game they were beaten by interests which had been playing it much longer than they and which were much more adept in calculating its shifting factors.

Had they stuck to their principles it is possible that popular disgust with the war would have shortened its course considerably and created a social network of governments throughout Europe which in turn would have enabled the moderate Kerensky in Moscow to survive against any Bolshevik threat, created a new global agreement on a mechanism to prevent the recurrence of war, created syndicalist and cooperative forms of economic activity to counter the instabilities of 'free' markets, and generally to have written the twentieth century in terms of the dawning triumph of man against the scourges of war, poverty, disease and ignorance, as well as over-mighty technology, which still hold him in thrall. Instead their betrayal was enough to ensure that the rest of this century was written in blood which continues to spill.

It is vain now to blame them for this betrayal, what is much more important is to grasp the nature of the forces that led them to it and which will continue, as they do, to prompt them to further betrayals as long as their nature is not grasped. In each case they were leaders of mass parties and this meant that the quest for power was bound to be pursued in terms of the inherent logic of power on a mass scale rather than of any fidelity to moral principle about the brotherhood of man. Once they felt, however, mistakenly, that the chances of the power they sought were threatened by adhesion to principle, it was principle rather than the quest for power which was abandoned. They, in turn, could do this because owing to their grip on the party machines it was they who controlled them, not the members. If they had attempted to adhere to principle in the prevailing hysteria it is quite likely they would have been ousted by rivals within the leadership who would have sought to go along with the dominant majority mood.

It may be thought that this is to suggest that it *is* the people who control the leaders, but this is to misread the character of events. Even in the twentieth century the onset of a world war was a highly unusual event and one in which, in this case, emotions were so charged as to sweep aside the forces that normally prevail. Normally the membership of a mass party is docile and acquiescent towards the leadership and the leaders are able to manipulate it along virtually any course they wish; when this ceases to be so the leaders must either follow the wishes of the people or get out. In 1914 the wishes of the people were for war and not a single leader, with the possible exception of Jean Jaures, who was unfortunately assassinated only six weeks before it began, had the courage and the vision to try to persuade them to a saner path. When war came they abandoned not only their principles, but their pretensions to lead, yet they did so not from any sense of deference to the masses, they were deferring rather to power; and it merely happened to be one of those rare instances when they could conveniently defer to both.

The dichotomy of interest between the pursuit of principle and that of power is endemic in any mass society and in any mass organisation. This is why a Labour Party leader in modern memory at a party conference debate on the issue of nuclear weapons, instead of joining in a general act of repudiation of one of the supreme man-made horrors of war of all generations of man, finding himself and the faction he led to be in a minority on the issue of doing so, vowed to the conference, vowed to its face! that he would 'fight, fight and fight again' to get reversed the decision the conference had taken by a substantial majority for unilateral nuclear disarmament. He did too, for he saw, probably correctly, that the majority of the British *voters* would feel betrayed and defenceless without these terrible weapons in a world where other large powers possessed them. Mr. Gaitskell was not interested in the views of the majority of his party members on this issue, except to frustrate them, he was far more interested in the views of the voters, for their votes were the cobblestones of his road to power.

Gaitskell succeeded in reversing this conference decision for the simple reason that he had the backing of the party machine not simply as leader, but on this particular issue. For the operators of the machine saw, or believed they saw, with clarity, that no labour party could hope to win a general election with the albatross of a conference decision in favour of unilateral nuclear disarmament around its neck. It was necessary to reverse this decision as a precondition of gaining power, so reversed it was and it was the machine of the central party bureaucracy which did the job.

It may be thought that there was another possibility here; that a party with its often proclaimed concern for the brotherhood of man would recognise this question of nuclear disarmament as one of the supreme moral issues of our time and accept its own conference decision as a major plank in its platform. From there it might have proceeded to mount a prodigious campaign of political education to convert the mass of public opinion to the need for unilateral disarmament. This doubtless was the view of those muddle-headed idealists in the party who secured the adoption of the original resolution, but this course was just not on for two principal reasons.

First, however effective such a campaign would have been in Britain, it would certainly not have converted either the other European members of NATO or the government of the United States. When one views the extent of the influence of American bankers on British economic policy during the economic crisis of the 1930s, and of the effectiveness of American pressures, not to say threats, which secured the withdrawal of British forces from the madcap folly of the Eden government's attack on Suez, to make no reference to similar pressures on more recent events, we need to be under no illusion as to the way that power would have been used to secure a government more amenable to the Pentagon's ideas of statecraft, even if it meant instigating an economic crisis and a 'run on the pound' designed to bring about the downfall or the compliance of a government committed to unilateral nuclear disarmament.

The scenario for these events is not difficult to imagine, for with this formidable opposition from abroad the Government would have found itself confronted by the high-powered opposition of big business and banking interests at home, and with them would have been harnessed the power of the media. *The Times* would have thundered about the grave dangers to national safety of an irresponsible government controlled by demagogues and 'extremists', and the mass circulation dailies would have pulled out every stop to arouse the fears of their mob readerships about their safety, the imminent prospects of a Russian assault, and the threat to their pockets and stomachs caused by the waning credibility of the pound as an instrument of purchase.

Of course these pressures would have succeeded, if only because of factors relating to the second principal reason, which revolve on the nature of any mass political party's organisation. Long before the unilateral issue reached the party's conference it was already an issue around which alignments in the jockeying for power within the party machine had been made. Had the party machine decided to back the conference decision we may be sure that those who aligned themselves with Mr. Gaitskell would simply have seen their defeat as the prelude to the next round in the struggle.

It is an inherent defect of all voting procedures that they tend to divide rather than unite. It is impossible to apply consensus politics on a mass scale and voting nearly always has the effect of polarising views, emphasising differences rather than areas of agreement, which those who differ may share. So that the 'Gaitskellites', backed by a large minority of those who at the time shared their views, would have been in overt alliance with the opposition forces outside the party, and they would have ensured that the life of the unilateral government would have been short-lived, if only by projecting the sacrifices the government would have been compelled to demand from the electorate as the price of its policies as being as needless as the policy was harmful.

What then of the 'prodigious campaign of political education'? Again we need to remind ourselves, however repetitively, that party machines are not geared to the pursuit of idealistic principles, but to the pursuit of political power. The Party's main source of power in this instance is not from its individual members but from its Trade Union affiliates. Sooner or later these elements, seeing the prospects of power being jeopardised by the pursuit of principle, would have begun to apply their own pressures, for no mass education campaign can be waged without money, which in this instance only the trade unions could provide.

In a mass party organisation political education is not, indeed cannot be, an end in itself; the end is always power and if education fails to serve this end, or indeed, as in this case, actually threatens to subvert it, the more power-conscious elements in the party, especially within its bureaucracy, which will find ready support from the party's internal opposition, will assuredly act to ensure that the ends of power are restored to their primary place. The language of power is the religion of all bureaucracies.

All this must have been foreseen quite clearly by Mr. Gaitskell, and he must have also seen quite clearly that the least of the evils confronting him was that a 'unilateralist' party would have assuredly split to such an extent as to make its prospects of power negligible. On the other hand, by openly rallying his followers to fight against this resolution he knew he could attract sufficient support from within the party *and* without to give him a good chance of defeating the unilateralists whilst yet containing them within the party, maintaining an external facade of unity and achieving his quest for power at the polls. It was this knowledge which led to the otherwise astonishing spectacle of his open and uninhibited defiance of the Party's own conference decision. The event justified his prescience, whatever it may have done for his moral stature and the fate of the unborn; the decision was indeed reversed at the next conference and had he lived there is little doubt that in the ensuing general election he would have emerged as the Prime Minister of a Britain fully armed with nuclear weapons.

As we have said, it was in fact the party's own machine which was the principal agent in securing this reversal, and again it is this machine which largely controls the party member when he is elected to parliament; it controls, through some party functionaries called, with metaphorical aptness, 'whips', his goings out and his comings in, and the pressures they can bring to bear are considerable.

The member will be an M.P. usually because he has some ambition, but his ambition is not normally satiated when he reaches the legislative chamber, he will want to climb higher, to employ the usual adverb for this transition, he will want to become a member of the government, of the cabinet, and perhaps even become the prime minister himself. His conformity to party policy and to party decisions is also the price he must expect to pay for such minor forms of patronage as being included on visits of parliamentary delegations abroad. If his disagreements with the party's policy are so deep as to prompt him to vote consistently against it he can, as an ultimate step, be suspended from membership or even expelled.

Some people have been known to have suffered this fate and to have survived at a subsequent election by standing as an independent. But they have been exceptional cases. Elections cost money and require a fairly strong local organisation to ensure it is spent effectively. There is no point at all in printing forty or sixty thousand carefully worded election addresses if there is no supporting organisation of people available who will address and pack them for ensuring they reach the individual members of the electorate.

It may be that a local party to a man may be in complete accord with the policy views of a recalcitrant member who represents them in parliament. They may decide after his expulsion to continue to give him their support, which in effect will mean that the local party machine is at war with the national party machine. How will this be resolved?

The latter will seek to persuade the former to courses more amenable to it; if this process of persuasion should fail the national body will then proceed to 'disaffiliate' the local body, which will then, in its eyes, have no standing and no power to speak or act in the name of the party.

A local organiser will then be appointed by the national party charged with the task of forming a new local party in which the leading lights of the old party will be carefully excluded, if for no other reason than that it is an observable principle of the dynamics of group psychology that hostility to *former* members of a group is always greater than it is to those the group may be formally established to oppose (and in this case the 'old' party members will be filling both roles). He will generally succeed, for it is a rule of politics that the machine invariably wins any contest with its own or its former adherents.

The member may, on the other hand, feel quite happy in his role as a back bench M.P.; his very rare interventions in debates, his occasional questions to a minister during the special time allocated for such enquiries, as well as his work on numerous committees and sub-committees connected with the work of parliament, to say nothing of his contributions to the meetings of his parliamentary party, his occasionally reported speeches and perhaps even his possibly once-for-all appearance on television, will bolster his sense of taking a useful and influential part in public affairs which is its own justification.

If, on the other hand, he agrees with all his party says and does there is of course, for him, no problem. He is not sand in the works, but oil, and his progression will be accordingly smooth, or his quiet life of undisturbed equanimity on a back bench, if that is all he wants, assured.

At this stage a note of realism should be sounded. Our civilisation is foundering. The evidence is so multiple that it takes a positive act of closing eyelids not to see it and mark its import. The questions of war, population excess, resource wastage, pollution and human alienation would, in any particular, bespeak a situation of the utmost peril; taken together they indicate either a breakdown of the collective will to live, or a breakdown of the prevailing mechanisms of government by which the problems of the social order are located, defined and resolved. The writer believes the latter projection to be the case; policy formulation on basic issues is reaching the public consciousness in far too predicated a fashion to permit a significant enough alteration of their effects in the ensuing legislative processes to make alterations to these disastrous trends possible.

Already, for example, governments and legislatures are having long, solemn discussions on the effect of multinational corporations on their national economies. There has been no discussion as to whether such immense empires of private power and interest should be allowed to exist at all. Parliaments have equally long, solemn discussions about how to end the mounting perils of nuclear and thermonuclear weaponry. Not a single parliament in the world ever discussed the *principle* of their manufacture before their existence became part of the nightmare backdrop of our time.

This matter of nuclear weaponry is of such fundamental concern to the future of humanity, as well as to the thesis being argued here, that we need to focus more closely on just how it was foisted on the British people in the first place. The British involvement in this issue was not, apparently, even discussed in full Cabinet before the crucial decisions were taken in 1948, and there is still a great deal of ambiguity as to precisely what transpired even at cabinet level. There was, it seems, a Cabinet Committee on the matter and, "when the minutes of the Committee came before the Cabinet, the Prime Minister (as Mr. Crossman puts it) did not feel it necessary to call attention to this item".[7] Attlee's silence was a calculated ploy. The minutes, like a mass of other documents, had been previously circulated to Cabinet members, and the bomb was well buried in that mass. Mr. Attlee later told a parliamentary colleague that he did not want to discuss the atom bomb in full Cabinet as "I thought

[7]Andrew Roth, *Can Parliament Decide*, London, Macdonald, 1971, p. 27, I am indebted to Mr. Roth for his trenchant account of the workings of the British Parliament in many parts of this essay. He writes as a working journalist with a considerable experience of parliamentary reporting.

some of them were not fit to be trusted with secrets of this kind".

But let Mr. Roth's abler and more closely observant pen take up the rest of the story. "If", he writes, "Cabinet members and Privy Councillors bound by the Official Secrets Act were not to be made privy to much of the awesome secret it was certain that M.P.s would be kept in almost total darkness. It was decided, at the above mentioned full cabinet meeting, that it would be risky to manufacture the atomic bomb wholly without informing Parliament. It was also decided that it would be unwise to call attention to it. Therefore a planted question was arranged. George Jeger, a loyal Labour backbencher, asked the Minister of Defence, A.V. Alexander, on 12th May 1948, whether he was 'satisfied that adequate progress is being made in the development of the most modern types of weapons'. To this A.V. (later Lord) Alexander replied. 'Yes, Sir. As was made clear in the Statement Relating to Defence, 1948 (Command 7327), research and development continue to receive the highest priority in the defence field, and all types of modern weapons including atomic weapons, are being developed. In short, disclosure came in a parenthetic remark in what appeared to be a routine statement.

"In subsequent arguments against the thesis that the Attlee Cabinet was too secretive on this matter, George Strauss, who participated in the Cabinet decision, pointed to the above disclosure and raised the question of why it was not followed up by nuclear pacifists. In fact, Mr. Strauss did not call attention to the supplementary question and the reply. Mr. Jeger asked: 'Can the Minister give any further nformation on the development of atomic weapons?' The reply came: 'No, I do not think it would be in the public interest to do that'.

"Nor, indeed, did Mr. Strauss, in his various efforts to acquit the Attlee government of hiding its A-bomb development, point out that A.V. Alexander continued to stonewall later efforts to secure further information. Over a year later the left-wing pacifist, Emrys Hughes, asked on 27th July 1949: ' . . . in view of mutual obligations under the Atlantic Pact, what further expenditure is it proposed to incur on the atomic bomb?' In short, if the Yanks under Nato have to protest us with their A-bombs why should we waste money by making our own? The Defence Secretary stiffly replied that he had 'nothing to add' to his single answer to George Jeger fourteen months before".[8]

[8]*Ibid.*, pp. 27–28.

Mr. Roth is rightly concerned here with the evils of secrecy on major public issues, and his strictures extend to the total secrecy that preceded the Suez fiasco, the various musters for the move into 'Europe' and the Official Secrets Act. Yet our problem is deeper and more complex than this, and Mr. Roth touches on some of it when he refers to the changes in the assumptions made by various Prime Ministers, changes which they did not always see fit to communicate to their colleagues.

These assumptions generally refer to foreign policy issues, but many of the basic assumptions about the wider field of economic activity are not being made within the precincts of any part of the political machine at all.

We are constantly in the position of moving by an apparent, but generally induced, consensus, along paths laid down for us long before we become aware we are on them. Once we have taken them we find a whole host of pressures, party machines, media influences, career prospects and so on, are to hand to prevent any attempt from deviation succeeding. It is a primrose path and the peoples of the developed world are drifting along it in an induced euphoria of consumer gratification which is being used to lure them into situations which on a rational assessment they would never have dreamt of entering.

Yet even on the back benches there is disquiet, about thermonuclear weaponry for example, or about pollution,[9] but what can these powerless people do? To make a stand of principle on thermonuclear weapons is to risk all the dangers of expulsion from the party and probably, at the next election, from parliament if the party's power position in the House is threatened by it. If it is not so threatened he will be ignored—in either case he is reduced in power terms to a nullity.

In the case of pollution a survey of the problems involved indicates inescapably and unmistakably that what is at issue here is the whole direction, momentum and destination of our civilisation, but the majority of the voters are, or have been induced to be, quite quiescent on this, and any attempt by a government to stop increases in

---

[9] A big argument is at present raging in Britain as to whether huge super lorries should be allowed on the roads as they are in other countries. No parliament began to discuss this problem until monster lorries were already on the roads! Once again parliament is discussing effects rather than causes, what size shall they be—not whether they should exist at all.

industrial production, for example, far less to cut them back and base production on self-renewing rather than finite resources, would be, to put it mildly, to risk displeasing them and losing power.

It will be seen then that whichever way our member of parliament turns, unless he decides to go along with the dominant forces which are ordaining the pattern of life around him and which have brought him very largely to where he is, he is powerless. He may in consequence take up some relatively minor issue of public life, divorce law reform, the plight of the homeless, the proper care of deprived children, and so on, issues which are often not the business of a central parliament so much as of the numerous local authorities scattered about the land; he may well succeed in making some impact here, of alleviating some causes of distress, but in moments of truth it will be borne in on him that his fidelity to these issues and the gratification he derives from serving them is largely the result of a compensatory psychological mechanism activated by his failure to register any impact on the mainstream of events; he will be seeking to trim the banks of a minor stream, whilst, further down, the river of which he is a guardian is flooding and beyond control.

There is, of course, another avenue open to our powerless back bencher; he may well feel that his next step is to gain promotion and that by becoming a member of the government or of the cabinet he will be at last in a position to influence the course of events. In reality this is simply to extend the area of his self-deception, for in taking this step he enters a virtual conspiracy of silence with regard to his own thoughts; henceforth he must speak only in terms of agreement with cabinet policies, policies he has had little, if any, influence in determining, and he will be beholden moreover to a team of top civil servants who will be constantly at his elbow to advise, caution, encourage and even perhaps undo him. This latter prospect, of course, is not in the canon, but it happens all the same.

"The volume of official work which calls for decisions affecting the public is nowadays such that it is physically impossible for a Minister to give the decision except in the most important cases," remarked an official document on the civil service,[10] published over fifty years ago, and thereby pointing out the extent to which a Minister is far more dependent on his senior advisers than they are on him. Is it to be supposed that when there is a conflict of

[10]Royal Commission on the Civil Service (1929), *Minutes of Evidence*, p. 1268.

views that the advisors will always refrain from using their power? The essence of the position of a top civil servant such as a permanent secretary is, after all, that he is *permanent*.[11]

In Britain at least, he will find that nearly all policy considerations are based on the estimates for expenditure drawn up by the Treasury but we are discussing here where power really resides, so we need to ask what opportunities does a minister have of changing the estimates? Again he will find much of the situation is predetermined by factors largely beyond his control, or by assumptions he is unable to question. Yet who or what is the all powerful Treasury? From whence the estimates originate? We are back to the realm of full-time, highly-paid, and exceedingly influential bureaucrats, even though none of them has ever received a single vote from the electorate. We are in a realm of confidential minutes and memoranda, secret committee meetings and conferences where the estimates are hammered out. We are certainly not in an open field of public discussion where the assumptions on which the estimates are based are under public scrutiny. Inevitably the cabinet minister becomes a creature of this secrecy rather than an exponent of what he thinks he stands for. How can it be otherwise? Having 'arrived', as it were, as a minister, one of his major concerns will be to ensure he stays. This means he will normally need to keep the good opinion of his Prime Minister, of most of his cabinet colleagues, and of his senior civil servants. By now he has surrendered his freedom to speak his own mind to the doctrine of collective cabinet responsibility, and it will be a matter of major concern that he does not 'rock the boat'.

And, of course, he will ordinarily take care not to; if he feels deeply about any matter of policy on which his cabinet colleagues do not share his views he can only remain quiet—as far as the public is concerned—or resign. If he resigns it is frequently the end of his public career, although there have been notable exceptions; if he remains, the public at least will assume he is fully in accord with his colleagues. Either way he finds his power is not so much increased as enclosed within a gilded cage of cabinet office. This incidentally is one of the main reasons why in meganations there is nearly always

[11] As so often, nomenclature is misleading here; the designation 'Permanent Secretary' may suggest to the uninitiated a non-temporary short-hand typist; in fact a Permanent Secretary is a member of the top rank of the British Civil Service and as such probably wields more power than a Roman pro-consul ever did.

projected a front from the top which is blankly uniform and united but which in reality is wholly false and misleading.

There is, of course, a far more potent reason for this than the manner in which government estimates of expenditure are drawn up and submitted, and this is the undoubted impact of the ballot box on the fortunes of a government. In terms of the change/no-change dichotomy there is, and it is another general characteristic of any mass society, a large area of middle ground consisting of voters, frequently the majority, who do not feel committed to any of the main political parties. This leads to an even greater weakening of concern for principle in politics, for what in fact is happening is that the main parties are seeking strenuously to capture this middle ground of allegiance. In doing so neither can afford to stress its own basic principles, since it is part of the given situation that the uncommitted voters either know all about these and are not converted, or they are simply not interested, or might be hostile if made aware of them.

Hence the struggle will centre on how to impress these voters in other ways. In doing this *both* parties are virtually the prisoners of the assumptions the general body of the electorate makes about its pattern of life; and whilst the parties are able to influence those assumptions they do not create them; that task is largely performed, so we have noted, by the advertising industry. In practice the parties seek to create an image of being experienced, trustworthy, reliable, statesmanlike public servants, full of moral rectitude and financial probity, in whose hands the destiny of the nation can safely be placed. They will also each seek to portray their opponents in the opposite terms, and since the gullibility and superficiality of this section of the voters is manifest, campaigns[12] are increasingly conducted in terms of vague and unrelated generalities, as a result of which, as numerous voters rightly complain, both parties come to sound and look increasingly alike.[13] And of course, in fact,

[12] It was said that the fine margin by which Mr. Nixon lost the 1961 presidential election was a result of his last-minute appearance on T.V. with a 'five o'clock shadow' suggesting he had not shaved. Sufficient voters were impressed by this apparent personal slackness to vote for his opponent, who may well have shaved but omitted to have polished his shoes!

[13] It would make an interesting exercise to ask voters today to identify which party had used which slogan in elections in Britain. Under whom had we 'never had it so good' ? 'Let's go with X' 'Life is better with X! X cares'. Who, on these and other cases was X?

they *are* more alike, both are pursuing power as an ultimate goal and, when necessary, at the expense of whatever principles they may profess.

It is worth asking in this connection whether the history of Britain since 1945 would have been significantly different if either of the main parties had wielded a monopoly of power and stayed in office continuously? Would the crises which have affected the fate of the pound sterling been very much different? Would the issues of war, of pollution, of resource management, of urban planning, or of entry into the Common Market have been different in effect? One must surely be sanguine to suppose so. The strong temptation to adduce the abundant evidence to support this conclusion must be resisted; there are no doubt a number of marginal issues where the main parties differ; they do, presumably, have to differ about something, if only for the sake of some degree of apparent credibility, but on all the main issues of government and statecraft, issues which are shaking the foundations of civilisation to pieces, it is difficult to see, especially on the basis of the record, where they differ at all or where they would have produced different results.

It is this which makes the position of a cabinet minister so unreal in terms of power in contemporary circumstances; his power, like that of the M.P., or even of the individual voter, is largely the power to agree, to concur and to acquiesce with the prevailing stream. The economic interests and their publicity mercenaries in the world of advertising are setting the key and the tempo of the tune the masses have been taught to sing, as well as the direction they have been taught to march whilst they sing it; the cabinet minister may be responsible for any amount of welfare for the marchers, his civil servants may appear to defer to him endlessly in consequence; his voice may be as loud as any man's in the dispensing of new dignities or in changing the details of government expenditure to suit his own department, he may be a respected figure in the land and widely acclaimed for his services to the nation, but when it comes to seeking to persuade people to stop and ask themselves where they are going and why, to reconsider the whole momentum and direction of their lives, he is as powerless as a ploughboy and of no more account in the scheme of things than an old boot.

Even if he should reach the apparently top job of Prime Minister he will find he is the prisoner of the country's precarious foreign trade position and, in Britain especially, spectres such as inflation, devaluation, mass strikes in key industries, and the latest figures on the overseas trading account will give him more sleepless nights, and the reactions of foreign bankers and financers will give him more nightmares, than even the inevitable swings of opinion against his party or the loss of seats at by-elections.

And not without cause; for once in office he is the prisoner far more of these considerations than even of his electorate. He can, after all, pull the wool over the eyes of the electorate any day of the week; how else will he have achieved top office without having done so repeatedly? But the 'Gnomes of Zurich', he will soon find, are another cup of tea. Their information about his situation comes from sources beyond his control altogether and their reactions are generally in the same category.

We need to bear constantly in mind that the power of the 'Gnomes of Zurich' is not the cause of prime ministerial powerlessness over many key areas of policy, but a consequence. The cause lies in the assumptions millions of people have been manipulated into making about the pattern of their daily lives. It is the expectations derived from this pattern, which is the basis of political power. This is the basis of the electoral support a politician needs to gain office at all, but these expectations are also the bars of the cage within which he is trapped, and within which banking and other interests are able to manipulate him.

CHAPTER IX

The Will of the People

"It is the custom of my nation, when any new subject is brought before them, to put questions on it."

Chief Sechele of the Bakwena quoted by David Livingstone,
Missionary Travels in South Africa, 1843.

What we are observing here is men in different positions, as candidates, members of parliament, ministers, cabinet ministers, and prime ministers, making certain initial assumptions about society and its political and economic workings which effectively ensure that on whatever rung of the ladder to power they may find themselves they are powerless to change the general direction in which it is moving; it is clearly heading towards quite terrible forms of breakdown involving the most extreme kind of suffering for masses of largely innocent human beings, but, despite their apparent power, and because of the nature of these initial assumptions they bring to its use, they find at each stage that they are responding to a variety of pressures, from ambition, overmighty civil servants, misleading ideas about ministerial team spirit, and to a fair degree of brainwashing[1] to which everybody in a mass society is subject (how many cabinet ministers eat cornflakes?), pressures which make it virtually impossible for them to use their power, if they have to, in any genuinely constructive accomplishment.

In terms of these pressures around them their power is not unlike that of the House of Lords as defined in relation to the House of Commons. If they disagree with these pressures they are open at some point to the charge that they are obstructing the will of the majority; if they agree with them their power is superfluous.

It will be noted that the charge of 'obstructing the will of the majority' is one frequently thrown at any minority reforming interest in a mass society. Indeed our Labour Party friends are as apt as anyone to throw it, and it points to a terrible fallacy about the

[1]Advertising itself is, of course, a power as old as society, but the growth of its influence to a point where it conditions and controls the quality of people's thinking, and their disposition to react in one way or another at the deeper levels of consciousness and motivation, constitutes not only an institutionalised affront to freedom, but, it is not too much to say, a constantly exploding depth charge against man's biological stature. All biology is based on the free development of variety, all advertising is based on the need to promote uniformity of conditioning and response. No society can claim to be free where advertising (or propaganda) takes precedence over information, if only because the forces behind such interests cannot operate if the citizen is free. In modern times the destruction of the power of large-scale advertising has become a principal pre-condition of freedom.

workings of any mass society. *All* reforms and reforming innovations are the work of once-reviled minorities, and in the nature of things all interests concerned with the *quality* of things are minority interests; so is any field of original ideas and research. Today, now that the power of judgement of the majority in a mass society has been suborned by the mass manipulators and persuaders, these elements have constituted themselves as an almost impenetrable barrier to progress. No society can thrive on conformity, however induced.

Indeed it would be possible to write a history of civilisation simply in terms of how much minorities have struggled and persevered with their beliefs until the dominant groups have been won over to acceptance of them and proceeded to make them part of the prevailing orthodoxy. This must have been true of early agricultural innovations (the more recent ones have needed nothing more than the spur of the profit motive), ideas of warfare, of buildings, of mathematics, philosophy, religion and even painting and music. But not least it has been true of politics. Again and again one can point to a ferment created at first by a few gifted and far-seeing individuals on a particular issue, such as the need for free and organised schooling, or a more general body of ideas such as socialism or communism, which in turn has come to win acceptance, even if of an exceedingly questionable nature, often after a bitter struggle in terms of power.

Whatever the cause at issue all these initiatives have always been dependent on one cardinal and indispensable factor for their subsequent victory, and this factor has been the power to communicate. Today that power has been dangerously eroded by three other factors.

First, we have seen how simply as citizens people are no longer on a daily basis (with their families of course) of intimate hobnobbing and conference. They meet, increasingly, in a variety of separate and distinct categories. In each case they are meeting a different set of people in different circumstances, so that in general terms they can, or are disposed to, talk only about the matters of immediate concern in that particular field of which they have common experience, or of matters which are irrelevant to a comprehensive view of their lives and any attempt to assess its pattern in value terms. If they *should* seek to do this it will be an effort largely without point, for at scarcely any stage will the citizen be in a position to initiate effective remedial action. As a worker he can only use his union organisation, if indeed he can do so, to achieve marginal improvements in his terms and conditions of work. A union which sought to take a broad view and to accept, let us say, reductions perhaps of wages in order to help a firm to pay for anti-pollution measures, or to lower levels of production for the same end, or to pay higher prices for raw materials from third world countries from motives of common human justice, would be regarded as suffering from a form of collective insanity. A judgement not without point since its membership would either rebel or desert it to a union which behaved more in accordance with market pressures. The ordinary logic of unionism makes it unavoidable that all unions in mass capitalist societies are creatures of the impoverished ethics of prevailing mass market forces, just as in communist countries they are creatures of the dominant political machine.[2]

One may apply the same reasoning to a consumer; in terms of the global ecological dangers confronting us from a vast array of the wares in our shops just ought not to be there at all, or they ought to be made of quite different materials or by different and less harmful processes. But how can any shop respond to such needs, or indeed any business, without putting itself out of business? And given his fragmented role in society, how can the citizen bring pressure to bear? Attempts to create such pressures are, of course, constantly being made, but very often they are attempts to correct abuses the very workings of society themselves have created. They are attempts, as it were, to stop the shoe pinching at a particular point with seldom any vision of the need for a different shoe altogether.

This breakdown of the capacity of individuals in the mass society to communicate with each other from a basis of integrated social experience, a basis which is prerequisite for making such communication meaningful, springs from an even more portentous cause, for the mass society itself is the chief consequence of the destruction of human communities which technology and modern bureaucracy has helped to accomplish.

When Mahatma Gandhi declared 'you cannot have communism without community' he might have added that you cannot have a society based on any moral objective without community, and without community you cannot have genuine human communication either. It is this factor, incidentally, which probably accounts for the apparent decline in the arts of conversation and letter writing.

2With the now glorious exception of the Polish Union the heroism of whose members may yet prove to have changed the course of world history.

If conversation touches on public affairs it is generally an exchange which echoes the newspaper headlines which both parties have read, rather than an exchange based on direct experience, which both parties will generally lack. Mass literacy has not led in consequence to the release of hitherto untapped sources of human creativity and expression for which its sponsors looked, it has simply cheapened, degraded and vulgarised such standards as the communities of pre-technological mass societies were able to establish. The modern equivalent of Dr. Johnson's letter to the Earl of Chesterfield is all too likely to be two monosyllabic expletives.

Second, we are faced in this context with a factor already discussed, and that is the power of the dominant forces of the economic and bureaucratic sectors to pre-determine the social values by which the individual citizen lives and is even ruled.

Third, we are confronted with the rapid monopolisation of the media of communication, as well as its dominance, by the power of advertising. This process is both creating and being conditioned by a common factor which in a mass society is inevitable, and that is the cow-like passivity of the consumers. When people have no power over the various mechanisms, of society which dominate their lives their attention becomes focussed instead on the incidental trivialities of those mechanisms such as scandals about royalty or the private lives of political leaders, to the exclusion of the serious import of the workings of these mechanisms. Or they avert their gaze and focus instead on the commonplace incidentals of their own lives and propensities.

It is no accident at all that today newspapers (we do well to reflect on the ordinary meaning of the word), even when catering for supposedly enlightened readerships, rarely devote more than a small proportion of their space to news, or even to background material which helps to make events more intelligible. It will surely be a matter of wonder to future historians to note how, in an historical period when all the elements that bind society together are rapidly and disastrously dissolving or corroding, so-called newspapers rarely contain any meaningful news about the nature of the crisis amid which our civilisation is foundering at all. He will surely look at the pages of 'shopping news', 'fashion news', 'travel news', gardening, cooking, property advertisements, sports pages, as well as something called 'motoring', and marvel at the imbecile triviality of its import in relation to the terrible dangers in which people are rapidly being engulfed, and marvel too perhaps at the extent to which people who are products of the highest forms of education, and of institutions with a lifespan of centuries of consistent development and improvement behind them, can so sedulously repudiate their heritage and so thoughtlessly forswear their future and that of their children by permitting themselves to become engrossed in such matters to the exclusion of concern for real news in terms of the needs of our time.

It has been well said that journalism today trivialises the sensational and sensationalises the trivial, but we need to see this decline in the quality of journalism in terms of the overriding need of mass newspapers to win the unending race for higher circulations. At once we are reminded that the situation parallels the quest of the politician for power and makes both inevitably indifferent to questions of quality, and helpless to exercise any real influence to that end. The powerlessness of the masses made it inevitable that, despite the formal advances in educational attainment, the quality of the political process and of the press should become increasingly vulgar and offensive; neither can afford to appeal to the highest in people, for the highest things are generally the most uncomfortable and demanding to live with, and are thus inevitably minority concerns. So both are left with little alternative but to pander to people's baser propensities; in doing so they cut the ground for progress in either sphere from under their feet. A mass society of its nature has no moral standards and *mass* organs of opinion which seek to promote them are doomed to inevitable defeat. Triviality is all, and all minorities are submerged by the mass except those minorities who have the reins in their hands and are able to manipulate the mass.

It is surely a matter for astonishment that in an age when the technical means of communication have multiplied and reached unparalleled degrees of sophistication, and at a time when the growth of scale, of bureaucracy, and of other impersonal forces in the lives of people, make it necessary, if only in the name of freedom, to communicate more and more, that in reality people are communicating with each other less and less. The monopolisation of the media, whatever its form, ensures that although people are being communicated *with*, they are not communicating more with each other. The media is, in fact, little more than a commercialised or bureaucratic means of manipulation of the masses, as a result of which the business of communication is largely a one-way traffic from the top down.

There would not be the least difficulty in remedying this state of affairs if every parish and village were to have a centre, perhaps in the local post office, in which each citizen could have his own 'pigeon-hole' for receiving any communication from any other citizen, and where each citizen could collect such communications as a matter of course without the need for postage stamps and the like. It is the task of government to keep out of the way of the free communication of its citizens, not to hinder it.

In the same way each street could have its own large notice board on which citizens were free to put up whatever announcements, or comments on the events of the day, they saw fit. This would perhaps provoke argument and debate, from which could well come a much better informed consensus of opinion on public affairs than the mass parroting of newspaper headlines which prevails.

Unfortunately in today's crowded urban centres, space, even wall space, represents property, and hence money, and citizen affairs are crowded out by commercial or 'official' announcements. Again, the citizen is being communicated with, he is not communicating with his fellows, or they with him.

The de-personalisation of life from the democratic potential of personal relationships in, let us say, a city-state society, has not resulted, as the personal element has been destroyed in the mass society, in greater democratic safeguards, but in a pronounced erosion of democracy itself. The debate on public affairs is conducted at the top from a topside view of things by topside people. The citizen is no longer a participant in the process, but an onlooker for the most part, a passive onlooker at that, for whom the assumption has to be made that he is looking at all.

The development of policy regarding supersonic aircraft may be taken as a convenient example of what happens in consequence; it is convenient because it is a quite new innovation and not a matter which has developed over the years by degrees and which has been infiltrated gradually into public consciousness in a way that enables the citizen to be persuaded, or to persuade himself, that the matter has been decided on good grounds, perhaps by his grandfathers, permitting him a comfortable but usually entirely erroneous conclusion that he is going along with a democratically-established consensus.

As a preliminary perhaps we may postulate some of the stages of democratic decision-making which might be expected to operate in any society where freedom is a reality. If a society is confronted by a need to take a decision on a policy of some importance it is surely reasonable to suppose that a fair number of citizens are aware or persuaded of this need and are clamouring for it to be met. There are a number of public forums in any free society where such matters are discussed by the general citizen body, ranging from school debating societies, political party meetings, journals, newspapers and elected bodies, to casual exchanges over a convivial pint in a pub. From here, again, it is reasonable to assume, organised political bodies will begin to take up positions in relation to the proposed change until ultimately a debate ensues in the legislature which will enable the government of the day to take action in accordance with the majority decision, which in effect will mean to give policy directives to the administration accordingly.

It is instructive to relate this theoretical process to the actuality surrounding the decisions taken in relation to the development of supersonic aircraft. This form of aircraft had various aspects which marked it out as a radically new departure in aircraft policy. That it was going to fly faster than the speed of sound meant that research and development costs were bound to be astronomical even compared with those which had been devoted to other forms of flying. Again, the fact that speeds were to be maintained in excess of 1,000 mph meant that the projected aircraft would create a sound effect along the entire length of its flight path as its passage breached the sound barrier.

The choice of nomenclature in this instance gives a revealing glimpse of the power and the disposition of the manipulators to manipulate simply by their choice of words. To breach the sound barrier is not only a quite prodigious feat involving a considerable expenditure of energy resources, it is also an extremely noisy one which produces a sound not unlike a violent thunderclap. But it is a thunderclap with a difference, for whilst a thunderclap may reverberate for a few seconds and then die away, the effect of supersonic flight above the sound barrier is to create a continuous wave effect much as a ship will as it passes through water. Again, a thunderclap is generally preceded by some warning signs such as a lowered sky and flashes of lightning, but for anyone in the flight path (95 miles wide!) of a supersonic aircraft he is liable to be assaulted with no warning at all, by the sound of a sudden bang which is not unlike the firing of an anti-aircraft gun in the immediate vicinity. The aircraft itself may be twelve miles up and out of sight in the stratosphere.

One can imagine the earnest discussions that must have taken place on this subject; how to describe the sound of a major explosion in such a way that it sounds like something infinitely more modest? Without, one must suppose, a move of face muscle or any shift of gaze, they decided to drop the term earlier current, the sonic bang, and to call it a 'sonic boom'. A boom! A boom has an onomato-poetic gentleness suggestive of waves breaking on a distant shore or the *remote* noise of guns. The generality of people had little idea of the nature of sonic sound, so a 'sonic boom' could be counted on to raise no awkward questions.

From here the progression of events was almost exactly contrary to that outlined above. The first people to raise the matter were not ordinary, disinterested members of the public who might begin to activate the interest and enthusiasm for this new development in flying among their friends, neighbours and acquaintances, and who felt the entire future of our civilisation rested on the capacity of a microscopic minority of people to travel faster than the speed of sound, it was in fact the aircraft industry. Even so, it did not occur to them to start a nation-wide campaign in favour of their project. Why should they? To get the money they needed they went to the people with the power to dispense it, they went to the bureaucrats, who in turn formulated proposals for their political 'masters', and in due course certain proposals relating to the project and involving the expenditure of vast sums of public money, sums subsequently to be increased by leaps and bounds as successive estimates were shown to be utterly inadequate, were placed before the people's elected representatives in the House of Commons.

What is noticeable here is that the vote for these monies was duly passed with scarcely any serious public debate outside the legislative chamber at all. The people were never invited to consider the matter, and it is safe to say that not a single local political party, trade union, or co-operative branch discussed it or resolved a viewpoint on it.

Even more noticeable is the fact that it was passed without any serious debate inside the legislative chamber either. It is quite certain that supersonic flight in commercial terms is a non-starter, yet the vast sums involved do not reflect the outcome of a public debate or any desire on the part of the public in either Britain or France even to become involved in the matter at all, yet here is a clear example of technological objectives being pursued to a point where action ceases to bear any relation to reason.

There are two further points about the Concorde affair which are worthy of more than passing note; the first is that the wisdom which opposed the whole project did not spring from hindsight, but from a clearsighted view of the situation and the factors involved from its very inception. Indeed as public expenditure mounted into the kind of regions in which the plane was designed to fly, a special group was formed to oppose the entire project and to put a stop to it as soon as possible. Initially it was composed of ordinary citizens of no particular national note and the Secretary was a schoolmaster who subsequently resigned his job in order to devote himself more fully to the campaign.

The literature put out by the Anti-Concorde project was unequivocal that the plane was a disastrously conceived project which was doomed to failure and gave chapter and verse as to why it was quite unacceptable owing to its cost, its noise, its inherent commercial non-viability, its gross distortion of social priorities, its ecological dangers, and its wasteful use of resources. What is being stressed here is that those in high places who were making the decisions could not plead that the case against the project was not being made, or indeed heard. What resulted was not an adult discussion on the full merits or otherwise of the matter, in which the pros and cons were carefully weighed in a public forum or where public attention was as fully focussed on it as the extent of the commitment of the public purse warranted. The experts, the bureaucrats and the cabinet ministers had decided the project would go ahead. The matter was not, therefore, in their view, open to discussion or even question. So what ensued was a barrage of officially inspired, tendentious, and frequently abusive drivel designed to discredit and silence the opposition. It was a barrage in which the good sense, the patriotism, and even the sanity of the project's opponents were made matters of central concern, and which did not hesitate to suggest that any attempt to discredit the project, which was, it was affirmed, a sure sign of Britain's greatness and technological supremacy, its faith in the future, its belief in progress, and much else besides, was conduct little short of treason. Once the decision had

been taken, a decision on which the public had had no real opportunity to participate or to weigh its merits, any desire by those
responsible for it to ascertain the truth regarding the value of the
scheme gave way to an overriding determination to push it at all
costs.

'At all costs', the phrase can scarcely be described as hyperbolic,
the total development costs of the Concorde at the time of writing
are now approaching one thousand million pounds.[3] These costs are
not recoverable even if the machine is put into commercial production, for there has been no sign at all that any airline is prepared
to pay for a machine even priced simply on production costs alone.

Nevertheless, from the word go, officialdom presented a solid
front of uninhibited confidence in the wisdom of the project and the
media did not hesitate to give it unstinted support. Once again
'conventional wisdom' was being created from the top down with
no meaningful citizen participation at all. Secondly it should be
noted that the opposition to the Concorde project did not come
from within the ranks of the nation's elected representatives; indeed
at no time in the entire record of the affair could a majority have
been mustered in the House of Commons to oppose it, although
from the year of its inception (1962) there have been two Conservative and two Labour Governments. Yet the parliamentary system
is reputed to rest on the opposition being the nation's watchdog and
the House of Commons itself having control over the Executive by
virtue of its surveillance of public expenditure. The essential powerlessness of individual M.P.s and their general failure and inability
to fulfil either of these roles has rarely been more glaringly demonstrated. Even as late as 1972, ten years after the inception of Concorde,
the Anti-Concorde Project, by now one of a number of similar
organisations in Europe and the U.S.A., had an advisory committee
comprising many prominent scientists but which did not include a
single Member of Parliament.

It is quite possible when democratic methods are pursued that

[3] This figure is nearly double the sum spent on new houses by public authorities
in 1972 (£569 million), it is nearly three times the total expenditure on all agricultural support costs and estimated for 1973–74 (£340.8 million), it is more than
the British public's expenditure in butchers' shops in 1972 (£972 million), it is more
than the entire income of British farmers for the same year (£986 million), and is
about equal to the total tax paid by British people on beer, spirits and wine in
1972–73 (£1,070 million). All figures, except for Concorde costs, from the *Economists Diary*, 1974.

big mistakes will be made, that is in the nature of things. But since mistakes are part of life they can also be part of the educational process; yet in this case what lessons were being learned? And, more important, who was learning them? The experts, presumably, have merely learned not to back horses from the same stable; that they have learned to pursue more democratic methods is highly unlikely. The abuse of democratic government processes that surrounds the whole Concorde affair will be noted by a few members of the electorate and that will be all. The powerlessness of the individual citizen matches that of the M.P.s, he will be as powerless to apply the lesson as he was powerless to prevent it.

This form of procedure whereby the normal processes of democracy are reversed, so that the citizens are largely ignorant of vital matters at issue until they pay their taxes is now becoming a standard feature of life in the developed countries. In Britain one may see it in relation to railway closures, a policy which has resulted in the destruction of a considerable proportion of one of the best equipped railway networks in the world. Again the people were not consulted in any real sense on this at all, and most people were ignorant of what was afoot until closures of their local lines were imminent. Discussion is now revolving on a need to reverse this wasteful policy as a result of a rapidly dawning recognition of the ecological dangers of mass motoring, and the sudden awareness of the finite nature of the world's oil resources.

Another example may be seen in the decision over recent years to drop the names of telephone exchanges in many countries, and to substitute all-figure numbers instead. Again the move was from the top down. To the experts in telephone engineering the matter was simple, direct and conclusive; all-figure dialling systems meant that anyone could, in time, pick up the telephone and dial a subscriber in practically any other part of the world. What could be more in keeping with progress, the advance of technology and any other ritualistic phrase used to describe some fresh inroad into our lives or some fresh act of bureaucratic presumption?

When some more perceptive citizens began to complain that they did not want this further advance of streamlined technology at the expense of an enormous increase in the anonymity of their locale by losing the name of their telephone exchange, the high priests of technology were outraged. It seemed to them a typical instance of the kind of sentimental, backward-looking Ludditism which they view as the main enemy of progress everywhere. They moved smartly over to the attack from well-prepared positions of considerable strength (a strength based on the citizen power the citizen no longer possesses) and proceeded to push through their scheme without the least difficulty.

It never appears to have crossed the minds of the bureaucrats and the experts that there were far deeper issues at stake here than mere technological ones, that technology is, after all, for men and not otherwise, and that the idea of community is one of such supreme importance for the well-being of the human race that where it comes into conflict with technology it is surely the forces technology which should give way. Or that the name of a place has meaning and importance for the people who live there, in some ways as important as their own personal names, and no more to be substituted for a number on grounds of technological progress than on any other without their free consent.

Of course, the retention of names would mean 'more trouble'; of course that small minority whose lives are incomplete without frequent recourse to the international telephone system would be inconvenienced, however minutely, but what is this when set against the sociological impoverishment of the entire community, the increasing and dangerous sense of anonymity and alienation, and the desperate sense of loneliness which is overcoming modern man as he becomes more and more the creature of these blind forces? Is it too much to suppose, to hope even, that this decision might have been one for the majority of those in each local community involved, so that instead of wangling the matter through an almost powerless centralised legislature it was necessary for the initiators to run the gauntlet of genuine public opinion? Would not this be a more humanist procedure leading to a more humane society? By the same process postal addresses are now being reduced to codes which have only a bureaucrat's relationship to the name of places and streets, customers in computerised banking systems are losing the names of cheque depositors and payees on their accounts, and no doubt will soon find they are losing their own; numbers and anonymity are taking over in tax offices as names become lost in tax codes, in rating schemes, in medical and welfare structures, car licensing and so on.

Again, no substantial body of citizens has ever agitated for these changes, they are simply made from the top down in the confident expectation that the general body of citizens is too involved in meeting the complex demands of day-to-day living to spare the time and energy to join the easily ignored minority which has the gumption to protest. In the days of Rotten Boroughs' electors at least had to be bribed, today, on all matters of substance, they are merely ignored.

One may see this process at work in many other less specific and more intangible matters. Matters of economic policy, for example, in relation to agriculture. One might suppose that the idea of a small farmer on the land seeking to supply the needs of his family and to produce a modest surplus with which to sell to the market and to obtain the means to buy those other necessaries of life which he cannot produce by his own efforts would represent, even in the eyes of the most besotted planner, some sort of economic ideal.

This is to reckon without modern wisdom on the subject, and in particular without Dr. Sicco Mansholt who was formerly the Vice President of the Commission of the E.E.C. It is doubtful if many small farmers have ever heard of Dr. Mansholt, which does not really matter, for whilst he or at least what he represents, has become one of their biggest enemies they are quite powerless to do anything about the influence he has wielded over their way of life and the source of their livelihood.

The Mansholt 'Plan' for 'European' agriculture includes a proposal to 'retire' two and a half million farmers and farmworkers by 1980, to step up the size of farms, to increase the use of inorganic fertilisers and to promote a host of other measures which, as a way of producing food, are already causing considerable alarm to increasing numbers of environmental scientists.

Dr. Mansholt is, one must assume, not mad, but his proposals are; his difficulty is that his fundamental assumptions about politics and economics were formed at a different stage of our rapidly moving history. Since he is in his mid-sixties when he formulated his proposals they were formed when capitalism was still in its hey-day and when careless assumptions about the need for maximised production on a maximum scale were unchallenged, and when the human and environmental hazards involved had scarcely begun to raise their heads. It just happens that these factors are now staring us in the face and indicating that unless we rapidly change our ways we are heading for a global catastrophe in which millions will starve, and that the era of capitalist and communist global exploitation must now give way to an era of global conservation if man is to survive at all; Dr. Mansholt's ideas are based on a different era.

All this is as may be; what needs asking is what possibility does any small farmer in his capacity as a citizen possess to persuade Dr. Mansholt and his colleagues to drop their mad schemes and mind their own sensible, small-scale, mixed farming business? Put the question another way. What small farmer ever asked Dr. Mansholt to interfere in the first place? Did Dr. Mansholt *begin* by asking the farming community of his native Holland what they wanted and whether they approved of his destructive and pernicious proposals? Did he seek to convert the members of his local political party to his views as a prelude to canvassing a wider audience?

One has only to pose such questions to see how the principles of democracy are being subverted or ignored in a matter pertaining not only to an entire way of life of millions of citizens, but to the most basic and consistent form of human activity which has marked the slow, sporadic emergence of civilisation down the centuries. Surely, of all the symptoms of the on-rushing decline of civilisation now in process, nothing is more incredible than this determined attempt to undermine the ordinary balance of rural to urban life by pushing millions off the land into already overcrowded and decadent urban areas, in the hysterical, greed-besotted pursuit of monoculture of various forms which is already showing signs that it is one of the most dangerous and destructive assaults on the environment, the biotic potential of the soil, the ecological balance, the vital delicate life-support of the planet and the implacable forces of nature, that man has ever mounted.

Our question abides. What can an ordinary citizen in a mass society which takes a curious pride in calling itself democratic do to arrest these insanely dangerous forces? The answer, it would seem, within the present framework of the modern mass society, is nothing at all so long as present assumptions about the economic goals of society and its political and economic structure hold sway.

One need only pause to contemplate how this kind of proposal would have been dealt with in an African tribal village to see how far removed from any pretence to democracy such a process is. One can well imagine in the village how the elders would have listened long and carefully to any such proposals, however they would have deliberated among themselves at seemingly endless length, carefully weighing the *pros* and *cons*, seeking to establish the truth of the matter, the truth as it affected the entire village membership, and how the younger men and the youths of the village would be listening with attentive ears, learning how to consider, how to weigh the various factors at issue, knowing that in due course they too would be taking a full and responsible part in such discussions. To the apostles of Western hustle the proceedings might appear to be interminably tedious and they might be given to wondering again and again just when a vote would be taken that would settle the issue. But no vote would be taken at all. One object of these lengthy discussions would be not to arrive at a parting of the ways but at a general consensus of view of the village as a whole, and only when that point was reached would the proceedings be considered to be concluded.

This surely is a form of democracy which accords fully with the spirit and the letter of the word. Dr. Mansholt and his associates throughout the entire works of European 'unity' surely represent, in their methods as much as in their objectives, a standing repudiation of both. They have power, these people—the power of big money, big business interests, mass militarism and the control of mass party election machinery—and from such a vantage point they can proceed to organise their schemes for the ultimate damnation of civilisation, secure in the knowledge that as far as the ordinary citizen is concerned their power to do so is inviolable and impregnable.

Yet need this be? Does not the citizen have some power to act? To answer this question it may be worth looking more closely at the structure of those bodies which ordinary citizens themselves have created to protect their interests. Outwardly, to take a prominent example, the trade union world is as impressive as it is imposing, with large, efficiently run central offices, immense funds and memberships which may well run to millions, and usually a legally defined place at the negotiating table where issues of wages and conditions of work are settled. Why then is this not enough? Why in fact is the individual who is a member of these mass organisations virtually powerless to affect their course? We are back again to the issue of size and to a further example of how democratic practice becomes a virtual impossibility as growth proceeds. A national union of only a few hundred members would be hard put to operate democratically if those members were scattered over a wide area with little chance of direct communication, for the central leadership group would have an obvious advantage in selecting and shaping the issues which it thought best to raise and the policies it thought best to pursue, whilst the members would be hard put to communicate with each other on the matters of their common concern.

For a union of several hundred thousand, or even a million or more, the enormous centralised machine staffed with full-time salaried executives which is called into being becomes a virtually supreme power in its own right. Indeed, how can it be otherwise? Union branch meetings are notoriously badly attended, a regular gathering of one per cent or less of the branch membership is common and tends to be the field of those seeking a political end, or who may have ambitions of place within the union hierarchy. Hence many of this one per cent will in fact simply be locked in conflict with the existing leadership for the control of the union power, composed for the most part of the ninety-nine per cent who seldom bother to attend a branch or any other meeting. For the ordinary citizen in a mass society will normally only attend his union branch meeting if he is seriously disgruntled about something such as his wages or conditions of work, generally he will leave the burden of running the organisation to others.

Every union has an elaborate facade of democratic decision-making, but since only a few members bother to use it, those who do tend to find themselves waging a constantly unequal battle with the central controlling office over issues of policy, and to find too that the top leadership is virtually a self-perpetuating oligarchy which they can only influence by joining, if they can, and thus become oligarchs themselves. It should be remembered that in Britain, as in many other countries, union membership is obligatory to many jobs and that dues are frequently deducted from the members' salary or wage by the employer as part of his conditions of work and of union membership.

The union leader thus has an assured membership from the operation of the 'closed shop' principle (i.e. all in a given workshop must join the union as a condition of work) and also an assured income for his organisation paid into union funds by the employers. As a free gift he has membership of whom seldom less than ninety-nine per cent take no part or even interest in the day-to-day course of union affairs. But since a union with a mass membership is a potent form of political and economic power, it will be used to further the interests of those engaged in the pursuit of power. This is what it will be used for primarily, all other issues such as wage agreements, overtime, holidays and so on, will be secondary, so that if a proposed agreement on any matter, however advantageous it may be to the workers, is incompatible with the power interests of the union leaders it will not normally be pursued.

It is not simply the indifference of the average member to union affairs which makes him a tool of the leadership rather than vice versa, for even if he were a dedicated union member devoting much of his time to its affairs, he would still find that he and his union brothers would have no real control over the content of the union journal (which is managed of course by the union bureaucracy), over its policy or executive committees, over the organisation of annual conference and its voting procedures, over the union's relationship with the Labour Party and other organisations. The union, like any other mass organisation, is structured for central control and centralised decision-making and on a mass scale just cannot be conducted otherwise, which is why here as elsewhere mass democracy is a contradiction in terms and why any supposedly democratic structure within it is a sham.

It may be argued that this contention is invalidated by the 'democratic' voting procedures which are followed, but again, such voting procedures as are followed are a facade, behind which union leaderships are able to maintain their position and power year after year with ease. The limitation on a member's power in the matter of nominating and voting for the union's top offices become apparent when the procedures followed are examined in detail.

Any ordinary union member can nominate people to any important office of the union, and may well do so at the appropriate branch meeting when the branch mandates its delegates as to whom they shall vote for to the union executive committee, let us say, at the annual conference (and the practice of delegates ignoring their mandate, or even voting contrary to it, is by no means unknown). The individual member at his branch meeting will thus be confronted with a list of nominations from which to select, made by different branches across the country, which may well run into scores or even hundreds of names. How can he possibly choose intelligently?

How can he, ordinarily, weigh the merits of Brother X nominated by a branch in Liverpool, and Brother Y nominated by one on the Clyde? He may by a rare chance, know both personally, but ordinarily his ignorance is part of the price he is paying for being a member of a mass at all; it is part of the price of his anonymity and that of his fellows. But if *he* cannot judge who is who and is commonly reduced to voting, if at all, blindly, there is one element which knows precisely who is who in terms of what it wants, and that is the existing leadership, and their knowledge from their vantage point at the centre, is generally expressed year by year by the ballot results which keep them there.

There are only two ways in which the average member of a mass organisation can escape from his situation of powerlessness. The first is by himself becoming a part of the leadership group, in which case he will cease to be an average member, and the second is by securing the fragmentation of the organisation so that it becomes a loose federation of strictly autonomous and self-governing local groups, in which case it will cease to be a mass organisation.

The democratic theory of mass union organisation, so far as it seems to have one, presupposes that all members will be equally concerned with the affairs of the union. Even if masses of people were conditioned like the babies in Huxley's *Brave New World* to a general level of involvement of this order it would still prove unworkable in democratic terms. Union membership is only one facet of a member's life; he is a citizen, perhaps a parent, a consumer, a traveller, a resident, a taxpayer, a ratepayer; he may be a churchgoer, a football fan, a darts player and any number of other things, all of which involve organisation and all of which, democratic theory assumes, will be subject to his continuous concern and involvement. The logic here is that his evenings will be spent successively at meetings of his union branch, his parent-teacher association, his co-operative shop branch, his political party (which proliferates sub-committees faster than the fission process produces neutrons), his amateur dramatic society, his electricity consumers council, his works social committee and so on. A man would be mad to attempt to keep up with such a round (although some lonely souls do try), so that we may say democracy in a mass society is unworkable simply because most people are sane.

Another leading organisation thrown up by people in mass societies is in the field of co-operative trading. Again we may see how the workings of these bodies on a mass scale invalidates democracy in practice. The writer has a vivid recollection of an occasion when he attended a members' meeting of the London Co-operative Society at which a group of members was seeking to persuade the Society to support a boycott of goods from South Africa by refusing to stock such wares in its shops as a protest against that country's apartheid policies.

He had gone along fully imbued with the myth that the Co-ops were a workers' organisation and that as such they were models of the democratic spirit in practice. In a working lifetime of attending meetings of many kinds and for a variety of political purposes, he was astonished to discover the 'platform', and in particular the Chairman, behaving towards the meeting with an arrogance and an overbearing spirit of rudeness which had not the remotest parallel in any other public occasion in his experience.

Quite clearly the members of the management committee on the platform did not want the resolution to be passed and the chief reason advanced was that it would create trading difficulties in the shops. The rights and wrongs of this issue are not here our concern; what is of importance is to understand why a group of people, supposedly elected by democratic means by the members, felt it could display a boorishness that would not be out of place in a totalitarian structure, and express a manifest contempt for ordinary standards of behaviour and for the people to whom they were behaving, and which incidentally expressed a total indifference to the power of the meeting to seek any redress, which could only (as it did!) spring from a conviction that the power they weilded was unassailable.

Some remarks from the platform led one member to make a brief interjection, the chairman at once threatened to close the meeting if there were any more interruptions. This caused those who were seeking to promote the resolution to make whispered appeals to their friends not to give the chairman any grounds to take such a step—and in the event they did not do so.

But the writer could not help noting this anxiety and wondering about its sources; after all, the people on the platform were dependent on the votes of the people on the floor for their positions of authority as chairman and as members of the management committee; why therefore was it not the platform making a bid to placate the floor, or, for that matter, simply making a pretence of doing so? Why this curious reversal of roles?

The answer here, again, lies in the realities of democracy as practised in a mass society—and in vast metropolitan areas at that, compounded simply of a mass, and where nearly all localised community structure, the only kind of structure able to put teeth into the power of democracy, has been obliterated.

On paper the constitution of the London Co-operative Society is a model of democratic intent, and in a small town where people lived, worked, played, worshipped, studied and carried on all the other aspects of their citizenship within a network of relationships which gave people a fairly personal knowledge of each other, where they were neighbours of a neighbourhood rather than anonymous particles of a mass, such a constitution might work perfectly well in practice.

The key to the situation lay in the fact that the members of that meeting were largely strangers to each other and to those on the platform. When Co-op. elections are held the small group of those already on the management committee are fully aware that of the tiny percentage of those who will bother to vote, most of them will vote for those already in office and whose names, however, vaguely, are familiar to them.

Policy issues relating to the running of co-operative shops are nowadays generally too technical and abstruse to involve the interest or concern of the ordinary member, the result is a considerable empire of economic power run by a board of directors whose power in turn depends on placating a miniscule group of local co-operators who turn up for the regular co-op meetings held at the local branches. When a wider policy issue arises which arouses the concern of members from the general ranks of co-operators, the ruling group is able to ride roughshod over this temporary wave of concern, if it is its interest to do so, knowing that come the next election it will be back in office as a matter of course.

In this instance the co-operative scene has been complicated by the way for some years its elections had become a battle-ground of minority communist attempts to take it over. This has, or had, resulted in ardent lobbying by the communist factions to secure the election of their list of candidates. The non-communists, on the whole, held their ground with ease, but the faction fighting gave an easy handle of abuse to *any* opposition they encountered from any source, they had only to dub it 'communist' to put it out of court for any serious consideration by themselves and their friends. Needless to say the epithet 'communist' was hurled with some frequency from the platform at this meeting even though none of the main proponents of the resolution could be remotely described in such terms.

The interest of the communists in such a takeover needs no explaining, they had in fact done precisely this several times in the trade union world; what needs more focus is how, when the great majority of members might be presumed to be opposed to communism, a communist takeover was in the field of practical politics.

Again we are compelled to a consideration of the mechanics of democracy in a sphere where they are notoriously inapplicable, that of the mass society, or any organisation with a mass membership. As we have seen, the mass just does not involve itself, except on rare and special occasions, with the power considerations implicit in the governance of a mass organisation or a mass society. We need not pause to consider why this should be so, we can only point to the evidence in all such structures that this in fact is how it is.

This means the field is open to any power-seeking minority to obtain the power implicit in the existence of the structure for its own ends. The 'democratic' machinery of the structure becomes then a lever in the hands of those who are most adept at grasping it, at organising voting cabals, at manipulating the media for their publicity purposes, at creating an understanding with that tiny minority of people who actually vote and so on. This is the source of their power, once they obtain it they can afford to treat the *unorganised* mass of members however they see fit; and if long years of wielding power on this basis corrupts them, as it surely must, then a certain disdain and contempt for the views of the general body of the membership, an incapacity even, to extend to it the normal canons of courtesy pertaining to civilised intercourse, can be expected to ensue as a matter of course.

The central point that needs to be grasped is that union or co-operative leaders are, simply because of the size of their organisations in a mass society, only subject, if at all, to the most tenuous forms of control by their memberships.

If the organisations were susceptible to genuine democratic control, a control which can only be exercised on a modest and localised scale, it would then be possible for the members to influence their workings towards goals based on moral considerations. On such a basis it would be possible for the members to consider the wider import of the workings of their organisations in society, to take account of war dangers, resource wastage, pollution and other factors. They would be able to consider long-term factors, as well as the immediate ones surrounding their conditions of work, to take note of the way an increase in wages which is not accompanied by an increase in productivity (assuming that in today's over-developed societies such increases are desirable anyway) will tend to increase unemployment and so on.

But in the absence of any capacity of the members to frame policies based on moral considerations, or even the long as opposed to the short term effects of policy, given the existence of the mass organisation, what else can be expected to supervene on the basis of their virtual powerlessness but a mere struggle for power and place at the top to which all other considerations are subordinate?

The union leader whose members are employed on making weapons of war, for example, cannot concern himself with the global danger of a world war his members are helping to create, he can only pursue his struggle for power on the basis of seeking more jobs and always higher wages for the members and thus on the basis of a complete acceptance of the dominant forces within his society however dangerous, destructive or evil those forces may be. To seek to contract out of those forces would mean he would need to contract out of his struggle for power, which in turn would mean he would simply cease to be a leader.

CHAPTER X

The Nation

We are now in a better position to observe how the factor of citizen power-disenfranchisement in a mass society operates, or fails to operate, when the mass society in question is a nation, a meganation or a continental meganation.

We have noted earlier that the power of a community is something more than a simple summation of the power of each single person in relation to it, so that the whole, far from being the mere sum of its parts, is in fact much greater. We have indicated how in economics this is clearly observable in Adam Smith's famous example of pin production, and concluded that the political division of labour when applied to administration, war, law enforcement, and other factors, not least that of citizen anonymity in a mass society, clearly yields a similar increment over and above the sum of what each person could accomplish separately. The factor which registers such as increment, and which is not susceptible to statistical projection, is of course political power.

Where is this power located? It is not enough to say 'in the people', for, as we have seen, it resides also in institutions such as the monarchy or other titular head of state, the church, in various assumptions about government, and indeed about life in general in certain established customs and usages, in the ownership of wealth, in the organs of administration and so on and so on; but straddling all these factors is that embodied in what Rousseau called 'the general will', the will that is, of all the members of society having a mind to express it regardless of rank, status or influence. Yet even though the general will may be said to have predominated in much of city state life, there was clearly a division between the power it embodied and the power inherent in the other factors referred to above.

What is crucial to a clear grasp of the modern predicament is that whereas in a city state, if the general will did not prevail over the other elements (perhaps because of the dominance of a single family, such as the Medici's in Florence, or of other factors), the city state structure provided at least the possibility for it to prevail. Indeed we may go further and assert that under such a form the occasions when the general will did not prevail were the exception rather than the rule, whereas, and this is the crunch-point, in modern meganations not only does the general will not prevail, but except for occasions of extreme emergency (such as war), it cannot; the occasions when it does being the exception—and generally of a very short-lived duration. In other words, in city states the idea that the preponderance of power was with the people was at least a ballot box possibility, (not forgetting that other forms of democracy as in independent artisan and peasant power, to say nothing of the dispersed nature of economic power were, part of the very fabric of city-state life) whereas as the structure of government grew the power of the people, despite the growth of certain forms of democracy such as the ballot box, ceased to be preponderant. The general will may be said to prevail in a mass centralised state during a war or a major state emergency for a very simple reason; in such emergencies there is a transitory convergence of interest confronting the government and the governed. In this instance the convergence rests on a common imperative, survival.

The tilt in the balance of power away from the people was one of the most momentous events of the modern age and it has gone almost entirely unremarked. It has failed to be noted because the appearance of things nearly always suggested exactly the opposite. The emergence of centralised nation states upon the scene with the growth of mass parties, the rise of trade unionism, the development of co-operative societies, the extension of the franchise, the eruption of modern means of communication, the expansion of knowledge and technology, the humbling of former ruling groups and aristocracies before the power of popular tribunes, the advancement of literacy, the apparent destruction of privilege based on ownership, titles or position and the progressive taxation of wealth, all this and so much more, suggested that the general will was being enthroned at last as the formal arbitrator of the destiny of the people and that a new age of peace, freedom and plenty was being born. The spirit of the age is well caught in the words of one who was virtually the 'progressive' spokesman of his time, "We have dreams; we have at present undisciplined but ever increasing power. Can we doubt that presently our race will more than realise our boldest imaginations, that it will achieve unity and peace, that it will live, the children of our blood and lives will live, in a world made more splendid and lovely than any palace or garden that we may know, going on from strength to strength in an ever widening circle of adventure and achievement? What man has done, the little triumphs of his present state... form but the prelude to the things that man has yet to do."[1]

It is bemusing to reflect that those words were written between the two world wars, and in retrospect it is only possible to marvel at the extent to which men were so blind to the awful lessons of the horrors of the first, for if that war was not a gigantic intimation that our mass societies were no longer susceptible to the control even of those who were supposed to be ruling them, far less of those who were ruled, what was it? The ostensible causes of the First World War were too absurd to carry conviction with a cow-girl, yet the numbers killed and maimed ran into millions; man did not want it to start, and once it started many of conscience and foresight did their utmost to stop it. By 1916 its wasteful, pointless and destructive futility was obvious to anyone on either side of sound mind, yet it dragged on for two years more, wasting the combatants morally, spiritually and physically until it ground to a halt largely because neither side had any further reserves or energy, or even credibility, with which to continue it.

It is not too much to say that this sustained barrage of militarised imbecility wasted much of the moral capital of Europe that had been accumulated over nearly two thousand years, it paved the way directly for the monstrous horrors of the Stalin and Hitler dictatorships, and helped to deprive men of any realistic terms of reference with which to judge the political actions of these sadistic psychopaths; and it led no less directly to the multiplying villanies of government that swarm about our living clay today. We are in the grip of that moral exhaustion still. The roars of life-affirming outrage at the spectacles of governments manufacturing such satanic megadeath devices as a thermonuclear bomb, which Werner Pelz has so aptly described as 'the swollen belly of an emaciated imagination', are non-existent; we have instead the pitiful squeaks of outraged and mostly middle-class morality, the special pleading or the stony silence of political placemen, and a vast fateful, bovine indifference from the masses of people. And yet, by an extraordinary stance of unreason, and a sheer incapacity to digest the lessons of contemporary events, there continues to prevail a common belief that our trend it still towards 'progress' and that there is nothing

[1]H.G. Wells, *A Short History of the World*, Cassell & Co. Ltd., London, 1922.

It may be worth noting that in later editions this quotation was deleted.

fundamentally wrong with the forms of what we are doing, the framework within which we are doing it or where we are going.[2]

In justice this belief has taken some hard knocks and there are numerous signs that it is at last beginning to crumble, when it does it will clearly create some very acute problems of personal response to the social order and there are increasing indications already that to live in a society, especially a mass society, that has lost hope in itself is likely to prove a chilling experience.

How did the transference of the locus of power, once implicit in the general will even as late as the Renaissance city states, come to be located decisively in the grip of centralised controlling mechanisms of society as it has in the modern nation state, which has in turn created this terrible situation? That it has done so is today a matter of common observation and the cause may be traced to a number of factors.

First there is the matter of simple arithmetic. As we have already suggested, a community of one hundred adults may be said to enjoy a one-hundredth share of the power to determine the shape of things within it. Similarly a community of one thousand will enable each member to enjoy one-thousandth the share of the controlling influences, and we may continue to project these figures upwards as far as we may. It is reported that the population of China today is around eight hundred million people, if we assume therefore that its adult population is five hundred million, we may say that each adult Chinese enjoys (if that is the verb to convey the contemplation of so

---

[2]The reader who would like to pursue further the question of *why* big states are more war-prone than small nations is urged to consult a republished work by Professor Leopold Kohr entitled, *The Breakdown of Nations* (Carmarthenshire, Christopher Davies (Publisher) Ltd., 1974) especially chapter two dealing with the power theory of aggression in terms of his concept of 'critical magnitudes'. In this important book Professor Kohr effectively puts the skids under most current theorising about the problems of power, especially in relation to the problems of war and social misery.

One might have thought that the appearance of this book (it was first published in 1957) would have created a tremendous furore in many centres of learning and wherever the pursuit of truth is venerated (drives unfortunately not quite as dualistic as one might like to suppose), instead it was greeted for the most part with silence, a silence which suggests that academics share a common response with politicians when in a quandary. The latter, as we have noted above, when confronted with citizen demands which conflict with their quest for power and the former when confronted with ideas which conflict with their preconceived theories, both react in the same way, by ignoring them.

stupendous a morsel) a one five-hundred-millionth share in the process of government. This absurd conclusion at least illustrates one obvious but continuously overlooked principle, *that a member of a small community enjoys a bigger share in the control of its government than a member of a large one and that on the basis of this principle it is possible to extend the size of a community to a point where the individual share in its control becomes so small as to be meaningless.* It becomes meaningless, be it noted, regardless, as to whether the 'community' in question is a 'free democracy', communist, fascist, welfare-state socialist, liberal or whatever.

Second, we have to look at other factors that attend the process of growth. We stated earlier that a community represents an aggregation of power which is greater than the sum of its individual parts, and we saw how, as the size of a community progressed from a clan to a tribe and thence to a city state, there was a pronounced growth in the number and complexity of the institutions of government conducted from the centre. Clearly, this process of development at the centre is a function very largely of the growth of the size of the community itself and for that reason we should expect, with further growth, that the central functions also continue to grow, *and that since the whole is more powerful than the sum of its parts that this latter growth will be more than proportional to the growth of the former.* There are few analogies in nature for this because it is a profoundly unnatural process. It is as though as body becomes larger and larger it proceeded to surrender all the localised controlling mechanisms of its functions to a single organ of control. It is in fact a form of cancer, where growth takes place where it should not, starving the organs of the body of vitality and proliferating to a point where it chokes its normal functioning to a terminal stage of total collapse.

This development is precisely what has been allowed to happen in the sphere of politics, and it is a development which is now reaching a stage where it is showing itself to be fraught with the most terrible peril.

The reason for this peril again, is a simple one. As power has accrued to the centre it has been removed increasingly from the locus of citizen control, and this has happened, as we have seen, regardless of the formal mechanisms of democracy which have been devised and established in an effort to make citizen control effective. Even in the days of the city state this was a far from healthy condition of affairs, but its potentiality for mischief was checked by the small

scale of the operations of government, the dispersed nature of economic effort and its ill effects mitigated by the extent to which society
was still based on personal relations rather than institutional structures. What is one to say when this process is allowed to operate in
mass societies numbering many millions of citizens, when national
governments commonly abrogate to themselves powers to control
local hospitals, local schools and other local matters, and powers
which also encompass the horrors of hydrogen bombs and other
equally evil devices?

In the mass society such mischief becomes the everyday reality
of its workings. Power is amassed to huge proportions, but the
capacity of the citizen to control it declines to a point where he is
unable to determine any of the basic drives to which its social
mechanisms are subject. Perhaps we should not be so sanguine as to
imagine that so long as the citizen retains *some* power he is able to
influence matters. Mass societies know nothing of consensus politics,
politics that is, where all views are considered and help to determine
the policies adopted. Their procedural approach, where it adheres
to democratic forms, is in fact sharply divisive and based on the
crude realities of the arithmetic of voting. This means that bare
majorities have the say so and there is an end on it; an approach
that, on its own logic, can effectually block the capacity of at least
49 per cent of the people to influence matters.[3]

Even this, however, is subject to an important qualification. The
real power in a mass society is rarely susceptible to an arithmetical
expression or measurement. How can one so measure, for example,
the power that set in train the social catastrophe of mass motoring?
Or the obtuse drive to 'unite Europe'? Or the unreasoning folly of
supersonic aircraft, that 20th Century equivalent to the Pyramids of
Cheops? (The Pyramids may have helped to bring about the economic ruin of the Egypt of the Pharoahs as indubitably supersonic
aircraft are helping to bring about that of the England of the second
Elizabeth, but the death-worship of the ancients had at least the
element of the rational in the sense that death is a condition to which
all men must come, and with which an attempt to come to terms with
is at least explicable. But nobody at all *need* travel at speed, far less
supersonic speed, and the matter is one at which we may be sure

---

[3]Sometimes not even bare majorities. At the time of writing there are at least
six governments elected on minority votes in Europe alone, ignoring the empty
rituals that pass for elections in the communist countries.

only a quite tiny group of the teeming multitudes of humanity is ever likely to travel). In all these and many more matters the citizen has been an accessary after the fact, which has been accomplished by very real forms of power of which, for the most part, he is only dimly, if at all, aware.

Perhaps at this stage of the argument we are able to see a little more clearly how we have arrived at the incredible position where the whole world seems to be moving towards an armageddon of war and social collapse which nobody wants, and why masses of people are equally powerless to alleviate the other terrible evils of our time. We hope that by focussing on this factor of growth it will yield even more clarity, for by the time we reach a stage in growth from the city state to a nation state the nature of the power equation has undergone some changes which are as significant as they are indicative of the real nature of our problem.

The rival groupings within a nation will at first reflect the predominantly personal nature of the relationship we have noted as prevailing within the city state. The groupings will be modest in size and numerous, personalities within each will be well known to one another even, and this is what matters to people, at the base, and decisions will be made in this light. Nevertheless there will be a tendency for these groups to coalesce, to become larger *and fewer*. Since the dissemination of information has become increasingly a matter not of the power of conviction of the disseminators so much as of the power implicit in the technology of dissemination, what Marshall McLuhan refers to when he says 'the medium is the message', and since technology costs money, it follows that information will increasingly reflect the views and interests of those with the money to purvey it.

A number of factors peculiar to the modern era are at work to promote the depersonalisation of society in this way, technology, advertising, the cash economy, the development of the principle of the division of labour to a point where the significance of the contribution of the individual becomes marginal—and thus diminishing his significance as an individual, the dominance of the market by a few firms rather than the dominance of many firms by the market, all this and much more results in society, in this case the nation, being increasingly an expression of the wishes of a few powerful sectional interests rather than of the numerous individuals who make up the citizen body.

It might be thought that in the interests of democracy the development of these new forms of power would lead to new forms of citizen control of them, but in fact the reverse has happened. This control of the institutions in the market was once taken to be enthroned in what was called 'the sovereignty of the consumer'. This has now become very largely the sovereignty of the seller, who pays the advertisers to manipulate consumer preference on his behalf and in his interests.

Above all, in the modern era, there has been a growth in the functions of the central government far beyond that of any comparable growth in the past. The nearest historical parallel to this development may be seen in the theocratic civilisations of, for example, the ancient Egyptians and the Aztecs of Mexico, where the coming and going of ordinary people, the rules and conditions of work, economic objectives, social behaviour and institutions, and much else besides, were regulated by the central government, itself a priestly institution.

One cannot of course discuss the growth in the size of units of government in a vacuum or as some theoretical political abstraction, without much fuller reference to the factor which has not only made the modern expansion possible but which in the modern era has given it a distinctive character and form, and that factor is technology.

Technology and growth are the two dominant leitmotifs of our era, each has a separate significance but each has reacted on the other to make contemporary developments possible, yet despite the extent to which they are so closely intertwined hardly any attention has been focussed on the dramatic changes which the factor of growth itself has had on the workings of political institutions. Obviously a nation in its formative stages can take a variety of forms, monarchical, republican, capitalist, socialist, peaceful, warlike, rich, poor, conservative expansionist and so on, but the one characteristic all of them will tend to acquire increasingly as their populations increase in numbers is an accentuation of different forms of centralised power; the power of the central organs of government will grow at a proportionately faster rate than the growth rate of the nation in terms of numbers and wealth.

Is centralisation caused simply by an expansion of numbers and wealth? An affirmative answer can be ventured to this question with an important qualification, that it is so unless there are powerful structural forces pulling in a contrary direction.

Switzerland is an, it may well be the only, obvious example of this contrary trend. In political terms at least (but not alas, economic), power is firmly lodged first in the small communes, secondly in each of the twenty or more cantons and only residually in the central organs of government. Well into the twentieth century this structure has continued to function smoothly, efficiently and successfully even although all other countries (the writer at least knows of no exceptions) have pursued an exactly contrary path of increasingly centralised power, with the central government taking action and determining policy on a host of matters which would, if the Swiss government sought to act in a similar manner, be regarded by any of the citizens of one of its canons as a fundamental threat to his rights and liberties.

The British or the French governments have ministries of education and local government with wide-ranging powers in these respective spheres, and the citizens of either country regard it as normal, natural and laudable that officials of these centralised ministries should apply the most detailed rules and regulations to local schools or elected (sic!) councils. In the Swiss cantons this would be regarded as abnormal, unnatural and deplorable, as well as being to the highest degree presumptuous, to say nothing of being utterly unconstitutional.

We need to note one curious aspect of size in relation to technology; before the advent of mass technology many nations had all the behavioural characteristics of meganations! Many European countries which once had modest populations of around five million betrayed all the belligerence and expansionist tendencies of a modern meganation. Why should this have been? Why are modern nations of the same approximate population size by contrast so pacific and unwarlike?

It would rather seem that the *effective* size of a nation of 5 million in pre-mass technological times was much bigger; so that the centralised government of Britain enabled it to wage war on France for more than a hundred years, and the same overspill of power was observable in the Balkans and in Scandinavia, where tremendous battles were fought repeatedly on issues about which nowadays nodody knows or cares.

What seems to happen is that technology, especially in the field of communication, makes it easier to find other outlets for surplus energies and at the same time, by increasing up to a point the effective terms of democratic rule, enables the general desire for peace to prevail. Democracy in a medieval centralised nation was impossible simply because the means of communication which alone make democracy in such a unit effective were just not available. This is why at that time the only forms of democracy which prevailed were to be found in some of the city states.

Yet, paradoxically, technology besides *decreasing* in relative terms the effective size of a political unit and providing outlets for surplus energies which might well otherwise be squandered on war, also enables a far greater degree of centralisation of power to be achieved. Indeed for political purposes this may be said to be its principle effect.

The centralisation of power has two contrary effects; as we have noted, by making communication easier it enables those forms of democracy which depend on communication to prevail with greater facility even though the numbers within a political unit may be growing. With hindsight we can judge this in terms of the quarter of a million inhabitants of a city state as compared with the six or even ten million of a modern nation.

But as growth continues in numbers contrary and very powerful *anti*-democratic forces are brought into play. The freedom, for example, of the modern printing press to provide for a large variety of newspapers and journals to flourish in a nation becomes in a meganation the freedom of a handful of powerful press lords or of political bosses and aparatchicks to dominate and manipulate. This technological backlash is entirely a product of growth.

We can see more clearly now why in the modern era the nations, as distinct from the mega and continental meganations, have become increasingly peaceful, liberal and democratic. Scandinavia, Austria, Iceland, Luxembourg, Switzerland, Greece, Holland, Belgium, when did these countries last attack anybody? It is true the last two have been involved in wars with their former colonies, but these were wars of disengagement rather than of expansion and clearly they are unlikely to be repeated. It is also true that many of these countries have been attacked, but that is another story, centring on the power not of nations but of mega and continental meganations.

If a great many nations then, as a matter of general observation, are the only political units that show themselves to be free of the propensity to make war and certain other civic vices such as totalitarianism and backward-looking social practices, we need to ask again and again 'why?'. Is it a mere coincidence, or is it something which we may expect to stem naturally from their *size* that it is the *nations* of Europe, such as the Scandinavians, the Dutch, the Belgians, the Austrians and the Swiss who have taken the lead in abolishing flogging and other gross forms of punishment in both civil and military life, who have abolished the beating of children in school, who have abolished capital punishment, who have led the way in the humane reform of penal institutions, who have been foremost in acknowledging the equal rights of women, of homosexuals, of drug addicts, of racial or religious minorities and others who, in *bigger* units such as mega, or continental mega-nations, have achieved, if at all, only the tardiest practical recognition of their rights? Why is it that in these nations religious or political persecution is unthinkable? Why is it that they have been foremost in championing the arts, in making bold experiments in the field of mental health, in the provision of housing, in social welfare, and in the field of education? Why is the record of these nations not only in self-development, but in giving aid to help other, poorer, nations to develop so relatively generous? Why is the home of the Red Cross in Geneva rather than in Moscow or Madrid?[4] Why have the *nations* of Europe, as distinct from their mega-brethren, seen none of the religious or political fanaticism which has marred the modern era? Why is it that their currencies, almost without exception, have proved far more stable, less prone to violent fluctuations in value on the money markets than the French franc, the pound sterling, the West German mark or the Italian lire, to say nothing of the almighty dollar?

These questions are posed in the main in relation to Europe not because the present writer is more familiar with that part of the world than with any other, but because the countries of Europe have in large measure shared a common history in terms of politics, economics, religion, culture, and philosophy which makes comparison between them more realistic than if the net were spread wider to draw in countries with quite different antecedents, differences which might be held to invalidate the conclusions that

---

[4]It does need to be said however, that Switzerland's record in the matter of foreign aid, for what is one of the most prosperous countries in the world, is simply disgraceful, a matter which may be accounted for in part by its land-locked geographical position and its sheer lack of contact with poorer countries.

might otherwise be drawn.

Nevertheless, and even if one swallow does not make a summer, it is worth drawing attention to the experience of the modest island nation of Mauritius. Despite its small size, a mere 40 miles by 30 in the Indian Ocean, it has a population of rather less than a million, made up of Indians, Africans, Creoles, Chinese and Europeans. Two points of significance strike the visitor to this former British colony; one is that its economy is a developed one to a far greater degree than is the case with other and territorially larger former colonies, the other is the remarkable degree of stability and tolerance that prevails.

There is no instance here of any part suffering from peripheral neglect because it is too remote from the centre. This is not to say that poverty has been abolished, indeed there remains scattered pockets of backwardness and poverty for a very good reason. A small country cannot build a school, a welfare centre, a clinic and a community hall in every village all at once; what is impressive in Mauritius is the extent to which realistic plans have been drawn up for accomplishing such building over a period and the extent to which that programme is already advanced.

The development of the economy is hampered not so much by any dearth of skills and resources as by the unfortunate extent to which, during the colonial period, its entire economy came to be centred on the production of a single cash crop, sugar. Indeed the entire cultivated area of the island is apt to give the impression of being a vast sugar estate.

Nevertheless strenuous attempts have been and are being made towards diversification of the economy, if only to counter the fluctuations in the price of sugar on the world markets. What is significant is the extent to which Mauritius is proceeding to accomplish all this especially when contrasted with the relative failure of territorially vast Zambia, for example, to achieve the same goal in order to reduce its reliance on copper production.

What is at issue here is the extent to which control can be effectively exercised over economic life so as to yield the fruits for which people commonly quest; and what is being emphasised is the extent to which smallness is a far more effective key to riches than bigness which, given the relativity of the factors involved, must need to be seen as giantism. So that just as tiny Denmark 8.5 million can boast a higher per capita national income than

giant West Germany, 61 million, (in 1976 £3,764 as against £3,572
—*The Economist Diary*, 1979) even though Bismarck dallied with
the temptation to join the Zollverein on the grounds that it would
make Denmark richer, it is now possible to see that in relative terms
it would have made Denmark poorer. This of course is the writing
on the wall for all those dreams of European unity, the loss of
control through giantism will make all the members of the new unit
relatively not richer but poorer.

Our central concern here is to extend this analysis from the
economic to the political sphere and to show how the same loss
of control, the same inability to achieve the fruits of sound civic life
as peace, liberty, tolerance and stability ensues when political
growth proceeds beyond a given stage.

It is possible to argue this case from analogy, as we have done
with reference to economics, it is possible to argue it from pragmatic
observation as has also been done; but there remains a need to
argue it dynamically, on its own grounds as it were, and this has been
done so far only in part.

The crucial factor, the most dynamic one that generates loss of
control has to be seen primarily in moral terms. Peace, liberty and
tolerance are, after all, cardinally matters of moral import. We
want peace, for example, because killing and maiming is a morally
abhorrent business which is generally accompanied by many forms
of human suffering.

We need therefore to put under a moral microscope what is
happening when growth of a political unit continues beyond limits
which ensure sensible human and moral control. The key factor to
discern from such a scrutiny is the quest for power. This quest is
present to a greater or lesser degree in every kind of political unit,
whether in a small clan or tribe, or in a continental meganation.

The difference between small and large units would however
seem to amount, in terms of the quest for power, simply to this: in
the smaller unit this quest is subordinated to the problem of ensuring
the general well-being of the unit. We have emphasised insistently
that in the smaller units the mainspring of the forces which shape
their pattern as much as their destiny is the personal, as distinct from
the institutional, relationships of their members. In the small unit
Lenin's 'who? whom?' makes sense, in the larger it becomes simply
'which? what?.'

In larger units institutional power realities come to prevail over personal relations so that all moral questions are bound to become dominated not by considerations of whether A or B thinks this or that policy is right or wrong, but by whether a given policy best suits the power interests of the leaders (or the would-be leaders) or not. Power is all. This, as we have sought to show elsewhere, is simply because in themselves personal relationships are a vital form of control. A village may number three hundred or so people—the modern era speedy travel, television and mass marketing and persuasion have done much to weaken the multiple bonds which combine a village into a unit having a distinct moral character.

But three hundred or so men, or women, thrown together from diverse backgrounds into a military barracks constitute in no sense a village, and such moral character as the unit will have will be drawn from a rapidly dwindling stock of moral capital itself derived, where it exists from the community relationship and conditioning such people may have enjoyed in their home districts.

The moral significance of a military barracks lies in the fact that it is a microcosm of the mass society, the morality of the members of both is endlessly subject to perversion and manipulation by forces beyond their control or even, so conditioned are they, their concern. Hence when a political unit reaches a given size the forms of control which operate from the observance of a common moral code are thrust aside by those forces pursuing the goals of power (of which profit is simply one variety). A would-be leader in a democratic nation must acknowledge the imperatives of the prevailing moral code or else he will discover his prospects of election diminishing.

The leader of a mega or continental meganation dare not (although he must continue to appear to) give precedence to such imperatives without risking his electoral prospects. In these cases the leaders are concerned not with moral suasion or affirmation, but with the quest for power as an end in itself. So they will be concerned with their own and their party's image, with all the tricks and deceit involved in the manipulation of public opinion, with concocting an artfully worded party programme and so forth.

Whence does this difference arise? It arises from the fact that the meganation is no longer dominated, in politics or economics, by personal relationships so much as by impersonal institutional forces. The distinction, although it needs to be made for the purpose of analysis, is not, of course, as clear-cut as a verbal expression might suggest. Britain is a meganation, but the play of the 'old boy' network on public life is still considerable, and quite small nations are capable of demonstrating the kind of thrust stemming from the impersonal relationships of institutional forces as their larger brethren. Woolworths, Bata shoe factories and other multinational institutions are as much at home in nations as in meganations.

Nevertheless the distinction is as vital as it is valid and it leads to the conclusion which may be regarded as the central concern of this essay; that once the forces of profit and power-seeking are released from the constraints of a community moral code then the main drift is for everything to bow to the pressures these forces mount for their self-realisation, and a world dominated by such forces, if only because of the competitive dynamics they embody, is a world out of control and devoid of genuine moral objectives.

What else can ensue but horror? What else are we witnessing as the 20th Century unfolds but a cumulation of horror which contains all the portents of a civilisation gone berserk? Morality is the key to control, but morality in a situation where the relationships of individuals are subordinated to forces embodying nothing more elevating than a lust for money or power becomes simply a facade and but one element in a complex 'rape of the masses'.

The leaders of meganations swear their fidelity to the cause of peace and mount an elaborate and wholly futile (as well as dangerous) exercise in world unity, complete with ambassadors, assemblies, endless committees and sub-committees, a charter and an expensive international staff, meanwhile they do their utmost to join the nuclear club, if they are not already members, a club whose ultimate service to mankind can only be mega-death.

CHAPTER XI

The Meganation

Everything that exceeds the bounds of moderation has an unstable foundation.

Seneca

We have discussed the particular conditions that prevail in the widely differing circumstances of political units comprising the tribe, the city state and the nation; we have seen how even in a nation the effective practice of democracy is made very difficult if government is over-centralised or if communication techniques are poor, we have stressed that the basic condition of democracy is that there should be a large degree of citizen decision-making on the numerous issues that arise in his daily life, and a considerable degree of direct citizen involvement in the process of government itself. We have urged that even in a nation difficulties in making democracy an effective force begin to emerge against which we need to be on our guard; difficulties relating to the monopolising tendencies with which modern technology has so powerfully armed both economic and political forces, so that democracy is assailed by both the dominant belief systems of our times, by both capitalism and socialism to an extent that both become enemies of democracy, not from what they believe, but from the scale on which they act. If all this, and a great deal more, is true of a nation, which we have defined as a political unit having an upward limit of six million or so, what on this reckoning can we expect to find in a meganation, a unit which may contain thirty, fifty or a hundred million?

Would we not expect democracy to become more of an abstraction and less of a reality? That the overspill of power from over-growth would be leading to larger, and therefore less controllable aggregates of military and economic power which would lead in turn to more and bigger wars, and increasingly uncontrollable fluctuations in economic affairs? How does the record stand?

The populations of Britain, France and Germany number 55, 50 and 77 millions respectively and may be taken as not untypical examples of meganations. Both Britain and France have been or were, colonial powers for centuries, and this fact alone means that some degree of their power as meganations must have been weakened by it, especially as advances in technology enabled their power to be multiplied.

But not weakened as much as one might suppose. Despite its vast size the British Empire absorbed astonishingly few British subjects. We need to distinguish between colonial administrators, soldiers and settlers; of the three the last were the most numerous and most important, especially where they eventually became self-governing and ceased to be British. The soldiers were a quite modest factor in terms of size, especially once the colonial power had been established, (by 1946 the number of *British* officers and other ranks in the Army, Navy and Airforce in India was less than eighty thousand), the relatively minute units of the dominant power being buttressed by the recruitment of local subject peoples. And the administrators? The total number of British subjects in the Indian Civil Service in 1946, the year of India's independence, was a mere 1,640.

The figures for other parts of the former Empire must surely be equally miniscule even by these standards, and it is doubtful if the figures for the French colonial involvement differed significantly until the Algerian war.

Germany became a meganation too late in the day to engage in really substantial colonial adventures and what we have to see is that despite this expenditure of national energies, still the major powers were able to engage in full scale wars between themselves repeatedly. Indeed the war-making record of these three meganations in the modern era has been colossal.

Britain was fighting in the Crimea in 1846 and the Boers at the turn of the present century. In 1914 she was a major belligerent in the First World War, a war so ferocious, futile and destructive that even now, more than half a century after the event, the European peoples affected by it have digested neither the reasons which led to it or the full extent of the destruction of their common moral and spiritual heritage it accomplished. In 1939 it was again a major belligerent in the Second World War and its armed forces were used subsequently in Malaya, Kenya and elsewhere in colonial wars.

On the economic front, by the mid 1850's, it had secured for itself a pre-eminent position in the application of technology to industry and this brought it enormous riches as well as giving it a pre-eminent global position in terms of banking, insurance and other lucrative sources of invisible trade. Despite this its agricultural record was one of almost continuous depression and the lot of the newly industrialised workers was so wretched as to have provided half the material for Marx' *Das Kapital*. The First World War rescued its economy from a slough of despond and brought about some improvements in the conditions of its workers, to say nothing of its farming community. It is not for nothing that farmers are reputed to raise their glasses to the toast of 'here's to a wet harvest and a bloody war'.

Immediately after the First World War, despite the fact that the market was flooded with large numbers of ex-soldiers who had received varying types of technical training during the war and who might have well served to have filled the land full of 'homes fit for heroes' as Lloyd George had promised, the economy was plunged almost at once into a depression which led in 1926 to a general strike, and the economy continued to hobble along until it was engulfed in the world economic crisis alleged, but not by the present writer, to have been caused by the Stock Market collapse in New York. The economy continued very largely in the doldrums until armament expenditure began to revive it in the 1930's and during the war period itself. It is worthy of note that in both world wars, despite rationing and shortages, the British workers found themselves enjoying much more generous standards of consumption than they had known in the times of peace which preceded them.

After the Second World War there was a mini-boom under Labour governments which became a maxi-boom under Conservative governments to the extent that ever since British Prime Ministers in a variety of accents have been able to tell the British people 'you have never had it so good'. But good must always be getting better and the 60's and 70's were marked by a hitherto unknown condition where rapidly rising prices were accompanied by a fair amount of stagnation in the economy and an increasing incidence of unemployment.

France emerged from the Napoleonic frenzy weakened and exhausted but also with a government far more unified and centralised under the Napoleonic code than it had ever known and was thus ripe, as soon as its economy had recovered, for all the forms of militarisation that one might expect from its consolidated meganation status.

Germany at that time was an assortment of dukedoms, grand duchies, principalities and small kingdoms numbering more than thirty. As soon as Bismarck unified these sensible small-scale units there followed the Franco-Prussian war of 1870. This led in turn to the second Franco-Prussian war and both sides continued to confront one another in a state of mounting armed belligerence for decades,

and which made the ensuing world conflict of 1914 as inevitable as
the currently increasing armed belligerence is making the third
world war inevitable. The aftermath of the First World War, despite
the moral and physical exhaustion of both countries, saw them
continuing the policy of rearmament and arms accumulation, the
accumulation of military potential which could not fail to erupt
into conflict as it duly did in 1939.

After the Second World War France engaged in a costly and
wasteful colonial war in Indo China and Vietnam and again in
Algeria, to say nothing of lesser colonial wars it fought elsewhere.
Germany by this time had been rather sensibly divided and the
dividing line between the two Germanies became the frontier of
the global cold war which has ensued. East Germany became an
active party in the Warsaw Pact, West Germany became, (as did
France), a major partner in N.A.T.O., and it is probable that the
respective armed forces of East and West Germany are larger and
more powerful than were the forces of united Germany under Hitler
in 1939.

Economically both the peoples of France and Germany, despite the
expansion of their economies before the First World War, endured
a quite unnecessary degree of economic hardship and suffering, especially among the industrial workers. After 1918 the economies of
both countries virtually collapsed, very largely owing to the inanities
of the Treaty of Versailles. Like Britain their economies were also
submerged in the world economic collapse of the late 20's, but
Germany began to recover much more quickly because she began to
prepare for the Second World War more ruthlessly and determinedly
and she was helped in this by having an economic wizard at the
head of her affairs in the form of Dr. Schacht. It is noteworthy that
in this period of the 30's the German economy was already virtually
a siege—one in the grip of a totalitarian political party. This meant
that the economy was subject to a degree of control and direction
which was only realised in other countries after hostilities actually
broke out and it meant that the employment of national objectives
was facilitated to an extent that would have been impossible in the
free market economy of any other meganation. A similar result was
achieved by Mussolini in Italy. After 1945 the French economy
began a period of slow expansion which by the 50's became extremely
rapid until it ran into the quicksands of inflation and rising unemployment. The German economy arose Phoenix-like from the ashes

of its total defeat in war and a subsequent policy by the victors of industrial dismemberment, when much of Germany's heavy industry, its factories and docks, were deliberately blown up, proceeded to accomplish what the Germans called a *Wirtschaftswunder* and what lesser mortals call an economic miracle. Aided by sizeable investment from the Marshall Plan, Germany's industry soon became one of the most modernised and best equipped in the world and within a couple of decades was able to secure a pre-eminent trading position even among its former victors.

Today the economies of all three countries, increasingly being made to interlock through the medium of the European Common Market, are confronting problems of prosperity coupled with inflation and unemployment they have shown not the least sign of being able to resolve.

In all three meganations there has been a sharp increase over the past few decades of government intervention and control at the expense of citizen democracy. In both France and Britain there has been instituted a changeover which, rather bemusingly, has been labelled 'local government reform'. What in fact has been accomplished is the virtual destruction of local government and the establishment of large-scale centralised provincial government machines which have usurped many of the localised decision-making powers of villages, city wards and small towns' powers the latter had exercised previously for centuries.

The same is true of many other aspects of citizen life, whether one looks at the forms of taxation, of education, social welfare, trade, health, transport, housing, one finds the long nose of central government increasingly inclined to poke and the net result of this is, as it can scarcely fail to be, a pronounced erosion of the liberties of the subject.

What this brief survey of three European meganations surely serves to show is, whether we look at their military adventures their economic performance, that for all essential purposes they are out of control, their governments are quite unable to employ their respective national resources for purposes which are rational and constructive, or which give their peoples any long-term prospect of peace, bread or liberty. The prospect instead is one of war, economic dislocation and the onward march of totalitarian forms of domination and control by government of the ordinary citizen.

The factor of control is linked directly to that of size. If a nation, as we have defined it, finds it difficult to order its affairs in democratic terms because of its growth as compared to the size of a city state, then the answer to this major problem stares it in the face; either it should fragment itself into city-state size units in order to reap the advantages of both democracy and control that such a human scale is able to yield, or it should go for a policy of maximum devolution and non-centralisation of power of all kinds, so that only the most tenuous and residual forms of power remain at the centre.

Most nations have in fact pursued a policy almost precisely the opposite to such a prescription and have been even advanced to such undemocratic lunacies as *national* education systems, *national* social welfare policies, *national* police forces and so on, all in the name of democracy of course.

Again it might be thought that adhesion to democratic principle, the desire for some effective control in the ordering of its affairs so that war, inflation, unemployment and other evils were avoided would lead the peoples of meganations to insist even much more sharply on a policy of devolution and non-centralisation.

Tragically, despite these dangers, they have not simply followed the path of the nations, they have pursued it even more intensively, so that if we want an explanation of why a monstrous psychopath like Hitler could regiment an entire German generation to his will for war, indoctrinate millions of children with his evil thinking without having to obtain the permission of countless autonomous localised school boards to gain access to them, to telegraph his orders and instructions across the meganation without having to secure permission from numerous autonomous, localised and demo-cratically elected consumer councils to do so, and similarly from local railway board or highway authorities, to move his troops and supplies, it is surely here as much as anywhere.

The horrors of the twentieth century stem not from the excesses of democracy (which can be real enough) but from a failure to apply it in terms which can make it effective.

We have here too an explanation of the unbelievable imbecility with which the brainwashed millions of the meganations were induced to accept, and even vote for, membership of the European Common Market. Wordsworth was moved to write an ode when the Napoleonic hysteria induced the senators of the proud, rich, republic of Venice (the 'Eldest Child of Liberty'), with over a thousand years of continuous democratic rule behind them, to vote for its own extinction.

"...Men are we, and we must grieve
When even the Shade of that which once was great,
Has passed away."

No Wordsworth, possibly not even a Shakespeare or a Milton, could do justice to the tragic drama of the contemporary European folly where its nations and its meganations are blindly surrendering such prospects of democratic control as they still retain into the oligarchic maw of a centralised European power which will simply multiply the mischief-making possibilities of war-making and economic anarchy.

The lessons writ large in the record of the continental meganations as already exist have no illumination for them; an awesome capacity, linked to a no less awesome propensity, for making war, a sheer inability to organise economic forces for sensible economic goals, so that even where riches are amassed, as in the USA or India, they simply mock the misery of irredeemable poverty mutiplied a millionfold and more within their own borders and which they are incapable of ameliorating, mass unemployment, currency fluctuations which make a mockery of wage levels, and the always imminent possibility of a catastrophic economic collapse which only war or war preparations seem able to avert.

Is this what the people of Europe want? Of course not, but he who wills the ends must will the means. We now know to our bitter cost that peace and plenty are not fruits for free picking, however deep the desire in men's hearts for them may be, they are, if men so will it, products of human management and control which can only be achieved through a human scale of political and economic organisation.

In any case, we need to recall that the dynamic of democracy springs from a need for the workings of society to be subject to the control of the generality of its members so that those workings may be responsive to their moral promptings and expressive of their value judgements.

One result of any form of growth in size is to make this more difficult, and as growth continues beyond certain limits, to make it impossible; for the concomitant of growth of any social structure is that it becomes more impersonal in its operations. This means that instead of the citizen body making continuous judgements, forces are set in motion, generally on the basis of elitist minority judgements, which have a momentum of their own and which have the effect of, as it were, suspending the general judgement or of making it powerless or irrelevant. This can be more clearly seen if we take two extremes. A candidate for public office in a city state will generally be known to his supporters in the round; they will know him as a family man, an employer perhaps, a churchgoer, a patron (or not) of the arts, and his views on a multitude of other questions not directly related to the question of office perhaps, but relevant to their estimation of him as a human being. They will *know* as much as they know anyone in their circle, whom they are electing. It will be noted that the elective process is assumed to be based on this kind of knowledge, or else how can the choice be assumed to be meaningful?

Contrast this with the opposite extreme, with the election of the President of the United States, a country of 260 million people. The presidential candidate makes appearance on television, doubtless carefully rehearsed, and at this and other public occasions he makes speeches.

Does he write them? Are they his own thoughts? And if they are, to what extent are they assumed in order to meet some vote-governing exigency of the hour? Is he a man of honour, or a crook? Does he go to church, and if he does is this a matter of conviction or electoral convenience? What things are capable of making him really angry? Is he an alcoholic? Is he a good family man? In short, what is he really like? How many people in a multimillion electorate can possibly know? Most of them in fact have to be content with an 'image', an image sedulously concocted by specialists in the art of projection of such matters through the mass media. Such people will write his speeches, draft messages for him to sign, and arrange for him to be seen publicly in electorally propitious situations. They will inform the media what the candidate does or does not eat and drink, so that whilst he may be a consummate *bon viveur* they will not hesitate if it suits the book, to project him as a spartan ascetic who lives frugally on a diet of porridge and peanuts, nor will they hesitate to reverse the picture if the terms are otherwise and need arises.

Whether the image projected corresponds to the real man or not is a matter of complete indifference to the projectors, who are in business to secure votes regardless of any consideration of truth or falsehood; what is important is that the electorate is convinced he corresponds with what they want to see in him. To this end the projectors will be ready to fake his utterances, his beliefs, his ancestry, his daily habits, his life-style, his medical history, his physical condition, his political record, and as he is prepared for the T.V. cameras, with a judicious use of cosmetics, even his appearance.

A stranger is elected by strangers, as a democratic exercise it is a total travesty, for it repudiates the cardinal assumption of any democratic elective process, which is that the electorate should know who (or what) it is voting for (or about).

In the absence of this knowledge popular participation as a process becomes a ritual devoid of all but negative significance as the rival candidates, subjected to the same conditioning process, create an all too accurate impression of tweedledum and tweedledee, and confirm that the real locus of power lies elsewhere than in the hands of the voters *or even in the hands of the man they elect.*

If this conclusion should appear questionable we might do worse than reflect that one U.S.A. party alone appears to require an election fund of \$45 million simply to elect the President.[1] And one authority, described in *Time* as ' . . . the nation's leading scholar on campaign financing,' whatever that may mean, has calculated that the total cost of campaigning for the United States' 500,000 elective offices in November, 1972 was of the order of \$ 400 million.[2] Most of this money is spent on advertisement, and what else is advertisement in a mass society but deception? Nor should the contrast be overlooked between the men in the Greek city state so reluctant to take office that special rules are devised to ensure everyone takes turns to serve, and that of the spectacle of men competing for high office, spending vast fortunes and organising tremendous campaigns of lies and pretence simply in order to secure election.

Next we have to consider how the pattern of economic interest impinges on the democratic process as growth proceeds. In a small-scale society it will be more normal or small-scale economic interests that dominate events. Production at this level tends to consist of the efforts of a large number of small producers rather than a small number of large ones. Since the productive process itself will thus, because of its small units, be more human-centred, given the close inter-relationship of political and economic factors, the essential humanism of the political structure will also tend to remain intact.

[1] Henry Fairlie, *The Spectator*, 9 September 1972. Mr. Fairlie is referring to the Republican Party.
[2] *Time*, 23 October 1972, p. 20.

Of course, there have been exceptions to this, and some very prominent ones, but we are seeking to detail here the general trend, and a
general trend in human affairs to which no exceptions could be cited
would cease to be such and have instead the character of an immutable law, and it is possible that the only immutable law about the
general characteristics of human communities is that they have no
immutable law.

Again, with the growth of the size of the community, there tends to
be a growth in the size of the economic units which serve it. Or vice
versa, for initially at least this is very much a business of trying to
decide whether the chicken or the egg came first. At a later stage
there is no such difficulty, as may be seen at the time of writing in
the attempt to achieve the political unification of Europe by its
dominant economic interests. As we have noted elsewhere, the
immediate result of an increase of economic scale means that instead
of affairs being dominated by the personal relationship of the members of the community, *and thus subordinate to their moral judgements,*
they become dominated by the vastly more powerful impersonal
forces of the market. Inevitably, if it has not done so already, this
creates powerful pressures to make the same kind of impersonal
relationships prevail in politics.

At one time in economic matters men dealt with each other on a
personal basis, or at least were encouraged to, in terms of moral
prescript based on personal production and service as well as within
the constraints of formidable social pressures, and even legal sanctions, according to such concepts as a 'just price'. Company A
now orders goods from or signs a contract with Company B strictly
in terms of prevailing market conditions (which the activities of
both are helping to determine) and may otherwise be perfect strangers to each other.

In more general terms we may assert that the growth of scale in
economic units reduces the significance of the individual contribution
of both the producer and the consumer.

Small units of production nowadays bespeak an era of master
craftsmen, each of whom would be the master not only of his craft
but of the workshop in which he practised it. This microcellular
structure of industry was in the nature of things far more stable and
assured than anything of which we have experience today. A single
craftsman may not be able to produce the quantity of goods within
the capacity of a modern factory (any more than the latter can

achieve the quality within the reach of the former) but neither did his work result in sudden and violent fluctuations of prices and employment which the dominance of big units today sets in motion as a matter of course.

It would be tempting to suggest that the small-scale craftsman plays a larger role and is thus more significant, in the affairs of his local community than a factory worker, but the element of truth indubitably present here is obscured by the fact that we are not comparing like with like and that in general terms factories do not belong to an era of community life but to that of the mass society, and the mass society is an expression not so much of the vitality of community life as of its negation and destruction, a result the factory has largely helped to accomplish. This question of the greater significance of the individual in smaller units holds true even for the larger number of workers who as the jargon has it, are semi-skilled or unskilled. The errand-boy cum floorsweeper cum tea-maker in a small workshop may seem of little overall account, but he plays a role, dignified by the fact that he is needed to do so, which makes his individual contribution something to be taken into account in any appraisal of its functioning. He may be a school drop-out, he may be semi-literate or even a half-wit, but he has something to offer his workmates which they are happy to receive, he counts for something in the general scheme and his need to be needed is fulfilled.

The modern factory will not need an errand-boy, or thousands like him, as big brother on the intercom and the loudspeaker replace him, the floor may be swept by some vacuum machine, and another machine may be there to dispense some rather dubious cordials or instantly tasteless cartons of what used to be called tea or coffee. By now the 'boy', he was of course often a man, if his wits are in doubt, is kept in some institution full of those similarly afflicted where the cost to his former workmates through their taxes of maintaining him there is greater than that of having one of their children educated at Eton. It is possibly a sign of the times that at least one specialist in mental health has raised the question whether it really is the patients in these institutions who are mad rather than the medical and service staffs who run them or society at large which establishes them.

The significance of the worker in the work process may appear to be a minor question which need detain nobody, but it is at least possible that its importance is such that the way in which it is answered may make or break a civilisation. The factory worker in a mass society may seek to buttress his dwindling significance, his instant replaceability in a mass production process where the significance of machines is far greater than his own if only because they cost more, by joining a trade union. But the union itself is another mass organisation and as such far from affirming his individual significance will simply emphasise its opposite. It is not for nothing that those who work on the factory floor are no longer known as workmen, with brutal but quite unconscious accuracy they are described as 'hands'. A modern factory does not need the full humanity of a worker, how can it when it needs to slot the worker into a pattern of production which can only function by making all the essential aspects of his humanity superfluous?

It needs to be emphasised repeatedly that the central issue here is not that of technology as such, but the scale on which it is used. Work and production are essential features of any civilisation, and technology is an obvious aid to both, but to allow technology to assume a dominant place in the scheme of things at the behest of annual exercises in double-entry book-keeping and at the expense of the general humanity of those who work is to raise a question about the goals such a civilisation may be setting itself. Indeed a civilisation which has already hared off a long way along this path may be said to be doomed simply because it is indicating yet again that it is out of control. That control can only be regained when Protagoras' wisdom in asserting 'man is the measure of all things' is acknowledged and when industry is organised to fit the needs of man, as distinct from a situation where man is expected to fit the presumed needs of industry.

We are back again to considerations of size and scale, and if this is true of man in his capacity as a producer, it is no less so in his capacity as a consumer. The essentials of democratic life have become so obscured by contemporary political and economic sophistries that we are in constant danger of forgetting what in fact they are. Beside that danger the risk of being repetitive on the score must be accounted a minor one as we reassert that democracy is a business of choice and free choice at that. No assembly elected or otherwise, can possibly embody or control the entire field of choice confronting the citizen and those which presume to try, such as in the so-called communist countries, merely indicate that they are moved by a spirit as profoundly anti-democratic as any other example the long history of human societies can possibly show.

In the field of consumer choice it is the trends which have developed over the last couple of generations in the capitalist world which we need to scrutinise in terms of the democratic ethic, especially since the 'communist'[3] world is always rather ineffectually seeking to emulate them.

These trends may be summarised briefly as moves towards continuously greater standardisation of wares offered, a continuously increasing restriction of choice and a pronounced shrinking of the area of local community involvement in the management and control of local consumer marketing and merchandising.

It is possible today to travel across the entire length or breadth of even a continental-sized meganation such as the United States and find oneself confronted with an almost identical range of merchandise in the shops. This will be a matter of pride to those who promote it, they will point to the ease, convenience, cheapness and economy with which people are able to shop, able to recognise instantly the range of wares offered so that quick decisions are facilitated. What they will not point to is the dreadful cultural impoverishment that is entailed in such standardisation. Until the modern era practically every locality in almost every part of the world could boast of its own distinctions in matters of dress, cuisine, pottery, furniture, architecture and so on. However tragic the loss of these distinctions may be what we need to note here is the power ordinary people have lost to create what were in effect their own cultural patterns. They are no longer creating markets to meet the needs of their tastes and preferences, markets are being established by non-localised forces to manipulate people's tastes and preferences into standardised artifacts as best enables profits to be realised. Power is not in the hands of the majority of people, it is in the hands of non-localised profit makers. It is doubtful if a single text-book on politics in any country has noted the political implications of the loss of power here by people and the way it has accrued to an unrepresentative and non-elected minority.

[3]The very language of modern politics is so full of falsehood that it is impossible to use the words in common currency without some kind of qualification. The word 'communism' is a good example, for what is indicated by the word is the precise opposite to what those countries which are supposed to be applying it do in practice. Communism, having things in common, a common understanding and consent, a common share in the power of rule, these are the last things we can hope to see prevail in those countries which have purloined the name.

It might well be argued that this new, power minority is indeed elected, since it is elected by the shareholders of the companies who manage the operations pertaining to this result. The point needs to be answered, if only because the conduct of private companies in relation to the powers of the individual shareholders represents a model of what is happening in the direct political process itself. The government of a company, the board of directors, is usually elected by the shareholders of an annual general meeting; the pattern of shareholding will differ from company to company, at one extreme large blocks of shares may be held by a tiny group of owners, whilst at the other extreme there is the theoretical but rather unlikely possibility that there will exist as many shareholders as there are shares. We may take it that most companies have a pattern of share ownership somewhere between these two extremes, but what does shareholding in terms of voting and decision-making on a democratic basis (and as carefully provided for in-company law) mean in practice?

As far as the ordinary individual shareholder is concerned his power to influence the policy of the company is virtually confined to the annual general meeting. The key nature of this meeting is such that certain minimum conditions for its conduct are legally required to be observed; due notice must be given, the accounts presented must be properly audited, elections to the board must follow a prescribed procedure and so on. Given the importance of the meeting in terms of the disposition of the power of control in the affairs of the company it might be thought that it would be extremely well attended, but what in fact happens?

Precise figures are not easy to collate, but the general experience is that company meetings are seldom attended by more than a handful of shareholders and those that do attend are often relatives of the directors and who may be looking foward to the lunch which is likely to follow the exceedingly brief proceedings as much as any other item on the agenda. The meeting is generally regarded as a legal formality which must be processed with the minimum of fuss and the maximum despatch and any ordinarily competent company secretary will normally see to it that fifteen minutes will more than suffice to cover the entire proceedings.

There are of course, exceptions to this, when annual general meetings can become crowded and perhaps heated affairs, the company's situation may be in the doldrums, there may be a juicy take-over bid in the offing, the board may have entered into some very unpopular (i.e. unprofitable) arrangements and so on, but a discussion on general trends need not be detained by exceptions, what merits emphasis is that ordinarily shareholders are content to take no part in the running of companies in which they have invested money, none whatsoever; and it should be further noted that any particular minority shareholder faced with this massive indifference of his fellows, would find it very difficult to take any such part even if he sought to do so. So that power is firmly lodged in the boardroom and only residually and legally with the shareholders; what then is that power, in the field of merchandising, being used for? It is being used of course to maximise profits and to this end it needs to achieve the maximum economies of scale that may be realised through growth, and the elimination of as much market uncertainty as possible through the establishment of standardised products. The economies of scale to be achieved may, as common sense suggests, be wholly illusory beyond a certain point of growth, but even if they are it does not matter since growth in itself produces another fruit no less sweet, power.

The advantages to the seller of marketing standardised wares are equally obvious: accounting systems are simplified, advertising budgets can be streamlined, price policies 'rationalised', and the costs of stock movement and control reduced. And if, as in the case of foodstuffs, the shelf life of standardized products can be lengthened, yet another market uncertainty is either reduced or eliminated.

This factor of the quest for longer 'shelf life' in foodstuffs has, incidentally, sparked off one of the greatest revolutions in eating habits in human history. Any foodstuff has a natural life span during which it loses its freshness, stales and finally begins to decay. In the nature of things, since the human frame is a part of life, it needs life to sustain it, and not least in the foodstuffs it ingests; but in general terms food which has been 'preserved' has less vitality, less 'life', in it than fresh food. So that all tinned and almost all 'processed' foods which are processed to ensure a longer shelf-life, are denuded of some of those mysterious, elusive, ineluctable and unanalysable forces which constitute life itself.

What in fact is the difference between life and death? Nobody, thank goodness, knows; and how much wiser we would all be if we did, even though when we meet either state we are able to recognise it at once. So preservatives are added to wheat flour after it has been robbed (there really is no other verb which will serve here) of its natural and rough elements which keep the digestive tract in tune, milk is made inert, cereals are subjected to tremendous steam pressures and baking processes to create 'corn flakes', 'shredded wheat' or similar fantasies which are devoid of any possibility of nourishment, and so on and so on. The result is a mass ingestation of products as far removed from being real food as it is possible to imagine.

But they do have a longer shelf life! They may, as the evidence increasingly suggests they do, cause constipation, haemorrhoids, ulcers, varicose veins, heart disease, dental decay, baldness, cancer, the impairment of sight, sound, smell, and hearing, and speed up the degenerative processes of the body to an astounding degree (how many people of fifty in developed countries today look less than seventy, or, to allow for the extent to which familiarity breeds insensitivity on the point, how many people of seventy in undeveloped countries where a simpler diet prevails, look more than fifty?).

Our main concern here is not so much with the disastrous change in dietic habits which has occurred over the last two or three generations, but with the forces which have promoted it. Again we are not observing a process of citizen decision-making at work, we are observing a process of mass citizen manipulation largely through the medium of advertising.

It is true of course, that each person does have certain powers of independent judgement, but for judgement to operate effectively it needs to be fed with truth, not lies, and what the success of the advertising industry demonstrates is that falsehood can be so sedulously propagated that it ceases even to be questioned and becomes part of the prevailing orthodoxy. Most hospitals, for example, serve unnatural and devitalised foods such as white bread, white sugar, processed breakfast cereals, tinned foods and so forth, with no apparent awareness that they are undermining the health of their patients and doubtless aggravating the symptoms that such dietic folly promotes and what may well have brought them to a hospital bed in the first place.

It may be supposed that the wide range of foodstuffs on display in modern 'super' markets is sufficient to indicate that far from restricting the field of choice they enlarge it. This conclusion is illusory, for not only has the variety of retail outlets sharply diminished, and this itself bespeaks a loss of citizen power to choose and decide of considerable dimensions as he finds he is left with a modest number of stores which are often national semi-monopolies, these giants do not even try to provide the variety of wares formerly available.

One has only to think of a modest market town in France today, where the small shopkeeper still thrives, albeit with increasing difficulty, and to note how one 'crémerie' alone will be retailing nearly a hundred different cheeses, or to reflect on the astonishing (at least it is astonishing to we children of progress) variety of localised foodstuffs which were once freely available and which have now disappeared in the maw of standardised retailing. Where are the York hams, the Aylesbury ducklings, the Cornish pasties, the Romford patties, the Chelsea buns, the Eccles cakes, the Melton Mowbray pies and so on and so on, vanished or now debased tokens of bygone glories of regional cuisine which once flourished? Or the enormous variety of fruits and vegetables which are literally ceasing to exist as standardised hybrid varieties replace them?

It may appear that the power of choice in consumer markets is of a different order to that of political power, and even if this were true there is the danger of assuming too lightly that political power itself can determine wholly the nature and pattern of the social order. The Russian Empire is just about as totalitarian as it is possible for any modern political unit to be; for well over half a century it has waged a ruthless and unspeakably cruel struggle to stamp out private economic enterprise, artistic freedom and religious belief, yet the signs are multiple that capitalism in one guise or another is slowly gathering strength and momentum within its borders, that most of the work of its secret police centres on attempts to throttle increasing manifestations of artistic independence, and religious activity continues to grow, with churches packed to the doors Sunday after Sunday.

The fact is that power in human societies is all of a piece, and where the power to decide is usurped, sidetracked or repressed in any one part of the body, forces are set in motion which will come to prevail over the rest unless the unaffected parts assert themselves with sufficient vigour to reverse them. Mass societies are afflicted everywhere with increasing areas of non-citizen participation and decision-making, like the eruption of some noxious plague sores on the body surface; we need to ask just how far this process can go before the body succumbs, whether government is based on freely elected parliaments or not. At any rate nobody can legitimately complain if as a consequence the citizen is less and less involved in or concerned with the governing process.

The most important aspect of the monopoly developments in merchandising is the loss of local control and decision-making involved in the management of local enterprises. It was not so long ago that the local high street was dominated by the family butcher, the family grocer, the family baker and so on; whether the adjective implied the concern was owned by a family, as it invariably was, or that it served local families, as of course it did, is of no great moment; what is important is the extent to which it was for centuries a self-sustaining system of localised ownership, management, education (through shop apprentices), and community service. How often do we learn of councillors, aldermen and mayors who were also local tradesmen and who were also active in numerous other local spheres, from restoring the church roof, organising hospital carnivals to raise funds, or leaving handsome sums to local charities? The standardisation of the face of the local high street, so that it carries the same names and sells the same wares wherever one goes, involves a degree of impoverishment of local community life and culture which as yet has scarcely begun to be computed. What we have to note here is the brutal fact that it also involves a quite crucial loss to the local community of political power.

When localised control prevailed the citizens themselves decided the shape and pattern of local merchandising; they decided which shops should or should not be patronised and their demand preferences were one of the blades of a pair of scissors (the other being supply) which helped to determine prices. The forces of the market were part of a citizen weapon of attack as well as of defence. Today they are neither.

A similar degree of citizen involvement and power was to be observed in political affairs, citizens with a grievance would put matters right directly, or chivvy action from their elected man, with always the prospect of a mass demo if they achieved no result (within full hailing distances of all the government officials involved in the grievance), today they will be referred to a government department, the appropriate officer of which is away at a conference, or otherwise engaged, they will be assured eventually that the matter will be looked into, or worse, that it *is* being looked into, which means it is *sub-judice,* which means there can be no action,

no comment even, until the investigation is complete. The department concerned may well be hundreds of miles away in a remote
capital, the grievance may require legislation, the legislature itself
may well be in recess, the legislation may involve other matters
which effectively inhibit action. What are the other matters? It
may not be in the public interest to disclose them.

During its ensuance, to take a specific example, a majority of
the American people were reported to be against the continuance
of the Vietnam War, that majority was spread across the biggest
part of a continent two thousand miles across. It was in dispute
with its own administration, but how could it register its opposition?
Especially when both established parties were representative of
background forces (which supported the war) on which they
were dependent for sums like $45 million simply to get their own
men elected as president?

We need to bear in mind, astonishing as it may seem, the war
never really happened. Only congress has the legal right to declare
war and this it never did! The point illustrates with great eloquence
the futility of supposing that once a political unit exceeds a certain
size, written constitutional provisions are sufficient to guarantee
that events will be governed by them, or that value considerations
will prevail over the quest for power or the actions men take in its
pursuit or protection. So, should they, could they, the members
of this numerous war opposition, have formed a new party? Modern
history is equally eloquent of the futility of seeking to organise a
mass political party around a single issue, especially when the
issue is as transient as a war, even a major war; for mass political
parties tend to be representative, after a fashion, of long-term
entrenched interests having a significance which is apt to be measured generationally. For reasons which will be discussed in greater
detail, this is an almost inevitable aspect of mass politics, and there
is not a single instance whereby a mass party has been successfully
launched on a single issue once the field has already been occupied
by established parties. The war was not, in the event, terminated
by the pressure of 'public opinion' in the U.S.A., but by the stark
realities of military defeat in the field. The British people were
impaled on a similar hook on the issue of joining the European
Common Market. Until the mass persuaders set to work, financed
by some dominant economic interests, the majority was decisively
opposed to this step, but neither of the two main parties would

unequivocally support their views so that the issue went against
its wishes by default.

To whom could the U.S. citizen who sought to end 'his' country's
involvement in the Vietnam War turn? What influence could
he have exercised to prevent that involvement in the first place?
There was literally no one to whom he could turn, he is trapped
by the impersonal forces that dominate mass societies and which
pursue courses which are boundlessly indifferent to citizen wishes
or well-being. The war-involvement situation simply grew out of the
basic forces which certainly do not include the power of the people;
for to these forces the 'power of the people' is simply another factor
to be juggled with as they quest for their own sectional ends. It
was these forces which infiltrated U.S. power into Vietnam and
the troops there were called 'advisers' throughout.

This does not mean the citizen is totally powerless or totally
without recourse, but these are matters which need to be reserved
for discussion at a later stage when a clearer picture of the predicament has emerged.

In the light of the foregoing, we now need to ask, what is the
object for which this power-at-the-centre is used? In the case
of the smaller-scale communities prior to the city state there is no
problem; such power as resides at the centre is used to secure and
promote the well-being of the members as a whole. Whether
in fact it does so is not a matter which need detain us now. People
can always make mistakes about what constitutes the well-being
of their society, but the important thing to note is that it is rare
for some sectional interest to intrude itself between the members
of society and the governing mechanism. When we reach the stage
of the city state such intrusion becomes common-place. Despotic
princes, presumptious political prelates or military or merchant
parvenus will arise, and the renaissance is studied with its Medicis,
Fuggers, Richelieus, Wolseys, and similar characters. Yet for
all their apparent power and the harm they could and frequently
did do, their influence was of an order which the society of the
period could contain. A man might amass great riches, he might
use his power to engage in destructive wars, or he might pursue
some dreadful religious inquisition; but whatever the form of
imposition or exaction, it seems, in retrospect at least, even if the contemporary people—especially the victims—had an understandable
disposition to think otherwise, to have been an activity which was

marginal to the main business of society. The record may appear
to speak in different terms, there was, after all, always a war going
on somewhere; but somewhere is not everywhere, and if a record
of the periods of peace people enjoyed could be made it would
show a far longer and more widespread incidence than our history
books seem to indicate, just as a reading of divorce and traffic
cases in newspapers is apt to make one unmindful that a tolerable
degree of happiness is still the product of most marriages and
that quite a number of people reach their destinations after a car
journey with a fair degree of safety.

The main business was, after all, the small-scale production
and distribution of food, and the rural technology, the horseshoeing,
saddlemaking, wheelwrighting and so forth that went with it. Even
most of the wars of the time have a retrospective air of some extra-
vagant business with crowds of film extras whose contracts could
only start after the spring ploughing and sowing, and who had
to pack up and return home before the harvest whether the business
in hand was finished or not. The continuous all-encompassing
horror of a modern war was beyond any pitch of feasibility for a
city state, not that at times they did not strive very earnestly to
prove the contrary, as the long drawn-out struggle between
Venice and Genoa serves to show. In this case both were trading
entities struggling for the rich pickings of the Mediterranean and
the Levantine trade, and foolishly squandering such resources
as it gave them to do so. But by and large such profligacy was
beyond the reach of local resources, simply because production
and distribution, and numerous allied economic activities, were
on too small a scale to be harnessed for very long to any centralised
destructive purpose, be it political despotism or religious racketeering
at the hands of an ecclesiastical Mafia masquerading as an inquisition. Localised societies could suffer such ordeals and still encompass them without changing their essential characteristics.

In a new secular age religious imposition became impracticable;
but war and tyranny became matters which engulfed societies
and created new attitudes and new forces within them long after
hostilities were supposed to have ceased. After the city-state
stage of growth these things ceased to be contained by society,
they came instead to contain society within their maw, as modern
life has been dominated for more than a generation by something
called 'the cold war', and which one day, quite inevitably, unless

men change the nature of the forces within their societies to achieve a different result, must prove to be the prelude to a new 'hot' war. In their blindness men took no note of this momentous change and so contrived no new forms within their societies to contain the terrible dangers that change has created. As a result two major world wars have already ensued in the modern era and there is only just time, given the requisite change of heart and mind, to avert a third.

CHAPTER XII

The Continental Meganation

Why do the nations so furiously rage together?

The Psalms

The answer to the Psalmist's question with we begin this chapter is that the nations are not nations at all but meganations or ever wors, continental megenations.

If a meganation is a victim in many more senses than one of its size, what are we to say of political units which have expanded to the colossal size of an entire continent, to become what we may call continental meganations? In the nature of things there cannot be many such units in the world and there are in fact only four, China, India, the Russian Empire and the United States. In geographic size, Australia may be said to be another, but owing to the aridity of its vast central desert areas, its sparse population (it numbers only fourteen million), and the fact that this 14 million is very widely distributed mainly in its lengthy coastal areas, which themselves are divided into territories with considerable powers of self-government, it tends to have all the power characteristics not of a continental meganation, nor even of a meganation, but simply of a nation. Australia has participated in two world wars, but its participation has been due not to an overspill of uncontrollable power from within its frontiers, but to historic ties of kith and kin with Britain and the Commonwealth, and also to its fears of the far-reaching expansionist aims of Japan (population 101 million!) entertained until its defeat in World War II. Far from expanding its territory as a genuine continental meganation might be expected to do, Australia has in fact contracted its territory by ceding its former control of various areas such as Papua, New Guinea, and the Solomon Islands in the Pacific. This is a behaviour characteristic of a nation, not of a continental meganation. There is also a fifth continental meganation currently in the making, namely Europe, and on this we shall have something to say in a later chapter.

In the light of the thesis that we have been advancing what would we expect the dominant characteristics of a continental meganation to be? Would we expect it to be pacific, tolerant, stable, democratic and liberal? Or would we expect it to be belligerent, war-like, unstable, totalitarian and pronouncedly anti-liberal? Again, how does the record stand? Let us look at the four continental meganations in turn. The Russian Empire, for example, itself an enforced union of subjugated peoples of many different races, has expanded its territory since the so-called revolution, (if indeed it *was* a revolution, for what has changed in terms of human freedom?), and now sits firmly on the necks of the formerly free and formerly quite prosperous peoples of Latvia, Estonia and Lithuania; since the Hitler war it has expanded by grabbing territories of several of its European neighbours, in addition it has engaged in border disputes with every single one of its neighbours, and the most ominous of these, its disputes with China, another continental meganation, threatens continually to erupt into a new world war.

To contemplate this particular dispute is surely to contemplate an enormous streak of insanity in human affairs. The Russian Empire has been described as 'the Socialist Sixth of the World'; this may not say much for socialism but it does at least say a great deal for the evils of political giantism. The rival continental meganations whose territories are so vast as to be quite beyond the power of their hapless inhabitants to govern them wisely, or even at all, are locked in a border dispute involving a few miles of empty frozen, artic tundra, a dispute which may quite easily bring about a third world war. And those dewey-eyed advocates of 'one world' who imagine that the answer to our problems is for all political differences to be merged into one unified authority had better take note that these two nations are supposed to be practitioners of the same political credo! No doubt we can conclude sadly, as doubtless did Shakespeare, that 'the nearer in blood the nearer bloody', but does anyone suppose that this kind of rivalry can be regulated by a supra-national authority which speaks and acts for some special interest groups of mankind rather than for mankind as a whole?

There has already been a United Nations war in Korea and another in the Congo. In both cases United Nations soldiers were not fighting for the general interests of mankind (how could they? how could anybody?) but for the special interests of nations dominated by capitalist systems of economics who have a headstart over the rest of the world in terms of economic development. This does not necessarily make these nations baddies, for presumably each nation is entitled to adopt the economic system it wants; but it does make them unrepresentative and quite unable *collectively* to speak for mankind as a whole. The reason for this si simple : world unity in these terms of fighting and authority inevitably becomes an issue of ideology; in the nature of things there can be no collective ideology without the most preposterous intellectual and cultural impoverishment of mankind. This is precisely what the communist empires are discovering, for in seeking to impose their ideological straight-jacket on their unfortunate peoples they are compelled to disown and repudiate their greatest original and creative thinkers, their writers, artists and intellectuals. Stalin felt driven to murder almost the entire soviet artistic and creative elite of his time (along with millions of others) simply to stay in power, and his heirs have no scruples to this day in hounding and persecuting the most outstanding man of Russian literature (again, along with many others). In Alexander Solzhenitsyn they have a writer whose powers illumine as a matter of course the progression of developing consciousness of all mankind, yet because he is genuinely creative, because what he has to say is genuinely new, it does not, indeed it cannot, fit the ideological framework of an established power system which seeks to proceed by a preconceived and static ideology.

Any 'world government' would be bound to proceed by the same route and reach the same deplorable end. The constraints of the United States continental meganation on its subjects are of a different order, but they achieve substantially the same ends, the paramountcy of mass conformity and the silencing, stifling or the reducing to impotence of original, creative workers who do not 'fit' the ideological model of the prevailing power structure. One thinks of the thousands of gifted people who were hounded from their jobs and livelihoods, or who were jailed during the Macarthyite witch hunts of the fifties, and if the overt acts of domestic persecution now appear to be less, let it be remembered that the poisonous obscenities of orthodoxy and power still reign supreme in other ways, not least in the barbarities inflicted on the people of Vietnam, and that in securing an attitude of passive conformity to the goals of state power and the power of the dominant interests, economic, military and political, the USA has shown that what the jackboot and the mailed fist may fail to achieve, a plethora of consumer goodies based on an uninhibited rape of the world's finite resources and the suborning of the economic structure of many poorer countries may achieve without difficulty.

The spheres in which man needs to achieve unity are not in the realm of ideology at all, not at provincial, national, continental or world level, where it can only be achieved by a betrayal of the holy grail of man's own humanity. They are in fact simply in the rather mundane spheres of functional requirements of transport, communications and related matters.

People never will be all of one mind about political questions, just as they never will be all of one mind about religious matters; the mere notion that they might be is absurd, yet most forms of 'progressive' opinion, and those who drool with such empty, sentimental silliness about 'unity' in Europe or the world, make this absurdity the basis of their so-called thinking.

There are, it would seem, two ways of looking at the world of politics. One, followed by nearly all established power systems, is from the top down, and is, whatever it presumes to call itself in spirit and practice, utterly undemocratic. The other is from the bottom up, and is the basis of all democratic theorising since the Greek city states. The Sino-Soviet quarrel is a typical product of 'from the top down' politics; it is not a quarrel between *people*, it is a clash of power systems. Left to themselves the peoples of Sinkiang (at present a subject colony of the Chinese communist empire), and of Kazakhatan, Kirghizia and Kazikistan (at present subject colonies of the Russian communist empire) would have two choices about this border dispute, assuming they wanted to pursue it at all. They could settle it by peaceful negotiation, or they could go to war.

If they decided to go to war what a pity that would be; they would be pursuing a folly that has dogged all human history. Yet one needs to remember that they might at least get some fun out of it; the frontier is well away from any big centres of population, and the combatants might find blazing away at each other with Boer-war-period rifles quite entertaining. Of course they might kill quite a number of themselves before the steam ran out of the whole thing, but at least it would be a *local* war run by *local* people for *local* issues, and it is not difficult to visualise how they would eventually agree on some basis or other to live and let live.

Unfortunately, it is not their frontier, but the frontier of power systems whose centres of decision-making (one dare not say control) are thousands of miles away. The border peoples are neighbours, but Moscow and Peking are separated by about four thousand miles, as well as by a vast confusion of contradictorily crossed i's and dotted t's in the Marxist-Leninist hagiography and all the infinite torrents of vituperation which the propaganda hate machines of rival megacontinental state power systems can produce at will. Who is likely to get any fun out of a war proceeding from that? Who can prevent its seeming inevitability, and who will be able to stop it once it has started?

Or let us look at the record of China itself. After many decades of civil war, foreign invasion and local war-lordism, the empire was forced into a national unity under communist leadership in 1949. Estimates of its population vary from seven to eight hundred million or even more, and the wastage and destruction of war, famine and river flooding would, one might have thought, have given it ample cause to concentrate for another hundred years or more on tasks of national reconstruction and construction.

Not a bit of it. Its record since 1949 is one of almost unceasing hostility and belligerency to the world at large. Not satisfied with having the largest population in the world to care for and worry about, it proceeded to invade and subjugate the proud, independent people of Tibet, it has invaded India over the issue of some border posts so high up in the Himalayas that nobody in his right mind would dream of living within a hundred miles of them, it has intrigued and conspired in the quarrel between India and Pakistan, it became embroiled with the U.S.A. over the fate of Korea. It was involved in a conflict with the U.S.A. over Vietnam which prolonged a war in that tragic country for more than a quarter of a century and destroyed the greater part of its economic life, it has a finger in the pie of the affairs of every country in Asia, and is busy establishing some sort of diplomatic presence and ideological front in many parts of Africa; it is also busy championing countries such as Albania and Rumania against its rival imperialist power, Russia, in Europe and, just to keep the pot boiling as it were, is making the usual imperialist noises in respect to some purely imaginary claim to the island country of Taiwan.

Whatever the fate of Taiwan under Chinese dynastic rule of former centuries, in an age which talks so much of respect for the principle of self-determination, let it at least be acknowledged that Taiwan, which is over one hundred miles from the Chinese mainland, belongs to the people of Taiwan, and China's claims that it is 'theirs' are as inherently absurd as the late Chiang Kai Shek's claims were to be the legitimate ruler of China from his Taiwan vantage point. Taiwan belongs to the people of Taiwan.

One would not ordinarily suppose from its actions that China, after nearly a quarter of a century of communist rule, still has one of the lowest gross domestic products, *per capita,* in the whole world. According to figures published in the London *Times* (September 25th, 1972) China's G.D.P. is a mere £41. It is lower than that of many poor African countries such as Botswana (£42), Zaire (£94), Swaziland (£79), Mocambique (£90), Egypt (£68) or Libya (£766). Yet, such is the sheer pressure of overspill of its power it has financed and built an enormous railway through Tanzania (£35) and Zambia (£127)!

None of this should be taken as belittling the very real and positive achievements of the Chinese people since they were unified—if indeed they were unified, under Chairman Mao's rule—especially in the field of food production and the improvement of their consumption standards, which most visitors and observers seem to be agreed upon. It is note worthy that this has been accomplished on the basis of two very commendable principles; one is a considerable devolution of power in relation to economic activity so that in quite small district communes there appears to be a marked degree of localised decision-making with regard to agricultural and industrial production. We appear to have none of the rigid centralised 'five year plans' that have afflicted the Russian revolution, plans which have never failed to go awry and which compel Russian leaders to report on them to a succession of docile mass meetings of party representatives in the Kremlin with speeches of quite breathtaking boredom stretching over several hours of delivery, year after year to the general effect that they have failed.

The second is a very real respect for the principle of equalitarianism expressed in the personal life-style of China's leaders of all ranks and in the commitment of all ranks to the principle of the dignity of labour expressed in the expectation that everyone should take his turn at manual toil.

The ideological strait-jacket which has secured the acceptance of these attitudes may not be everyone's cup of tea but it has the apparent credibility derived from any successful effort—it works, apparently.

It works however against a vastly different background to that of the Russian revolution, for whereas Russia is still emerging from an exceedingly primitive and even barbaric background, China is one of mankind's oldest and most resplendent civilisations. Russia's vodka-sodden peasantry has no parallel in China, so that if we can view Russia as still struggling to emerge from backwardness, China by contrast is recovering from the decay of its former imperial greatness which set in with the period of foreign invasions. It was a greatness based on a developed rural economy of immense wealth which had been developed over many centuries and it helps to explain why, whereas the Russian revolution was an urban pheno- menon imposed on a rural people, the Chinese revolution was a rural one which stormed the cities. China's rulers have thus one outstanding advantage the Russians have never known, a people accustomed to the idea of collective discipline and social effort at village level. It is to the credit of China's rulers that they appear to have been able to harness this national trait to the task of largely ending the poverty and exploitation of former times and to give their people a new sense of purpose and self-respect.

It may be thought that its apparent success in ending the bane of civil war and war-lordism which has afflicted Chinese life for so long is a telling point for the kind of unity which a frightened and rapacious capitalism is seeking to impose on Europe; the realities of the matter are a trifle more complex and suggest other conclusions. Freedom does not consist of a single high road but of innumerable small foot-paths in human affairs, and national unity on such a scale as in China's case, which really amounts to the unity of a number of nations—as it does in any other continental mass—has always been an *imposed* unity, imposed at the price of freedom.

This does not mean that freedom precludes any form of unity, far from it, and the Swiss are not alone in having discovered it is quite possible to have a quite exceptional degree of national unity with no loss of freedom. But in the Swiss case unity is by the free consent of the people from the base upwards, and as such imposes, in the name of freedom, the most rigorous constraints on govern- ment power *from below*.

Unity imposed from above has, in the past, given China some long periods of stability even though in periods of crisis the unity has proved very brittle. Today such forms of unity have become anachronistic and are proving, to put it gently, to lack the stability of past forms.

And why should we expect it to be otherwise? The idea of freedom has taken a firm grip on the human imagination and is not likely to be easily surrendered. So that indubitable as China's achievements in the field of agricultural and industrial production may be, even its most ardent admirers can scarcely fail to concede that its national scene has been one of one convulsion after another since the revolution. The ideological terms in which these convulsions are expressed are benumbing in their obscurity to the outside observer but there is little reason to doubt that all of them have centred on struggles for power within the top hierarchy of China's leaders. These matters are wrapped in obscurity because of the strict censorship which prevails,[1] and their continuance would seem to indicate that the power-struggle at the top has not been resolved and that possibly on its present basis it is unresolvable, simply because the concentration of power is too great, covers too vast an area, and because men everywhere have come to recognise freedom and, imperatively, to want it.

China's successes, such as they are, stem largely from its authoritarian rigidity, an authoritarianism constantly threatened by the universal wind of change emanating from men's quest for freedom and a rigidity under repeated assault from the faction struggles of the top leadership groups. How these matters will be resolved it is quite impossible to predict, but the mere untenability of much of China's ideological basis in the outmoded constructs of Marxist-Leninism and the ordinary mortality of its leaders suggest that the days of fundamental change in China are far from being over and that we can anticipate even greater political convulsions in the future.

What surely needs to be stressed is that because of its size the power stemming from so much centralised control will inevitably continue to spill over into foreign military adventures as a matter of course whatever ideology is used to rationalise the policies of the leadership groups.

But perhaps Dame Barbara Ward derives her inspiration for the prospects of peace with a United Europe from the performance of non-communist megacontinental states? There are only two others, India and the U.S.A. Is the peace-keeping record of either of these entities such as to justify optimism?

In the 25 years of its independence India has quarrelled with every single one of its neighbours. Its row with Pakistan over Kashmir has been endemic, for years it was in a state of belligerent confrontation with Ceylon, it took over Goa from the Portuguese, on

[1] It was two years (sic!) after the event that news of the attempted coup and subsequent flight of Lin Piao and his associates, which led to their deaths when their plane crashed, was released in the Chinese press.

the plea of self-determination. To whom does Goa belong—to India? To Portugal, or to the Goans themselves?); its forces have been in constant conflict with the ancient hill tribes of Nagaland, it can make no peace with China, it is already in a state of acrimony with the fledgling state of Bangladesh, it has had disputes with Nepal and it is acting as ruler to the numerous hill states of its northern frontier which enjoyed a measure of peace, stability and prosperity and independence when India was under colonial rule which they have never enjoyed since.

All this needs to be seen against a background of poverty so widespread, so chronic and so abysmal that not only is it almost the poorest country in the world in terms of its per capita G.D.P. (£38), its economic problems show every sign of getting worse, and several parts of its territory are showing such unmistakable signs of total collapse that the late Sir Julian Huxley was moved some years ago to urge that the U.N. should have a special disaster task-force ready to move in to Calcutta at short notice when the worst happens. India is a land of famine, communal strife, mob violence, corruption and poverty; its people, by the million, are cliff-hanging at the brink of a chasm of destitution the like of which is unknown anywhere in the world, yet it has the time, the energy and the resources to behave like a snarling tiger to most of its neighbours most of the time and has now joined the nuclear club and continues to spend more than half its annual budget on war preparations. And of course, not one of its cities lacks statues, pictures, museums and other memorials to a saintly bespectacled semi-naked figure in a loin cloth and sandals who brought a message of peace and non-violence to all mankind of such awe-inspiring dimensions it has yet to even begin to digest.

When we reflect on this extraordinary juxtaposition of phenomena in the poorest by far of the continental meganations it should give us some foreboding of what to expect in the wealthiest and by far the most powerful continental meganation the world has ever known, or is possibly ever likely to know.

In the short space of a couple of centuries the U.S.A. has irredeemably ravished the resources of an entire continent and created a lifestyle for its inhabitants which in turn creates a disproportionate, insatiable and entirely selfish demand for the resources of the rest of the planet. It is a demand quite impossible to fulfil in generational terms and it is already clear that America's golden age, such as it was, is already over.

The early settlers entered a continent whose inhabitants had created a beautiful and delicately poised life-style based almost entirely
on the consumption of self-renewable resources. The finite resources
of the continent, its oil, its coal and its ores, were virgin and
untouched; so indeed were many of its self-renewing resources, its
forests, its fauna, its waterways and shore fish resources, its birds
and its natural beauty.

There is a glory about any open space, and perhaps in temperate
climates with a normal vegetative cover that glory is more pronounced
than elsewhere; certainly the America of that time, when vast herds
of bison roamed its prairies and only a few million Indians at most
culled them for food and clothing, or trapped its plentiful game, or
fished from its amply stocked rivers, and lived a corporate existence
in their varied tribes which was so profoundly religious, so complex
and sophisticated in its refined subtlety, and so hauntingly compelling in its dignity and grace that it still retains its power to command
loyalty from their descendants or emulation from those of their oppressors to this day, it must have been as near a form of paradise as
men have ever known.

We need to recall this setting, and to recall too the people who went
there to settle. These people, in the early days at least, stemmed from
a Europe which had cradled the Renaissance and nourished it to such
heights of human excellence in almost every field of human endeavour that urban beauty was a commonplace in the merest village, and
other forms of beauty, especially in painting, sculpture, music and
literature, were so profuse in their abundance that in retrospect it
sometimes seems men were living as a matter of course in a careless
rapture of delight in the sheer enravishment of their own senses and
the very joy of living.

They came, these people, from the Europe of Leonardo da Vinci,
of Michaelangelo, Shakespeare, Bach, Thomas Tallis, Byrd, Titian,
Diirer, Rembrandt, Cervantes, El Greco and so many others so gifted
that the life of that Europe seems even now to have been ablaze with
jewelled fire from a luxuriant profusion of gems of human accomplishment. It was a Europe of glory, and if ever a people had seemed
equipped by their tradition and antecedents, poised to struggle their
way to the highest heavens of invention and achievement, it was
surely these followers of the original boatload of pilgrims that sailed
from Plymouth in the year 1620.

The first settlers, it seems, were kindly received by the Indians, and in one dire winter were saved from starvation by timely gifts of food from them. Was ever a generous act repaid with such bitter fruit? Within a few score years these gracious tribesfolk were being hunted down everywhere like carrion; genocide followed one broken 'treaty' after another, and where it did not succeed was followed in turn by forced evictions, starvation and attempted slavery. We may wonder the more at the way of life these Indians evolved for themselves that all attempts to compel them to any form of slave labour failed utterly; if not flogged to death, they sickened and died from the mere deprivation of that freedom they and their forbears had always known and assumed as a precondition of life.

There is no space to go further into the details of this crime, quite one of the most dreadful in the entire catalogue of human depravity. The interested reader may like to consult some of the works of John Collier, especially his *The Indians of the Americas*[2]; we can only stay to reflect that to this day there is a manifest streak of insensibility in the quality of American life which prompts no proper recognition of the enormity of what was done, no spirit of atonement, and no desire at all to make amends to the survivors for the wrongs from which they still suffer.

In viewing what was done to these people it gives us a grim intimation of what was done to the land and its flora and dependent fauna. The vast herds of buffalo were the first to go, and the price, in terms of ecological disruption alone, is surely vast beyond any possibility of reckoning; a wide range of entire species of life is known to have disappeared and that is a toll which continues to this day. Forest cover was stripped from the land at a rate which discernibly altered the climate and prompted widespread flooding and soil erosion; farming methods were pursued which resulted in the murder of the biotic potential of the soil in many places and the appearance of vast dust bowls in which not a blade of grass will grow, the ores and fossil fuels of the earth's treasure were despoiled with a wantonness and abandon which cannot but fail to impoverish the entire posterity of the continent; rivers, lakes and seaboards were overfished to the point of exhaustion and subsequently, and frequently simultaneously, were polluted with the by-products of factory processes and insanitary forms of urban living which, in the case of some of the largest lakes,

[2]John Collier, *The Indians of the Americas—The Long Hope*, the New American Library, 1947.

has transformed them into vast open sewers which makes even their shores repellent to human habitation.

It would be wearisome to extend this terrible catalogue, even though it would be easy to do so and doubtless needs doing, but what, it should surely be asked, is the justification for such an appalling desecration of the heritage of a once almost virgin continent? Perhaps it is to be found in the figures of what economists are quaintly prone to call the 'standard of living' when all they are talking about is the standard of consumption.

Today the American people, if the editorial section of the *Economist's Diary* of 1979 is any guide, are the biggest *per capita* users of private cars, television and radio sets; they are the biggest consumers of electricity, oil and coal, they also fly more miles, visit more places and publish more titles of new books.[3] It goes almost without saying that its national income *per* head is not only higher than that of any other country, it is very much higher than even that of the other members of the rich man's club, it is, for example almost double that of the U.K. (and it is about sixty times that of India).

There are many people who doubtless suppose that this degree of material affluence fully justifies all that has gone to promote it; yet perhaps we should have a care, and since economists are prone to suppose that these figures really are indicators of the standard of living perhaps we should consider what life is actually like in the U.S.A. in the terms that people live it.

The perceptive traveller to the U.S.A cannot fail to be struck as he goes about the continent, by the irredeemable ugliness and tawdryness of the urban scene, its vulgarity, its monotony, its dispiriting lack of concern for any human values and its total disregard of man's stature in the majestic evolution of his own biology. One American writer has been driven to describe his country as an 'Air-conditioned Nightmare', which is not really exact since even in America air-conditioning is an exercise for the well-to-do. But let Mr. Miller's pen take over, he is, after all, an American citizen. Writing of a visit to Ohio (not that it matters, in this context it might be in any part of the continent's appallingly uniform scene), he comments:

"The saddest sight of all is the automobiles parked outside the mills and factories. There they are, thousands of them, in such profusion

---

[3] A typical economist's non-statistic. Do the titles follow the literacy traditions of *Wuthering Heights?* Or the *Adventures of Andy Capp?* It would seem to an economist a book is a book is a book . . . .

that it would seem as if no man were too poor to own one. In Europe, Asia, Africa the toiling masses of humanity look with watery eyes towards this paradise where the worker rides to work in his own car. What a magnificent world of opportunity it must be, they think to themselves. (At least we like to think that they think that way!) They never ask what one must do to have this great boon. They don't realise that when the American worker steps out of his shining tin chariot he delivers himself body and soul to the most stultifying labour a man can perform. They have no idea that it is possible, even when one works under the best possible conditions, to forfeit all rights as a human being. They don't know that the best possible conditions (in American lingo) means the biggest profits for the boss, the utmost servitude for the worker, the greatest confusion and disillusionment for the public in general. They see a beautiful, shining car which purrs like a cat; they see endless concrete roads so smooth and flawless that the driver has difficulty keeping awake; they see cinemas which look like palaces; they see department stores with mannequins dressed like princesses. They see the glitter and paint, the baubles, the gadgets, the luxuries; they don't see the bitterness in the heart, the scepticism, the cynicism, the emptiness, the sterility, the despair, the hopelessness which is eating up the American worker. They don't see this, they are full of misery themselves. They want a way out: they want the lethal comforts, conveniences, luxuries. And they follow on our footsteps—blindly, needlessly, recklessly.

"The most terrible thing about America is that there is no escape from the treadmill which we have created. There isn't one fearless champion of truth in the publishing world, not one film company devoted to art instead of profits. We have no theatre worth the name, and what we have of theatre is practically concentrated in one city; we have no music worth talking about except what the negro has given us, and scarcely a handful of writers who might be called creative. We have murals decorating our public buildings which are about on a par with the aesthetic development of high school students, and sometimes below that level in conception and execution. We have art museums that are crammed with lifeless junk for the most part. We have war memorials in our public squares that must make the dead in whose name they were erected squirm in their graves. We have an architectural taste which is about as near the vanishing point as it is possible to achieve. In the ten thousand miles I have travelled thus far I have come across two cities which have each of them a

little section worth a second look—I mean Charleston and New
Orleans. As for the other cities, towns and villages through which
I passed I hope never to see them again. Some of them have such
marvellous names too, which only makes the deception more cruel.
Names like Chattanooga, Pensacola, Tallahassee, like Mantua,
Phoobus, Bethlehem, Paoli, like Algiers, Mobile, Natchez, Savannah,
like Baton Rouge, Saginaw, Poughkeepsie: names that revive glorious memories of the past or awaken dreams of the future. Visit them,
I urge you, see for yourself. Try to think of Schubert or Shakespeare
when you are in Phoebus, Virginia. Try to think of North Africa when
you are in Algiers, Louisiana. Try to think of the life the Indians
once led here when you are on a lake, a mountain or river bearing
names we borrowed from them. Try to think of the dreams of the
Spaniards when you are motoring over the old Spanish Trail. Walk
around in the old French Quarter of New Orleans and try to recon-
struct the life that once this city knew. Less than a hundred years
has elapsed since this jewel of America faded out. It seems more like
a thousand. Everything that was of beauty, significance or promise
has been destroyed and buried in the avalanche of false progress.
In the thousand years of almost incessant war Europe has not lost
what we have lost in a hundred years of 'peace and progress'. No
foreign enemy ruined the South. No barbaric vandals devastated the
great tracts of land which are as barren and hideous as the dead surface of the moon. We can't attribute to the Indians the transformation
of a peaceful, slumbering island like Manhattan into the most hideous
city in the world. Nor can we blame the collapse of our economic
system on the hordes of peaceful industrious immigrants whom we
no longer want. No, the European nations may blame one another
for their miseries, but we have no such excuse—we have ourselves
to blame.

"Less than two hundred years ago a great social experiment was
begun on this virgin continent. The Indians whom we dispossessed,
decimated and reduced to the status of outcasts, just as the Aryans
did with the Dravidians of India, had a reverent attitude towards the
land. The forests were intact, the soil rich and fertile. They lived in
communion with Nature on what we choose to call a low level of
life. Though they possessed no written language they were poetic to
the core and deeply religious. Our forefathers came along and, seeking refuge from their oppressors, began by poisoning the Indians with
alcohol and venereal disease, by raping their women and murdering

their children. The wisdom of life which the Indians possessed they scorned and denigrated. When they finally completed their work of conquest and extermination they herded the miserable remnants of a great race into concentration camps and proceeded to break what spirit was left in them."[4]

If these lengthy extracts give the flavour of Henry Miller, a writer capable of describing an American civic park as 'a circumscribed vacuum filled with cataleptic nincompoops' they also convey some of the real flavour of U.S. life. Miller however was writing over fifty years ago and modern reports, if less rumbustious, are somewhat more ominous.

Even from a casual reading of newspapers it is impossible not to conclude that American civic life is deteriorating at an alarming rate as social problems of every kind, accompanied by a decay of the sheer fabric of the cities themselves, multiply to a degree which makes them insoluble. Crimes of violence have reached a pitch where few feel safe to walk abroad after dark and where in New York City alone an average of twelve people is known by the police to be murdered each *day*.

So far has this decay gone that a recent report on New York's police force[5] declares that well over half (sic!) the police force were involved in one form of corruption or other, extending from the simple receiving of bribes to the selling of narcotics, including heroin, and murder. This report appeared before a fresh development in which it was revealed that large quantities of confiscated drugs to the value of 30 million had disappeared from police security stores.

All police forces of course have their ups and downs, but today across the length and breadth of the U.S.A. such evidence of official corruption by law enforcement agencies (among others) has become so commonplace as to cease to arouse comment. Even more sinister is the growing readiness of law enforcement officers to resort to violence and killing, to show a casual disregard of human life, or to connive at the killing of 'awkward' individuals in custody, or to enact farcical courtroom trials involving heavy prison sentences or other penalties for people involved in political trials.

[4]Henry Miller, *The Air Conditioned Nightmare*, London, Panther Books, 1965.
[5]The third and final volume of the report of the Knapp Commission which was set up in 1970 by the Mayor of New York, Mr. John Lindsay, to examine police corruption in the city.

One recalls with grief the murder of George Jackson, allegedly, in a phrase made odiously familiar by Hitler's thugs in the thirties, 'shot whilst trying to escape' from San Quentin Prison. Jackson's published letters from prison, where he had been held for nine years after involvement in the theft of about *ten dollars* (nine years!), showed a sensitive, noble man who had matured from a background of poverty and illiteracy to an accomplished man of letters with a world-wide audience. To have achieved that in the confines of one of America's most vicious, violent and race-ridden jails is surely a measure of the stature of this man who, even so, was still only in the early reaches of his development. He had all the promise of becoming one of America's greatest sons and they shot him down whilst a prisoner in one of the most closely guarded jails in the world with no more compunction than with which a wanton boy would squash a fly. It is a measure of the spiritual corruption and inhumanity that infests the system that not a single voice in the official world was raised to utter one syllable of regret, the explanations of his jailers were accepted without question and the facade of a routine event (sic) calling for no special comment or condemnation was maintained throughout.

George Jackson's murder was not an isolated event, the deaths inside San Quentin alone over the years make clear that violence and murder are an established part of the ethic of the American prison system as it is of American life; what is the dividing line between an occasional murder, which is a kind of statistical inevitability in any mass society, and this growing toll of life where teenage students are gunned down in universities by their own government troops, where city riots lead to whole areas being razed to the ground and the death toll counted in scores, with multiplying Mafia elements in hard drug-trafficking, trade union government associated with, to quote one report,[6] 'corruption, misuse of union funds, a fraudulent election with violence and with murder,' an escalation of figures for crime, mental illness, suicide and social disorientation, what is the dividing line between a degree of such events that bespeak a society with manageable problems and one which is irretrievably breaking down? A society that frequently and blindly boasts it has the most, if not the best, of everything?

And when one contemplates this degree of violence, the massive

and unappeasable anger of racial discords, the strident and murder-
ous frustrations of the generation gulf, the festering injustices inflicted on numerous ethnic minorities, and the determinedly mindless
readiness to meet their every manifestation or protest with violence
and death to any degree that may be required, what is the dividing
line between social dissolution and civil war?

If this is an indication of some of the dominant aspects of America's domestic life, what is one to say of its external actions in relation
to other countries? Like all continental meganations it is not satisfied with the extent of its problems or its territory but is driven by
internal forces beyond 'its'[7] control to extend both as far as its gigantic physical force allows. So that in the last 100 years America has
acquired control of Alaska, Haiti and Puerto Rico, Samoa, some
islands called 'Trust Territories' in the Pacific, the Virgin Islands,
the Panama Canal Zone, Guam, Arizona, Colorado, Hawaii, Mon-
tana, New Mexico, North and South Dakota, Oklahoma, Utah,
Washington and Wyoming.

It goes without saying, we should note in passing, that this has
not led to any addition to the diversity of American cultural riches,
rather the reverse, in a mere extension of the bland uniformities of
the 'American way of life', its drinking and eating habits, its drug
habits (which often amount to the same thing), its newspaper and
journals, its cars and car accidents and so on.

It has also involved itself in two wars in Europe, in three wars in
Asia (against the people of Japan, Korea and Vietnam), it has engaged
in a power struggle against China, in another against Russia and another against Cuba; it has been the instigator or a powerful background
presence in almost every violent event in Latin America leading to
the overthrow of governments, or their subversion (or their support if
local popular forces should threaten to weaken them) it is the principal supplier of arms to Israel, was one of the chief props to Franco in
Spain and the Fascist military regime in Greece, it was largely in-
strumental in securing the re-establishment of large-scale capitalism
in Western Germany after the Hitler War, its arms were the principal
instruments with which the semi-feudal Indonesian Government
murdered over a million so-called communists in 1965, it is the main
source of the arms which enables the military government of Taiwan
to pose some sort of military threat to China, it has sponsored an

[7] It is part of our difficulty that the personal pronoun is quite non-indicative
and non-definable, who are, or who is, 'its'?

attempted invasion of Cuba, its agents have invaded Panama, it was extremely active behind the scenes in promoting the defeat of Biafra in its first war of independence, it played a large if hidden part in the murder of the only freely elected President of the former Belgian Congo, Patrice Lumumba, and the jockeying into office of President Mobutu in his place; it insisted on buying large quantities of chrome from Rebel Rhodesia in defiance of a United Nations sanctions resolution, and its agents and money played a prominent part in the Chilean coup of 1973 and the death of its democratically elected Premier Allende.

Wherever any political situation shows the least fluidity, there U.S. agents are busy with bribes, corruption, intimidation, threats and outright assault in the form of individual murders or wholesale invasion against any genuinely popular or representative feeling. Haiti poses just about one of the most corrupt and oppressive governments in the world and exceeded as such, if at all, only by Liberia, both governments are creatures of American power, a power wielded largely through that empire of power within an empire, the C.I.A.

So vast is American power it has lost control even of the agents of its own policies; the C.I.A. is notorious for pursuing policies over which its parent government has no control, and for feeding the government with false information which in turn has a calamitous influence on major policy decisions. The 'Bay of Pigs' attempted invasion of Cuba would certainly not have been mounted if the late President Kennedy had access to more accurate and reliable intelligence report.

Let it not be thought that this is a matter on which remedial action could be taken, for what is observable here is a general principle of the operations of meganations, far less of continental meganations, that the different sectors of the state apparatus tend, with the growth of the parent unit, to get increasingly beyond its control. Kennedy's predicament was an integral part of his situation as President of a continental megapower.

This terrible truth is even more evident in relation to the way the U.S.A. has conducted war in the Pacific for more than a generation. The conflict between President Truman and General Douglas MacArthur over the conduct of the Korean War is now part of history, but its implications in terms of the power line-up of a continental megapower are still very much part of the living present. General MacArthur was finally sacked as American Pro-

Consul in S.E. Asia, but not before his bombing policies, waged contrary to Presidential policies, and contrary to the general weight of world opinion, had brought the U.S.A. close to open conflict with China and the almost inevitable prospect of another world war. A British Prime Minister flew to Washington to disassociate his government from such madness, and the U.S. President flew to see his Pro-Consul (it was not the other way round!) before deciding to destroy his authority to act. The evidence suggests he was only just in time.

The same unwieldy relationship on this scale between the chief executive and his military has dogged the Vietnam War. In U.S. constitutional parlance only Congress has the right to declare war; since it is doubtful if Congress could at any time have been persuaded of the wisdom of declaring war on North Vietnam, another solution to the problem of using the quicksilver spillover of U.S. power had to be found, it was found by fighting a war without formally declaring it. Even such cumbersome instruments of democracy as a continental megapower possesses have not been used to sanction this war, the greatest undeclared war in history, and one which makes most of its declared wars look like fist fights in terms of the agony, destruction, killing, corruption and despair it unleashed.

Again, this war was characterised by a sheer failure of Presidential or Governmental control, air strikes took place without even the knowledge, far less the consent of the administration, and on one notorious occasion, heavy raids on Hanoi were ordered by the President and carried out by the air arm without the knowledge of the Chairman of the Joint Chiefs of Staff. This was subsequently denied by the President's office, but no explanation of why the statement was forthcoming in the first place was made. We have to recall other details of the effects of this spillover of power. Mai Lai was a hamlet where all its inhabitants were massacred by American troops, men, women and children; it was an atrocity. It was one for which the officer concerned was courtmartialled and found guilty. World opinion was shocked, yet there is abundant testimony that far from being an isolated incident it was a normal product of a process of brutalisation and contempt for the value of human life in a war which had no legality, no morality and no humanity or even sanity. Some of the war criminals and atrocity mongers of Nazi Germany were hanged after the Nuremburg trial. Lt. Calley, who was found guilty of the Mai Lai Massacre, is today a free man and publicly honoured by President Nixon.[8]

It is due in part to the flaccid intellectual climate of our period that the deep questions which inevitably arise from a consideration of these appalling phenomena are seldom asked and never adequately answered. Behind all the bustle of political and economic organisation in nearly every country is the unspoken assumption that political and economic centralism plus an untrammelled concern to push the production of goods and services to the highest level that practical conditions permit to be reached is the way forward to happiness, social fulfilment and self-realisation.

Yet the evidence is surely now unambiguous that such an approach, far from realising such goals, positively negates them, and that far from realising the life abundant it is the highway to hell. What is happening in our universities all over the world that the lessons of this experience are being so sedulously ignored or side-stepped?

The very word 'university' connotes from a concern for those matters which are universal, the concerns of all men everywhere and not simply for the transient concerns of the moment, but for as wide a span of time as a concern for history and the effects of today's dominant trends on the world of tomorrow may permit.

Almost without exception the teaching of politics rests on a survey of the workings of those institutions which prevail today. The libraries of books that pour yearly from university and other presses are rarely concerned to evaluate, or to relate the major problems

[8]These words were written before the Watergate "scandal" broke in the U.S.A. What transpired is that the American Presidential election of 1972 was conducted by methods so fraudulent and corrupt as to make its result invalid even in terms of American Law, and President Nixon's resignation or impeachment inevitable as a matter of course.

Since he resigned the presidency there has been a general disposition to condemn him as a bad guy and to assume the answer to the problem lies in substituting him with a good guy. The fact that the American *system* produced Nixon's presidency and is too vast to be made susceptible to the influence of the private moral judgements of its citizens, especially in relation to the major power drives that dominate it, will be ignored. Watergate was not an aberration of the system, it was a natural fruit, and an indication not of a temporary defect but of one aspect of its total breakdown. In this sense it is not a 'scandal' any more than a scratch on a decayed corpse can be described as a blemish. These words were also written before Vice President Agnew resigned the Vice Presidency and pleaded guilty to charges of tax evasion and corruption.

of our time, problems such as war, to the workings of these institutions, and such evaluation as is attempted generally proceeds on precisely the approach of viewing such problems 'from the top down', rather than 'from the bottom up'[9] which has largely created them in the first place. It follows as a matter of ordinary consequences that what they have to say is generally beside the point (the point being how to resolve the problem of power in the mass society) and thus of no serious import.

In economics the same blinkered negativism prevails. It is common today for economics departments to be furnished with elaborate statistical sections and expensive computer devices to service the quest for truth, one must suppose, in the field of what is called 'micro-economics'. The macro-economic field being dominated by resolving questions on how the economy behaves as a whole in terms of the most ordinary utility, we have surely reached here the end of the road, and economists appear to have acquired the mantle of those medieval divines who were wont to discourse on the number of angels who might comfortably be accommodated on a pinpoint.

The depressing catalogue of some of the dominant aspects of the politics of the four continental meganations that dominate the globe is already as long as it need to be for our purpose even though it could without difficulty be made a great deal longer. What we need to ask in the light of it is why?

Why are these matters so prominent in the record? Is there something peculiarly evil about communism, for example, that makes such war policies and such horrors as mass domestic purges inevitable? Are the Indians of the Asian subcontinent a people with a peculiarly war-like propensity and war-making disposition which makes it impossible for them to settle and develop the arts of civilisation? Are the American people the victims of some peculiar form of depravity stemming from their addiction to the evil arts of capitalism?

These questions may appear rhetorical, but they are often asked in

9I am borrowing here the usage of Ian Bowen Rees in his illuminating book *Government by Community*, (London, Charles Knight and Co. Ltd., 1971). Mr. Rees is himself a senior officer in local government in Wales and has written a work on the general aspects of his professional concerns which, to quote Professor Max Beloff ". . . should be compulsory reading for all those entering upon a career in either central or local government," adding, ". . . it is likely to do them more good than all the economic text books and manuals of management they are ever likely to see."

all seriousness by different adversaries of each of the different countries. Nevertheless they are rhetorical, and rhetorical nonsense at that.

Communism is one of the noblest political ideals conceived by the mind of man, and some of the greatest moralists and thinkers have given it their allegiance. India is the cradle of one of the world's oldest civilisations and its achievements in the fields of art, philosophy, architecture, poetry, religion, music, dance and dress, stretching back over thousands of years, mark its people as one of the great cultural benefactors of mankind. And as for capitalist America let us recall that under earlier stages of capitalist development, men have reached the sublimest heights of their inspiration and creativity and that the dreams of democracy and liberty which inspired the Founding Fathers and produced the American Constitution make it a significant step in the moral progress of mankind.

Again, anyone travelling to these countries does not find that its people are full of bellicosity, jingoism and merely destructive anger directed at the peoples of other countries. Quite the contrary. The writer happens to have travelled extensively in both India and the U.S.A. In both countries he enjoyed bountiful and freely-given hospitality from numerous people in many spheres of life. He was not blind to the violence and the tension that exist in both countries; but the idea that the assaults of the Indian Government on the people of Nagaland, or that the desolating mockery of all standards of civilised conduct as represented by the barbarism of American actions in Vietnam is representative of the generality of people in these countries is merely absurd. One surely needs only a modicum of faith in human nature to make similar statements about the peoples of China and Russia. And if that faith is insufficient, perhaps the reader will bear with me for a quotation from the life of a young Russian poet:

"In '41 Mama took me back to Moscow. There I saw our enemies for the first time. If my memory is right, nearly twenty thousand German war prisoners were to be marched in a single column through the streets of Moscow.

"The pavements swarmed with onlookers, cordoned off by soldiers and police.

"The crowd were mostly women—Russian women with hands roughened by hard work, lips untouched by lipstick and thin hunched shoulders which had borne half the burden of the war. Every one of them must have had a father or a husband, a brother or a son killed by the Germans.

"They gazed with hatred in the direction from which the column was to appear.

"At last we saw it. The generals marched at the head, massive chins stuck out, lips folded disdainfully, their whole demeanour meant to show superiority over their plebeian visitors.

" 'They smell of eau-de-Cologne, the bastards' someone in the crowd said with hatred.

"The women were clenching their fists. The soldiers and policemen had all they could do to hold them back.

"All at once something happened to them, they saw German soldiers, thin, unshaven, wearing dirty blood-stained bandages, hobbling on crutches or leaning on the shoulders of their comrades; the soldiers walked with their heads down.

"The street became dead silent—the only sound was the shuffling of boots and the thumping of crutches.

"Then I saw an elderly woman in broken-down boots push herself forward and touch a policemen's shoulders, saying 'Let me through'. There must have been something about her that made him step aside.

"She went up to the column, took from inside her coat something wrapped in a coloured handkerchief and unfolded it. It was a crust of black bread. She pushed it awkwardly into the pocket of a soldier, so exhausted that he was tottering on his feet. And now suddenly from every side women were running towards soldiers pushing into their hands bread, cigarettes, whatever they had.

"The soldiers were no longer enemies. They were people!"[10]

There is surely a wider import to this passage. *Official* communist morality still sees nothing wrong with the organised humiliation of masses of people in a 'victory' parade; not dissimilar to that inflicted by the Romans on their defeated adversaries two thousand years ago. So that the Russian people were showing their humanity *despite* their government, not because of it. And we need to see that there must be very few travellers in other lands who have not witnessed similar acts of quite spontaneous humanity transcending barriers of nationality and race without inhibition or reserve.

The writer well recalls a journey on a crowded, slow-moving

[10] Yevgeny Yevtushenko, *A Precocious Autobiography*, Penguin Books, 1965.

British troop train into Germany shortly after the Hitler collapse. Somewhere beyond Hanover the train lurched into yet another seemingly interminable halt; as it did so a train crawled alongside from the opposite direction which was full of German soldiers. It needs to be remembered that this was during the closing stages of a long and terrible war during which the opposing state organs of propaganda had been hard at work for years seeking to portray the adversary in the most lurid and unfavourable terms.

It took the well-fed and well-clothed English soldiery but a few moments to grasp that those German soldiers were hungry and that many of them were wounded; it was in fact a make-shift ambulance train. In no time at all pockets and knapsacks were being emptied of chocolate, tobacco, food packages and even money, and passed to those whose need was so evident. I recall looking down between those two trains at that long line of hands stretching out to give and to receive, and observing the rough attempts to jump the language barrier with the signs and gestures of goodwill from both sides and suddenly feeling I was in the presence of something older and deeper in the scheme of life than any force of war, something universal to the human condition which is infinitely more expressive of truth than any amount of fighting or killing can ever hope to be, and for the first time since I had begun to see those miles upon miles of cruelly devastated towns and cities of bomb-battered Germany I felt my spirits soar with a gladness and gratitude that life was shaped so to its profoundest base with such a un'versal instinct for fellowship, decency, and, dare one say it, love, which, and I have no *reason* for adding this at all, is, I am sure, indestructible.

What then is wrong that these continental meganations fail to express in their official actions the ordinary humanist realities of their peoples? We need to see they are not wicked because they are communist or capitalist, or because they are too rich or too poor, nor because they represent different branches and traditions of civilisation, or even because they profess Christianity, Hinduism, Mohamedism or Atheism, for none of these factors do they have in common sufficiently to account for this uniformity of phenomena in their behaviour. The one factor which they do have in common is that they are all too big, they all have machines of state power which are largely out of control in terms of determining and achieving humanist goals and which, because they are not controlled by their peoples and in fact control *them*, they all behave in terms which tend to deny rather than express the humanity of their peoples.

Miss Ward sees something of this. She refers to the democratic anomaly of an out of work American citizen having a vote theoretically equal to that of a Henry Ford, when the latter enjoys so much more power, wealth and influence, yet despite the obvious fact that the unemployed worker can exercise no influence on the conduct of the American Government it is worth noting she is still able to write, ". . . a whole range of intermediate political institutions between the family at one end of the scale and any ultimate world authority at the other is here to stay."[11]

She is, of course, out of date at one end and quite unrealistic at the other. The family as meaningful social unit is being pressurised into extinction by the forces of giantism in the modern world, and as it happens it is in the process of reducing all intermediate groupings up to the level of state power to a powerless and anonymous nullity. The state power is all, and citizen control over it vestigious.

One must assume in this context the inevitable decline of even the presumed socialistic morality of Marxian communism in both Russia and China, just as the fire in the belly of the French Revolution faded with the passage of time. Indeed the main fuel for the maintenance of apparent revolutionary zeal in Russia to this day comes not from within but in response to hostile attitudes from without.[12]

In due course the major differences of the political giants will cease to be ideological, for all will express the workings of the question for power as a matter of course, and since centralised power tends to be far more manipulatable in capitalist forms, and since it tends to promote far more problems of the management of the masses under communism, we must expect a historical drift, as a matter of course, to use the jargon of contemporary unreality, from 'left' to 'right'.

In mass societies all forms of authority are right wing.

[11]Barbara Ward, *Spaee Ship Earth*, London, Hamish Hamilton, 1966, p. 33.

[12]The writer happened to be present at a reception to mark the 50th anniversary of the Bolshevik Revolution. It was held in a posh hotel in the capital of one of the smaller African countries. Of the hundred of Africans and Europeans present, only one person saw fit to don the standard bourgeois uniform of a black dinner jacket, white shirt and black bow-tie, and that was the Soviet Ambassador.

CHAPTER XIII

Eurogiantism

"All we like sheep have gone astray."

Isiah

In 1975 a referendum was held in Britain to determine whether or not it should become a member of what was called the 'Common Market'. Some unkind souls have since been inclined to dub it the 'Common Markup' but even though the original name itself is now falling into disuetude (it is giving way, as the top manipulators always intended it should, even though during the referendum they blandly declared it wouldn't) to the title, 'United Europe', to, that is, the political, military *and* economic unification of at least Western Europe.

Yet the title 'Common Market' has its own significance, one that should not be put entirely out of mind. What is a common market? It is, at least in this case, a trading relationship designed to protect the interests of its members; so that in global terms, in terms of the global distribution of wealth and poverty we need to ask, do those interests *need* protecting? And if so from whom? From other rich nations? Or from the mounting anger of the poor?

Before developing this point we need to focus on the general move for European unity and what it means, for there can be no doubt that the result of the common market referendum made a black day for the people of Britain, for the people of Europe and for the people of the world. The forces that make for progress, and even sanity in human affairs suffered a tremendous set-back, a set-back from which it may take decades to recover; and given the powerful spirit of sheer irrationality and of uninhibited economic and political power-lust that has prompted this step, and which we may now expect to flourish as a consequence of the defeat they have inflicted, it must be regarded as an open question whether indeed our civilisation can survive such perils as a new global war it will indubitably provoke.

To grasp the magnitude of the problems this step has created, (and not simply to be able to say at some future date we told you so!) some of its immediate consequences need to be spelt out.

It is part of the general intellectual chaos that has produced this result that we should find the famous historian Mr. Arthur Bryant writing in the *Times* the day before the referendum saying that if the historic sovereignty of Parliament is incompatible with member-

ship of the common market then the answer on whether to join or
not would be undoubtedly 'no'. Yet by some quirk of logic Mr. Bryant seemed to be suggesting that a 'yes' result was justified whilst
in the same issue of the *Times* Mr. Bernard Levin was exulting in
the prospect of a 'United States of Europe' as the logical outcome
of a 'yes' vote. How right Mr. Levin is. He speaks in fairly full
knowledge of the forces ranged behind the whole European concept
and is delighted that they should be working for a U.S.E., to be
realised as soon as they can manage it, which, from all the signs,
will not be very long.

Strangely enough, in making their different cases both Mr. Bryant
and Mr. Levin express a primary concern for freedom, and since
everything in politics is presumed to stem from such a concern, which
is one reason why so much was sacrificed by so many in at least one
world war, their concern is not misplaced. What then are the consequences of Britain's endorsement of the common market likely to be
in terms of freedom?

It is here that, as Mr. Bryant and others clearly see, the sovereignty
issue is crucial. The working usage of the word means simply the
power to decide, and that power effectively, has long been assumed
to reside, in constitutional parlance in "...the Lords Spiritual and
Temporal, and the Commons, in Parliament assembled".

A growing body of evidence over recent years has indicated that
in practice this has been a truth of decreasing content, and that
whilst the hullabaloo of mass electioneering and the apparent power
has been steadily passing into the hands of the bureaucracy and to
interests outside Parliament and, in the case of multinational companies, outside Britain. So that if there were any substantial body
of concern to ensure that parliamentary sovereignty was preserved,
we might have expected to see a powerful campaign launched with
this vital point as its objective. We have instead seen the matter
treated with silence and indifference by every major political organisation. Let historians, if no one else, note that the forces which manipulated the assent of a majority of the British people to surrender
of their sovereignty in Parliament in 1975, accomplished a massive
erosion of esteem for that sovereignty in the first place, to say nothing
of an equally massive erosion of its working effectiveness.

In any event a number of factors, such as the growth of population,
the further development of the media as an instrument for the manipulation of people's minds, (exemplified so well in the referendum

result itself), the concentration of capital in the fewer and fewer hands of large institutions, the same process applied to retail and wholesale trade, to manufacturing and almost every other facet of economic life, the growing centralisation of nearly all forms of power, especially political power, with its inevitable debilitation of the entire democratic process, not least in the realm of local government, as well as the rapidly increasing tempo of both production and consumption, especially in the field of manufacturers, which produces the same problems of representation and control as an increase in human numbers, were all making the overhaul of centralised government, and the need to restore the vitality of parish, village and urbanward democracy, a matter of unquestionable urgency if our historic ideas of freedom were not soon to be snuffed out.

Instead the reverse has been put in train; instead of less centralisation, less bureaucracy, less sterile and conformist patterns of life, less giantism and less remoteness, we are now going to have a great deal more. Mr. Levin and others see a U.S.E. as a bulwark of freedom to the challenge of soviet-style Communism, they appear to overlook altogether that the objectives of a U.S.E. are themselves based on a denial of individuation and freedom and can only be achieved at the expense of freedom. The very idea of a continental exercise in economic control for example, especially in agriculture, presupposes a readiness of individuals to conform to continental regulations emanating from a single centre and an equal readiness to compel if that spirit of conformity should prove lacking.

This is happening at a time when capitalism is showing every sign of crisis, a crisis which itself stems from the same cause, the collapse of effective human control which ensues from overgrowth in the size of units and the acceleration in the machine tempo of the economic process. The simplistic socialist disposition to think and talk in blanket terms of economic categories leads some to suppose that capitalism is collapsing when what we are witnessing is a virtual breakdown of some of the more imposing forms of *large-scale* capitalism. But the dinosaurs of capitalism will not give up without a fight, which is one principal reason why the European exercise was launched in the first place. Such a struggle will involve even further attempts to manipulate social mechanisms to end. Unemployment and inflation are as old as economic history, what is new today is the scale of the operations promoting the present massive incidence of both, and the readiness of the big-timers to make ever-increasing inroads into the shrinking arena of choice open to ordinary people in order to remain topside, and there to impose their solutions. The mere fact of the crisis is bound to create a need for more compulsion and centralised coercion in the hope that it will reduce the number of variables being grappled with and then make the crisis more manageable.

Siren voices from almost every point of the political spectrum, concerned with the size of spiralling wage claims, although seldom with the profits that provoke them, can be increasingly heard calling for a wages policy. They do not mean what they say and are using words to conceal rather than express their intentions, for what they really have in mind is a *compulsory* wages policy. We have come a long way from the capitalist theory which urged that the forces of the market when left to themselves can safely take care of such matters. The ganging up on both the labour and the capital sides of the market has clearly left the capitalist battalions in a relatively weaker bargaining position. So of course, to restore the parity at least, if not the capitalist superiority, of the *status quo ante,* the political mechanism must be used to bring the organised workers to heel.

But one thing is apt to lead to another; wages may be defined in policy terms by edicts from Brussels, endorsed or not by something called a Parliament in Strasbourg, but supposing workers rather than accept the prescribed levels of remuneration in a given sector of industry prefer to drift out of it altogether? With compulsory wage levels, can the compulsory direction of labour be far behind?

Yet even this is but to view the matter in terms of traditional theoretical concepts and to ignore that there is something quite new on the stage today. The threat of ecological disruption, a threat which capitalism itself has largely created, which poses in turn a threat to the very existence of the organised societies in which we live, is creating a deep-rooted crisis of confidence within the upper echelons of the capitalist world, as well it might. Capitalism is accustomed to coping with a state of crisis, a phenomenon which is largely a by-product of its own operations anyway, and in the past it has always managed to weather such storms. But all the pointers suggest that the factors making for the present crisis are not going to go away but that they are to become more imposing.

This is a crisis for which the psychology of capitalism has no capacity to deal with whatsoever; all its instincts serve to make its reach perpetually beyond its grasp, forever to expand to the utmost limits within its powers as rapidly as possible until such a headlong rush

for the trough brings its inevitable anti-climax of doubt as to whether
expectations will be fulfilled causing the stampede to stop in its tracks
and then become a rout until confidence picks up again.

Yet the pointers, in terms of diminishing finite resources, overpopulation, pollution and human alienation (an urban-industrial
pollution of the human soul), are portentous in the unified message
they convey, that along this road we have already travelled too far,
and that we are doing so at a speed too excessive for comfort, safety
or survival and that unless we modify our momentum and restrain
our rapacity we will surely smash both our conveyance and ourselves.

Hence the idea that the regulatory mechanisms being cooked up
in Brussels will be applied on the benevolent basis of the soft sell,
endless consumer manipulation which assumes its own justification
in the production of a plethora of shoddy consumer durables and
other manifestations of what passes for affluence, and a general advance in what passes for standards of social welfare, all on the lines
of the U.S.A. model, is probably in for some hard knocks.

It may well be that for a decade or so Europe may be able to protect its consumption standards (in the quaint belief that they represent its living standards), and that it will find the energy and raw
materials to maintain its industries against the rising tide of discontent and revolt of less happier lands, but at what cost?

Such an effort will soon be seen to require a prodigious degree of
military preparation (in the defence of the free world, of course) and
this in turn will inevitably create the tensions and the attitudes of
mind which provokes its use. This is not prognostication, it is history,
and modern history at that. A military machine is not a neutral integument of power which is packed in cold grease until it is required,
it is itself a potent, perhaps the most potent, force in generating the
conditions which prompt its own employment.

NATO is a military pact between a number of European states,
as such it is seen as essentially a holding operation against the presumed communist threat from Eastern Europe and is under the chronic constraint that any one of its members may pull out at any time,
as France did under General de Gaulle.

What are the consequences likely to be when a fully united Western Europe emerges with its own integrated and unified military
power? A trading unit whose export trade is already four times greater than that of the U.S.A.? How will the Russian Empire react
other than by greater suspicion and belligerency, and with greater

military preparation, even greater repression of its own people and of any sign of dissidence; and how can a continent of rich nations who have ganged together to get more cake whilst millions starve for lack of bread, fail to discover that in various parts of the world it has 'interests' which need preserving, when indeed they are not being promoted?

Will the U.S.E. navy have a role to play in the Indian Ocean as well as the Mediterranean? In the Pacific as well as the Atlantic? Who will get the oil? And how will they get it? By trade? Treaty? Force? Who will do the fighting? Elitist mercenaries or underpaid conscripts? What we are witnessing here is surely nothing less than the unrolling of the back-drop of the Orwellian strategic scenario as written for 1984; but there will be this difference. Orwell envisaged monster political units able to sustain a global power struggle for decades, whereas what would appear to be emerging is a general breakdown of civilised social organisation due primarily to a collapse of the morale and even the will to live (if the figures for drug addiction, alcoholism and suicide are any guide) of its members. Such a collapse is unlikely to be able to sustain a widespread military effort or indeed any other kind of effort. What is much more likely to ensue is a sporadic chronically fluctuating form of localised warlordism whose power in turn will derive from such stocks of sophisticated weaponry as it can accumulate, a ruthless and unhesitating resort to terrorism of civilian populations by torture and assassination, looting of foodstocks, exploitative manipulation of the machinery of civil and commercial government (including of course a lucrative monopolisation of traffic in hard drugs). Much of this is already emerging in the Middle East and in South East Asia.

If this is the future prospect for peace and liberty, there can be little confidence that the prospects for bread will be any better. Again we have to see this problem in terms of traditional as well as distinctly novel dangers. The mere size of Europe as an economic unit will ensure that attempts to organise and run it as a single entity fail. The beef, butter, egg and wheat mountains, to say nothing of the wine lake, the Common Market has already produced are not simply the growing pains of a new body, they are the inevitable consequence of seeking to control too great a magnitude encompassing too many variables, and they betoken the prospect of more hyperinflation, greater and more violent economic fluctuations, massive waves of unemployment and the general escalation of food prices behind a high tariff barrier, a barrier which will not only keep out food produced more cheaply elsewhere, but which will bar access to those producer countries who have hitherto sold their produce to Britain.

Again this is no mere exercise in futurology, for it is already happening. The Lome Convention was held out as a triumphant affirmation by the Market of the reality of the concern of its members for the well-being of the less-developed countries and was hailed as generous, statesmanlike, far-seeing and all the rest of it. Two days after the British referendum result, Mr. Forbes Burnham was reported from Guayana as being deeply disturbed by the way the Brusselariat was dragging its feet in implementing the terms of the agreement. "The Lome Agreement" he is quoted as saying, "must not be allowed to become a mere exercise in European Public Relations." Unwittingly or otherwise he was hitting the nail exactly on the head, for this is precisely all the Convention was ever intended to be. One of the disquiets widespread in Britain in the earlier stages of the referendum campaign centred just on this point: Was not Britain joining a rich man's club which would proceed to exploit the poor or ignore their needs even more than it was already doing?

The much trumpeted Lome Convention was the much quoted answer to such misgivings; it must have stilled the doubts in many an academic breast and won over a great many doubtfuls. With the referendum in the bag the mask could safely be allowed to slip. Dr. G.K.T. Chiepe, Botswana's Minister for Commerce and Industry, informed a press conference on June 12th (we are still in 1975) that the E.S.C. levy on meat spelt disaster for his country's cattle farmers and that some 80 percent of all the people of Botswana would be "deprived of their livelihood in the next few weeks," adding that the proposals by the E.E.C. to reduce the levy for certain cuts of meat "had only scratched the surface of the problem." Botswana, despite its enormous undeveloped mineral wealth, is among the poorest countries in the world with a *per capita* G.D.P. of £42 per annum. (Compared with France's £1,314 and West Germany's £1,467.) On June 18th the Tobacco Farmers of Zambia (G.D.P. £127) most of whom are small cultivators, were told they were unlikely to realise any profits on their sales owing to the swinging import tax imposed by one of its chief customers, Britain (G.D.P. £887). Britain of course, was upping its import taxes in line with E.E.C. regulations.

The African-Caribbean-Pacific (ACP) group of developing countries issued a communique after a two day meeting in George Town on June 8th (3 days after the referendum). They made two points about the E.E.C.; one expressed 'serious concern' at the lack of adequate consultation between the E.E.C. and the 46 A.C.P. states in settling the interim arrangements of the Lome Convention; another 'deplored' instances of the E.E.C.; action inconsistent with the spirit of the Convention, which had created 'grave difficulties' for certain A.C.P. states. The communique was issued only four months after the signing of the Convention.

Is this another instance of 'growing pains'? Or an illustration of the patent fact that what is inspiring the whole European exercise is the lust for power, whether expressed in terms of profit, or place, or both? And that therefore the only chance the poor (and therefore weak) nations have of getting a square deal, much less a generous one, from the rich nations is in the unlikely event that they can wield a similar ponderance of power?

In the absence of any such prospect why should any of the top boys of Europe give a rap what happens to the under-privileged milions of the globe? They have organised the Euro gravy train for their own benefit, not for that of those in far-away places whose fate is a matter for their own local politicians to worry about.

After Mr. Chiepe's protest, the E.E.C. Commissioners agreed to reduce the levy payable on Botswana beef (by the Botswana producers of course) to 10 per cent of the original figure. Is this a new policy? Or simply a temporary modification of the old one under pressure? Press reports said the reduction was agreed only after an 'impassioned plea' for a more generous policy from the British member. Previously the Commissioners had replied to protests by saying that the trouble arose not from the levy itself, but from the fact that since Botswana had to pay the levy before her beef was admitted to the British market, i.e. before it was actually sold, this created for Botswana a liquidity problem which the Commissioners graciously indicated they might be prepared to assist in solving.

What needs noting here is the general drift, that drift is to use the terms of trade and other devices to penalise poor countries and benefit the European rich. When food prices in Britain are eventually adjusted to correspond with the high prices of the rest of the continent, we must expect as a matter of course that concern about the size of levies on food imports will decline regardless of the fate of Botswana beef producers or of producers of any other primary product in poor countries.

What in fact then are the forces which have helped to accomplish this result and which are pushing the whole Euro-exercise?

Right at the top of the list must come the wielders of power—the world of capitalist finance and control, the board-room buccaneers, of giant capitalist undertakings (one can no longer call them enterprises, for here we are in a realm of monopoly or oligopoly where power is simply begotten by power), whose operations are frequently on a global scale. Computer technology and other developments have now made it fairly easy for such people to control or dominate world-wide markets, they operate from a pinnacle of power which is answerable to only one criterion of efficiency, that of profitability; frequently they operate on annual budgets which are higher than that of many governments, which is one reason why governments find themselves spending more and more time considering problems, such as transport, pollution, resource utilisation, inflation, strikes, unemployment and so on, which they very often create. "What is good for the multinats is good for Europe" is one blazing falsehood their spokesmen frequently declaim; but assuming they believe their own lies (and in justice to them they like to think such sentiments are true), why should any of them bother at all about the price of beef as it affects Botswana? Or the price of any other commodities poor countries produce?

Another element which helped materially to achieve the success of this unbridled exercise in effrontery and democratic denial was the bureaucracy. Warning voices have been raised repeatedly over the last few decades pointing out the dangers to liberty of an overmighty bureaucracy—itself a product of grossly overcentralised forms of government; and on the whole these voices have been totally ignored. Even the publication of the Crossman diaries, with their breath-taking revelations of the extent to which ministerial power (to say nothing of Parliamentary power) had been eroded by top bureaucrats have gestated no proposals from any quarter as to how this power might be checked and cut back; now this particular chicken has come home to roost with a vengeance, for if democratic realities have been sedulously undermined by this form of privileged power-mongering on a national basis, what will be the consequences now that it has been a major element in accomplishing the civicide of the nation and helped to create an even vaster, more powerful and more remote basis for its operations in Brussels?

Next there are the militarists and their fantasy projections of a future war. There is a disposition to assume that in Europe at least these people are the silent subservient servants of whatever group of politicians happen to be currently at the top of the greasy pole. This is a very dangerous misconception. At any given moment a politician may appear to be in the key position of having the say so on a particular issue of some importance. But how did the issue arise at all? What were the pressures on the politicians which created it? Who prepared the position papers and who listed and spelt out the options? Who did Prime Minister Eden listen to when deciding to join France and Israel in the abortive invasion of Suez? Who have Prime Ministers Wilson, Callaghan and Thatcher listened to on Rhodesia over the last decade, or on NATO and its problems? Historians were wont to debate at great length on the colonial record as to whether the flag had followed trade or trade the flag; no doubt they will argue with equal inconclusiveness about the relative roles of the military and civil arm in the drive to unite Europe, but there should be no illusion that the roles of the two forces are other than relative and equally imposing.

To the big brass of the commercial and military spheres we must of course add the politicians. It is possible that leading politicians, at least in the modern era, have tended to be pretty second-rate and rather unworthy types, lacking the sophistication even to be aware of the intrinsic nature of their own chronic insincerity and utterly unable to discern or appreciate the boredom and envy their flatulent egotripping is all too apt to create, or perhaps it is simply that their pretensions have worn so threadbare as to be obvious to all but the willfully blind among their own followers, but it can scarcely be gainsaid that a spectacle of the leaders of both parties actively participating in a prolonged and agonising nightmare of national betrayal in support of a change neither of them believed in, a change involving the abject surrender of a national sovereignty which has endured for a thousand years by means of a manipulated referendum makes it impossible for any literate adult to view party alignments and posturing any longer with the least credulity.

What has happened here is a particularly outstanding example of a very general trend. The top money boys (and the military brass) put the pressure on to secure a given objective, the politicians, whether they agreed with the objective or not, were thus confronted with a choice, to accede to the pressure or to oppose. In the event they divided and the majority opposed the changes and the loss of sovereignty involved; Prime Minister Wilson, for example, declaring it was a national surrender in exchange for a mess of economic pottage. But the pressure mounted steadily to a point where a victory for the pro-market forces was seen to be inevitable. One rule in politics is that power begets power, and the bigger the interest involved the bigger the pull of power it is therefore able to beget. So it need occasion no surprise to discover that numerous members of parliament were suddenly able to discover all sorts of virtues in the idea of national betrayal in the guise of a united Europe which had hitherto remained concealed from them. The drift to the Euro gravy train became a panic-stricken stampede which soon left only a modest principled minority on an exposed and increasingly uncomfortable platform of opposition. To their credit this minority, which included the members of the Scottish and Welsh Nationalist parties, stuck to their guns. However bitter the pangs of disappointment they may now feel, they may take comfort from one solid assurance, that history will indubitably justify their stand. The whole idea of Eurocracy is shallow, emphemeral, rootless, unprincipled, worthless and un-workable; it springs from the arrogance and presumption of power derived from money and place, it proceeds on a basis of an ingrained contempt for the dignity and worth of ordinary humanity and a belief in its infinite capacity for being manipulated and a brazen readiness to employ the instruments of persuasion and even coercion it owns to that end. It just happens that there is a rather sizeable fly in the Brussels ointment, for the concoction is utterly incompatible with the spirit of freedom which has come to dominate world history over the last two centuries and which people everywhere are seeking increasingly, and in many ways successfully, to assert. The day will surely come when the sudden flight by the band-waggon boys to Brussels will be matched by an equally sudden return flight to base and the entire scheme will be seen for what it is, a tawdry attempt to direct the mainstream of history into an authoritarian and money-dominated backwater.

'The Perfect Result' was the gleeful headline in one newspaper on the referendum, and we need to ask how a result so 'perfect' for the proprietors of the leading organ of capitalist opinion in the Western World, and so portentously inimical to the interests of the people, and to their prospects of peace, freedom of bread, was accomplished?

One answer is to be found in the cartoon published in the *Times*, showing a worried boardroom member enquiring of another "Is there any way we can recover some of the money we spent on the referendum campaign?" It is part of the malaise of our time that this ponderous cynicism is assumed to be a form of humour, but it points too to a very grim reality, that considerable sums were indeed spent by capitalist interests to accomplish this result. Bankers, industrialists (Lord Stokes of British Leyland (sic!) splashed £40,000 on an advertising campaign in the latter part of 1971), insurance companies spent freely.

They were not alone. The Government was spending public money with equal lavishness on propaganda for the cause, but there was also a third major element, the C.I.A. and the American Government. Why fight expensive wars against communism when with a quite modest outlay a political force can be organised which can be relied on to do the job much more effectively? This has been State Department thinking on Europe for a generation, and as far back as the early fifties it had organised and financed a front organisation which later became 'the European Movement'. Initially of course it was a movement not of men but of money. And it seems that the money in question was being channelled through the C.I.A. Of course the American *people* knew nothing of this at the time, any more than did the British people, and there is a grim irony in the reflection that the C.I.A. should be helping to assist in the creation of a governmental structure in Europe not dissimilar to its own, one which had, of course, spawned the C.I.A.

By 1971, according to Andrew Roth (*Can Parliament Decide ?* London, Mac Donald, 1971) "it seemed as though about £1,500,000 was being spent to persuade Britain it was worthwhile joining the Market." In the same year the same authority estimates the anti-Market bodies were thought to be budgeting about £30,000. The pro-Market forces were spending fifty times as much cash on propaganda as the modest organisation trying to stop them. There must be millions of British voters who fondly suppose they made up their own minds to vote 'yes'.

The E.E.C. itself was reported to have increased its 'information' budget from £2 million to £7 million during this period largely, one must suppose, to help the British public to make up its mind, and it is worth noting that the only two areas in which a negative result was registered were those in the remotest parts of the U.K. *and the furthest away from the influence of the manipulators*. With such lavish resources at its disposal for the sole purpose of manipulating mass opinion on a single issue how could a campaign for Europe have failed? The question is not theoretical, given the weight of opposition and public, indifference to the whole question for it could well have failed. It succeeded in part because the European Movement took great care to protect itself behind a number of front organisations, so that overnight almost, the press was loaded with reports and large, expensive advertisements (at special discount rates?) from 'Writers for Europe', 'Socialists for Europe', 'Lawyers for Europe', 'Students for Europe', 'Youth for Europe' and even, so help us all, 'Christians for Europe'. There were of course no 'Farmers for Europe' for that would have been treading on too painful a corn.

Yet all this is by the way. What really settled the outcome was not these insolent manoeuvrings and the plentiful hard cash behind them, nor even the way in which the referendum question itself was artfully structured to induce an affirmative vote from the unwary. The real cause of the failure to stop these enemies of the people, the enemies of their peace, freedom and bread, from prevailing, lay in the near total confusion of mind and purpose of the opponents of Eurocracy.

The mere fact of the European Campaign, the way it was mounted, the way it was conducted and the way in which it secured its objective was, given the nature of that objective, the screams of a warning siren that freedom was in deadly danger. Yet, apart from a few isolated instances that had no perceptible influence on events, those screams were utterly ignored. People were persuaded to debate with endless, earnest-minded fatuity about the consequences for farm prices, the outlook for the white fishing industry, whether 'sovereignty' really resided in parliament, or in the monarch, or in the cabinet or possibly in the discarded old boots of the Lord Chancellor's deceased grandmother; whether one of the richest nations with a headstart of inherited skills second to none in the world and the kind of competence that, however economically idiotic, could produce the technical miracle of the Concorde aeroplane would 'survive' if it did not join Europe, and so on and so on. The rights, liberties and traditions bequeathed by a thousand years of continuous history were under the deadliest forms of assault they had ever known; what ensued was not a debate about the central issues (which indeed were largely suppressed) but a media-conducted yakety-yak conveying scarcely more than the verbal parameters of somnambulism.

The people of Britain have a large number of organisations through which they are able to express their opinions, when they have any, on matters of importance. Let it be noted that none of its local political parties, trade unions, coops or any of its multitudinous civic organisations had a single word to say about uniting Europe, not that is, until money, place, position and power began to move on the subject.

From the outset it was not a campaign so much as an exercise in manipulation by top people for top people's interests, and the mere fact that such an operation could be mounted at all suggests some terrible fractures in the structure of our freedom. It was the blindness of those who opposed Eurocracy to this cardinal point that made them so ineffectual in the struggle.

The blunt fact is that due largely to overcentralisation and an overgrowth of scale of most of the artifacts of national life, which include not only business and commercial enterprises but political partie and trade unions, the power of the people to create their own pattern of life, and hence to exercise control over its different aspects, has largely been destroyed or reduced to proportions of the most residual significance. Hence the argument about having the Parliament at Westminster or at Strasbourg was without meaning simply because the major question-mark hanging over Westminster is how to devolve most of its powers downwards to the local organs of government where it properly belongs before democracy and freedom succumb to the grip of bureaucratic strangulation. It was this failure of perception which made the ensuing 'debate' in all leading journals of opinion arcane, trivial, silly and irrelevant, and of course unable to provide any answer to the dangers which had been mounted.

There is no need to discuss in detail the role played by the press, with one minor exception it pleaded the case for Eurocracy; it is the exception that needs to be noted; despite a temporary lapse when it advised in an editorial that there seemed no alternative but to join, a stance from which one may guess the anguished cries of its readers compelled it to recover, the *Spectator* was the one serious organ of opinion which voiced opposition to Eurocracy. Its case was almost entirely economic and mainly in conventional terms, with occasional forays into the 'sovereignty' aspect and the theme of partriotism. That was all. It never seems to have asked itself what would happen if the people were persuaded to vote for Eurocracy and what its own policy would be in consequence. Its attitude now is one of mere acquiescence. No doubt it will seek to criticise the bluntness of the axe from time to time, but effectively it has now put its own head on the block.

It might be thought that help would be forthcoming from that voice of the middle-aged intellectual trendies, the *New Statesman*, which has an entirely unfounded reputation of being 'the voice of the left'; in reality it is a voice from another perch in the plush glades of privilege, a fact which became clearly apparent to those who might have missed the obvious on earlier occasions during the referendum countdown. Its final editorial, "The Case for Voting Yes" was a monument of pompous obliviousness to what was at stake and a tribute to the efficacy of the media manipulating skills of the Eurocrats. Its case for going in rested essentially on the *tu quoque* that it was not possible for Britain to stay outside! As one angry reader was not slow to remark, this was not the first time the *New Statesman* had betrayed its readership at a time of crisis but why, we need to ask, did it respond to events with such egregious pusillanimity? It did so because of a defect in its outlook it happens to share with almost the entire modern world: this springs directly from a crisis of power. We are in the final stages of the consummation of that crisis and it may yet produce an apocalyptic form of armageddon for the human race. But for the 'left' this crisis, if it exists in their minds at all, is purely peripheral to other issues such as the class war, nationalisation, equality, world unity and similar shibboleths.

Ask any of these gentry why we have had two world wars, the generation-long horror in Vietnam, the world slump of the thirties, the establishment and proliferation of the nuclear club, or any other repudiation of the people's desire for peace, liberty and bread, and they will answer with endless chatter about the evils of capitalism and betray no inkling of awareness that these tragedies are direct consequences of this crisis of power, and which in turn is being promoted by the sheer size and scale of over-centralised political and economic power, and the rapidity with which the revolution in technology over the last century has enabled fewer and fewer hands to grasp control of that power and use it for furthering the pursuit of power as an end in itself regardless of any other interest.

It is this cardinal factor which negates nearly all contemporary political discussion. Does Leftie want the new Europe to help the poor nations? His desire is irrelevant because he has no capacity to influence an agglomeration of power of this magnitude for any particular purpose *at all*; those who wield such power are beyond his reach. Do Rightie or Leftie want freedom, or peace, or bigger battalions, less inflation, and subsidies for small enterprises? Again they are pipe-dreaming, it does not matter what they think on these or any other issues for on such a scale power is an end in itself and will pursue only those goals which will yield this particular fruit.

Ah yes, says our brothers-to-all-men-parliamentary-soft-of-centre-do-gooder, that is why we have formed our wonderful socialist-liberal-tory party, so that we can secure the reins of power in our own hands and thus achieve these objectives. This is the para-illusion of all illusions of contemporary politics. Has he forgotten that the leaders of mass socialist parties are building hydrogen bombs and Polaris submarines? Is this to further the brotherhood of man? Or to keep our great leaders in office?

Has he forgotten that until their power interests dictated otherwise it was the tory leaders who were the greatest exponents of national patriotism and how their public meetings were apt to begin with a rendering of the national hymn as though it were their personal property? Who was it upheld the virtues of all things British and sneered at 'foreigners' and all things foreign?

The lesson is simply this; in any mass society politics is not the art of the possible, but the art of manipulation and all mass parties are basically an instrument of that process, a process which manipulates people along the courses best suited to keep the power-mongers in power.

This is why in any mass party, when the members differ with the leaders on any matter of moment the latter simply proceed to ignore the former. The Labour Party went so far as to call a special con-ference of its members to make a decision (once for all?) about the Eurocracy project. By an overwhelming majority the members voted against it. By then the Labour Government was set on a quite con-trary course and the effect of this conference vote on its actions could not have been more contemptuous of both the conference and this collective decision, indeed a small group of ministers who tried to work in accordance with conference decision (of their own party) were roundly accused in the public prints of disloyalty to their government colleagues!

If the lesson, with all its horrendous implications, that in mass parties the leadership manipulates the members when it can and ignores them when it can't, and that in no sense worth relating do the members control the leaders, continues to be lost on the bulk of progressive opinion then it will continue to act as a stop to an open door ushering in ever widening eruptions of betrayal and disaster for the peoples of the world.

What is at stake here is a quite basic issue of intellectual clarity about the nature of the power that dominates the modern world. The two principles that need to be grasped and which almost all political theorising ignores, are (*a*) on a mass scale power is no longer susceptible to *any* form of democratic control and (*b*) that democracy can only be effective when the political unit is modest in size. (For those who love numbers we may say that a unit of five or six million seem about right given the facility for common action which modern technology makes possible, as the Scandinavian experience indicates; ten million is getting a bit much, although the Swiss seem to manage superbly with twelve million bearing in mind that Switzerland is not a nation but a *confederation* of largely self-governing countries).

The modern era is peculiar in the extent to which it has turned its back on the one rule which accompanies growth throughout the natural order; it is a rule which applies equally to chemistry, biology, zoology, plantology and the expansion of numbers of any group of living creatures, *as numbers increase, in order to achieve a continuity of self-control and self-manageability of the unit the unit must divide.*

A failure to divide would lead not simply to loss of control, but to a loss of the features which give the unit its distinctive character. A herd of zebra, for example, conducts itself in terms of grazing, mating, defence, especially of the young, leadership selection, restraint of numbers and territorial occupancy according to a complex pattern of behaviour mechanisms which have developed over centuries of evolutionary impetus.

For a herd simply to multiply its numbers in the mindless manner that has emerged in mass human societies over the last two centuries would be to put an unbearable strain on the behaviour mechanisms that govern the life of the herd and face it with the prospect of extinction.

Hence when numbers increase it brings into play certain restraints on its breeding habits which put a brake on reproduction. (When will our population alarmists begin to stop bothering about pills, rubber sheaths and mass sterilisation programmes, and begin to study behaviour mechaisms which have controlled the numbers of different species of animal life for many centuries with the most

superb effectiveness? Is it perhaps because all animal life has a basis
in the organic grouping of its own kind, a grouping which is the
framework within which numbers are controlled and because it is
considered 'impractical' to relate such reasoning to human life?)

Or it divides.

It *never* proliferates in a mass unless the unit is such as, for example,
when cells, (themselves of course a process of division), multiply in
a sick organism as in the case of a cancer-like growth. Need we add
that in all such cases such proliferation is invariably a terminal stage
in the life of the organism?

So that when we see a proliferation of human numbers within
one state unit that may run into many millions or even hundreds of
millions, we are not observing a process of burgeoning power, growth
and progress, but simply one of decay and quite inevitable collapse.

Hence Eurocracy is in no sense a sign of advance towards visionary
realms of tranquillity and plenty, but a lurch towards cancerous
forms of militarism, bureaucracy and repression which cannot fail
to kill the host body as a matter of course.

One of the most extraordinary aspects of modern political theorising is that it is unable to give any explanation for the major crises
of our times, of the world wars and world economic depressions
which have stunted so much of human life and its possibilities. It is
assumed that *somehow*, though quite how is never precisely indicated,
these tragedies are products of the normal workings of human nature,
as though the teaming masses of humanity could possibly want world
war or world economic collapse as a way of life.

This failure springs directly from a refusal to take into account that
there is such a political or economic phenomenon as overgrowth at
all, or an inane readiness to assume that any form of such growth
is *ipso facto* a sign of advance. What now needs to be grasped, not
least by these forces seeking solutions to world problems, is that *no
progress in human affairs worth the name can be expected to ensue unless this
factor of the optimum limits of growth is made one of central concern to all
analytical thinking.*

To say as much is to pose a gigantic moral and intellectual
challenge to the progressive forces of humanity. The phenomenon of
decadence which now dominates human affairs has its origin in the
vast institutional changes in human life which for the most part
were initiated in the nineteenth century. It was this century which
saw the refinements of capitalist and socialist economic and political

analysis which provided the theoretical framework for the mass
parties of the 20th. The very profundity of the contemporary crisis
in human affairs, of which the move to unite Europe is but another
symptom, indicates that the theoretical framework is utterly inadequate as a basis for action and that mankind's prospects of survival
now hinge on its capacity to abandon swiftly the former intellectual
constructs which constrict it and an equal readiness to seize on
these new forms which hold out the prospects of liberation.

It needs to be asserted with measured emphasis that political
parties based on the theories of yesteryear, whether they are capitalist
or socialist, communist or fascist, liberal or libertarian, are simply,
because they are based on the centralised manipulation of a mass
membership, an organised repudiation of democracy and its prospects, and far from holding out any prospect of resolving our major
problems can only betray us. That is what modern history is all about.

What must man *create* today by way of social forms which will
rescue him from the thraldom of power? The post gives some clues.
The fact that man, not just 'leaders' but man in general, will do the
creating suggests it will be on a small scale, and is it not indeed the
case that the supreme triumphs of the spirit of human life, whether
in terms of architecture, sculpture, painting, poetry, philosophy or
music, have invariably emanated from city-state types of civic life
which were modest in scale? By a happy chance the title of the late
Dr. Schumacher's book appears to have given a new phrase to the
language—'Small is' indeed, 'Beautiful,' to avoid large-scale errors—
not to say disasters, and altogether more seemly to the human condition, not least it is the indispensible prerequisite to any form of
successful social action or enterprise.

How then do we proceed? It is impossible here to think in terms
of grand strategy, about which there is always more than a whiff
of fascism, whatever political label may be attached to it. The
approach will be necessarily pragmatic and piecemeal, depending
on the opportunities available and the forces which can be expected
to manifest themselves.

These forces are by no means slight. One of the really interesting
aspects of the Eurocracy conspiracy is the way in which its work-out
has been accompanied by a resurgence of small ethnic or national
groupings all over Europe, and indeed in many parts of the world.
In essence this resurgence is simply a continuation of the historic
drive for freedom, a drive which also found expression of a kind in all

the principal revolutions of the modern era from the English Civil War, the French Revolution, the American War of Independence and the emancipation of subject peoples from colonialism of our own day. The Communist revolutions of Russia and China do not, of course, fit into this pattern at all, whatever state propaganda machines may assert to the contrary. Both represent the replacement of a weak and antiquated form of colonial authoritarianism by one that is infinitely better organised, far more ruthless, and blatantly contemptuous of the value of human life. The cause of colonial liberation inside the Russian and Chinese empires has yet to be asserted, far less accomplished. Hence first and foremost we need to become the champions of these peoples and their struggle for freedom in every way we can. Already the freedom forces in Scotland have helped to change the political face of Britain and it is another irony of the Euro-conspiracy that whilst it seems to be achieving some of its biggest triumphs, the dominant aspect of Spanish politics should be a new wave of cruelty and repression against the increasingly resurgent Basques.

In the perspective of history what cause is more likely to prevail, that of the power and wealth at the top, or of the people at the base?

We need here to rush forward a revolution of consciousness. At present this world-wide struggle is buried under layers of ignorance, indifference and spurious fears of 'Balkinisation', as if the conflicts which once afflicted that region were the product of any other factor than the intransigent interference in their affairs by what used to be called the 'great powers'.

There are also imposing barriers in people's mind arising from erroneous notions about economics. It is *assumed* rather than discussed, that political giantism is the key to economic riches, but it is an assumption which flies flat in the face of the evidence. All the giants are miserably poor and are in the lower, if not the lowest, bracket for per capital G.D.P. figures in the world. The exception appears to be the U.S.A., but given its considerable level of affluence, itself based on the headless rape of the resources of a virgin continent, why are the poverty levels of millions of its citizens and the meagreness of its social furniture so appalling if it be not that its mere size is so huge and uncontrollable as to make such a degree of public squalor amid its private affluence as inevitable as it is ineradicable?

People who call themselves left-wing badly need a refresher course in economics based on observable facts. For a start they need to digest the implication of the fact that nearly all the really prosperous nations in the world are quite modest in size. There is nothing exceptional, for example, about Denmark. It has a G.D.P. of £1,393, which is among the highest in the world. Yet it has a population of a mere 4 million.

The magnitude of the task of achieving this change of consciousness need not be gainsaid, but neither too must its necessity. We are at the brink here of a major world disaster and an immeasurable degree of human suffering may be avoided if a large section of that thinking minority which takes the lead in political matters will devote its time to ensuring the need for these changes is understood. We need not in this regard, be overmuch concerned with the imposing and apparent immutability of the prevailing power structures; it is scarcely a quarter of a century ago that the world appeared to be dominated, by a number of equally imposing and apparently immutable colonial empires. Where are those empires today?

Essentially what is at stake here is a battle for the mind and a need to illuminate consciousness throughout the world with the imperative need for small-scale political and economic structures as the indispensable basis for peace, liberty and material sufficiency.

Very often the people in the thickest part of the battle, for example the Basques, the Ukranians or the Nagas, appear to have the least knowledge of each other's struggle for revival and the relevance of that struggle to the general drift of world events. It is here that those less immediately involved can assist. The need for example, to bring together representatives of these resurgent nations, the Fourth World no less, has now become one of great urgency. They need to exchange information, to confer, to plan ahead, to establish their own modest organisational structures and generally to assert themselves on the world scene as a force for progress. If only a small number of those earnest souls who talk so windily of setting up a socialist Europe, workers control, state ownership of everything (leading doubtless to personal responsibility for nothing) and other shibboleths of the so-called 'left' would take the lead here, they might well have the kind of effect on the course of history they seem always to quest for without ever coming near to achieving.

Again we are confronted with a prodigious need for many forms of research into a new world political and economic order based on a human scale of operations; we need more journals for both propaganda and intellectual clarification, to monitor the elements of this world-wide struggle and to make known the good news of peoples' liberation. There is here a major task of organisation and of action, it cannot be done by one group of individuals however devoted they may be, it can only indeed be done at all, by many many small groups of people being prepared to devote their energies and talents to the task with the kind of inspiration that has accompanied the attempts of our forbears to change the direction of human society in other ways.

At the local level there is the need to establish the kind of parish, village or city-ward structures which will reflect our liberation and democratic aspirations. These are already emerging in multitudinous forms, but the central debate about power and how to resist the boundless presumption of those centralised forms which pose such onerous threats to freedom from a basis devoid of genuine democratic content has scarcely yet begun. It is vital that we create these new forms for community life, for housing, education, health, trade, culture, neighbourhood welfare and so on, but such approaches will have little vitality and less viability if their protagonists do not also at times lift up their eyes unto the hills to take a perspective of the wider scene, if only to establish where in general terms we are heading.

However much each of us concentrates on doing our thing, the general problems of power, peace, pollution and population will not just go away; localism needs to be matched by a world view and *vice versa,* to ignore either is to cripple both.

The same is true of national affairs; if freedom continues to have any significance they are clearly going to be a great many changes in the powers of centralised governments over the next generation, if only because many, if not most of them, are incompatible with its ordinary working. But whichever way it goes there are bound to be national units, and however imposing and exciting local problems may be, there does also need to be a concern to resolve the problems of national life in terms of liberty and democratic responsiveness.

What, for example, are the limits beyond which the power of a national government must on no account be allowed to intrude? This is not a new problem so much as a very old one which has been forgotten; one of the most extraordinary aspects of more than a century of socialist theorising is the extent to which it has been assumed that the power of the state is always of beneficial import when in socialist hands. Never has it crossed the socialist mind that once that power exceeds a certain size, extent or tempo of activity it simply ceases to be even capable of being responsible to popular control.

Yet it is precisely this factor that is binding liberty in chains in our own age; it has permitted the authoritarian posturings of the labourites over the European issue, and enabled them to betray the powerless manipulated millions to courses which serve no other purpose than to keep the power freaks in power, and even now they are still at it, for the 'left' labourites are calling for more and more authoritarian schemes of nationalisation. The result of the referendum has of course led to a cruel exposure of the shoddiness of their intellectual assumptions; previously they were 'against' British membership. So what will they do now? They are going to try to create socialist majorities in the European Parliament and other institutions.

The implications of the fact, that for all their socialist majorities in Britain they have been unable to prevent external forces manipulating British mass opinion into a surrender of its historic birthright of sovereignty, that they cannot prevent Britain from building more and more nuclear weapons, poison gas and germ-warfare weapons, researching genetic engineering, the poisoning of farmland, waterways, seas and airspace with non-bio-degradable by-products of industry, or even stop Britain behaving like a greedy pig in face of the dire lack of food and other necessities in the poorer countries of the world, seems to escape them altogether.

Just in case they do not comprehend the implications, let them be stated again in terms which may even penetrate the well-organised defence mechanism of *New Statesman* addicts;

   i   Power relationships change as units of politics or economics grow in size.

   ii   Growth itself causes more power to flow to the centre and away from the people.

   iii   Hence as growth continues, power tends increasingly to be lodged in unrepresentative and non-responsive hands.

   iv   These statements are not invalidated by existence of the traditional mechanisms of representative democracy.

   v   Such mechanisms simply become additional perches on which elitist leaders can climb and from which the arena fo the manipulation of the mass can be extended.

vi   Hence with continued growth the particular colour of the
     ideology of the manipulators matters less and less, the fact
     of their power perch and the powerlessness of the masses
     matters more and more.

vii   Overgrowth leads to authoritarianism.

viii   Mass democracy is a contradiction in terms.

ix   As the Russian Mensheviks of 1917 discovered to their cost,
     an ideology in a given situation is of no account if one
     lacks the power to practice it.

x   Unless the declared objective be to destroy democracy the
    power to implement any ideology in a democracy is of no
    account if it is based on institutional realities which negate
    the power of democracy itself.

This is not the place to push this analysis further, badly although
it needs doing, the cardinal consequence is simply this, that on a
modest human scale it is possible for moral judgements as expressed
in an ideology to take precedence over mere power-mongering,
but when the scale is too large then moral considerations are always
subordinate to the quest for power as an end in itself. This is the
chief symptom of the sickness of overgrowth which leads to wars and
economic crisis. The aetiology of this sickness does not stem from
human wickedness as such as from the mere fact of overgrowth.

These considerations call for a considerable overhaul of traditional
thinking about political and economic matters. We can no longer go
on discussing intelligibly such blanket categories, as 'socialism' or
'capitalism'. What we have to ask is, is the socialism small-scale
and therefore subject to the control, which need not always be
expressed in formal terms, of the people, or is it large-scale and
therefore an element in the manipulation of people rather than an
expression of their wishes? Given the pronounced dangers to liberty
that stem from a huge centralised state apparatus, what forms of
popular control shall be exercised over institutions such as railway
networks and electricity grids which are large-scale by the very
nature of their operations, to prevent them being used by power
freaks as instruments of oppression or constraint?

Again, when we speak of 'capitalism' are we speaking of it in
its original sense of a large number of small-scale entrepreneurs,
or are we talking of the world of monopoly or semi-monopoly
control of the multinationals and the huge private institutional
investors and other products and apostles of giantism? We really

must clear our minds of generations of accumulated cant on this subject. We must see that our tame acquiescence to the capitalist giant is as dangerous to liberty as our hostility to the freedom of the small entrepreneur.

Small-scale economics is as vital to liberty as small-scale politics; that is why the champions of the Fourth World should not hesitate to make common cause with small shop-keepers and small business men. The question of whether an enterprise is publicly or privately owned is of infinitely less importance than whether it is large or small. If it is small it is susceptible to local community control, if it is large it isn't. Hence progressives should not be deterred by sneers about 'populism'. Populism has become a swear word used by the Eurocrats to denigrate any form of opposition to their schemes. Quite right too, the word relates to peoples' power, of which they have just cause to be afraid. Opposition to Eurocracy needs to make common cause with small-scale entrepreneurs in the struggle to defeat giantism, they represent a potent source of assistance which up to now has been largely ignored.

Progressives need also to make common cause with rank and file trade union members. All too often trade union organisation is a fix, a large-scale fix controlled by privileged power elitists at the top who are virtually irremovable. As in the field of mass political parties, the democratic forms are ostentatiously observed whilst their democratic content has become vestigial. But the Augean stables cannot be cleansed without a clear vision of the new order that is to prevail, otherwise, as so often has been the case in the past, we shall simply end up with the mixture as before.

The primary need here is to democratise trade union power; that means making it locally autonomous so that instead of local branches being a footstool for power freaks in a rigid bureaucracy they are autonomous decision-making bodies in their own right. In time it is to be hoped that they will come to see that generally they have more in common with members of other unions in the same locality, than with members of the same union outside it. This is another potent source of power for the realisation of Fourth World objectives which at present is being largely ignored.

It would be possible to make similar points about other forms of power which need to be democratised, such as local government and numerous ministries of the central government, as well as the power of parliament itself.

The sovereignty of parliament has been largely destroyed from above by overloading it with functions which only an army of bureaucrats could operate. The citizen surrenders power to parliament in the belief that M.P.s will act in his name only to find that despite the formalities of the matter to the contrary, the bureaucrats are the real masters and are responsible only to themselves.

When the crunch finally came on the question of Europe the citizen discovered that the power of his M.P. was illusory and that the people who really had the power, the bureaucrats, had sold the pass long before. Far from being the expression of his collective sovereignty, parliament over the years had become an elaborately formalised ritual which confirms, or acquiesces in, decisions taken elsewhere. It was not in consequence difficult to persuade the citizen to acquiesce in a skillfully engineered campaign to transfer the residue of its sovereignty. Parliament today, if a contradictory metaphor may be permitted, is a haven of political eunuchs, and of no more consequence than the parish Council of Neasden. The Prime Minister went on record after the referendum, to say, "...14 years of national argument are now over." He can only be right if one assumes that the argument about freedom is now over. Indeed, as Brother Martin said after the burning of Saint Joan, "This is not the end ... but the beginning." The European trick has helped to throw into focus the real nature of the forces bent on destroying freedom, and men of political sensibility must now rouse themselves as never before to a major effort of mind and will to repudiate the path to damnation along which these bleak, destructive and profoundly amoral forces would drag us.

Having said this, it must be faced that the arguments for the unification of Europe which have been drummed up so assiduously, are accepted by many people and deserve to be treated with some care. Miss Barbara Ward in her book *Space Ship Earth*, has probably put these arguments as persuasively as anybody else and they may be worth examining in detail. In justice to Barbara Ward there is evidence that on many counts her thinking, especially in relation to the problems of ecology, has changed considerably since *Space Ship Earth* first appeared, but quite clearly many people are still influenced by her earlier writings.

She argues first that unification is the only way in which the curse of war between nation states in Europe can be lifted.

In view of the fact that two major world wars in this century have originated in Europe, it might be thought that Miss Ward is on firm ground, but she appears to ignore totally what in fact has been the real cause of these wars and to assume that their origins are identical with the origin of, let us say, the Boer War or even the wars of the Roses. What distinguishes modern wars from those in the past is that today nobody except a tiny handful of people at the top *wants* war. This is not to say that people do not want, if they can get them, the fruits of war; what is obvious is that the vast generality of mankind has developed a considerable awareness of the value of peace which makes it esteem its fruits even more than those of war.

If the generality of people in Europe had been given the option to fight or not to fight in the two world wars, we may be sure that the majority would have decided against fighting. This, presumably, is why *all* armies found it necessary to introduce conscription. We may go even further and say if the generality of people had been asked whether they approved of the preparations for either of the two world wars they would have registered strong disapprobation. Whereas in the past there was an appetite for war, and many people wanted to fight if only for the rich pickings that were offered them in victory, the generality of people today do not decide these questions at all because, as we have repeatedly asserted here, they live in societies so large that it is impossible for them to make their interests predominate over the interests of the centralised power machines which run the state.

The generality of the people of Europe, and indeed the world, is confronted with state machines which are out of control simply because they are too large. Miss Ward's solution to this frightening state of affairs is to merge some of the existing units into a single giant one, she sees that this is an inevitable march of history towards a one-world government. This is of course not argument, but incantation. The question should at least be asked, if people cannot control meganation-state entities of the size of France, Germany and Britain, what possible prospect is there that they will be able to control a bigger empire compounded of these and other units, and what prospect is there that the generality of people of the world will be able to control a so-called world government, established with the kind of centralised authority Miss Ward appears to have in mind?

In politics if we want the ends we must create the means; if we want peace the way forward is not to conclude that since meganations make war as a matter of course despite the wishes of their subjects therefore we must unite them into continental meganations, for all we are then doing is not uniting for peace so much as for a propensity for more and bigger wars. A glance at the record of any of the major continental meganations will indicate that at this level war becomes even more terrible and even more immediately inevitable. However that may be the very nature of the attempts aimed in the long run to make Europe a military, economic and political whole, confirm in almost every respect the political aspects of the thesis we have been arguing here. The military case for such an entity was spelt out with a fair degree of exactitude by Mr. Edward Heath during some lecture he gave to an American University audience in 1969. The Americans, it seems, felt the time had come for Europe to look to its own defence in terms of a possible war, with the enforced union of non-Soviet, non-Socialist Republics, of the Russian Empire. To do this Europe must, it was assumed, unite its military forces. This is and has always been one of the primary considerations underlying the entire exercise.

It will be noted that there was no question of consulting the people. It may be argued of course that it is a leader's job to lead, but, in democratic terms what does such leadership involve? Does it involve placing clear alternative courses of action before the people, and even urging the adoption of one rather than the other as a prelude to acting in honest terms of the people's considered verdict? Or does it involve manipulating the entire apparatus of the power of the state towards an objective predetermined by the 'leaders' before the people have been consulted, and engineering its adoption through the legislative machine in defiance of the people's wishes? Britain's 'leaders' chose this latter course and in doing so have betrayed not the slightest inkling that the principal victim of this shoddy trick has been democracy itself. Today the increasing resort to violence and even killing to gain political ends by ordinary citizens is manifest, so too is the growing contempt for politicians of all colours of ideology. Political leaders view this development with pained surprise, seemingly unaware that when people feel driven to such violence they are now using the only power they believe themselves to possess and are thus repaying the politicians in their own coin.

This move coincides with two developments on the economic front which make the idea of a United Europe not only infinitely more attractive but, from the viewpoint of certain powerful interests, imperative. First is the sudden break-through of computerised technology in the sixties which at a bound had made the management and exploitation of world-wide markets a practical matter of everyday happenstance; second is the growth of economic institutions to match this degree of scale, the multinational corporation. It is true that there is nothing particularly new about multinationals as such (nor, for that matter, about computers, of which the abacus is possibly the earliest example), what is new about today's multinationals is that in the past they were established mainly to exploit primary products and resources, or to build and operate public utilities. Hence they might exploit Iranian oil, Zambian copper, Malayan rubber or West Indian sugar, or they would build railways in the Argentina or Tzarist Russia, so that generally they confined their activities to a single-crop or resource, or to a single utility. Today they are rapidly moving towards a complete grip on the entire consumer market, which in turn means they will be determining the general pattern of consumer preference and, with the passage of time, consolidating themselves as a pronounced political factor in a sphere even further removed from the political control of ordinary people.

Inevitably this means that political unification is seen as a desirable objective by these special interests and we do well to consider that in Britain this call came, as it doubtless did in other countries, entirely from the military, industrial and commercial interests. Once *they* decided on this fateful step they proceeded to unleash a barrage of skillfully tendentious propaganda to convert the people to their viewpoint. In Britain, as in other countries, an abundance of public money was shamelessly poured out in this wholly partisan project, industrialists and others also dipped deep in their coffers to pay for the leaflets, posters, books, 'campaign' centres, and for special radio, television and press 'features'. Newspapers such as the London *Times*, which for generations had maintained a facade of independence in the reporting and explaining of events to their readers, suddenly betrayed the trust their readers had learned to repose in them and became brazen organs of propaganda for the new conspiracy and no form of persuasion which could be used to condition public opinion into accepting this move was neglected.

Two features marked the campaign; first was the quite dishonest effort to pretend that no surrender of the power of parliament was involved in the new relationship, so that the whole issue of British sovereignty was pushed into the background. A host of side issues was given prominence, issues such as agricultural policy, off-shore fishing limits and so on. By this means the basic issue of the Common Market and the tremendous degree of surrender of sovereignty, and thus of democratic control involved, was skillfully played down. Again we have to see here the usual method employed on a major issue, one of which had on this occasion the effect of undermining not only the sovereignty of parliament but the democratic rights of the people. The basic issue of principle was, should the British people surrender its sovereign power to run its own affairs as it saw fit to a remote bureaucratic complex or not? All the guns of propaganda were brought to bear, not on the argument about this basic point of substance, but on minor and relatively trifling side issues which carried with it the implication that the major decisions of principle had in fact been taken and that this surrender of sovereignty was as inevitable as it was desirable and meritorious.

The second was the extent to which the entire campaign for this move emanated from the top levels of British society, and from the top levels of hierarchical societies abroad. At no stage of the opening moves was the generality of people *informed* on the matter, far less consulted about their wishes, and most of these moves, and the subsequent negotiations, were conducted in such conditions of secrecy that even members of parliament were unable to gain a clear picture of precisely what was afoot.

The propaganda campaign which accompanied them was financed and conducted from three main sources, first there were the moguls of private industry interests such as British Leyland, whose full-page advertisements in the *Times* were drumming up the cause of British entry with pronouncements saying, "we feel sure it will be good for Britain, good for Europe and particularly good for British industry and ourselves." Statements which prompted Mr. Andrew Roth to wonder parenthetically whether it was not "an unconscious parody of the American car magnate's classic remark: 'What's good for General Motors is good for the United States'."[1]

Second were the organisations which were established to promote

[1]Andrew Roth, *Can Parliament Decide*? MacDonald, 1971, p. 156.

the pro-market campaign among various sections or special interests such as students, youth groups, management, research and so on under the umbrella of the 'European Movement'. In 1971, the same authority[2] declares, it was estimated the movement budgeted to spend about £250,000.

The third source was the taxpayer, of whose money the government admitted having spent £645,000 up to 15 July 1971, on its pro-market campaign. Bringing the estimated total of money spent on propaganda for the campaign to something like £1,500,000.

Inexplicably something went wrong. People seemed to be relatively unaffected by the barrage of propaganda directed at them and instead insisted on making the basic point of principle the central issue. We can see here a classic instance of how the forces of power in a mass society will resort to every trick of the trade they can think of to persuade public opinion to their own way of thinking: if, however, they should fail, as in this effort they failed, they have another weapon in their armoury. They proceed to ignore it. Opinion polls in Britain for years consistently showed that the great majority of British people did not wish Britain to enter the Common Market, nevertheless, a determined Prime Minister of a divided cabinet, and of an even more deeply divided House of Commons, pushed the measure of access through the legislative process against the wishes of an even more divided country.

We should pause to contemplate the enormity of what has been done here. For what the top-side centralising interests are saying is that they are only prepared to go along with democratic procedures provided public opinion wants what they want, or provided, if they do not, that the mechanism of democracy can be used to achieve the results they want regardless of the democratic views of the majority. It is difficult not to conclude that in a real sense when the promarketeers celebrated Britain's formal joining of the Common Market what in fact they were celebrating was a deathblow to the mechanisms of democratic procedures which had been developed in Britain for many centuries, and one of the grossest acts of national betrayal in a millennium of continuous history.

In the abandonment of principle for special interests there are depths below depths it would seem. As these words are written the media is expounding at great length on the virtues of a 'European Parliament' and the unwisdom of certain Labour Party elements in

[2]*Ibid.*, p. 162.

refusing to send delegates to Strasbourg to sit there. It seems to cross nobody's mind that if people have so little control over a Westminster parliament which they have, in formal terms at least, elected themselves, what point is there at all in seriously discussing participation in an even remoter body composed of people whose responsiveness to popular wishes is so manifestly irrelevant to what they want? It should be noted that this so-called parliament is utterly bogus. It has the power to dismiss the Commission which runs it, on a vote of no confidence, which is rather like saying the House of Commons can dismiss the monarch, it can reject the budget as a whole (as if it would! What parliament in all history has ever done so?) it can 'amend' some items in the budget amounting to 20 per cent of the total, and that is the limit of its defined powers. It is graciously allowed by the Commission to advise it and to be consulted and that is all. It is a talking shop with less power than a primary school management committee; the real power is in the Commission. What then is the Commission?

The extent to which the processes of government in Britain are no longer susceptible to genuine democratic control have rarely been so conclusively demonstrated as by the open contempt that former Premier Heath and his associates showed towards the real wishes of the people as indicated in successive opinion polls. They *used* Parliament and its enacting machinery to override those wishes, and the people, despite their formal powers of self-rule enshrined in Parliament, were utterly powerless to stop them.

In this context we need to recall again that these wishes were being expressed, and we do well to bear in mind that a similar situation existed in other European countries where the issue was foisted upon an unsuspecting public, after the deployment of a degree of brainwashing and other techniques of mass persuasion for which it is doubtful if all recorded history can find a parallel. At every turn the common man was being assured this was the path of peace, progress and prosperity, that to refuse to tread it was a sign of weakminded confusion, of a failure to grasp the realities of the time, and an indication that he was out of step with all responsible, expert and authoritative opinion.

Again, let us pause to contemplate how a democracy is supposed to work. A man has an idea, a scheme perhaps, the adoption of which, he is convinced, would lead to a considerable increase in the wellbeing of his countrymen. He lives in everytown and he walks round the corner to discuss it with his neighbours, he writes to the local press, he canvasses on an increasingly wider front, delighted that his neighbours and acquaintances share his opinions and his enthusiasm to get them adopted. His union and co-operative branch take it up, the idea takes wings, it becomes a national issue, a matter of national debate and, ultimately, it is reasonable to say, of national decision.

We ought to note that there is an underlying supposition here which is fully justified and which has a long and respectable ancestry, that truth is something which has an innate strength of its own which enables it to make its way despite whatever obstacles ill-disposed persons are prepared to put in its path. Truth does not need to be drummed at people like a campaign to promote the sale of an item of rubbish from the supermarkets masquerading as food. Truth, it may be said, has a presence, a majesty even, of its own which only needs to be perceived to be acknowledged. The fact that so much modern merchandise is founded on fraud and deceit is why an advertising industry exists at all, to manufacture the lies and cozenage by which a gullible mass audience may be duped into accepting it. A great poem or any great work of art makes its own way into public awareness and acceptance: because it is a singular work of creative imagination and not a mass product, no amount of advertising can make it acceptable if it is bad and no amount of hostility in the media can prevent its acceptance if it is good. And it does not *need* the media if it is good. There is a hunger in men's souls for truth in these as in other forms which ensures it will be sought out and accepted—whatever the obstacles. We may be sure, for example, that the writings of Solzhenitsyn are read and esteemed in Russia wherever they are able to circulate despite the fact that Solzhenitsyn himself has been deprived of his nationality and forced into exile.

As far back as 1946, Mr. Winston Churchill sent up his first balloon on the subject. Speaking at Zurich he said, "My counsel to Europe can be given in a single word: Unite!" From that date the top-side campaign gathered momentum to its culmination in the calculated treason of the Heath Government of 1973. Yet a search of the conference agendas of the intervening period, of the resolutions of local branches of political parties, trade unions and other local bodies reveals no echo whatsoever until the latter part of the seventies when top-side began to impose the issue on the attention of the people. From then onwards, as we have seen, the majority verdict on the whole project remained negative until the artificial stimulus given to the issue by the referendum had brought about a change in the situation.

There are many who suppose that a United Europe will somehow (quite how is never precisely indicated) smooth the path to the creation of a world government under which men will then be able to live in peace for evermore.

A world authority, as conventionally envisaged, could not fail to reflect little more than the top-side interests of the present continental megapowers, and no consideration of these megapowers relating to a proposed authority above them can be entertained without reference to the almost complete lack of democratic control of their workings by their own citizens below them.

At no stage, like the entire weight of orthodox conventional opinion on the subject, does Miss Ward show any disposition to do this. Her view is very much, if she will forgive me saying so, that of an expert viewing matters from the top down at a time when the whole burden in the modern crisis of authority indicates that people of every race, colour and creed the world over will be content with nothing less in the running of public affairs than an approach as viewed from the base upwards. Her authoritarianism goes so far that she freely declares, "World institutions will need to be mediated to ordinary citizens through secondary authorities just as the Chinese Emperor's control was exercised most of the time through provincial officers."[3]

All such approaches implicitly assume that the *common* concerns of mankind are primarily ideological (and hidden within this assumption is the deeper one that the ideology in question is rightwing, authoritarian, centralised and, on the whole, capitalist).

Yet the truth is otherwise; neither Europe, nor mankind as a whole, is ever going to be of one mind about matters of ideology, not even though all continental megapowers attempt to assume that the subjects of their own area are, and deploy their power largely on that basis. So we are presented with a situation where masses of people are being pressurised to accept an ideological unity they do not want and which demeans their humanity, whilst being denied those democratically functional forms of unity or co-operation they need.

Europe, for example, badly needs a democratically controlled European Air Service which will organise all internal air services

[3] *Ibid.*, p. 33.

in the continent and such international services as are needed, in terms of its membership of an international or intercontinental air service. How such a structure will be made and kept subject to genuine democratic control is a matter on which much more needs to be said, but if anyone supposes that such control is impossible or that it can only be exercised through our increasingly useless and futile parliaments they should at least frankly acknowledge the Chinese-Emperor authoritarianism that is the alternative and stop talking about it as though it were progress and as though tyranny, far from being a bold, exciting step into the future, were not one of the oldest and most discredited forms of government known to man.

Yet Miss Ward and her numerous top-side fellow travellers seem to assume, if only tacitly, that the loss of liberty is a small price to pay for the prize of peace they believe a United Europe will accomplish. Again, where is the evidence on which this easy and fashionable notion is based? The wars that have plagued Europe in the last century have not been caused by *small* nations, but by meganations. Switzerland, Liechtenstein, Monaco and the Papal State of the Vatican have not been involved in wars during this century. None of the four Nordic nations, nor Iceland, Luxembourg, Holland, Belgium, Austria, Yugoslavia, Albania, Czechoslovakia, Hungary or Greece has attacked another nation in this century, and not one of them has shown any serious disposition to initiate a war. Many of them have, of course, been attacked and even temporarily conquered, but in each case this has not been done by *small* neighbouring states, but by the giants. Both world wars in this century were started by the 'big' powers, not by the small nations.

There is a disposition to dismiss scornfully any discussion in terms of smallness as being 'Balkanisation', as though wars sprang from small power entities. Yet the record is conclusive that what made events in the Balkans spark off, for example, World War I, was the intrigues by the mega-powers in their affairs. Without those intrigues Balkan differences would have proved as containable and harmless as those in Scandinavia.

This is not to say that small nations can be trusted not to make war, of course not. What is asserted, and again the record is unambiguous, is that small nations are far more to be trusted to refrain from war than are large ones. Indeed the record permits an even stronger statement; that whilst the risk of war from small nations is less, and that when it occurs it is containable, in large nations that risk becomes an inevitability, and when war breaks out it becomes uncontrollable. Let the reader test that generalisation for himself and then ask, does this point to the need to create from the nations and meganations of Europe a new continental meganation which will inevitably be drawn into an uncontrollable war with other continental meganations (and does it really matter which ones they are?). *Or does it not point to a need to break up the existing meganations into human-sized and humanly-controllable entities of at most a few millions in population each, on the lines of the Scandinavian nations.*

Even at the risk of repetition we must insist on the reason for this. Peace is not a beatific state of nature; it is a value judgement made by human beings about their relationships, and such judgements are only operable, can only be operable, when people control the societies in which they live. If they don't control them then their value judgements have no effect and the workings of the mechanisms of society proceed in ways, as all modern experience indicates, which make those judgements irrelevant. To step from a meganation to a continental-meganation is not to reduce the prospects of war by making it impossible for the meganations in question to fight among themselves, it is to combine the war-making capacity of each meganation to a continental dimension where its use is even more beyond the power of ordinary people to control and thus even more remote from any application of their value judgements.

The people such as Miss Ward who blindly suppose that a United Europe will be a power for peace ignore too the realities of European history; when Bismarck tricked, bullied and impelled the German speaking principalities, dukedoms, grand duchies and kingdoms into a single sovereign entity these were precisely the kind of arguments which were peddled, it would stop these small powers from fighting among themselves, it would speed up economic development, it would present the different elements with a splendid opportunity to influence the councils of Europe and much of the rest of the claptrap that is being drummed into our ears today. Bismarck's achievements led directly to two world wars—a double tidal wave of human massacre and misery, and all the traumatic horrors of Hitlerism; and what single part of East or West Germany today can boast its standard of consumption is all that different (for better or for worse) than that of the tiny kingdom of Denmark (population under 5 million) which Bismarck would doubtless have liked to include in his Zollverein?[4]

Those who, again like Miss Ward, fondly imagine that the establishment of some kind of international authority will suffice to end the problem of war have given insufficient thought to the origins of the problem as it exists today, as well as to the consequences of the remedy they propose.

The First World War was the clearest possible demonstration that men were living in meganations they could not control and that the power even of meganations was being expanded to hitherto undreamt of proportions by advances in technology which made them even more uncontrollable. Men had allowed their political mechanisms to expand to a point where, far from directing them, they were being directed by them.

The first Christmas of World War I saw British and German soldiers abandoning the sterile idiocies of the war foisted upon them by powers beyond their control and instead getting stuck into a sensible game of football in no-man's land. This was common people responding to a problem of human relations in a way which might have worked if they had been living in a city-state scale of power. But they were living in meganations where a clash of interests could only be resolved by a meganation scale of massacre. When the high commands on both sides heard about the football they were equally furious and ordered this 'fraternisation with the enemy' to cease. Had it gone on it might have spoilt their war.

The Vietnam war, to take a more recent example, has demonstrated that the idea of imposing a given concept of law and order by force does not work. Vietnam is a tiny underdeveloped country, the U.S.A. is the wealthiest and most powerful nation the world has ever known. Yet not all the bombs, guns, 'rockets, planes, helicopters and, of course, money, that it expended in Vietnam over more than a decade of involvement could bring that country to its knees and make it accept a concept of law and order that was different to the one it has chosen for itself. Attempts to blunder into a world government by compelling the different nations of the world to accept the diktat of a majority of the continental meganations just will not work either and will only produce a new tidal

[4]National income per head 1970: Denmark £1,210; West Germany £1,125. (East Germany's is much lower). Source: *Economist's Diary*. 1973.

wave of tyranny.

In this respect we are in the same boat as those eager, earnest and
ardent revolutionaries who fought for the triumph of the Russian
Revolution in 1917. They believed they were fighting for a new
order in human affairs, for justice, equality and brotherhood among
men. They fought and toiled in their tens of thousands against the
cruelty, tyranny and corruption of Tzarism convinced they were
forging an internationale which would unite the human race in a
brotherhood of freedom and progress.

There is no need to dwell on the horrors and the disillusionment
that ensued under Stalin which sent millions of people to perish
before firing squads and in the cruel miseries of artic labour camps,
what we need to ask is, where did these innocent and gullible revolutionaries go wrong? What was their mistake?

The fact is they made the same mistake that our European fanatics
and our dewy-eyed one-worlders are making today; they assumed
their *intentions* in creating an institution were in themselves sufficient
to ensure that once established the institution would fulfil those
intentions *even though they had no real power of control over it and no way
at all of ensuring it would respond to their wishes.*

They overlooked altogether that any unit of power once
established follows first and foremost the laws of the pursuit and
perpetuation of power rather than the aims of its founders, even if
they are driven to adopt policies which are quite contrary to what
the unit was founded to promote in seeking those ends.[5]

How many millions must perish or suffer unspeakably at the hands

[5]This is true of even quite obscure non-governmental organisations conducted
on a mass scale. Even a modest body such as the British Royal Society for the
Prevention of Cruelty to Animals is not immune to the operation of this law.
Some years ago it suffered a long-drawn out internecine quarrel which was sparked
off when one of its members in all innocence moved a resolution at its annual conference urging that the banning of fox hunting be made part of the society's aims.
Unwittingly she unleashed a tornado, for it appeared that most of the Executive
Committee were fox-hunters; or supporters of this pastime. The row grew, and grew
subsequent annual conferences were disrupted and one' was even abruptly cut short
by its chairman. The upshot was a victory for the old guard who continued to
refrain from banning fox-hunting, and the hiving off of the anti-fox-hunting
members to form a new association.

Here we have a microcosm of the whole difficulty of organising a mass movement
in a way which makes it subject to genuine democratic control. The key factor to
this particular situation was that the society was a *Royal* society, meaning it had
at its head a royal patron who could be expected to appear on important occasions.

of continental or planetary megatyrannies in the future simply because Miss Ward and her friends are indifferent to the task of doing their homework on the deployment of power in overmighty institutions and because they fail to note the inevitable centralisation of that power in the hands of special and quite unrepresentative interests; interests whose dominant drive inevitably become the pursuit of power as an end in itself regardless of any moral consideration?

This pursuit, we may be sure, is the dominant factor of political life in Washington, Moscow, Delhi and Peking today; it is also dominant in London, Paris, Bonn, Rome and the capitals of other meganations. The difference between these two groups being merely this, that whilst some vestigial forms of control or influence remains in the meganations there is none worth remarking in the continental meganations.

This gave it a much sought-after social cachet and its Executive Committee was full of distinguished names of people from the gentry and the nobility of the land of quite the most eminent respectability.

But most of them were keen supporters, like the royal family, of fox-hunting. The demand for the society to ban fox-hunting grew, so the powerful executive committee dug in and deployed its forces for battle, and even though one must suppose that any society opposed to cruelty to animals would have a majority of members opposed to fox-hunting, yet the Executive Committee views prevailed, some members arguing that foxes enjoyed the hunt as much as the hunters! The Executive Committee controlled the agenda of the annual conference of the association, its members largely determined what material should appear on the ballot papers in relation to candidates seeking election to the Executive Committee, they controlled the contents of the society's literature, and they briefed the press on matters relating to the society. Since however their views on fox-hunting made them a decided minority in the society at large how did they manage to prevail?

They were aware, as any organisers of any body of opinion with a mass membership is aware, that by and large the majority of the membership is extremely passive, if not wholly indifferent to the question of the detailed running of the organisation. It is the silent passive majority in any mass organisation which enables the power of the top group to be consolidated and perpetuated year after year.

In this case, as in many others, the membership was a widely scattered one whose only real common channel of communication was by post through the headquarters of the organisation. Hence it was quite possible for the majority of members not to know how the society was being shaken by this row and it is doubtful if many of them grasped the full scale of the division until the row erupted in the press. What is important to note is that in reading of it in the newspapers individual membership saved them nothing to counter their isolation and anonymity, which was part of their powerlessness to influence the issue until the press gave it the treatment.

Again, one has to go to the nations, especially of Europe, to
see the extent to which certain real forms of influence and control
of government machinery still remain under some form of genuinely
popular control. In the Scandinavian countries, for example, or in
Switzerland, where centralised control is so minimal that the Swiss
are able to dispense altogether with the need for a ministry of
education and a ministry of local government (if all local government is locally controlled what is there for a ministry to do?), or
in Luxembourg (population 336,500), where the Minister of
Foreign Affairs also holds the portfolio for Physical Education and
Sport, where the Minister of Economic Affairs doubles up as
Minister for Tourism, Transport and a portfolio rather bafflingly
described as 'Middle Class', and where the only lady in the government has the onerous responsibility of looking after Youth, Health,
Culture and Religion.

It is characteristic of much of the muddled thinking on this
question of power that only the other day the London *Times* was
regaling its readers with the profundities of one of its political
commentators who was moved to remark that in the light of the
outrageous bombing attack on Hanoi at Christmas 1972 by the
U.S. Airforce, "there must be many in Western Europe who are
happy to see the chance of gradually becoming more independent
of an America which is still capable of doing what it did in North
Vietnam last month."[6]

Not for a moment does Mr. Bonavia, the author, stop to ask himself why, if the U.S.A. is big enough to perpetrate such atrocities,
a United Europe would not be disposed to do the same. In all the
discussion about the new power monster of Europe there has been
no examination at all of how the warmaking potential of its burgeoning industrial-military complex will be subjected to democratic
control or of what precautions will be needed to ensure it will not
be abused.

In 1956 the British and French Governments conspired with the
Israeli Government to launch an all-out military attack on Egypt.
This act of quite incredible folly was only checked by the American
Government which, for sundry weighty reasons relating to its own
power interests (it was assuredly not concerned with the morality
of the matter), insisted on the attack being called off. Is it so very
difficult to envisage a united Europe embarking on similar follies,

[6]David Bonavia, *The Times*, 15 January 1973.

just as the United States embarked on Vietnam? And when it does so who will be able to prevail against it? Who was able to prevail against the Vietnam disaster? Or the Chinese invasion of Tibet? Or of the Russian invasion of Hungary?

The experience here suggests that the real solution for ending the danger of war lies not in aggregating political units into yet larger complexities, but to reduce the existing monster complexes such as France, Germany and Britain, to speak nothing of the bigger ones, to a size which man can control. War today is so evil and destructive that for the first time in human history there is massive concern to abolish it altogether which is world-wide. Despite the fact that this new ethic is probably shared by the overwhelming majority of the people of the world, the counterfact remains that they will never be able to abolish war until they are able to control the governments that wage it.

Another strand of Miss Ward's thinking which tends to lead her astray is her assumption that only vast continental meganations can really bring to bear the resources that will enable modern industry to develop its full potential. She appears to ignore altogether the experience of the small nations, whether in Scandinavia, Belgium, Holland, Switzerland, Austria and even Luxembourg or Liechtenstein, all of which have achieved satisfactory levels of industrialisation on the basis of comparatively modest domestic and international markets, to say nothing of quite modest resources, and all of which, incidentally, have a good record of peace-keeping among themselves, and of international voluntary service. The International 'Red Cross' originated and has its home not in America or the Russian Empire, but in tiny Switzerland.

Miss Ward's second major argument in favour of European unity rests on the belief that it will help to close the world poverty gap. She envisages that a United Europe will be able to make a bigger sacrifice for the benefit of the underdeveloped countries than the different countries of Europe do individually. One must surely ask what on earth is the basis of Miss Ward's arithmetic? Of course a large unit can handle and has at its disposal larger aggregates of money and materials, but this is simply to say that one and one is two and two is bigger than one. But of course 1 + 1 is still the same as 2. Numerical aggregation simply aggregates; of itself it does not increase what is around.

It is unfortunately impossible to state with any precision just what proportion of 'aid' figures today is aligned to the military or political purposes of the donor countries. The U.S.A. is reputed to be one of the major aid giving countries and its apparent total of sums of money donated exceeds that of all the main countries together (excluding the Chinese and Russian Empires).[7]

The figures quoted below are reckoned to be flows of capital excluding those for military purposes but when one notes that certain countries having a pronounced U.S. military presence figure high in the list of recipients, e.g. the Republic of Korea ($£114$ million), Republic of Vietnam ($£118$ million) and Indonesia ($£98$ million) compared with Latin American countries of which Brazil is the highest recipient with $£77$ million; with all the others around fifty million or well below; or the African countries, all of which with one exception, receive less than $£40$ million; it is clear that 'aid' is largely determined by the interests of the donors rather than the needs of the recipients.

What is even more important is to note that this factor intrudes itself increasingly as the size and power of the donor unit increases. Nor should we overlook that even on the level of these derisory figures the showing of the U.S.A. is as tight-fisted and mean as the other donor countries. If the figures from the same authoritative source are to be accepted, not a single country in the word gives as much as 1 per cent of its gross national product in aid. It is perhaps an indication of the unreliability of criteria applied to the collection of such figures the most generous donor country is shown to be Portugal (0.74 per cent!) and the next France (0.68 per cent), both of which of course have enormous colonial and neocolonial interests. But even the U.S.A. is shown as giving only 0.40 per cent.

It is surely to be expected that a developed country of say fifty million people will give bigger sums in aid than a developed country of five million people. But absolute sums are not the whole story. Miss Ward's argument appears to be that Europe would give more aid as an entity than the total sum at present given by its different member countries when added together. Again, the evidence points the other way, as can be seen from a glance at the figures of aid disbursements when presented as a percentage of the gross national product of each country.

In 1977 there were only three countries whose aid exceeded 0.7

[7]Total aid 2,618 million, of which U.S. A provides 1,327 (figure based on annual averages 1966-1969). *Economists' Diary,* London, 1973, p. 88.

per cent of their G.N.P.s, the Netherlands, Norway, and Sweden, and all of them modest in size. From a league table it may be seen, with the inevitable exceptions to any economic trend, that the smaller countries tend to give a higher proportion of their G.N.P. whilst the bigger ones give a smaller. In this table the U.S.A., the only continental meganation shown, gives little more than 2 per cent of its G.N.P. In addition to those mentioned, Australia, Belgium, Canada, Denmark, France, West Germany, Japan, New Zealand and the United Kingdom all give a higher percentage—in several cases double that of the U.S.A.

If Miss Ward really wishes to push the aid given to poor countries she should, on the above figures, advocate the splitting up of the U.S.A. into about fifty autonomous nations. This would appear likely to result in a doubling of the total aid given, whereas if Europe becomes united on this issue the same figures suggest that the aid coming from Europe will be more than halved.

Whilst we need to remember that in American terms 'aid' sometimes takes on some very curious connotations, Miss Ward ignores an even more disturbing factor, which is that the bigger nations are quite unable to achieve any reductions in the poverty gap even within their own frontiers. In the United States, for example, the figures indicate that poor people are poorer and the rich richer than they were two decades ago, and the same is true of meganations such as the United Kingdom and France. The same is also certainly true of India; unfortunately no reliable figures are available from China or Russia.

We do well to remember that 'aid' in the sense of one person or group seeking to give effect to a genuinely disinterested desire to help another is a moral question, a decision based on a given moral premise. But, as we have sought to show, the larger the political unit the more its central workings tend to be in the hands of top groups whose dominant common concern is the quest for power as an end in itself. If this is the case, and in the light of the available evidence those who think it is not are assuming an obligation to show why, then we must expect with the consolidation of Europe that the question of aid will be increasingly a matter not of morals, but of power politics.

And already the behaviour of the top brass of the E.E.C. is showing this to be the case. The really crucial question pertaining to aid is not a matter of gifts and handouts, but of adjustments in the terms of trade in favour of the poorer countries. The beggar who sells matches in the street is using the mechanism of trade to advertise his poverty in the hope that those who are more prosperous will give him more than an economic price for his matches as a way of relieving his plight.

Many underdeveloped countries are receiving not more than the economic price for their goods but less, and the 1973 negotiations for example, between the E.E.C. and the countries of Africa were conducted on a basis of uncompromising toughness about the terms of trade by the former to the helpless anger and chagrin of the latter. Miss Ward's dream of closing poverty gaps shows no signs of coming true, and quite a number of signs that the net effect of uniting Europe will be to create a monster trading complex which will be able (and willing) to extort whatever terms of trade will suit its (power orientated) purposes. Why should it not?

In any event if the more prosperous countries of Europe wanted to give more aid to poor countries by giving them better prices for their products what is stopping them individually from doing so now? And if it is argued that any country doing so would put itself in a disadvantageous trading position vis-a-vis its rich neighbours and rivals what is to stop them all, if they are really serious about aid, from setting up an 'ad hoc' committee in order to establish a common practice of generosity without further delay?

Miss Ward's argument is based on arithmetic, but the third argument that she advances, namely that it will help to sustain, and even increase, economic growth, is moonshine which is created simply by taking and assuming aggregates regardless of the composition of the aggregates. The level of industrial expansion in Germany, France, Switzerland or Denmark since World War II appears quite favourable, as indeed it is that of Japan, to that of the United States.

On the principle of 'much makes more' there is always a tendency for the factors making for economic expansion, when market forces are left to their own devices, to coalesce in a given locale rather than to spread evenly over an entire country. This maybe a result of the local availability of resources such as coal and iron, as in the Rhur, or of a local tradition of inherited skills such as watch-making in certain parts of Switzerland, it may be related to the preponderance of a highly centralised administrative machine such as West-

[8] *Midland Bank Review*, winter 1978, p. 9.

minster in relation to the development of South Eastern England, but probably the determinative factor in case of access and availability of transport. It will be noted that London possesses three of these four factors with its inherited skills of banking and insurance, its powerful administrative machine and its unrivalled transport facilities for land, sea and air.

This has resulted in a concentration of development for many years in the South East of England at the expense very often of other regions. Wales, for example, despite its wealth of natural resources, has achieved only a modest increase in its economic development, and the same may be said of Scotland and parts of Northern England. The forces that combine to pull development into a given region are numerous and of a kind that tend to achieve their growth from each other. London, for example, could not have become a vast trading centre if it had not developed its banking services, not have grown if there had been no expanding trade to service. But in a large centralised country the forces that pull development into one region tend to pull it away from others. Professor Kohr calls this 'the law of peripheral neglect'. Direct government intervention may do something to correct this imbalance but experience suggests that it is not very much, as the results in both Wales and Scotland appear to indicate.

There is a further point to be noted here with an obvious relevance to what is happening to Europe. The bigger the size of the political unit the more powerful the forces making for selectively localised, as distinct from generalised, development become.

This may be seen in the striking regional contrasts of wealth and poverty in the United States and India. The poverty, generational and apparently ineradicable, of much of America's Deep South in contrast to the wealth of New York State is simply the same principle at work that has led to the development of the Paris region and the stagnation of Brittany or Champagne. But with this difference. Since these contrasts are the result of the normal workings of economic forces coupled with political overcentralisation, it follows that the bigger the unit the bigger the effort and the bigger the degree of government intervention that will be required to ensure a more even spread of development. And if a meganation the size of France or Britain is unable or unwilling or both to muster sufficient resources to counteract the consequences of the free play of the forces of the market, and if the experience of the con-

tinental meganations of both the U.S.A. and India demonstrate
the task is beyond them, why should the experience of a continental
meganation called Europe prove to be any different?

On the level of moral considerations *why* should the forces seeking
to accomplish the unification of Europe show any more consideration for the poor countries inside Europe than they have displayed
for those outside? Why? These people are not a bunch of starry-
eyed idealists seeking to establish the millennium, they are where
they are and doing what they are doing for profit and power and
for no other reason. They are in the game simply for the beer and
any moral considerations that may be drummed up to support their
moves are simply the sugar gloss on a stale bun.

On the purely economic level the economic giants of Europe can
be counted on to become more gigantic, and in doing so to accentuate the polarisation of the regional poverty and wealth disparities
which already prevail. 'Growth' there will indubitably be, but
even if the growth in question represents something more than
the mere aggregation of existing figures (and the outlook for that
particular prospect does not look all that rosy) who will benefit
from it? The poor? or the rich?

Miss Ward's argument is not only moonshine, it is out of date,
and the objectives of economic policy she still appears to regard as
desirable make it dangerously out of date. Her book *Spaceship
Earth* was published in 1966. In the decade or more which has
elapsed since then a revolution has taken place in human thinking
which is now deeply alarmed at the consequences of maintaining even
the present level of industrial production in a world where words
such as pollution, resource-exhaustion and non-viable industrial
farming have suddenly become part of a new vocabulary which men
must learn to use. Instead Miss Ward's argument assumes there is
virtually no limit to the levels of industrial productivity that may be
achieved by the developed nations of the world. Yet an increasing
amount of evidence is pointing to the fact that not only are there
very striking limits to the production levels which man can achieve
if he is not to pollute irredeemably his 'Spaceship Earth', but that
in many aspects those levels may have already been reached or
passed. So that what is really confronting mankind today is not the
challenge to proceed with unlimited industrial expansion; but how
to relate the existing levels of production to the results, the conditions
and the life-support systems of the planet. There can be no excuse

today for any educated person ignoring the warnings which are being received on numerous fronts of research and scholarship in these matters.

Miss Ward's argument in this respect must be taken to be as out of date as pre-Copernican astronomy. Her fourth argument suffers from the same shortcomings as her third. She is concerned with the need to maintain an effective level of demand as a pre-condition of economic well-being for masses of people by achieving stable levels of production.

For some reason Miss Ward cites as the cause of the inter-war depression the malfunctioning of the economies of each of the countries of Europe. This is really to stand history on its head; it is true there were minor recessions in different European countries before 1929, and that in Germany there was a major economic collapse, but even Miss Ward would surely agree that the real cause of Germany's economic collapse lay not in its failure to be united with the rest of Europe, but because of the special conditions which prevailed in Germany as a result of the war, and the idiocy of the terms of the treaty of Versailles. If the different European countries had been as well versed in Keynesian economics then as they are today, it is more than likely that they would have seen the folly of seeking to destroy Germany's economic power, which could only result, if persisted in, in the destruction of their own and that they would have pursued wiser and quite different policies altogether.

Even so, if the German collapse was an economic storm, what hit Europe from across the Atlantic as the consequence of the collapse of the New York Stock Market in 1929 was a hurricane. But Miss Ward and her friends would do well to note that in the ensuing collapse it was the small nations of Europe which weathered the tornado best. Inevitably their economies could not remain unaffected, indeed in a world of large-scale international trade how could it have been otherwise? But let Miss Ward compare the percentages of unemployment in the small countries as compared with the large; the degree of social provision made for the unemployed and their families, and the extent to which agricultural production for the domestic market was affected; and also the projects to provide work to off-set the effects of the crash. She will see that in each case it was the small countries which fared best and it was the large countries where the effects of the collapse were the greatest. It is also of significance that politically the small nations weathered the economic storm with a remarkable degree of stability and even continued to develop their institutions on democratic lines. It was the big powers which tended to totalitarianism or, as in the case of France, administrative authoritarianism based on sheer political chaos.

One would expect this to be so; the larger the country the less controllable are its economic forces and the vast continental mega-nations like the United States suffered acutely, with millions reduced to destitution and enforced unemployment for long, bitter and unproductive years of their lives.[9]

The reason for this inability of larger units to exercise adequate control over their economic forces is not locked away in the more abstruse reaches of economic reasoning, but pertains directly to the kind of decisions people make according to the scale on which they are working. In this connection it is pertinent to note that the bigger a territorial unit the bigger the economic units *within* it tend to be. General Motors of the U.S.A. for example, is a giant even to British Leyland of the U.K.

If, therefore, we take the smallest scale of operations first, say of an individual craftsman-carpenter making furniture, we may assume him to possess a stock of timber and other materials some-what in excess of his immediate requirements. If trade is brisk his stocks may tend to be even higher and he may be able to take on an assistant or two. If trade falls off his reactions will tend to be gradual; rather than lay off his assistants he may fill up his store rooms with finished wares in the hope that things will improve. If they don't he will of course have to pay off his workmen or give them a holiday or reduce them to part time work, and if things get worse he may have to shift around for odd jobs himself, repairing joinery in his neighbours' houses and so on. If things strike rock bottom he may be forced to turn to cultivating his garden more intensively in order to provide much of his own food. The point to note is that even at their worst, trade conditions are unlikely to drive him down to total destitution; the results of his past pros-perity, the scale on which he is working, his ingrained habits of independence, provide him during a lean period with reserves and a base to which he may be pushed, but from which in time he can

---

[9]The total helplessness of ordinary people living in a supposedly democratic conti-nental meganation during an economic holocaust is depicted with poignant realism in Steinbeck's famous novel, *The Grapes of Wrath*, a work which emanated of course from the mighty U.S.A. and not, let us say, from Austria.

recover. His position contains inbuilt tolerances which enable it to give but not to break under strain; it is manageable.

Contrast this situation with that of a furniture concern with nationwide markets, perhaps with international markets, for its branded products and with a payroll running to hundreds, or even thousands, of workers. Let us suppose with its capital equipment and its capital intensive methods its output is equivalent to that of a thousand independent artisans; is it to be supposed that its stocks of timber are equivalent to the total stocks a thousand such artisans might carry? With its accountants watching the employment of every penny of capital? And as the same accounting gentry are busy sniffing every wind of changing market conditions, is it likely that factory workers will be employed a week longer than such conditions will appear to justify? And the factory worker, what is his fate as he pours out of his factory gate by the hundred for the last time until the gale blows over? What does he do for food in the high-rise apartment block in which he has his home?

He and his fellows, far from having any reserves, are all too likely to be in hooky for hire-purchase payments for some consumer durables, and the loss of employment generally spells total destitution relieved only by government doles.

In their folly even small countries are now trying to do away today with independent producers of all kinds and seeking to emulate the big ones in terms of factory production and other big-scale activity. Nevertheless if we take the two instances given as being merely extremes, it is not difficult to see how a large mass of small independent producers have more control of their economic fortunes than the members of a single mass labour force in one factory. There is a cushioning effect in a small scale of operations which is generally absent from the more brittle arrangements, in terms of stocks of materials, finished goods and labour employed, of a large concern. And when we are confronted with a continental meganation of big concerns where the production pattern is dominated by large concerns, we can see why such a nation's economic situation will tend to break under stress whereas those conducted on a smaller scale will merely bend before the storm and buckle down until better times emerge.

We really must grasp that if there is any way in which economic forces of continental megapowers can be controlled nobody, not even under dictatorship forms of government, has yet discovered what it is. As these words are written the Soviet Empire is in the throes of its second successive grain crisis and India is in the early stages of a famine for which figures of probable deaths running into millions of people are being predicted. The Soviet Empire is supposed to have established a new form of government giving its people all the blessing of huge scale 'scientific' planning. After more than fifty years of such scientific expertise a country which was before the revolution a major grain exporter, and was often referred to as the granary of Europe, cannot now feed its own people. Other aspects of the Soviet Empire's economy are shrouded in silence or falsehood and there is no reliable way of knowing for example its current figure of those unemployed. One can only assume it is severe; "men only wish to cover up that of which they are ashamed."

India's record of grappling with its terrible problems of poverty is marred at every turn by the inertia, corruption, inefficiency and the mesmerising stultification of initiative prevailing in the labyrinths of its grossly over-centralised and quite unmanageable bureaucracy. Over thirty years after its independence the consumption standards of the people of Bengal today are lower than they were before the intrusion of foreign rule in the eighteenth century, and all the pointers suggest that the future is one of growing social squalor and collapse. Yet Miss Ward is convinced that uniting Europe will accomplish a stable level of effective demand. Where is her evidence?

Economists do, of course, need to make a distinction between demand and effective demand. General demand, we may say, is measured by need, whereas effective demand is measured by the capacity of people to pay for what they need; the former is part of the universal human condition, the latter fluctuates alarmingly, but both have a relationship. If effective demands decrease we may suppose general demand increases; the reverse, however, is not the case. If general demand increases, as in a famine, it may have no effect on the level of effective demand, whereas if general demand decreases (a most unlikely event we must suppose) it would surely reduce the levels of effective demand.

This suggests the commonsense conclusion that if individual need has little effect on market forces, market forces do have a considerable effect on the extent to which real, as opposed to effective, demand is satisfied; it is the nature of the market forces which is decisive, not the extent of real need. Hence we are brought back again to a consideration of the extent to which an economy can be controlled to yield what Miss Ward rightly stresses as a desirable goal, a high level of effective demand.

To measure the level of effective demand in different countries is an almost impossible task, but a rough indication of the extent to which demand is effective can be gauged by some more accessible figures, such as those of the gross domestic product of each country.

Some published figures[10] give the following table of those highest in the league, those countries, that is, whose *per capita* G.D.P. is over £1,000 per year.

	£ Sterling
U.S.A.	1,932
Kuwait	1,877
Sweden	1,812
Canada	1,651
Switzerland	1,477
West Germany	1,467
Trucial State	1,407
Qatar	1,406
Luxembourg	1,397
Denmark	1,393
Norway	1,319
France	1,314
Belgium	1,196
Australia	1,172
Netherlands	1,080
Iceland	1,004

We may discount the three Arab countries (Kuwait, Trucial State and Qatar) for our purposes, all of whose economies are grossly distorted by the fact that they happen to be sitting on vast oil fields. The first point to note about the rest is that they are nearly all modestly sized countries. The exceptions are Canada and the U.S.A. and anybody who supposes that their record of feverish exploitation of the untapped resources of a vast and almost virgin continent can be repeated elsewhere knows little of history and less of geography.

Again, Australia may appear to be a large country, and in terms of physical size indeed it is, but with a population of twelve and a

[10] *The London Times*, 25 September 1972.

half million, (one-fifth of that of Western Germany and smaller than that of the Netherlands) it is really among the smaller nations. The only meganations in the list are in fact France and West Germany, so that taking this list of prosperous nations as a whole (but excluding the oil states) we have a breakdown as follows:

Continental meganations	2
Meganations	2
Nations	9

The next thing to notice about the list is those countries which are *not* included. They include three continental meganations—China (£41), India (£38) and U.S.S.R. (£596), and a great many of the developed meganations, e.g. U.K. (£887), Spain (£432), Rumania (£418), Poland (£427), Yugoslavia (£259), Italy (£758), East Germany (£667) and Japan (£934).[11]

Hence we may conclude that Miss Ward's plea for continental unity as a means of securing a high level of effective demand is also contradicted by the facts to an extent which suggests even the reverse of her argument may well be true. That is, to be specific, that a small political unit is more likely to achieve a high level of effective demand than a large one.

Again, all this merely reinforces common sense, a high level of effective demand depends on internal economic stability, a fairly stable measure of entrepreneurial and corporate confidence, and adequate reserves with which to meet the fluctuations of domestic and international trade. It would take us too far from our main concern to show in detail how small nations have the edge over big nations in these matters, but there is a valid short cut to the conclusion. The figures of the G.D.P.s referred to above have one weakness at least: since they are averages they give no indication of the disparities of wealth *within* each country, and it is this of course which helps to indicate the real extent of effective demand. Even in 1970 the U.S.A. had an unemployment rate of 5.9 per cent of its labour force whilst the U.K. rate was 3.5 per cent.

This is what we might expect, the smaller a country the closer the relationship between the locus of execution, the bigger play there is on the dynamics of the comprehension and creative capacities of the mind, a power no machine or computer can match.

[11]Figures from the *Economist's Diary*, 1973.

We should note however that there is one element which is tending to cancel out this advantage small countries have over large ones and that is the modern disposition towards centralised forms of control, together with a speeding up and standardisation of the economic process, whether in the public or the private sectors. Inevitably these trends make the factors of human judgement and control more remote from the field of action or narrow the scope of its play, so that such manifestations of a lack of real control, of which unemployment is only one, and of which business fluctuations and currency instabilities are others, are bound to increase.

Miss Ward's fifth major argument for uniting Europe centres on the need to stabilise liquidity and to liberalise trade. Again it is note-worthy that she makes only passing reference to the environmental crisis which, at last, men are aware is upon them; yet the lesson the environmentalists are pressing on us is that we cannot afford this 'liberalisation' of trade, the presumed need for which is based in turn on a presumed innate virtue of unlimited economic expansion.

How can our environmental dangers be squared with, for example, the Mansholt Plan requirement for the elimination of two and a half million small farmers from the European economic scene except on the assumption that the appalling dangers of large-scale industrialised farming are non-existent?

How can we square it with the desolating spiritual depravity which is descending on the modern urban scene in almost every part of the world (to such an extent that some governments are beginning to revert to the revolting practice of the public execution of those criminals it inevitably creates)? Or to the now quite obvious fact that the finite resources of the world just cannot sustain the levels of industrialised urbanism or farming that even now prevail?

We are going through an historical period when we have abandoned the centuries-old goals of economic effort for something quite different. Before the modern period men produced to consume, and their ideas of consumption were related to a scale of need which was sensible, susceptible to their moral judgements, and fully capable of realisation. Today men produce not to consume, but to trade, and the forces that control trade are concerned to multiply each individual's needs to well beyond any point where on a world scale they are remotely realisable at all. Miss Ward with her talk of liberalising trade is pursuing a chimera; we just cannot continue a process of making the luxuries of one generation the necessities of the next without sooner or later overtaking our resources, dehumanising our life pattern and destroying our habitat.

In fairness to her she is part of a large and imposing company. An issue of the *Economist*[12] can begin its opening article with "Britain has a policy of going for maximum possible economic growth . . . This is the . . . policy for which this paper has argued for many years." Yet it is not a policy at all, it is the development of a primitive animal instinct for acquisition, to which liberal shepherds doubtless give a grosser name, and which will assuredly accomplish the destruction of our burgeoning world civilisation if not checked and firmly subordinated to other considerations in time.

The Times, in a very special leading article entitled, 'No Alternative to Europe' pleaded substantially the same case, the need for major scientific investment, the need to keep pace, and preferably surpass, the other giant industrial groups of the planet, and trumpets, "Britain will not be 'all right' if the European negotiations fail. That would be a total, disastrous and unmitigated defeat for us, threatening our industry, our currency, our standard of living, our cost of living, our level of employment and even our political institutions with a crisis in the 1970s to which we have no apparent answer."

It is part of the bigoted unreality of our era that these words should be written at a time when Britain is a full member of the rich man's club of the world community in terms of its consumption standards, not only of necessities but of every kind of luxury. One only has to reflect, for example, that with one of the most closely woven railway networks in the world, and with a public transport system in its capital city with which no other city in the world can compare, it is yet . confronted with a 'car problem'. Where to build the roads for them? Where to park them? How to park them? How to make urban air more breathable after the effects of their carbon monoxide poisoning of it? How to reduce accidents? (currently killing more than 6,000 people per annum) and so on. When is enough, enough?

The value confusion here is total. It might be an interesting exercise to ask the authors of this kind of writing to survey the world in terms of its rapidly diminishing finite resources, its terrible problems of poverty, its areas of overcrowding and underdevelopment, and the extent to which a few rich nations are hogging the main

12*The Economist,* 20 January, 1973.

share of those resources, and then to ask them what they consider to be the elements of a civilised standard of consumption and how it is to be achieved for everybody. What, in their view, is enough? Two cars to every family in Greater London whilst impoverished nations struggle to accumulate the capital to finance their rural development programmes? Or do they consider such questions as simply irrelevant to the central problem of making the rich nations richer regardless of any effect their greed may have on the poor?

Miss Ward is, after all, a professional economist and a former Editor of the *Economist,* so that one can only ask how she can be so unaware of the realities of the power situation that will inevitably ensue. The essence of the E.E.C.'s policies is that they are protectionist and that its intention is to develop its *European* trade behind very high tariff barriers. Far from such a policy assisting the less developed countries, each of them will find that instead of negotiating with different European countries in matters of trade, development, credits, loans and so forth in a competitive market, they will be confronted by the most powerful, populous, wealthy and industrialised trading bloc the world has ever seen or is likely to see, with a clear head-start in development matters and with a capacity to dictate terms of trade to its own advantage which will almost inevitably ensure the efforts by poor countries, which are trying hard to develop their own industries in attempts to diversify their economies and to avoid a continued dependence on a single crop or product, will surely fail. What answers are they likely to get from European overlords to their requests for assistance to do this when the overlords themselves view these countries as the natural markets for their own manufactured products?

On which side of the tariff barrier, as well as the negotiating table, are Miss Ward and her friends, for all their verbalised concern for the welfare of the underdog, likely to be?

What is being engineered here is not, as they might aver, a wise development of the British or the European economy as a step towards the full integration of the world community, a pointless exercise in any case; rather it is a complex assembly of forces at work which, by over-production and over-consumption is creating strains and stresses in the ecosystem, in the social structure, and, not least, in the psyche of countless individual members of our so-called advanced societies which seem set to achieve nothing less than the suicide of a civilisation at the incidental cost of the continued impoverishment of the poor countries.

Behind all these dangerously futile economic arguments is the increasingly psychotic consideration of what is called with euphemistic self-deception 'defence'. It is the assumed military danger emanating from the Russian Empire which is urging our politicians and militarists to think in terms of a continental military organisation. How real is this danger?

For reasons already advanced we can accept that any political unit which gets too big can be expected to overspill into violence in one way or another. Nearly all the wars and violence of the last forty years have emanated from the continental meganations, indeed what is striking is the extent to which the smaller nations have everywhere managed to live in peace except when the giants have interfered in their affairs. Not one of the Latin American countries has attacked any other in this period and the same is true of Africa. Most African countries have populations well below ten million and what is striking is the extent to which where violence has erupted within particular countries it has been those which by African standards are the biggest, in Zaire—formerly the Belgian Congo (population seventeen and a half million), Nigeria (population fifty-five million), and the Sudan (fifteen and a half million).

There have been numerous coup d'etats and some tribally motivated massacres, but despite the aftermath of colonialism and the racialist infamies of South Africa, the general tenor of the relationships of the newly independent states is one of harmony and neighbourly goodwill throughout the continent. Exceptions to this statement will spring readily to mind. Exceptions always do, but that is what they are, exceptions.

We have the same picture in Asia, the giants falling out and prompting wars with smaller nations, and strikingly enough, the same is true of Europe, it is the *big* European countries which are invading small countries or making monstrous weapons of destruction. It was not Finland or Austria which invaded Hungary and Czechoslovakia but the frightened giant, the Russian Empire. And it was not Sweden or Ireland which conspired to fight against Egypt at Suez, but two of the four most heavily populated Western European countries, France (51 million) and Britain (56 million). And what wars and invasions have there been in Oceania where its twenty-four territories have only one 'giant'—Australia, with a population (twelve and a half million)—the same as Ceylon's? None whatsoever!

The outstanding war exception to all this is the Arab/Israel confrontation, yet here again, as in Zaire and Nigeria, or in Korea and Vietnam, we have a picture of local animosities which are blown up into a major war situation by the giants, who rush into hostilities beyond any capacity of local people to sustain them. How long would the Biafran War have lasted without the British arms to Nigeria and French arms to Biafra? And why is the Arab/Israel confrontation even now a 'threat to world peace' except because the giants insist on involving themselves in it and supplying arms to one side or the other and sometimes both?

The foregoing might well suggest that a Russian invasion of the small countries of Western Europe is a strong probability and that the latter is wise to organise itself into a strong defensive unit against this project. This is to ignore some current realities and some quite inevitable consequences of such a reaction. It is quite evident that the Russian Empire, as a machine for world revolution or anything like it, has ground to a halt. It seems equally clear that within the next generation China is only too likely to follow the same path, if indeed it has not already done so. As harbourers of a system of belief capable of commanding the free allegiance of the peoples of the world they have shot their bolt and are already decaying into mere systems of power which, all their rhetoric of revolution not-withstanding, are coming to centre their concerns on a mere quest for power as an end in itself. A quest which will involve the ultimate restoration of capitalism as a matter of course, if only because the quest for freedom is the subterranean force which conditions everything else in history, and experience has shown that the freedom of the debating chamber is impossible to sustain without the freedom of the market. In time the attempts to sustain a facade of ideology behind the realities of power-questing on such a scale simply become too much *bother*.

The same process has been at work in the organised churches of the Christian communion. These churches *preach* the most revolutionary gospel the world has ever heard, yet they have become more conservative, more timid, more quietist and conformist and more attuned to the power realities of their own decaying organisations than the politicians to theirs and as such represent today an organised betrayal of their own gospel. It was Lloyd George who described the Church of England as 'the Tory party at prayer' and in time, for history is such a patient soul and never fails eventually to give effect to what people really seek, as witness the bourgeoisification (in time!) of the French revolution, we must not be too astonished if the Russians and the Chinese come to adopt a not dissimilar posture.

The rival power quest between Russia and China is only too likely to result in the two giants attacking each other. Yet within this context one needs to bear in mind that both countries are in the throes of pronounced stresses and strains within the confines of their own systems. Despite the censorship and the ubiquitous secret police, it is widely known that there is a considerable restiveness among the various national minorities of the Russian Empire, and it is a restiveness which is growing apace.

And why should it not? For decades the Russian-subjugated peoples have had drummed into them the iniquities of 'imperialism, colonialism and neocolonialism', what then more natural than that as they see their national aspirations being repudiated by the Moscow machine as 'nationalist leanings' (sic!), chauvinism and so forth, they should begin to see a certain justifiable relationship in terms as those Moscow so freely uses in its foreign propaganda about countries such as Britain and France in relation to their former Empires? And stripped of its constitutional verbiage, the constitution purporting to codify the rights and liberties of those over whom its writ wins, produced at the height of the Stalin purges when life and liberty continued to count for exactly nothing before the blaze of his megalomaniac suspicions of any, however remotely, who might or might merely seem, to bar his arbitrary use of power, a constitution to which no Russian leader has ever given more than the most casual lip service and the provisions of which he has never hesitated to break, in what other light is the relationship of the Russians to the other peoples of the so-called 'Union' be viewed but that of colonies?

This, of course, is what they always were under Tzarist rule, and even the Tzars were confronted in the modern era with a growing restiveness at the Russian-dominated nature of the relationship. Today that restiveness is steadily ripening into revolt and 'Nationalism' (except for the Russians themselves) has now become one of the ultimate crimes in the Soviet calendar. The evidence now is overwhelming that ethnic, cultural and religious nationalism is a major problem in the internal affairs of the Soviet system, and that, as in other parts of the world, it is not one that can be resolved by palliatives or repression. On the contrary we can expect to see a growing power of resistance to Russian imperialism and colonialism within the Russian Empire which sooner or later will reach a stage of civil conflict.

The impetus behind this comes from mass literacy and education programmes, television, transistor radios, the very ubiquity of the youth revolt and the instinct of young people everywhere to challenge any form of authority and to disavow their allegiance to any society that produces such monstrously suicidal devices as thermonuclear weapons, and the lies and falsity of state propaganda as they become apparent from their own contradictions.

In short, with the passage of time, the Russian Empire is going to have its hands full even if it does not come into conflict with its rival communist imperialism in China or the renascent commercial imperialism of Japan.

Even if this were not so, is fear a worthy motive for making a major structural change in the organisation of European societies? Would it not be a more creative and realistic approach to espouse in every way the cause of freedom for the oppressed minorities of Soviet imperialism? This surely is the soft underbelly of Russian ideological pretensions. The anxious West European may point to the extent to which Soviet troops are massed in the territories either side of its western border, but is there any consideration given at all to what in fact is their role? Their primary task is to contain the threat of disaffection from the people of its Eastern European puppet regimes. Their major concern is to keep, by force if necessary, as in Hungary and Czechoslovakia, these governments loyal to the system the Russians have imposed on them.

Supposing a war between East and West were to occur. Are memories so short as to have forgotten what ensued on the last occasion? In Georgia and the Ukraine *millions* flocked to the standard of the Nazi invader in the hope of ending their sufferings at the hands of Stalin's henchmen. It was only the perverse ideological blindness of the Nazis themselves and the terrible sufferings they in turn inflicted on these helpless people that enabled Stalin to retrieve the situation, which might well otherwise have destroyed the basis of his empire. Today the number of potential defectors of the Soviet system inside Eastern Europe must comprise the great majority of the peoples of the Eastern European countries. The Berlin Wall and its extensions along Eastern Europe is not a symbol of the Soviet challenge but of its failure and of its fears. Its purpose is to stop people getting out—not in! The Russians, we may be sure, do not want a war in Europe and are not looking for one, and time, as always, given the chance, is on the side of moderation, accommodation and the desire to live and let live.

Human rights has currently become a political catchphrase. Good. But let us get on with it. Instead of organising armies let us start organising ideas. Let us trumpet the human rights of the oppressed nations of the Russian Empire as hard as we can, let us spend much more money on radio programmes beamed to these peoples by their compatriots outside, on organising well-published conferences which ventilate their aspirations and their wrongs. Let *us* attack 'colonialism' with all the weapons in the armoury of propaganda we can muster by marshalling them against the one great European power that still has the effrontery to practise it in 19th century terms of total domination. In doing so let us remember that the 'Soviet' troops which are presumed to pose such a threat are, each single one of them, human souls with a capacity to respond to the message of freedom, so that if they are sent to stations near the frontiers of the West let us make it our business to ensure that they receive the message of freedom from the West.

But we cannot begin to preach such a message with any hope of effectiveness if we proceed to deny it ourselves in our own practice. The vast, dotty, historic mischief of seeking to unite Europe can only be accomplished at the price of denying freedom to the resurgent historic nations of Europe which are increasingly seeking to escape the domination of the European meganations. How can we bring a message of hope and liberation to the peoples of the three Latvian republics, or to the oppressed Ukranians, Georgians, Tartars, Uzbeks and many other nations at present in the grip of the Russian bear if we deny freedom of self-rule to the Basques, Bretons, Walloons, Scots, Welsh, Serbs, Croats and numerous other nations of Europe which are seeking to reassert their historic identities? How can we, bearing in mind that these re-emergent old nations of Europe are themselves part of a world-wide change of human consciousness which is bearing the same fruit in many parts of the globe?

But what can we expect to happen in the Soviet system if Europe proceeds to forge itself into a new imperial power in terms of its military and industrial strength? What consideration has been given to the worldwide realignments that will inevitably take place once the new 'United Europe' is in a position to flex its muscles and to begin dictating its own military and economic terms? How can the Russians fail to see this as a threat to their system, and how can they react but by promoting an arms build-up and an increased domestic political repression of their own? Once begun how will this escalation of militarism be stopped before it achieves its natural consummation in conflict and war?

As we have already seen, once this degree of military and economic consolidation is achieved in Europe the natural desire of the people of Europe for peace will become irrelevant to the cause of peace, the leaders of two enormous giants, among the biggest in the world, will be confronting each other full of suspicion and fear about the security of the basis of their power, a power the common people in neither camp share. Their fears will lead, inevitably, to a heightened tension in every sphere where either side assumes it can gain an advantage over its rival, so that we can expect a new edge of bitterness and danger to accrue to the Arab/Israel confrontation, and a new wave of competitive neo-imperialism throughout the African continent for political control of the different countries. The old Franco-British imperial rivalries now neatly transformed into subtle undercurrents of rival neo-colonialisms will emerge as a neo-colonialist partnership determined to keep out the Russians, the Chinese and the Americans; the growing crisis of diminishing energy resources will fuel at least the bitter rivalries of the giants as they jockey to gain control (and deny to others) the remaining reserves in the Middle East and different parts of Africa. 'Europe' will discover it has 'interests', whether strategic, economic or political, in almost every part of the globe, the Sino-Soviet quarrel will be exploited and if need be fostered, to feel these 'interests'; Turkey and all the other lands of Asia Minor will find their internal affairs are being in large part determined by this rivalry and the number of flashpoints around the world which can be the centre of a potential conflict will increase.

Might it not instead be asserted that Western Europe, having saved itself from Hitler by its exertions, may yet save the world by its example? And what example can it best give to the world in the cause of freedom than to develop its practice? This cannot be done by drowning such freedoms as it has in a monster 'European' organisa-

tion centred on Brussels or anywhere else, for what example is that
to a Ukranian or Georgian nationalist, let us say, struggling to regain
his freedom from Moscow?

Nothing would contribute more to the break-up of the Russian
Empire than the spectacle of the multitudinous peoples of Europe
enjoying the reality, each one of them, of their own liberties and
independence, and seeking to foster the utmost cultural and political
diversity as each ethnic group may wish to aspire to. That is the
true path to freedom and social splendour. The path of unity is the
path to overgrowth, uncontrollable militarism, civic decay and
social collapse.

These words are not based on prophecy but on the observable
consequence of one continental meganation having already taken
this path in the U.S.A.

The people of Europe, far from having created a system of security
for themselves will find themselves merely in the wake of a monster
whose war-like propensities they have no means of even effectively
locating, far less controlling, and will find too that the danger of
war has multiplied incalculably. And for what ends? What ends
are those engaged in this unreasoned pursuit of power-consolidation
seeking?

They are seeking to increase even more the economic wealth of
the continent and to protect that wealth with a barrage of tariffs
and the tremendous advantage it gives them in trade negotiations
with other and poorer countries so that they may exploit the wealth
of poorer countries to enhance even more their own. This at a time
when the consumption standards of the individual European nations
are already way out in front of the vast majority of the people of
the world!

The per capita gross domestic product of the common market
countries is as follows:

	£ Sterling per annum
Belgium	1,186
France	1,314
Germany (West)	1,467
Italy	758
Luxembourg	1,399
Netherlands	1,080
Denmark	1,393

| Ireland | 539 |
| U.K. | 887 |

Only four of the 33 countries in the Americas have a G.D.P. comparable to these figures, and most of them have a G.D.P. much less than half of the Republic of Ireland which, at £539, is the poorest in the above group. Only one country in the whole of Africa (oil-rich Libya £766) belongs to this class, most of the rest having a G.D.P. below £100 and half of them below £50. Of the fifteen countries of the Middle East only Israel and three oil states are in the common market class, the rest having for the most part less than half of Ireland's standard. In Asia only Japan out of 26 territories which include China and India (£41 and £38) is a member of this rich man's club, and in eight listed territories of Oceania only Australia, New Zealand and the small nickelrich island group of New Caledonia are members.

So that of the 160 countries of the world most of the nine members of the common market are easily among the very richest, they are part of an island of wealth in an ocean of poverty; for on this showing, of the other European countries only Portugal (£285), Turkey (£169) and Albania (£198) are classifiable as poor. Yet in a world of rapidly diminishing finite resources, beset with ecological destructiveness, rocketing population figures and a growing gap between the consumption standards of the rich and the poor nations, the declared major object of the common marketeers is to increase their rate of economic development! To do that they are prepared to create yet another uncontrollable unit of power armed with thermonuclear weapons and similar suicidal fatuities in a situation where mankind has already teetered for a generation ever closer to the brink of a Third World War.

It may be asked, why, given the extreme unpopularity of the move to unite Europe, given that in some countries there was a majority in complete opposition to the move, there was so little effective opposition to it, so little that people allowed it to be imposed upon them with scarcely a sign of organised protest or revolt?

The reason for this is that people had no real alternative policy. Clinging to the status quo when its basis has been upturned by new developments is not a policy but simply an instinctive reaction to new dangers which assumes that things will calm down themselves, or that they will float back to harbour by a mere play of the very ideas that washed them out to sea in the first place.

The folly of such a stance is surely now apparent, for the forces making for a united Europe have their hands on all the controls of the commanding heights of Europe's economy, that they have no democratic base is beside the point, for their power enables them to override any objections to their policies based on mere inertia with ease. The only way the boundless effrontery of these forces can be checked is by a positive policy, and the only positives which will concern a modern humanist is one based on the power of the people to make their own decisions.

The fact is there really is no other form of power which can be trusted. *Vox populi* can be barbaric, especially if no serious effort is made to enlighten it or to give it leadership, or if it stems from political units which are comprised of such vast masses as opposed to genuine communities, that their members are inaccessible to the leadership especially the moral leadership, which every community throws up in every sphere of its concerns in abundance as a matter of course. But given this leadership who can deny that the common stuff of humanity is capable of reacting warmly, generously and compassionately to those who suffer or who are in want, or even for such great abstract principles as freedom and peace?

The extraordinary thing is that despite every massive force to the contrary, the power of *vox populi* is emerging now all over Europe just as it is emerging all over the world. I am not speaking of the mass-structured and machine-engineered leadership of mass political parties, which even at its best, where it has spearheaded the struggle for independence from colonial or other form of totalitarian rule as in Africa and Asia, is transient in its value and which, if within a generation or so it has not succeeded in developing its power into genuine community control, quite inevitably degenerates into mere power-mongering on western socialist or communist lines.[13]

13A good instance of this kind of power-mongering and the impossibility of stopping it by centralised, authoritarian means is provided by Yugoslavia. In an interview with President Tito a rather astute Yugoslav journalist, Dara Janekovic, raised a number of exceedingly pertinent questions about the quality of Yugoslav life, the anti-communist-party values of young people, the place-seeking in the hierarchy and at local party levels, the growing incidence of corruption at all levels and the increasing 'non-party' character of many of the members of the Yugoslav Communist Party itself. What must be done to check all this, asked the journalist and more to the point, ". . . which are the forces that will initiate the resolution of all these problems?"

Today it is scarcely possible to open a newspaper without reading of some protest or other form of self-assertion by one small ethnic group or another. In Europe alone one can read of Welsh language protests and court trials, of the persecution of Bretons by the French, of Catalans by the Spanish, of Serbs and Croats by the Yugoslavs, of long suffering Catholics in Northern Ireland, of freedom fighters in Wales, Cornwall, Brittany, the Isle of Man and Scotland, all seeking a renaissance of their common Gaelic tongue, of the desire for autonomy in Alsace and Lorraine, in Croatia and Macedonia, similarly among the oppressed peoples of the Russian Empire, the Latvians, Lithuanians, Estonians, Georgians, Ukranians, Berbers, Tartars, Turkmanians, Slovenes and hosts of others from that remaining outpost of the European colonial empires; and even in the heartland of the attempts to 'unite' Europe, in Brussels no less, the city is a no-man's-land between the rival peoples of Flanders and Walloonia who are tearing even the modest sized nation state of Belgium apart in their quest for independence. Without listing the names of many other peoples of Europe alone whose fortunes have long been submerged in the pretensions of the nation states, sometimes for centuries, and ignoring all those in the rest of the world struggling to achieve self-rule and independence, we can see that wherever the claims of the nation state are being repudiated by the peoples of Europe they are not being so repudiated to achieve a greater degree of unity in Europe but greater disunity and frag-

---

Sublimely the ageing President replied, "It is the Party that must get them initiated. No one else will."

Mr. Janekovic then pointed out that the President himself had observed that there are people in key positions who are obstructing this. To which the President retorted, "We are already doing something. First of all we are sending . . . a letter . . ." After more exchanges Mr. Janekovic returned to the point, asking, "In addition to the letter . . . do you envisage any other direct, concrete action . . .?"

The President replied, "All these matters will be discussed . . . we must have unanimous policies and we must work in union." And after a further question, "I have long been convinced that I must go (on) to the end. In any case I have not much time left. I am tired of constantly having to contend with these individuals, and that is why I must do everything in my power and why I can do it."

Here the interview concluded. The president of an all-powerful party is, as his verbal confusion might indicate, tired, tired of contending with corrupt elements in his own party; but he is determined to do something about it. He is sending a letter . . . he is going to have vigorous discussions . . . .

Socialist Thought and Practice. No 49, August-December 1972, Begrad, Trg Marksh Engelsa IV/V, P.O. B. 576.

mentation. The same is true of the rest of the world. People at last
have begun to see the true nature of the threat the overlarge nation-
state represents to them, and instead of falling into the seductive
trap of bigger conglomerations of power which hold out the promise
of more candy floss and inflated consumerism, as well as more war,
at the cost of their liberty and identity all as a part of a masquerade
of 'progress', they are taking the path of sanity and genuine progress
where things are measured not by cost-effective accounting or
productivity, but by the ordinary limitations of the stature of man
himself.

And this really is the way forward. There was a time when to
anticipate *the Breakdown of Nations*,[14] especially of the mega and mega-
continential nations, was merely to invite ridicule and to prompt
a reminder of the old anarchist slogan, "Be realistic, demand the
impossible." Today, however, we are moving into a new climate
of ideas. The world-wide crisis of power has at least the benefit of
prompting a re-consideration of the forms of power right down to
the fundamental assumptions on which its political structures are
based. So far most thinking has been prompted by an assumption
that the natural progression of power and of human need is towards
larger and larger units:this, it has been supposed, is the only way to
rid mankind of the destructive waste of war. This approach has
ignored one salient factor, that the danger to mankind from war
does not stem from war as such, but from monster wars waged by
monster states. If men are so foolish as to want to settle their differences by fighting then no power on earth will stop them, as a
glance at the wars of the last decade is surely enough to indicate.

It ignores too that in a world of small states the war problem is
containable and that since the fall of the Roman Empire all big
wars have been the product of big agglomerations of power (how
else indeed?). The First World War was not 'caused' by the murder
of a royal duke and his wife in a provincial Balkan city, any more
than ice which has been thawing for sometime is suddenly 'caused'
to crack when stepped on: just as the cause of the crack-up of the
ice is really the change in temperature which anybody who steps
on it at a critical stage is merely helping to register, and thereby
setting in motion forces of which the venturer may have no inkling;
so the political climate of Europe, dominated for decades by the

[14] The title of a sparklingly evocative book by Professor Leopold Kohr, first
published in 1957.

rivalries of great powers, whose armaments were being tremendously increased by the advances of technology, were heading for an inevitable conflict which only needed a minor aberrant political act to precipitate.

France and Britain, alone among the powerful nation states of Europe, have a lengthy history of national unity, more or less, dating back a fair number of centuries. The reasons for this belong as much to the framework of geography as the accidents of history. Men were not consciously weighing the pros and cons of such structures, they produced them blindly for the most part, in response to some transient challenge or need; political, economic, religious or social. Often this need centred on the desire to end the waste of localised wars with no realisation of the possibilities and dangers of making wars bigger, more destructive and more uncontrollable once such unity was achieved; but for the most part it sprang from the ambitious and the dynastic pretensions of upstart royalties anxious to extend the grip and girth of their power for no other reason than self-aggrandisement.

In France this holds true from Clovis, perhaps the first true king of the French, who died in 511, and his successors, it holds true of the Carolingians, of the Capetian monarchs who for over three centuries produced an unbroken succession in direct line down to 1328, through the so-called House of Valois to the advent of the Bourbons (to say nothing of the malignant Richelieu) and their eclipse in the revolution of 1789. Always the main impetus of this drive for the centralised government of a huge territory came from the top. For centuries, despite the existence of the central monarchy, provinces such as Burgundy, Flanders, Brittany and Aquitaine were able to maintain a separate existence which was prosperous, stable and peaceful. They did not voluntarily opt to join 'France'; in each case their fortunes, and the submergence of their independence, were determined by dynastic marriages or by wars of conquest, only Flanders prevailed into the modern era, when it was engulfed, like so much else, by the aftermath of the French revolution.

In not a single instance was the voice of the common people the determinative factor in the various territories comprising France at any time, or in the provinces it added to its main. Is it not now time enough to make it so in an age which talks more claptrap about democracy and self-determination than any other has ever seen fit?

A similar progression of events may be seen in English history, dynastic and faction struggles between various war leaders resulting in the supremacy of one who emerged as king and who proceeded to maintain an uneasy balance between foreign and domestic rivals. A perpetual struggle down the centuries between topside interests, with the commonalty cast as the soldiers who did the actual fighting in time of war or who paid the taxes in time of peace. The power struggles of church, over-mighty barons and would-be monarchs leading to the Wars of the Roses (sic!) culminating in the totalitarian clampdown of the Tudor despotism. The savage and repeated attempts at the subjugation of the neighbouring territories in Scotland, Wales and Ireland leading finally to the 'united' Kingdom the imposed unity of a king's power, not the free-given unity of people; whereupon the itch for fighting and conquest, being finally aborted in Europe for a time, especially by the earlier loss of Calais, found outlets in India, Africa and elsewhere.

Now these same topside interests, with the added might and power of interests thrown up by the technological revolution of the last two centuries, after spilling the blood of generations of conscripted common people in wars of nation state rivalry, are prepared to abandon the concept of nation statehood, which for so long has been the base of their power, at the drop of a hat from motives of avarice, fear and power aggrandisement.

Again, in their own interests, not those of the people at all. They are not doing this in order to restore the power of self-rule to the people, to whom it inalienably belongs, but to a super-grouping of topside interests which is seeking, it supposes, to unite in face of the assumed Russian danger to its interests.

There is only one form of opposition to the dangers of this policy which has any validity and even any sanity in terms of the threat to liberty and peace it poses, and that is an avowed campaign to consummate the logic of the long historical struggle for democracy to ensure the people everywhere in their rightful power to rule themselves.

The struggle thus becomes one to build man-centred, humanist societies of a sensible size that human beings really can control. We should note in passing that not a single form of the opposition to the topside unity of Europe was prepared to embrace such an alternative; at most they were concerned to insist stoutly on preserving the existing terms of the power struggle, a struggle in which

they themselves have a stake. This is the reason for the near total
ineffectuality of such opposition; it is based on the maintenance of
the *status quo* in a situation in which its basis has already disappeared,
or been discredited by the consensus that stems from the quiet com-
munings in each man's heart as he quests for truth with no other
thought but to find it. Our conservative Powellite imperialists who
wanted to go on dreaming of a *great* Britain, and our good old
Labour Party left-wingers who wanted to see the world safe for
labour mass-party, machine-run, socialism, were alike in the event,
hoisted by the petard of their own authoritarianisms. Neither
could make any noises that the people wanted to listen to despite
the fact that the majority of people were at one with them in opposing the whole united Europe exercise.

Having said as much it needs to be said that the people who
inhabit the British Isles, especially the English, have been landed
in a terrible historical predicament which cannot be resolved by a
policy of mere inertia. They are now in fact beginning to pay
the bitter price for the destruction of their own peasantry which
Oliver Goldsmith bewailed so eloquently over two hundred years
ago. Many are familiar with his famous couplet, but its setting
is no less pertinent.

> ... And trembling, shrinking from the spoiler's hand,
> Far, far away the children leave the land,
> Ill fares the land, to hastening ills a prey;
> Where wealth accumulates, and men decay;
> Princes and Lords may flourish, or may fade;
> A breath can make them, as a breath has made;
> But a bold peasantry, their country's pride;
> When once destroyed, can never be supplied.

Goldsmith was referring to an economy which was sensibly
based on a large measure of self-sufficiency and a peasantry given
to small-scale productive methods, methods which began to be
destroyed by the twin rapiers of imported cheap food and a concentration on manufactures for export with which to pay for it.

In the midst of these developments loomed another factor which
was even more ominous of trouble to come, an explosion of population which, with the onset of the last quarter of the twentieth
century, has produced a situation where Britain, with a popu-

lation of 55 million, is only producing half its own food.[15] This
in a situation where the prevalence of cheap food relative to dear
manufacturers has been reversed to one of increasingly dear food
relative to cheap manufactures.

Of one thing we may be sure, that relative to the price of his
other wants, the urban dweller is going to find his food increasingly
expensive, and today's occupant of the British Isles is so urbanised
that only 651,000 people, or 2.5 per cent of the total working population is employed in agriculture. It might be thought that it is this
sobering fact which is prompting the move to unite with Europe,
on the contrary the whole object is to accentuate it in line with the
Mansholt Plan to reduce the number of farmers in Europe (all in
the name of efficiency!) by two and a half million.

The blunt fact is that the basis of the cheap imports of food
on which Britain has built up its manufacturing industries for two
centuries is approaching a point where it must break. The next
two or three decades are going to witness an increasing scarcity
of food in the world at large as a result of population pressures and
the forms of intensive monoculture that have come into general
practice since World War I. The spectacular quantitative results
of such monoculture must not blind us to its inherent generational
non-viability over a period of time and the awesome strains, already
in some cases beyond breaking point, it is imposing on the ecosystem.

For Britain the choice would seem to be either to allow itself
to be made a part of the common-market, in which case some of
its problems will be solved by a population drift to urban centres
across the Channel, or to remain independent and to pursue an
energetic policy of population export to less densely populated parts
of the world until its numbers are low enough, parhaps 25 million,
to enable it to feed itself. The acerbity of the current debate about
'coloured' (are not all men-coloured?) immigration is a non-issue.
There should be no immigration for settlement into Britain today
except on compassionate grounds at all. Any alternative policy
is folly and invites the most imposing forms of historical retribution.
To proceed with its present numbers and dependency on foreign
imports of food is to pave the way for a situation where by the end
of this century, and perhaps well before, the rationing of bread and

---

[15] *Britain 1973*, an official handbook prepared by the Central office of Information, London, p. 311.

other basic foodstuffs will become a permanent feature of British life as mass starvation becomes a chronic feature of the world scene. There can be no escape from this fate for our immediate posterity, and even perhaps for ourselves, if the territories at present compri·ing the British Isles do not pursue a sensible policy of a rational population figures relative to the available food producing resources.

On his 85th birthday, Dr. Arnold Toynbee shows himself to be more aware of those underlying factors than most people in their prime. He forecasts that the age of affluence will rapidly draw to a close and that far from maintaining a policy of economic expansion the developed countries will soon be forced to slow down and contract their economies. This state of siege economics is likely, he thinks, to become permanent and the political consequences lead to the establishment of dictatorial and authoritarian governments with policies reminiscent of the authorities of the two world wars, with the difference that such austerity will become chronic and increasingly severe.[16] Even so he is not gloomy. He thinks it is possible for a society to be declining materially but ascending spiritually and of course he is right. If we are compelled to return to the labour-intensive and small-scale forms of production based on the use of replaceable rather than finite resources, of former centuries why should we not emulate and even surpass the glories they accomplished? But the key to this, which he does not mention, is a return to a smaller scale of *political* organisation.

Even if Britain finally opts to remain independent (for it is simply unreal to suppose that the signing of some documents in Brussels in January 1973 is or can be the last word on the matter), the way ahead points to even more changes than Britain has hitherto been prepared to contemplate. That Wales and Scotland must recover their powers of self-government is evident on a number of grounds, not least of which is the rising crescendo of demand which the peoples of these countries themselves are voicing. The same is true of Northern Ireland, although whether the Northern Countries remain separate from the South or, as is more likely, are linked with them, is a matter which the Irish people themselves will have to sort out.

And as for England, will it, can it, continue its pattern established for over nearly a thousand years of dominance from one geographic location in its South East?

16 Arnold Toynbee, *The Observer*, 14 April, 1974.

In the early stages that centralised dominance was weak; the monarch was 'primus inter pares' and liable to be undone, as occasionally he was, by his peers. Even after the Tudor despotism one king was toppled and beheaded by the rising merchant and gentry class, despite the new prosperity from expanding world trade and exploitation it was enjoying.

In the last two centuries or so centralisation has put any questions as to its legitimacy or practicability out of court by the enormous strides made in the accumulation of national riches which gave Britain a preponderant place among the nations of the world in wealth, trade, investment, manufacturers, banking, and in military and political power. Why change a system that has apparently been so successful? This must have been the answer to every form of criticism as its wealth grew, its imperial horizons expanded and its levels of domestic consumption rose to ever greater heights.

Today, it scarcely needs saying, Britain's position has been radically transformed. Two world wars have proved powerful asset strippers, the Empire has ceased as such to exist and Britain's *per capita* level of consumption, like its share of world trade and its annual 'growth' rate, are all declining in relation to those of other countries. These latter factors are far less important actually than people are apt to make them sound. The things of the good life, plentiful and varied food, a roof and some clothing need only the addition of reading, writing, carving, and other materials to enable man to create and to develop his inner life.

The vast, dotty mania for rushing about in lethal vehicles like a ceaseless horde of paranoiac morons is only a marginal aspect of the serious business of living, as is nearly two thirds of the contents of the average shopping centre, its gadgets, its 'gifts' (that nobody really wants), and its plethora of ugly, tasteless, and shoddy 'household goods' and all the meretricious salesmanship that goes with it, could vanish in a day and would scarcely be missed. A television set in a public place can well serve two hundred families; it makes no more economic or spiritual sense to have one in every home than it does to have a cow in every kitchen.

The average British citizen has the consumption standards of a maharajah! Like the rest of the minority of wealthy nations in the world, Britain derives its wealth in part from the share that poor countries are not getting and from hogging the rapidly dwindling reserves of finite resources such as oil the poorer countries are unlikely ever to see. As such, a drop in consumption standards of non-essentials, combined with more concern for proper provision of the basics (food, clothing and shelter) would doubtless improve the *quality* of national life considerably.

But if Britain is to cease to be besotted by the mad frenzy of getting and spending that has come to dominate the modern world, and which is leading it by the nose to its damnation, it must realise that it needs to accomplish a national revolution in the business of political and economic involvement in the lives of all its people.

This involves not only a bold decision to form a partnership of equals with the new nations of Scotland, Wales and Ireland, if they want it, but also *among* the English themselves. If Denmark for example can rival Britain in current prosperity, and even in some respects, surpass it, with a population of under five million people, then surely the same scale of economic and political localisation can achieve similar results in Britain.[17] A federated England of a number of self-governing regions of five or six million people would unlock a tremendous reservoir of localised talent, entrepreneurial, creative and administrative energies in each region which would transform each one of them in ways we can only, given the long nightmare of centralised presumption which continues to grip us, with difficulty appreciate.

Many parts of England are endowed with natural resources such as iron and coal of which Denmark has little or none, the difference of income today between the two, with rich little Denmark looking down at its poorer by-a-third neighbour Britain and with almost double Britain's annual growth rate, does not arise from the fact that the Danes work hard whilst Britons are lazy, but that the Danish *scale* is small enough to enable a much greater degree of its human abilities and resources to be fully used.

---

17 National income per head	*	Growth (average % per annum)
U.K. (Pop. 55 million)	1,965	1.5%
Denmark (Pop. 5 million)	3,764	2.9%
(Source : *The Economist Diary*, 1979)		

CHAPTER XIV

The Fourth World

The future of the World lies in the hands of the small nations.

Peter Ustinov
An address to students of Dundee University, 1968.

We have been dwelling at some length on European affairs, not simply because the writer was born in one of its chief cities and may possess a parochial obsession with the problems of that part of the world, but because what is happening in Europe today is clearly going to have a very important effect on the fortunes of the rest of the world and because that effect seems likely, at the time of writing, to be wholly evil and altogether inimical to the best interests of mankind as a whole.

Since the writer is an Englishman he has been writing against a background of his own national experience and has drawn his examples mainly from that problematical coign of vantage. The phenomenon of overgrowth is however not confined to England, Britain or Europe, it is of course world-wide, but if the problem is common to many parts of the world it does not follow that each part so afflicted can resolve it in the same way; the inevitable differences of location, history and stages of development, among other factors, are bound to create different problems of adjustment and different methods of approach if a desire manifests itself to create the kind of small-scale decentralised structures that are being propounded here.

Let us therefore make a very brief survey of some of the different regions of the world in the terms we have been discussing here.

In Europe there is no real problem; if we assume that the most manageable unit, in the modern experience, and taking into account the extent to which developments in communications enable a larger population to be meaningfully part of a community, is around the five million mark, we find this frequently corresponding to many of the borders of its historic provinces or regions. So that in recreating Sevoy, Lombardy, Catalonia, Waales, Flanders, Saxony, Bohemia, Bavaria, Macedonia, Naples and a host of other ancient regions we would be sensibly re-affirming our ties with the past and making a rational choice with which to face the future.

There is no political or economic difficulty here provided the will to accomplish such a solution is present, nor in sub-dividing each of these provinces into cantons or districts for the purpose of autonomous self-rule in matters of local government down to village, parish, commune or neighbourhood level. Such a step would not lead to the inflaming and recreation of ancient feuds and rivalries, there would be no outbreak of violence and there would be no economic collapse.

In fact, quite the reverse, for as we have sought to show, the deep-rooted desire for peace among the people of the world would no longer be cheated and frustrated by topside interests beyond their control, and all forms of economic activity would receive a considerable boost as local energies were more fully harnessed to local needs and local resources. It is the present super-scale structures which are hampering these developments today and creating problems which, in their blindness, topside people are persuading themselves can only be solved by a transition to an even bigger scale. The fisherman who finds his rod is too long to enable him to manipulate it to catch fish successfully does not solve his problem by lengthening the rod even more, but by shortening it.

The real obstacle to such a radical reconstruction of Europe to make it a peoples' Europe is one of belief and mental conditioning. All indoctrination (and all indoctrination in society on such questions now comes from the dominant central groups) seeks to persuade us that our salvation lies in bigness and growth. If we could persuade ourselves of the reality that it leads rather to social decay and collapse, if we could clear our minds of the accumulated cant of 19th century nationalist theorising, the way would be open for a wholly new era in European affairs, one based on peoples' power for peoples' interests and for economic objectives that corresponded to a sensible constraint in consumption, that observed ecological limits as a matter of course, that practised a pronounced degree of localised self-sufficiency in the interests alike of local political independence and international market stability (to say nothing of the drastic economies in transportation waiting to be achieved) and thus constituting the basis of a new renaissance of every form of human creativity, one which would surely outsoar all those reminders of a past renaissance which today continues to mock us with the sheer quality and profusion of its achievements.

Not least it would surely be a new dawn in the long march of human liberation and self-fulfilment. That prospect is there within our reach to take it if we will, and if we have the courage to repudiate the perfidious sophistries of those currently dominating claques of bankers, politicians and industrial tycoons and their lap-dogs in the advertising world, which we allow so gratuitously to imprison us in overlarge institutions which keep them rather than us in control.

In nearly every other part of the world these problems are compounded by other factors such as poverty, illiteracy, lack of resources or of development and, not least, by overpopulation.

In the continent of Africa, for example, the same problems abound except for that of population which looms at present hardly at all; of its fifty-seven territories only ten have a population of more than ten million, and even the biggest (in population), Nigeria, has only fifty-five million, which is about the same as Britain's. In relative terms Africa has no population problem worth talking about.

Yet Africa has a problem no other continent shares to anything like the same degree, and that is tribalism. To be more precise one should say tribalism in relation to current national boundaries. Less than a hundred years ago most of the present national boundaries were hacked out by the combating colonial nationalisms of Europe; as a result, those boundaries both divided and encompassed tribal entities which are still powerful political factors in the make-up of each, and for the most part newly-independent, nation state.

The effects of this may be seen in the civil wars and military take-overs which have marked the continent's history since the virtual demise of colonialism. In the Sudan, Nigeria, Burundi, Zaire (the former Belgian Congo), Somalia, Uganda and elsewhere events have been dominated by the attempts of one tribe or another to gain an ascendancy over the rest. It is this factor, plus the inheritance of a certain authoritarian ethos in some forms of tribal rule, which goes to make most African governments highly centralised, and suspicious of any questioning of their authority from any source.

The situation of Zambia may be taken as indicative of the general complex of forces within which many African governments work. As a country it has a decidedly awkward shape, being almost bisected by a 'waist' created by a gigantic pedicle which pushes down from the north to a point a mere 100 miles or so from its southern border (in a country five times larger than England).

This pedicle, a finger pointing deep into Zambia, is a monument to the greed of British commercial interests and those of Leopold II of the Belgians and the commercial empire built in the Congo before his death in 1909, even though the borders of the pedicle itself were not finally established until 1914. The general drift of the border is from East to West, the reason why it suddenly drops down sharply from North to South East is summed up in one word, copper. Belgian and British copper interests carved out this border in order to share the copper deposits on either side of it. The fact that the border bisects several tribal territories, makes no geographic sense and poses considerably internal communications problems for Zambia is today part of the price of Zambia's colonial legacy.

Within Zambia there are over seventy tribes, with three of them having a considerable dominance over the rest. The historic rivalries of these major tribal groupings are reflected to this day in underlying tensions, which occasionally erupt into the open to disturb or disrupt national life. As in other parts of the world there is also an alarming drift, one might almost call it a rush, of people from the thinly populated rural areas to huge urban shanty towns, there is an enormous disbalance between rural and urban life (compounded by the riches derived from mining copper), between rich and poor, and between literate and non-literate peoples.

It is on this basis, with no *national* traditions, culture, history or historic institutions, that Zambia is seeking to create stable conditions of life for its people and to bring them the mixed and sometimes dubious blessings of technology, modern education and modern concepts of living. Some of these goals may not be valid and will doubtless alter with time, but on the whole they reflect the wishes of the majority. Yet the nature of the tightrope on which Zambia seeks to accomplish these things can be inferred from the way tribal rivalries have erupted into civil war and the killing of thousands, hundreds of thousands, and even millions, in other African territories in recent years.

It is noteworthy that the two countries in Africa which have been most disrupted by war and economic stagnation and collapse are the two largest, Nigeria and Zaire. After a disastrous civil war in which the people of Biafra sought and failed to achieve their independence it became clear to the victors that the old structure of Nigeria, created of course largely by British Fabians with their usual authoritarian and centralising mania, would not work.

With a commendable spirit of magnanimity the victors proceeded to divide up this huge country into twelve regions, each with its own considerable powers of self-government. It is too early to say whether this experiment will work, what is noticeable is the theoretical trends which are apparent; giantism clearly does not yield results so let the giant be divided up into more manageable units. Will our Eurofanatics please note!

The estimated population of Zaire, and it must be an exceedingly rough estimate, of 25 million, live in a country larger by far than Europe West of the Urals! In the colonial era this vast region was allowed to stagnate except for some exploitation of its minerals and its rubber, and a certain amount of fringe activity by missionaries in the fields of education, health and nutrition.

Since it achieved its independence it has been involved in civil wars, mainly with its Shaba province, and with one form after another of political upheaval and economic collapse. The World Bank and others have poured in vast sums as loans and at present World Bank officials, in the faint hope of seeing something for the Bank's money are established in some of the leading ministries and virtually directing policy. There is now talk of raising more loans to get this gigantic economic structure afloat and we can say with unreserved confidence that the new loans will go the way of the old loans in a morass of incompetence, corruption, military adventurism and sheer political confusion.

Everything, it seems, it is assumed must be done to keep this creaking unweildy giant intact in one piece, and in making this assumption no one seems to grasp that this is the cause of the malaise. The peoples of Zaire are as wise, competent, able and gifted as any others on the planet. But a silk purse cannot be made out of a sow's ear, except possibly in a plastics factory, and no Zairean politician can devise a suitable instrument of government for a country which is ungovernable simply because it is too big. The one need that stares the peoples of Zaire in the face, as much as it does the mandarins of the World Bank if they want to see their money again, is the imperative need to divide the territory into governable and manageable units. It is a tragedy for the World Bank officials that all their training and conditioning leads them to suppose the bigger the better despite the fact that their experience in Zaire is suggesting precisely the opposite. It is of course no less a tragedy for the luckless peoples of Zaire.

We have been pleading throughout this essay for a maximum degree of decentralisation and of people's control, but nobody viewing the African scene would want to see such changes even attempted at the expense of the breaking of the still precarious and fragile unity of many of the smaller of those newly independent African states, and the inevitable aftermath of a general breakdown of the rule of law leading to the rule of the gun and the bayonet which would all too probably ensue.

Yet most African countries would do well to take note of the way in which one European country afflicted with the same problems of tribal division as well as linguistic, cultural, religious, ethnic and geographic barriers, has resolved them. For almost two centuries, Germans, French, Italian and other groupings have lived at peace within the borders of Switzerland, whereas outside them these same peoples have been at war repeatedly and disastrously.

The Swiss are justly praised for this creditable achievement, but strangely enough the means by which this has been done have attracted scarcely any attention at all. Swiss constitutional arrangements are in fact just about the most revolutionary and successful the world has ever known; they are also simple to state and easy to grasp.

First of all, Switzerland, itself is small, both in area and population (6·3 million), secondly, it is not a nation in the accepted sense at all but a *confederation* of different cantons, each of which is largely self-governing. This fact is of paramount importance to the system, for since the main ethnic groups are thus sub-divided into cantons the member tends to regard the powers and privileges of his canton to be much more important than membership of his ethnic group (which membership of course has no legal status). Hence the impetus for ethnic rivalry is defused by sub-dividing *from below* the level of such rivalry in the cantons, and uniting above it in the federal parliament. So that such rivalry is circumscribed by institutional arrangements from above and below; it is in no way suppressed, nor is any attempt made to, (and neither, let it be stressed, is there any need to in the interests of national unity), from above.

To reinforce the system of interlocking local loyalties each canton, of which there are more than twenty, is *'comprised of'* (the verb is important, it is not 'divided into') numerous communes—some quite large and some a mere village. These communes also have enormous powers of self-rule in the fields of local affairs, indeed far more than is to be found in any country in the world. In this respect the size of the Swiss Cabinet (or Federal Council) is noteworthy, comprising members whose portfolios cover simply the following spheres; Foreign Affairs, Public Economy, Justice and Police; Interior: Transport, Communication and Power, Defence;

Finance and Customs; and that is all. There is no minister of education, no minister of local government, nor is there any minister of health, social welfare or any matters of local concern. Despite these unique features Switzerland can justly claim that it is one of the most law-abiding, well-governed and prosperous countries in the world, where illiteracy has been practically unknown for two or three generations. Many people, as Professor Kohr has observed, assume from this that Switzerland is well-governed because it is prosperous, but they have it the wrong way round, it is prosperous because it is well-governed.

Europe is busy ignoring the challenge implicit in the success of these arrangements by haring off on a path of mammoth structural unity which can only compound rather than solve all its major problems and destroy its remaining vestiges of democratic government. But for Africa there are important lessons here which need to be learned and applied to its problems as a matter of extreme urgency.

Despite much rhetoric to the contrary, the most pressing need of the newly independent African states is not for continental unity but for national integration. Without exception each of them is top-heavy, fissiparous, weak and devoid of any deep sense of national unity or identity. A European reader may find this catalogue of defects astounding, but this is because in Europe most countries have so much national integration it has become a civic vice, cocooning the citizens in a plethora of decisions they have not made and posing as yet little-considered threats to their liberty. In Africa the opposite is the case. These governments are precariously poised so that when they fail the consequence is not the fulfilment of some European anarchist day-dream or a genteel change of tempo in the parliamentary minuet, but bloodshed, killing and suffering to a quite terrible degree.

Such governments cannot advance towards a photo-copy of the Swiss system in one stride, even if that were desirable or desired, what they can do is take note of its chief lesson in relation to their own internal tensions and divisions, and apply it. The lesson is that the divisive forces of tribalism cannot be arrested by mere suppression from above by an over-centralised administration, which will inevitably in due course, if they try to do so, provoke an explosion, *but by fragmentising the tribal areas from below into cantonal-type district structures with a large measure of local autonomy.*

Such a step would have several important consequences, some of which can be listed as follows:

(a) It would defuse the tribal potential for political trouble by creating more localised centres of political concern *within* each tribe.

(b) It would present the citizen with an alternative form of loyalty to the tribe which is meaningful to him and which in his mind he can grasp, if only because he can be intimately involved in its workings.

(c) It would create a vitally important focus for local economic development, especially in the rural areas, which at present is almost entirely lacking.

(d) Strange as it may seem, it would actually increase the stability of the central government by giving it a direct form of communication with local centres of power and administration which are much weaker relative to its own *and to that of big tribe groupings*.

(e) We can expect that the prospect of exercising local power for local economic development will put a pronounced brake on the present disastrous drift from rural to urban areas.

(f) Local decision-making will create local work situations and local incomes, which in turn will create local markets for local manufacturers and agricultural products and these in turn will generate the kind of localised civic development which today is so conspicuously lacking.

At present nearly all African governments are seeking to promote rural development from an all-powerful and very remote centre, yet despite the fact that rural development presents far fewer technical problems and makes much fewer demands in resources than urban development, it remains a field of conspicuous failure almost everywhere. What rural development is being accomplished is, again, almost everywhere, of the wrong kind, being in the form of large-scale monoculture of cash crops, or products which provide minimal rural employment possibilities, where the income generated is sent to the cities and frequently abroad (often in the form of dividends) and where the national economy becomes hamstrung by the need to import expensive machines and equally expensive inorganic fertilisers. Indeed we are becoming used to the spectacle of food being produced with the aid of urban factory-made machines and fertilisers and which is being used increasingly to make up for a food production shortfall *in the rural areas*. So that instead of the urban areas being enriched as well as fed, by a rural hinterland, urban resources are being used to feed rural people and to relieve rural destitution. No wonder rural folk are prone to pack up and catch the next city-bound bus!

Powerful central governments will never begin to resolve this problem until they grasp the nettle of the need to *share political power with rural people*. At present they can't, because there is no localised rural structure equipped with the authority to undertake its own decisions in the fields of development. In Zambia there are even greater barriers to a new approach arising from the fact that the authorities are clinging to the old structure of provincial government as established by the former colonial power. Given the enormous area covered by each province the provincial government is as remote from the people's lives as is the central government and, given the distances involved, as well as the poor roads and other communications, it could scarcely be otherwise. What is worse the effect is to make the provincial government not a two-way channel of communication but a two-way barrier, and as such, constitutes the biggest single barrier to both effective democracy and economic development. What is even more dangerous for Zambia is that the provincial boundaries are frequently those of the tribal frontiers; so that they also give the maximum stimulus to tribal feeling and the maximum stimulus to do everything but check it.

At least Africa has the excuse, in making such an error, that it is a long way from the straightforward simplicities of Switzerland. But what is one to say of France, Britain, Italy and Germany which are all, in defiance of the lesson of the Swiss success, erecting similar barriers? In the guise of a 'reform' of local government, which really amounts to much of its destruction, each of them is creating enormous multiplepurpose provincial-type administration structures which will be much more under centralised control. This is not government, it is a senescent withdrawal from creativity and a readiness to simply exist on the basis of accumulated social capital. In the nature of things that capital will one day be exhausted and people who have been made accustomed to living at the behest of bureaucratic decisions handed down from above, will have to pay a reckoning which is already being computed in the form of a despoiled ecology and other evidence of social decay.

This holds equally true for the communist countries. In 1957 when Khrushchev[1] sought to divide the Russian Empire in 105 semiautonomous economic units he was acknowledging an even more basic aspect of Soviet reality, that the Soviet Empire is too big. One has only to compare the economic performance of the Russian Empire and that of Japan since World War I, at a time when both were at a comparable stage of development, with their situation today to see the extent to which Japan has forged ahead. It is true that owing to its obsessive secrecy that Russian Empire statistics are not easy to obtain, and that allowances have to be made for the tendentiousness of state propaganda. The only figures I have immediately to hand are as follows:

	R.E.	Japan
[2]Per cent per annum growth rates	5.5	6.8
Motor cars (1970)	1.5	16.3
Television sets (1970)	21.6	23.5
Radio Sets (1970)	46.1	46.5
Telephones (1971)	7.0	42.6

Perhaps the first figure is the most significant. We have made it clear repeatedly in these pages that concern with economic growth, far from being an ultimate form of wisdom for human societies may well be one of extreme folly; nevertheless the rate of growth is the kind of criteria by which political leaders are prone to measure the progress of their societies and on this count the Russian Empire is markedly behind Japan which in fact has one of the biggest growth rates in the world. Another figure which helps to reveal the disparity is the *per capita* gross domestic product; this in the Russian Empire in 1970 was £596 and in Japan £934.[3]

[1]It is curious to note that at the time three of the empires of power in the world produced leaders who all seemed to be of unusual mettle, for Premier Khrushchev was in power along with J.F. Kennedy of the U.S.A. and Pope John of the Roman Catholic Church. All of them were beset with problems of size and all of them either tried, or in the case of Kennedy, seemed ready to try, solutions which had the effect of reducing the weight of power at the centre, Khrushchev was ousted, Kennedy was killed and Pope John died, before the work they tackled could have borne fruit. It is an interesting speculation as to what they would have accomplished in their respective spheres had they lived. Given the nature of Soviet Power Khrushchev's defeat would have seemed to be inevitable and it is probable that the same is no less true of Kennedy and the power structures of the U.S.A.

[2]*The Economist Diary,* 1979.

[3]*The Times,* 25 September 1972.

Well Khrushchev, who wanted above everything else to weaken the stranglehold of the vast Moscow bureaucracy on the activities of the 240 million peoples of the Russian Empire, failed. He rightly saw the need to weaken it as an indispensable prerequisite to the task of creating some badly needed dynamic in the system. However that may be, the Russian Empire is confronted with a problem which in some respects is similar to that of the African nations. The latter are all concerned to stress their own cultural history, but that cultural history is of course, tribal, just as in the Russian Empire it is national. So that whilst in Africa, where tribalism carries the sort of stigma that 'Trotskyism' did under Stalin, attempts are being made to emphasise African cultural riches, which of course, are tribal, in the Russian Empire the political bosses continuously vaunt the *cultural* achievements of Ukranians, Georgians, Armenians and other nations, whilst nationalism itself has become one of the main forms of anathema to be pronounced by the Russian authorities. Clearly this is, to use a favourite Marxist jargon word, a 'contradiction' and equally clearly it is one which is unlikely to hold much longer. We can, in due course, expect to see the struggle of these different nationalities for freedom from Russian colonialism succeed, for ulimately all forms of colonialism derive from the acquiescence, however reluctant, of the subject peoples. Modern history is eloquent that from the moment such acquiescence is actively withdrawn the game is up.

But in the Russian Empire what then? Some of these nationalities themselves run into many millions of people, as may be seen from the following table:

Republic	Population
Russia	130,697,000
Ukraine	47,496,000
Belorussia	9,074,000
Uzbekistan	12,143,000
Kazakhstan	13,230,000

All the remaining republics, Georgia, Azerbaidjan, Moldavia, Kirghizia, Tadzhikistan, Armenia and Turkmenistan have populations around or well below five million, and the same is true for the independent republics of Estonia, Latvia and Lithuania which are still under Russian occupation after the Stalinist invasion of 1940. Hence the break-up of the Russian Empire could well lead to the establishment of meganation state structures similar to those in Western Europe and with a similar propensity for war and violence. The answer to this is not to preserve the existing union in another guise, for as we have seen from the attempts to do so in Europe, this is no answer at all; for a unit of such a size will always be war-prone whatever the ideology of its Government. Here again, the answer to the problem lies in further division, doubtless along lines of the Provinces and Districts which already have a long history through Tzarist and communist rule, and at the base what better solution could there be than to revive the powers and functions, to say nothing of extending them, of the Russian Mír?

The Mir is the only form of Government the Russian people themselves have ever created, and its kinship to other units such as African tribal villages and the Swiss communes, in its sturdy spirit of communism (was it Gandhi who said you can't have communism without community?), self-help, self-reliance and democracy, before it was crushed by the juggernaut of Tzarist bureaucracy, is so pronounced one can but wonder at the course history might have taken if it had been allowed to develop along the lines of the Swiss model. How many lives of Russians alone might have been spared in the revolutions and wars of the present century?

The structure of the Russian Empire is at present based on the theoretical primacy at the base of the constitutional pyramid of the city and village soviets. These 'soviets' elect representatives to the next tier, the Rayon (District) Soviets who in turn elect to the Ablast (provincial) assemblies, who again in turn elect to the council of their respective republic. In practice of course, this is a mere facade, the transparency of which cannot conceal the fact that far from all power belonging to the Soviets, it is effectively in the hands of the leadership, the army and the secret police.

In terms of genuine democracy it is doubtful if there is any future at all for the present 'Soviet Union'. Nor is there any compelling reason why there should be. The Urals form a natural divide between Europe and Asia and when the different nationalities of European Russia have found each their distinctive voice one may suppose they will partake in specific European concerns such as a railway network and, whilst the wasteful irrationality of mass air travel remains with us, an air network, just as the Asian parts of the Empire will partake in Asian arrangements. But whether the present arrangements of Soviets remain is surely a decision which the members of the local bodies of that vast continent will decide for themselves. The situation is frozen at present by an iron grip from the top down; when the true voice of the people is heard from the bottom up we can expect some interesting developments.

The same is surely true of China. Westerners are all too prone to view China as a single homogenous unity, but a moment's reflection will be enough to show the absurdity of such a supposition. Europe (excluding the Russian Empire) has a population of 462 million. When one considers the diversity of language, dress, culture, philosophy, religion, architecture and other aspects of life prevailing among these peoples, is it not absurd to suppose that a similar diversity does not prevail among the 750 million people of China? (Or for that matter among the 130 million people of European Russia?).

I have no knowledge of the reality of the actual divisions, and even though China has a long history of unified rule under feudal forms of government, that is no reason at all for assuming that that diversity, as opposed to the feudal-minded uniformity of its present rulers, could not be made the basis of a new era of unity in freedom. Such a unity need not, indeed in the interests of freedom dare not, extend beyond a few areas of practical concern such as travel, communications and health matters, and on this basis one may confidently anticipate a time when the prevailing monocentralism will either wither away or be overthrown from below.

In the Indian sub-continent a similar solution is discernible. The inevitable break-up of the two wings of Pakistan which has resulted in the creation of Bangladesh out of former East Pakistan is of course, one may put it so, a very weighty straw in the wind. In Europe *Governments* are busy trying to unite themselves, in the sub-continent *peoples* are acting to break a unity they find intolerable. The establishment of Bangladesh has now been followed by moves for separation and autonomy in the different parts of West Pakistan, and there is now a ferment for separation and independence in Sind, Baluchistan, Punjab and the North Western frontier Province. Nor is India free from this move towards fissiparousness, for in recent years an increasingly insistent voice is being heard calling for local autonomy; this voice has erupted in Kerala, Orissa and Maharashtra, and now Andhra Pradesh is clearly moving towards a state of complete independence which will be accompanied by a division of the state into Telangana and Andhra Desa.

India's leaders are reputed to be afraid that this development will open a Pandora's Box of similar demands throughout the Continent, but why should they be afraid? This is the only development which stands the remotest chance of rescuing the sub-continent from its stupefying torpor of poverty and stagnation. The villages are decaying, and gripped in a fatalistic acceptance of social squalor and a psychological spirit of inertia and indifference which thirty years of independence has shown not the remotest sign of challenging. Indeed all the efforts of the Central Government are proving sharply counter-productive, for the more the Government acts and campaigns the more the villages assume they can leave things to it. The villager's horizons are limited to his village and its general squalor, even the revolutionary impact of the transistor radio, if it arouses discontent with his lot does not so much impel him to seek changes in the village as to leave it for the city. He feels he has no power to act, his life is circumscribed by the soldier and the tax collector, and that any improvements he seeks to make will improve their lot rather than his own. He has never known any other way of life, why should he care? It is the Government that sees the wider picture and the potential for rural betterment, but the Government is not in the village, it is elsewhere. The twain can only meet *by making government fit the village scale.*

This was the reason for the enthusiastic but utterly inadequate response to the efforts of that far-seeing Indian statesman Jayaprakash Narayan;[4] he had eschewed normal political structures and parties, going instead direct to the village in this effort to get schemes of self-help and co-operative village renewal under way. Wherever his workers had been they had scored successes. What limited that success was the pitiful lack of numbers of those who were prepared to devote their lives to this work. One wonders what the effect would be if all those people so active in the cause of so much futility in the mass party structures of India turned their attention to this need for generating the power to decide and to act at the grassroots level?

Shri Jayaprakash was seeking to create structures from the base upwards; in time he probably came to meet the limits of what I can only call 'the five or six million barrier', that number, beyond which, as a political unit grows in size, its members insensibly lose control of its workings to the polyarchic groupings at the centre. This difficulty

4 Jayaprakash Narayan died in October 1979.

is already rearing its head elsewhere. East and West Pakistan have become separate States, but the new entities remain enormous. Pakistan has a population approaching 70 million and Bangaldesh has one greater than 70 million. Similarly Andhra Pradesh, where there has been agitation for independence from India over the years, has a population of 36 million, and even if divided as indicated above these territories will still produce units too large to be fully manageable in democratic terms. One gets a clearer picture of the problem when it is realised that the total population of India, using Whitaker's 1979 figures,[5] is over 600 million. This is broken down into the separate states, disregarding a number of 'territories' such as Goa, as follows:

Andhra Pradesh	43,502,708
Assam	14,857,314
Bihar	56,387,296
Gujarat	26,697,475
Haryana	10,036,808
Karnataka	29,299,014
Kerala	21,347,375
Madhya Pradesh	41,654,119
Maharashtra	50,412,235
Meghalaya	1,011,699
Nagaland	515,561
Orissa	21,944,615
Punjab	13,551,000
Rajasthan	25,765,806
Tamil Nadu	41,103,125
Tripura	1,556,822
Uttar Pradesh	88,299,453
West Bengal	44,440,095

It seems probable that we can expect to see the sub-continent divide somewhat according to this table in due course if only because, increasingly, this is what people want. But if it is so divided it will run into many new dangers, not least will be the danger of war from many of the bigger states which, because of their size, will be not nations, but meganations. Their rulers, divorced by that gulf between Government and the governed which afflicts all monster states, will

[5] *Whitaker's Almanack 1979.*

dream of extending their 'interests', of combing with this or that shifting alliance in opposition to this or that rival State or grouping. There is no alternative here but to pare down power to around that handful of millions which reduces the gap between government and the governed, and which at the same time reduces the capacity to make war to such derisory proportions as to enable people's natural desire for peace to become the prevailing principle.

In doing this it will not be excluding the possibilities of democratic co-operation throughout the sub-continent for those matters in which people have a common interest. The most obvious of these is roads, railways and other forms of communication. So why not a sub-continent Federal Parliament simply for Transport and Communications? Why not another and separate Parliament for Monetary Affairs? Another for Health, another for Defence and so on? This means none of the elected people need be full-time, none of them need be paid, none of them need become a member of the non-productive parasite bureaucratic class that now dominates life in Delhi, and the people who do the electing could keep a close eye on how things were going. It would be a structure built from the bottom up, not from the top down. None of these Parliaments need be centred in the same city and since none would be able to initiate without reference to, or even with the consent of, the others in many matters, the prospects of serious armed conflict would also be reduced. Defence, for example, would doubtless need Transport's permission to move troops and Finance's concurrence to pay them.

It is not possible to attempt here a detailed examination of peace prospects along these lines in all the different parts of the world, all that the writer can do is to allude to those prospects in those areas of which he has some slight knowledge.

With regard to the United States of America, there is a difficulty not pertaining to other countries which makes an approach to organic political structures much more difficult. The main mass of the United States population has been derived from other parts of the world in successive waves of immigration in comparatively recent times, there is thus only scattered manifestations of a spirit of long established ethnic grouping and local loyalty to which they can look or respond. Yet even the United States of America has a long, even if greatly eroded, tradition of local power. In pioneer days the town meeting was the *only* source of local authority and to this day the issue of 'states rights' in opposition to those of the Federal Government, has been kept alive. It is true that those who have championed states' rights have done so often for dubious motives aimed at crippling the Federal power at times, such as under Franklin Roosevelt, when that power was being used in an attempt to apply generous social policies to which entrenched conservative interests in states legislatures were bitterly opposed. But if these people were right for the wrong reasons they were still right, for there is something fatuous about a monster Federal Government seeking to give effect to minute details of social legislation.

This is not to overlook that in certain spheres such as race relations the effect of Federal legislation have been markedly beneficial. Today it is probable that legislation to assist racial groups who have been victims of discrimination by the majority group have gone about as far as it effectively can; this is basically a problem of human relationships and further progress in resolving it must surely now be accomplished at grassroots level.

Despite the drawback to the creation, or recreation, of effective localised power, it need remembering that the path to this goal is not all thorns. The tradition of local power does exist, in however muted a form, and its revival and restructuring can be helped by the fact that out of its fifty-one mainland States only six have a population greatly in excess of five million. These are, in rounded figures:

State	Population (In millions)
California	20
Illinois	12
New York	18
Ohio	11
Oregon	12
Texas	11

Like all the Governments of continental meganations the United States of America is out of control, it is out of the control of its people and it is out of the control of the polyarchic grouping in whose hands much of the real power resides. If its people were wise they would do away with the present system of Presidential election altogether and have the President elected annually by a Cabinet elected in turn by the members of its two elected legislatures. In drawing up the powers of these bodies the people would do well to follow the Swiss practice and make them absolutely residual and mainly for purposes of internal co-ordination.

If the main centres of power and decision-making were in the States these two would need to observe a vital principle, and one which in the interests of functional democracy, is of general application. The channel between the lowest base of power, let us say the District, should be unimpeded to the State level. Any attempt to intersperse an intermediary elected authority would lead to citizen voting bewilderment, a loss of power from the base and proliferation of bureaucracy at levels beyond the effective reach of the citizen and a general gumming up of effective democratic control.

Whether the American people have the wit to grasp the need for a solution to their problems on these lines before their present monster system of over-centralised government destroys them is of course, as it is elsewhere, another question. To diagnose sickness is one thing, to persuade the patient to adopt the remedy is quite another.

CHAPTER XV

Conclusion

"If we take man as he is, we make him worse. If we take him as he ought to be, we help him become it."

Goethe

Very few of the appeals to urge other countries of Europe to join the common market fail to include some reference, usually as a rhetorical finale, to the extent to which Europe has always been united culturally, and with this whopping and egregious falsehood there is usually trotted out names such as Shakespeare, Goethe and Dante, with the suggestion that these people were true 'Europeans' and that the political unification of the continent is thus the end product of a long historical process associated with their greatness.

It would be difficult to locate a more wilful inversion of factuality. The splendours of Europe's cultural heritage come not from its mere continental and geographic identity but from its former fragmentation, independence and diversity. Dante was not first and foremost a European, he was not even an Italian, he was a Florentine, and was indeed but one of a host of men of genius nurtured in that amazing city. Shakespeare was neither European nor British, he was English, and even his Englishness pertains to a particular spot, his birthplace at Stratford-upon-Avon. And with what geographical expression is the greatness of Goethe usually identified? Europe? Germany? The Germany of Bismarck and Hitler? Or with his citizenship of the Weimar city state? It is possible to demonstrate again and again that the real cultural greatness of Europe is a compound expression of numerous *small-scale* city republics or of chartered cities, rarely exceeding a couple of hundred thousand people in number, which were, for the most part, self-governing and generally politically independent. The demise of Europe's great age of cultural splendour was coterminous with the demise of its independent city states and the growth of its nation and mega-nation states; from that time dates all the inhuman horror of magnified but uncontrolled violence which has reached its apotheosis in our own generation with political and economic institutions becoming more impersonal, more squalid and more demeaning of everything truly human, and more destructive and uncontrollable than any institutions have ever been in the human record. What is there one can say to those bigotted 'European' fanatics who are so ignorant of their own history and so unreceptive to its lessons as to wilfully, perversely and obstinately

proceed to the creation of a political monster which can only help
forward the potent forces of world anarchy and destruction, a tragedy
which has about it all the hallmarks of an apocalyptic Faustian
betrayal of the human soul and a cruel senseless denial of all the
elements of the true glory of human destiny?

What, after all, is basically wrong with this approach that it has
unleashed so much horror in the human record and will inevitably
unleash so much more if men persist with it? Surely it is possible
to assert that what has been overlooked in the modern era is that
however glittering the prizes of modern mass-production technology, however imposing the pomp and circumstance of state power
it helps to produce and sustain, if the scale on which it is conducted
ignores the sharply circumscribed limits of power and wealth which
man can control, ignores that is, that if man is not made central
to the purposes of its functioning, then it will inevitably produce
results inimical to man's true interests and well-being, and that it
will, with no less inevitability, extend its range and power until man
himself is victimised to the point of his own destruction.

"Man," said Protagoras, the first humanist and the first apostle
of a wisdom already so old that men have long forgotten it, "is
the measure of all things."

If we accept this, and on what grounds dare we refuse to do so? we
surely cannot fail to grasp that if we fail to practise it then it becomes
inevitable that *things* will be made the measure of man, things, whether they are economic systems or nation states; and that in displacing
him from the natural centre of reckoning they will disrupt even his
biological relationship with life, so that his God-given gifts of self-
awareness and comprehension are disastrously subverted by forces
his own kind has created and which collectively he can no longer
direct at all, far less towards any ends which serve his fulfilment.
"...What" asks Teilhard de Chardin, "is the work of works for man
if not to establish, in and by each one of us, an absolutely original
centre in which the universe reflects itself in a unique and inimitable
way?"[1] And what, we may add, is the point of *that* if man is unable
to master the forces he engineers for the fulfilment of his purposes,
be they ever so mundane as the means to accomplish Monday's
washing, or social artifacts which may well be glittering with the
majesty of the utmost reaches of his imagination?

[1]Pierre Teilhard de Chardin, *The Phenomenon of Man,* Fontana Books, 1955,
p. 278.

All we have sought to show in this brief essay amounts simply to this, that the malaise of our times, the giant evil that overshadows the entire human spectrum, is not something in our stars and not something beyond our wit to grasp or our power to control; it is a matter of human error, of human failure, both of which can respond to the capacity for human adjustment, if only men will make the effort of imagination and nerve to do so.

And why should they not? Men created and built splendidly once, as the achievements of Renaissance Europe, which are surely the true mark of man the builder and creator, abundantly testify; man mastered certain mundane aspects of his material environment and proceeded to build towns and cities which still dazzle us with the magic of their conceptualisation and the almost careless yet flawless lavishness of their adornment. The universities, palaces, cathedrals, mansions, museums, squares, halls and other structures were matched in their splendour by the soaring extravagance, based on discipline and poise, of their achievements in every sphere of artistic and intellectual activity.

We look back, and whilst in our secret hearts we marvel and wonder, all too often there springs to our lips a spirit of carping denigration at some of the more obvious shortcomings of these times, unaware that even as it does we are in fact simply increasing the stature of what was achieved despite them. We conclude, quite rightly as it happens, that we cannot live in the past, but then we make the terrible blunder of supposing that this ordinary fact of life is a justification in itself for compelling us to accept without question the horrible conditions of the living present, and condemns us perpetually to be a prisoner and a victim of those conditions into the future. It is then, as we survey the sterile oppressiveness of modern architecture, the grim and insulting uniformities of our modern townscapes, the emptiness of modern philosophy, the assinine betrayal of transcendent values by our religious leaders as they caper around on one trendy bandwaggon after another of ephemeral 'radical' causes, or slink by in a grotty torpor of chronic life-denying indifference, the blatant spiritual stinginess of our painting, music and poetry, the general suffocating stultification of our whole way of life, and the cheap compensatory refuge we are all too often prone to seek in whatever technological baubles are currently in fashion, that a spirit of pure despair is apt to invade us and subdue us.

Yet it need not be so. The great achievements of former civilisations, right up to the dawn of mass-production technology, were based on a common and largely unspoken principle which, had it ever been committed to words would surely have said, "never, on any account, allow any human propensity of any kind to achieve a dominance over the others in community affairs." In practice this meant that for long periods a balance, however precarious, was achieved and maintained. It is true that there were times when that balance was tilted disastrously towards war, but wars, as well as despotism and tyranny, have a beginning and an end, and once they had passed society regained its equipoise, and building and creating was renewed.

It was not until the eighteenth or nineteenth century that a single element in society was allowed, as a permanent feature, to achieve a dominance over the rest; hitherto society had controlled the propensity for economic gain by the intensely personal nature of its institutions and by the common acceptance of a moral code which the personal nature of society enabled it to maintain if not always inviolate, at least to general effect. The advent of the profit motive to an overall dominance has come near to destroying both community and the practical effects of its free and full working. With that terrible destruction there has been set in train the entire sequence of events which has led our civilisation at last to the verge of its own entirely gratuitous breakdown.

Again, it need not be so; all life is perpetual rhythm of renewal, and if in human affairs a great measure of that rhythm appears to have ceased, it is not because it was destined to do so, but we ourselves persist in courses that have unavoidably disrupted it.

Our civilisation is dying. The civilisation which has arisen on the basis of the single vision of man as an appendage to machines, and as an appendage to institutions based on mechine concepts, is clearly entering its last convulsive stages in which its propensity for war, for polluting the habitat, plundering finite resources, promoting overpopulation, economic instability and a psychic sickness in the soul of man himself, will finally tear down many centuries of accumulated social capital if man does not soon embark on a new mode of life.

The cause of this crisis stems largely from excess of many forms being promoted by the dominance of organisations, chiefly political and economic, which have been allowed over the last two centuries or so, to become too large for man to control.

The temptation to seek a way out by promoting institutions (such as a United Europe and world government) which are even more beyond anyone's capacity to control, will compound rather than resolve the problem and lead man into even deeper trouble. The real path to the future is not the suicidal pursuit of giantism, but the deliberate adoption of a scale of organisation small enough for man to be able to exercise over them the full genius of his powers of control. An organically structured 'Fourth World' can be an expression of the multifaceted gifts he has for social co-operation of many diverse kinds, give full expression to his instincts for love and compassion, and help him to realise the imaginative riches of his creativity. Not least it can be a world in which he will find freedom.

We say 'can', not 'will'. Little in human society is predictable, and there is no way at all of ensuring that if man finally achieves genuine freedom to choose, he will choose wisely and well. Man's interior world is not a placid realm of saintliness, at present being battered and abused by the forces of giantism; rather is it a battleground of good and evil, a struggle in which impulses which are squalid, vicious and destructive are locked in an unending battle for mastery with those which are noble, lovely and, (dare one say it?) divine.

Yet it is only on a small-scale of organisation and control that the battle between good and evil *can* be joined, a battle from which man's true moral stature is able to emerge; on the large-scale man is no longer the instrument of his own purposes, he is no longer able to assert a moral ascendancy over those who would make him theirs, he becomes instead the instrument of these giant forces which are all too apt to take no account of his moral questionings at all. That this leads to the enthronement of evil as inevitably as night follows day is the most obvious and potent fact of all the facts of man's existence in society today.

It is part of his cruel contemporary predicament that his own folly and greed have helped his outer world to acquire an institutional form which so sedulously negates his desire to serve the best in himself; but that folly and greed stem from a make-up which also embraces vision and understanding. And here the writer calls to the reader directly, to use both, while there is time, to free his mind of the intellectual shackles that bind him, to repudiate the bonds of habit, quiescence, conformity and fear, which modern life has imposed on him, and to reach out to those new forms of life which merit his service and idealism, which indeed wait on him to build.

It may well be that for many of our current modes of life look too imposing and powerful to be challenged, that any serious attempt to do so may appear hopelessly impractical and utopian, so that instead of affirmation there will be a disposition to cynicism, to despair, or to mere indifference.

This is understandable, but let it be recalled that imposing and all-powerful as the giant institutions of our time may seem to be, they are man-made, every one of them, and that many of them are now being used to lead man by the nose to his damnation is all too evident; they can perform this function because instead of serving the true needs of man, man has unwittingly allowed himself to be enslaved to the presumed needs of their functioning.

But let it also be recalled again that all forms of slavery and subjection rest ultimately on the acquiescence of the slave, and that once that acquiescence is withdrawn the days of oppression are numbered. To what else indeed is the collapse of the once seemingly impregnable colonial empires of the nineteenth century due but to this cardinal fact?

Men want, increasingly, to find the terms of the struggle of their interior world mirrored in the conditions of their external world; so that the battle between the forces of darkness and light in the former can also be fought on equal terms in the latter. It is only intellectual weakness and confusion, as well as mere timidity, that inhibits the fulfilment of this desire at present, but the very dangers and disasters that the old order has created are helping to clear our minds of the accumulated cant of an epoch and showing the way forward to a better order of things.

Increasingly this is seen, especially among the young, if only before they become embroiled in the business of getting and spending; nothing is more heartening than the total repudiation by so many of them of the entire works of the political decadence around them and their readiness to embrace radically new forms and structures of living.

Nothing too is more heartening than the readiness of so many ethnic groups in every continent, the very stuff of the organic world structure that is now struggling to emerge into what we are calling 'the Fourth World', to assert their inalienable right to be free, to be free above all from the monstrous pretensions of giantism that persist in overshadowing all our lives.

These shadows will surely pass, and with them so much evil and suffering which now so needlessly afflict us. And given that change, what lies beyond ? Today we are so encompassed by forces of decadence that we are all too prone to be unmindful of the tremendous spiritual achievements of the human race. Yet these achievements have already given us a measureless degree of splendour and happiness down the centuries and if we will the means to do so we can renew the quest which yielded them and reverse the tide of evil which is threatening today to submerge us.

This is no call to utopianism, the Old Adam in man is possibly as inalienable a part of the duality of his being as is the godhead of his own holiness. No social mechanisms can resolve the conflict between these forces and whatever form of society is fashioned, even at its best, will continue to reflect the duality of their eternal struggle of which man himself is surely the highest protagonist and expression.

And even if every generation is destined into perpetuity to be its own Sisyphus is there not always the prospect of a change in the terms of the struggle? The half god rejected by the gods need not always be striving through a barren mountain region tormented by heat and thirst, any more than he need abandon the struggle altogether for a living death of enervating valley affluence.

Mountains have their runnels of trickling sparkling spring water, the air can be soft and balmy with fragrance and freshness, there can be halts on the way in the shade of the most lovely trees where Ariel can play his pipe and Bacchus enjoy his wine as friends are met and spirits are restored . . . .

If man will but seize the means to do so, with institutions and social mechanisms which serve his humanity rather than mock it, he will find he has grasped the means to fulfil and to consummate what is finest and truest within himself, and that given this, far from viewing a retrospect of greatness that has gone for ever, he is but surveying a prospect of an infinitely greater glory that has yet to be.

Index